HOW TO THINK ABOUT CLIMATE CHANGE

Caught in the crossfire between climate deniers and catastrophists, the intelligent layperson is understandably bewildered when faced with the complexity of climate change. *How to Think about Climate Change* shows that economics provides not just a suitable, but an indispensable perspective to understand the root causes of the climate-change problem: scarcity of resources, externalities and free riding. Riccardo Rebonato argues that there are no silver bullets or easy solutions. However, he shows that the new-generation economics models offer a radically different insight about our best course of action from what most early models recommended – in particular, they suggest that fast and large-scale climate action can now be justified as the most cost-effective strategy without requiring the 'infinite altruism' of earlier models. Given the conceptual tools provided in this book, readers can decide whether they agree with these conclusions – and, if they do, what the most effective courses of action are.

Riccardo Rebonato is Professor of Finance at EDHEC and Scientific Director at the EDHEC Risk Climate Institute. He worked as a researcher at the nuclear research reactor at the Institut Laue Langevin, at Brookhaven National Laboratory and at Oxford University and has authored eleven books and fifty articles on finance, risk management and political economics. He is a current Board member of Nine Dots Prize with Cambridge University Press and a former Board member of ISDA and GARP.

HOW TO THINK ABOUT CLIMATE CHANGE

Insights from Economics for the Perplexed but Open-Minded Citizen

Riccardo Rebonato

CAMBRIDGE
UNIVERSITY PRESS

Shaftesbury Road, Cambridge CB2 8EA, United Kingdom

One Liberty Plaza, 20th Floor, New York, NY 10006, USA

477 Williamstown Road, Port Melbourne, VIC 3207, Australia

314–321, 3rd Floor, Plot 3, Splendor Forum, Jasola District Centre,
New Delhi – 110025, India

103 Penang Road, #05–06/07, Visioncrest Commercial, Singapore 238467

Cambridge University Press is part of Cambridge University Press & Assessment,
a department of the University of Cambridge.

We share the University's mission to contribute to society through the pursuit of
education, learning and research at the highest international levels of excellence.

www.cambridge.org
Information on this title: www.cambridge.org/9781009405003

DOI: 10.1017/9781009404983

First published 2024

Printed in the United Kingdom by CPI Group Ltd, Croydon CR0 4YY

A catalogue record for this publication is available from the British Library.

Library of Congress Cataloging-in-Publication Data
Names: Rebonato, Riccardo, author.
Title: How to think about climate change : insights from economics for the
perplexed but open-minded citizen / Riccardo Rebonato.
Description: New York : Cambridge University Press, [2023] | Includes
bibliographical references and index.
Identifiers: LCCN 2023019911 (print) | LCCN 2023019912 (ebook) |
ISBN 9781009405003 (hardback) | ISBN 9781009405010 (paperback) |
ISBN 9781009404983 (epub)
Subjects: LCSH: Climatic changes–Economic aspects. | Climatic
changes–Econometric models.
Classification: LCC QC903 .R426 2023 (print) | LCC QC903 (ebook) |
DDC 333.7–dc23/eng20230819
LC record available at https://lccn.loc.gov/2023019911
LC ebook record available at https://lccn.loc.gov/2023019912

ISBN 978-1-009-40500-3 Hardback

To Rosamund,
to Seba,
and to my perplexed but open-minded students,
for whom the time is out of joint,
and who are born to set it right.

Contents

Figures

Tables

Acknowledgements

It is impossible to give due thanks to all the people who helped me, directly or indirectly, in the writing of this book, but I'll try my best. Among my colleagues at EDHEC and EDHEC Risk Climate Institute, I would like to give thanks to Frédéric Ducoulombier and Nöel Amenc for making ERCII such a vibrant, exciting and a pleasant place to work; to Dherminder Kainth, Lionel Melin, Dominic O'Kane and Irene Monasterolo for their unparalleled intellectual input to our common research programme; to Lionel Martellini, Raman Uppal, Abraham Lioui and Gianfranco Gianfrate for the useful comments, pointers and suggestions they have given me. I am also grateful to Hersh Shefrin (Santa Calkra University) for robustly challenging my views on rational choice theory: sometimes we agree to disagree, but it is a pleasure even when we do.

Jean Czerlinski Whitmore Ortega has read an early version of the manuscript and given me really helpful suggestions and pieces of criticism. Jane J. Lee and Ian O'Neil (NASA) and Laura Kuenssberg (BBC) have provided me with useful information, and Dr Samantha Gross (Brooking Institution) has helped me with insightful comments about the differences in our dependence on fossil fuels and rare earths. NASA, the UK Meteorological Office, Science Direct, and Skepticalscience.com have kindly allowed me to reproduce important images – thank you. The excellent and always reliable organization Our World in Data does not even require to be asked whether their beautiful graphs can be used – a double thank you. One of the anonymous reviewers made some insightful comments about the 'learning-by-doing' process that have found their way into the book (see Chapter 1, footnote 10) – I am sorry, but the veil of anonymity prevents me from adding a name to my 'thank you'. My wife, Rosamund Scott, who is a professional philosopher, has helped me with the difficult Chapter 9 – I tried, with no success, to convince her to co-author this chapter: better luck next time. Among my students, a special thank-you goes to Alexandre Marchesin, Yann Lancrenon, Amanda Olofsson, Fanny Battle, Elsa Vermunt, Ia-Hue Salinas Sung and Mayeul D'Anselme for their comments and suggestions. Mr Luca Ossani and Jim Weisman have helped me a lot with their careful reading of the original manuscript. My teenage son, Sebastiano, has admirably played the role of the perplexed-but-open-minded reader, and mercilessly pointed out and torn to pieces the more obscure passages. If you still find the going tough in places, please have a word with him.

I would like to thank Cambridge University Press for finding three expert anonymous reviewers, and, of course, the reviewers themselves, who dedicated a lot of their time to reading the manuscript and to making very helpful and constructive suggestions. The book is much the better for their input. My sincere thanks also go to Robert Dressen, editor for Economics and Political Science, for the enthusiasm he has shown for the project, and to Fiona Cole for her accurate and thoughtful copy-editing.

And, last but not least, a word of thanks goes to Professor Don Knuth[1] (for TEX), to Leslie Lamport[2] (for LATEX), to the Gummi[3] developers and to the LaTeXila[4] development team for the LATEX editors that they have made freely available, and with which this book has been written. Game theory, extensively used in analysing climate change, does not explain well why they have been so generous, but they have: double thanks again, then.

Since this book is not aimed at a technical reader, my treatment has been in places somewhat imprecise. I have tried to simplify the handling of the material without ever making 'wrong' statements. Alas, the line between being acceptably economical with scientific correctness and getting something wrong turned out to be thinner than I wish it were. So, if, despite the help I received, I ended up stepping somewhere over the line, the responsibility is fully mine.

[1] www-cs-faculty.stanford.edu/~uno/.
[2] www.lamport.org/.
[3] http://gummi.midnightcoding.org/.
[4] http://projects.gnome.org/latexila/.

CHAPTER 1

Introduction

Or, Do We Really *Need Another Book on Climate Change?*

The time is out of joint – O cursèd spite,
That ever I was born to set it right!

— W. Shakespeare, *Hamlet, I, 5, 188–190*

If a man writes clearly enough anyone can see if he fakes.

— E. Hemingway, *Death in the Afternoon, Chapter 5*

IN THE RUN-UP TO THE 1929 MARKET CRASH FINANCIER Joe Kennedy remarked that, when you hear a stock tip from a shoeshine boy, it is time to get out of the market. Similarly, when you notice that the racks of your average airport newsvendor seem to hold more books about climate change than crime thrillers, it is fair to conclude that the market for climate-change books is truly saturated. Yet, I believe that there is room on the rack for one more book. This one. What makes me think so?

There is great uncertainty about the magnitude of the threat posed by climate change, with 'respectable' projections of climate outcomes ranging from the severe-but-manageable to the catastrophic. When many commentators routinely refer to global warming as a climate emergency, yet Yale Prof Nordhaus, an economics Nobel-Prize winner for his pioneering work on the modelling of climate change, recommends that our resources are best spent today on climate research, rather than on hasty and costly abatement, the intelligent reader to whom this book is addressed is understandably perplexed. How has this state of affairs arisen?

Partly this is because, while the science of climate change is reasonably settled, its economics and ethics appear to inhabit the land of 'anything goes'. In these 'relativistic' times, this seems to suggest to some that also when it comes to climate change we can interpret the evidence at hand to reach whichever conclusions we want. At the opposite end of the intellectual spectrum, the way the climate-change problem is often framed seems to imply that 'the facts' uniquely determine what we should do. Don't get me wrong: facts *are* extremely important, because they determine what is achievable, and what our real choices are. But facts do not determine ethical choices, and these play a key role in deciding what we should do to curb climate change. Providing facts is the job of scientists. Making ethical choices is the job of open-minded, inquisitive and intellectually honest citizens. The goal of this book is therefore to provide this open-minded, inquisitive and intellectually honest reader, not only with the key facts, but also with a mental compass to navigate the uncertain waters of the climate debate.

As she proceeds through the book, the reader will become progressively aware that making thoughtful decisions about climate change is no easy task. Faced with the attending choices, humans are today forced to make choices whose consequences could end up being farther-reaching than any of the decisions they have had to make in their history, as their actions can affect the outcomes not just for this or that group of people, but for humanity a whole.[1] We may even find it unfair that the responsibility for fixing a situation that, unbeknownst to us, had been getting progressively more serious since the start of the Industrial Revolution, should fall so heavily on our shoulders. Like Hamlet in the quote that opens this chapter, we may feel not just that time is out of joint, but also that it is a curséd spite that setting it right should be up to us. However, it *is* this generation that must make some of the key choices about what to do about climate change: again as in Hamlet's case, no choice is painless, and no choice is easy. But since Hamlet's reluctance to act ended in tragedy, this is where I would like the parallel with his predicament to end. It is exactly because the task is so daunting, and the temptation to do nothing so strong, that with this work I intend to give the reader some tools to make the task more manageable. And, inspired

---

[1] Searching in my mind for another such example, I can only think of the development of nuclear weapons.

by the quote by Hemingway that opens this chapter, I have tried to do so using the simplest and plainest language to convey ideas from a technical and specialized field. I have strived to do so because clarity, I strongly believe, is a necessary condition for honesty – whether I succeeded, of course, is an altogether different matter.

Let me manage, not only the reader's, but also my own expectations right from the start. If you are totally convinced that we are living a climate emergency, and that this is our last chance to avert an 'existential threat', you may well ask why we need to *write* more about the subject. Surely, if we are teetering along the edge of a climate precipice, it is now time for action, not for analysis. The only books we need now are 'activist pamphlets', written in the trenches of climate warfare, not the one you are reading. At the opposite end of the ideological spectrum, if you believe that the threat from climate change is an outright 'hoax', or that it has been blown out of all reasonable proportions for political and ideological motives, you will probably conclude that my book is not a dispassionate examination of the climate problem, but a thinly disguised ploy in the climate-change conspiracy. Much as I would like to, I doubt that I will be able to change the minds either of the climate-change deniers, or of the catastrophists-who-entertain-no-doubts. But, I hope, there is a large middle ground of genuinely concerned and perplexed citizens who would like to form a balanced view, based on facts and on clearly identifiable moral choices. This is the readership I strive to reach.

Does my readership really need convincing that swift and large-scale climate action is needed? If we leave to one side Hilary Clinton's 'deplorables' – whose mind probably cannot be changed anyway – aren't we all convinced of the reality and urgency of the climate problem by now? Yes and no. A perplexing narrative has recently gained wide currency, according to which it is the politicians who are dragging their feet, and stubbornly ignoring what 'the people' want: I am sure that Greta Thunberg's 2019 'How dare you' speech at the UN climate summit still resonates in my readers' ears, and the target of her tirade were, of course, the politicians gathered at the summit. Now, to paraphrase Warren Buffet, in the last decade or so politicians worldwide seem to have been hell-bent on discovering new ways to make themselves distrusted, when the old ones were working so well. However, if we exclude China and Russia, in the highest-emitting countries the politicians whose responsibility it is to enact measures to curb climate change are put in power by their electorates. Now, at the time of this writing the grand total of Green party representatives in the UK, France and Italy combined is one. Admittedly, in the 2021 elections the German Green party did much better than in the past, but even in its *annus mirabilis* its vote tally only added up to 15 per cent. Voters seem to like the idea of going green, but, when faced with job losses in coal mining communities, increases in fuel tax, restrictions on short-haul flight, or withdrawal of fossil fuel subsidies, they do not cast their votes for the parties that ask for real sacrifices: they vote, if at all, for those who promise big climate changes with little or no pain (planting trees is one of the favourite get-out-jail cards – not surprisingly, the Trump administration, not known for its unwavering commitment to fighting climate change, was a whole-hearted supporter of the Trillion Tree Initiative).[2] Yes, fossil fuel lobbies *are* powerful, but what stops politicians from taking decisive (and painful) climate action is not the fact that they are in the pocket of the oil lobbies, but that, when they present the electorate with unpalatable, if necessary, choices, they are routinely not elected. So, voters (in Europe at least – in the US the situation is far more complex[3]) do not need convincing *in the abstract* that we must act to curb climate change and that there isn't too much time to waste. However, they have been convinced, or have convinced themselves, that the transition can be painless, and the changes in our ways of living can be, if not cosmetic, certainly easily manageable. As I am not a politician, and therefore I do not have to run for re-election,

---

[2] US Department of the Interior, 13 October 2020, *Trump Administration Furthers Commitment to One Trillion Trees Initiative.* For a brief discussion of the Trillion Tree Initiative, see Chapter 15.

[3] Opinion polls conducted by the reputable Pew Research Centre in 2019 found that 49 per cent of conservative Republicans, who represent the party majority, believe that fossil fuel production must be *expanded.* And only about half of Americans believe that 'human activity contributes a great deal to climate change'. Twenty per cent of all Americans believe that the human action has a negligible impact on the climate (45 per cent when we look at Republicans), and 35 per cent that the main causes of global warming are 'natural'. See, www.pewresearch.org/science/2019/11/25/u-s-public-views-on-climate-and-energy/.

I intend with this book to change the minds of my readers on this important point, and to convince them not only that the changes ahead are indeed urgently needed, but also that they will have to be deeply upsetting.

How do I plan to achieve this ambitious task? First, I intend to convince my intended reader that, for once, the way economists think about the climate-change problem is both insightful and helpful – and, as an extra bonus, intellectually rewarding. But my contention is stronger. I want to convince the reader that looking at climate change through the lens of economic analysis doesn't just provide an alternative interesting vantage point. I want to argue that we cannot make sense of the abatement choices ahead of us if we ignore what economics has to say about three absolutely fundamental aspects of the climate-change problem: scarcity, externalities and strategic interactions. It is no exaggeration to say that we would not have a climate *problem* in the first place were it nor for scarcity; that the problem has arisen because of a massive-scale market failure (this is the externality bit); and that finding a solution is so difficult because of the free-rider problem (and this is where strategic interactions come to the fore). Dealing with these three features is part of the job description of any economist (but of no other scientist), and the discipline of economics has accumulated over decades valuable insights about how to handle them. Economists, of course, are far from holding all the answers. However, without looking at the problem from an economics perspective none of the answers we come up with is likely to make much sense. This is why I believe that understanding how economists conceptualize the climate-change problem – reductive as their approach may be – is indispensable if my 'model reader' wants to reach her own conclusions on the topic.

1.1 WHAT CAN ECONOMICS OFFER?

Convincing my reader that examining the problem of climate change from the perspective of economics is going to be not just rewarding, but actually necessary, is not an easy sell. Economists do not command the same trust or inspire the same confidence that 'hard' scientists do – and, if one casts one's mind to relatively recent economics-related events, it is not difficult to understand why.[4] However, for all its blemishes, economics remains our only port of call if we want to make sense of scarcity, market failures and free-riding. If this sounds a bit like a two-cheers-for-economics endorsement, well, yes, it is. But, blunt and crooked as it may be, economics is still the best tool we have to handle the three root causes of the climate problem.

1.1.1 SCARCITY. Let me start from scarcity. Economics has been defined as 'the science which studies human behaviour as a relationship between ends and *scarce means which have alternative uses*'.[5] Or, if we want to put the emphasis on the outcomes of economic policies – exactly what I am going to do in this book – '[e]conomics […] is characterized by the study of how to obtain the best possible result from *scarce* resources.'[6] Indeed, if our resources were unlimited, most of what today we recognize as economics would either not exist, or be extremely boring. The choices economists study with their models are forced upon us by the fact that resources *are* limited, and extracting them is painful. And this is exactly where the link with climate change lies: the decisions we are confronted with when faced with the problem of controlling climate change are hard exactly because our resources are limited. If we could throw infinite resources at the problem, we would not have a climate problem any more: we could remove CO_2 from the atmosphere and store it safely (the technology to do so has been around for decades – it is just rather costly); we could deploy all kind of sources of renewable

---

[4] In November 2008 Queen Elizabeth II interrupted her scripted speech for the opening of the London School of Economics's New Academic Building to ask the impromptu question 'Why did no one see it coming?' She was referring, of course, to the Great Financial Crisis of 2008 that, just a few weeks before, had just reached one of its defining moments (the default of the American investment bank Lehman's Brothers). As far as I know, she never received a convincing answer.

[5] Robbins (1932), page 15, emphasis added. If the goal of economics is how best to make use of *scarce* resources, problems in economics are naturally cast in terms of *optimization*. The Integrated Assessment Models we will discuss in detail in the rest of the book are exactly an exercise in optimization. Casting the role of economics in terms of optimal allocation of scarce resources is today widely accepted, but it must be acknowledged that before the 1930s this interpretation was not mainstream among professional economists. See Backhouse (2010), page 100 and *passim* for a good discussion.

[6] Forni (2021), page 4, emphasis added.

energy without worrying about their cost effectiveness; we could throw unlimited resources into research about nuclear fusion, or other energy sources: that is, we could get ourselves the best and cleanest energy that money can buy. Unfortunately, we do not live in such a world of plenty. In reality, we cannot avert future climate damage *and* enjoy the same level of consumption we could have enjoyed had fossil fuels not produced a dramatic increase in the atmospheric concentration of CO_2 (and of temperature as a result).[7] Whoever peddles the fairy tale that we can successfully tackle climate change with little alteration of our lifestyles is either naïve, or ignorant, or in bad faith. If we truly want to bring climate change under control, the commitment to the task must be substantial – I often refer to it as a 'war effort', and I don't use this grim term lightly. It is exactly because the required resource commitment is so large that we must allocate our efforts wisely. And this is why economics – the science of scarcity – can help.

Given this background of resource scarcity, let me give an example of why unstructured abatement action can be counterproductive, even if we believe that the climate-change danger is 'clear and present'. Take the cost of solar panels. This has plummeted by more than 80 per cent over as short a period as ten years.[8] This is excellent news, and gives us real hope that energy from renewables may be able to provide us in the near future with a substantial fraction of our energy needs. However, the very speed with which costs have fallen should give us pause for thought. The lifetime of a solar panel is approximately thirty to forty years. If five to ten

---

[7] Carbon dioxide is not the only 'greenhouse' gas, nor the most potent. One should actually speak of 'CO_2 equivalent', that is, one should convert the concentrations and emissions of other gases to the equivalent CO_2 concentrations and emissions that would generate the same climate (temperature) change over a specified time horizon. For simplicity, I will mainly refer to CO_2, but one should really talk of CO_2 equivalent.

[8] To be precise, it has fallen by 99 per cent over the last four decades (Chandler 2018). Over the period 2010–2019 Solar photovoltaics (PV) have had a cost decline of 82 per cent. International Renewable Energy Agency (IRENA) (2019), *Renewable Power Generation Costs in 2019*, available at www.irena.org/publications/2020/Jun/Renewable-Power-Costs-in-2019. And as a salutary reminder that all our projections are just that – projections – it should be noted that the 2020 cost of energy per kWh from solar is less than a quarter than the International Energy Agency (IEA) 2010 forecast, and less than half its 2014 prediction.

years ago we had rushed into the deployment of the then-state-of-the-art panels, we would now be saddled with less efficient photovoltaic devices *for which we would have paid almost ten times as much as we can pay now.* True, those costly and not-so-efficient panels would have still somewhat reduced our emissions in the last five to ten years, and therefore made the climate problem today a bit more tractable.[9] However, deciding where the 'sweet spot' for action exactly lies – to what extent the advantage of waiting until we are 'smarter and richer' is negated by having to deal with a more difficult-to-handle climate problem – is clearly not easy. Thinking at the same time both about the falling prices of solar panels (and wind turbines, and carbon sequestration technologies), and about the increased severity of the climate events we are already observing makes us readily appreciate the nature of the problem, and why its solution is not easy: *since we are resource-constrained*, we must choose carefully how our abatement bullets are used.[10]

1.1.2 EXTERNALITIES. Let me move to the second reason why looking at the problem of climate change through the lens of economic analysis makes a lot of sense: because the climate mess we find ourselves in directly results from a massive market failure. What does this mean? The green-

---

[9] Does this automatically mean that we would have been better off waiting and installing more efficient solar panels at a later date? Not necessarily. Solar panels have become as cheap as they have because so many of them have been produced, thereby improving our processes and our technological prowess. Innovations are not 'manna from Heaven', but are the fruit of what economists call 'learning by doing'. So, this example simply shows that, when it comes to abatement strategies, matters are always complex, and decisions have to be nuanced. For a discussion of learning by doing in the context of climate change, see, for instance, Messner (1997), who was among the first to introduce the idea that investment costs of technologies depend on the cumulative installed capacity, and van der Zwann et al. (2002) for a direct application to climate change.

[10] Matters, as usual, are a bit more nuanced. Suppose that we did delay the installation of the solar panels, waiting for more efficient ones to appear. As an anonymous reviewer of this manuscript pointed out, 'the decline in cost is also a result of the scaling and of the learning by doing and thus of someone investing sub-optimally. Could we have the prices of solar panel we have today if someone didn't invest sub-optimally ten years ago? In other words, pursuing the maximum efficiency objective may lead to a coordination problem whereby no one wants to make the first move, as it is suboptimal.' Excellent point.

house gases that we emit today will affect (negatively) the welfare of future generations, but these future generations are not compensated for the damage inflicted on them. The current price of a litre of gasoline comes from balancing *today's* supply and demand for gasoline (i.e., from the bargaining of today's buyer and seller), but no account is taken in arriving at this price of the huge unpaid bill left for future generations to shoulder. The existence of these 'unpaid bills' is well known in economics and the bills themselves go under the name of externalities. When the idea of externality first developed, the 1879 example was that of English cardiologist who could not hear properly the heartbeat of his patients because of the noise of the confectioner's machinery next door. Today, the textbook example of an externality is the noise the dwellers in the landing flightpath of an airport have to endure, without the ticket price negotiated between the airline and the passenger taking this into account. More generally, externalities arise when a transaction occurs between two parties (the purchase and sale of the litre of gasoline, in our example), but damages accrue to a third party who cannot have her say in the two-party bargain by seeking compensation (in the gasoline case, the third party today is the victim of pollution,[11] and tomorrow's third party are the generations who will have to face the costs associated with living in a hotter world). Economists therefore view as a key goal of the economic analysis of climate change the *pricing* of the externality arising from the emissions of greenhouse gases – a price that should take into account the damage they inflict.[12] Note that economists, being economists, do

---

[11] The pollution bill is not small: the WHO estimates that 4.2 million deaths per year are attributable to ambient (outdoor) pollution, and that worldwide air pollutants account for 29 per cent of lung cancers, 17 per cent of acute respiratory diseases, 29 per cent of strokes, 25 per cent of heart attacks (ischaemic heart disease), and 43 per cent of chronic obstructive pulmonary disease. We should keep these figures in mind when we discuss the pros and cons of nuclear energy.

[12] As usual, I am simplifying matters a bit here. In the domain of climate change, economists recognize three types of externality: the emission externality that we have just mentioned; the innovation externality; and the network-effect externality. The innovation externality arises because the benefits from innovations in climate abatement area are not fully appropriated by the inventors. This is why subsidies for research, when they fix this market failure, can make *market* sense. And as for network externalities, they are often associated with the building of new infrastructure, which will have to play a major role in the green transition. The classic example is that of electric vehicles and charging stations: installing more charging stations is held back by

not take a moralistic stance in arriving at this price: it is neither their intention nor their inclination to punish the 'bad' emitters. They simply ask the slightly otherworldly (and a bit 'impolite') question: for what compensation, paid by us today, would future generations accept the damage we are inflicting on them? If this sounds a bit crass and narrowly materialistic (and it is), let's not forget that if today's fuel users actually had to make this compensation payment, a very different equilibrium price for gasoline would be reached, and, as a consequence, we would immediately burn less fossil fuel. This would already be a big step in the right direction towards curbing climate change.[13] In reality the at-the-pump price of the emission externality is currently *negative*: large subsidies are enjoyed by the producers and consumers of fossil fuels – see the discussion in Section 12.4. No wonder we have the climate problem that we have: because we have probably engineered the greatest market failure in the history of mankind.[14] Prof Nordhaus (2021) puts it very clearly:

> Carbon capture and sequestration [CSS] provides a good example
> of this double externality. Economic returns on the research and

the small number of electric vehicles, and the production of electric cars is hampered by the scarcity of charging stations. In general equilibrium analysis one finds two equilibria: one with a lot of electric cars and charging stations; and one with few of both. Again, subsidies can help the establishment of one equilibrium over the other. For a good discussion see J H Stock (2021), *Driving Deep Decarbonization*, Finance and Development, IMF, September 2021.

[13] Let me be clear here: a market mechanism such as pricing today's emissions, and adding this 'emission tax' to the price of a litre of fuel works well in the idealized textbook world populated by *Homines economici*. Much as I think that market mechanisms, such as the establishment of emission markets, can to some extent help to tackle climate change, I do not think for a second that the invisible hand of the market has all the solutions to the climate-change problem. The reality of the 2017 *gilets jaunes* demonstrations in France are a stark reminder of how wide the gap is between the grubby sub-lunar world we live in and the rarefied world of the economics textbooks.

[14] I cannot be sure whether it is really the biggest market failure ever: however, the total world CO_2 emissions in 2019, including agriculture and land use, were over 40 billion tons. A *very* low estimate of the social cost of carbon puts it at around $30 per ton. (Some estimates are two-to-three times higher.) This means that the 'missing compensation' is at least well over one trillion dollars *per year*. This seems to me pretty large by any standards. To put the number in perspective it is the same size as the 'massive' infrastructure bill approved with bipartisan support by the US Senate in August 2021 – an investment that I do not think will be repeated every year.

commercialization of CCS spill over to other firms and future consumers. But the captured carbon is worthless in most countries because carbon emissions are drastically underpriced, which makes investments in CCS commercially nonviable – and therefore out of the question in corporate boardrooms. The same logic holds for advanced nuclear power, fusion power, and the burgeoning hydrogen economy: none of them have any advantage over fossil fuels as long as carbon prices remain low.

So, as we shall see, when economic analysis comes up with a way to 'price' this externality (the 'social cost of carbon'), it is not just coming up with an interesting descriptive statistic of the climate-change problem: it is trying to estimate an absolutely key quantity in the effective tackling of climate change. *How* this carbon tax can be levied in practice is a very difficult problem (also about which economics has a lot to say), but the implementation difficulties do not wave the problem away.

1.1.3 FREE-RIDING. This brings us to the third feature that makes handling climate change difficult, and economic analysis helpful: the free-riding problem. In essence, it all comes down to the fact that the cost of emission reduction is local (is paid by *you* here and now), but the emitted damage is universal – CO_2 molecules know no state boundaries, and mix very rapidly in the atmosphere, irrespective of where they have been emitted. So, even if you stop emitting altogether, your emission-free patch of land does not enjoy a better climate than the land of your polluting neighbour. The temptation, therefore, is for you to hope that your neighbours will curb (at a cost) their carbon emissions, and for you to enjoy the benefits of their sacrifice without doing your bit.

To analyze the multi-party free-riding problem economists have come up with a nice story (the diner's dilemma), that goes along the following lines. Suppose that you decide to go out to dinner with a large number of friends to a restaurant that offers two menus, a cheap-and-ok one, and a good-but-expensive one. You and your friends decide beforehand that you are not going to go Dutch, but you will split evenly the final bill. If you dined at this restaurant on your own, you would not choose the expensive menu, because you don't find that the better quality of the expensive food justifies its cost. But tonight you are out with a bunch of friends, and, you reason, if just this time you chose the expensive menu, its cost would be diluted amongst your friends. This being the case, you think, tonight it is worth going for the fancy menu. The fly in the ointment is that all your friends also think the same way, and therefore everybody chooses the expensive menu and ends up with a choice that *nobody* prefers. In the lingo of game theory the expensive-meal solution is strictly dominant – the strategy is better for one player *no matter what the other players choose* – and is a unique Nash equilibrium – meaning that no player has anything to gain by changing her own strategy. Choosing the expensive meal may well be dominant and a unique Nash equilibrium,[15] but the fancy words do not change the fact that it is also the collectively worst solution.[16]

Mutatis mutandis, this setting shares important features with many important real-life situations, such as, say, taxation: we all know that if nobody paid taxes we would have no hospitals, roads, schools, police, etc. This, we all agree, would be the worst possible outcome. However, if everyone else paid their taxes and you didn't, you would still enjoy almost exactly the same hospitals, roads, schools and police, but your current account would show a significantly higher balance: all moral aspects excluded, free-riding would be your ideal choice. Needless to say, if everyone reasoned in the same way, we would quickly end up in the worst state that we all wanted to avoid in the first place. As Prof Nordhaus says, 'the result of pervasive free-riding is that international climate policy has reached a dead end.'[17]

Getting out of the free-riding problem is particularly difficult because, in these situations, perfect rationality, the distinguishing feature of *Homo Economicus*, offers no way out of the impasse: if anything, it is a coldly rational appraisal of the problem that leads us to the bad solution in the first place. How do we get out of this impasse (how do we avoid, that is, the worst-outcome situation)? Perfectly rational actors require, *and*

---

[15] For the interested lay reader Axelrod (1984) is the most rewarding book on the topic I am aware of.

[16] Individually, someone could be even worse off: that would happen, for instance, if a single diner went for the cheap meal, and everyone else chose lobster with foie gras. In the climate-change context, this would correspond to a single country going for a costly abatement programme.

[17] Nordhaus (2021).

will ask for, a co-ordinator to 'force them to make the right choice'.[18] This can work well when the problem is local (say, national), and one can therefore empower a national coordinator (the government and the judicial system) to 'force us to make the right choice' – one can think of this as a variation on Hobbes' solution to the Leviathan problem. But when the problem is global, the enforcement of global coordination becomes extremely problematic, as recognized by Nordhaus (2021).[19] Perhaps international institutions such as the World Trade Association could provide the required sticks and carrots, but the difficulty of the task should not be underestimated.

These insights have profound implications when it comes to choosing the right mechanisms to tackle climate change: since the temptation to free-ride is always present (both at the individual and national level), pure market solutions, with no government interventions, would not work *even if every citizen were perfectly informed and unerringly rational.* Yes, in some cases the power of the market can be harnessed, for instance by setting up the trading of carbon permits. But even in this poster case of how markets can help in curbing global emissions, an external rule, that is, stipulating that you need a permit to emit at all, must be put in place and enforced beforehand by the 'co-ordinator' of choice. And since the free-riding problem is pervasive in strategic interactions, not surprisingly economics has a lot to say about all of this.

---

[18] Some people say that we are not only motivated by our gain in making social choices such as paying our taxes or not. A moral or social code also plays an important part in determining our choices. This is certainly true, but an economist would answer to this that, if part of your utility is derived from observing moral or social norm, then we should change the payoff matrix of the 'game' and, when we do so, we probably no longer have a diner's dilemma setting any more.

[19] 'Countries rely on others to act, a tendency that undermines the strength of climate agreements. Given these […] problems, it cannot be a surprise that the world has made so little headway in slowing climate change. … Noncooperative approaches to issues as diverse as tariffs, ocean fisheries, war, outer space, and climate change lead to outcomes that leave most or all nations worse off. The result of pervasive free-riding is that international climate policy has reached a dead end. The fatal flaw in the 25 UN conferences leading up to Glasgow is that they are essentially voluntary. Countries may agree to take action, but there are no repercussions if they withdraw from the accords or fail to keep their commitments.'

1.2 GLOBAL WARMING AND INEQUALITY

I debated a lot whether a better title could be found for this section, because, as it stands, it reads like a naked attempt to grab the reader's attention with the two 'trendiest' topics in current social debate. However, the point I want to make here is that there *is* a deep link between tackling climate change and inequality. This being the case, a simple heading that brings the two concepts together is, after all, the most appropriate one.

Inequality has become one of the most pressing topics in economics. If you look up a standard undergraduate textbook in economics written in the closing decades of the last century, you would be hard pressed to find any mention at all of inequality. The new, 1,000-plus-page book by the Oxford Core Team that tries to set the standard for modern teaching of economics introduces inequality on page 3, and, so to speak, its authors never look back.[20] This is certainly a welcome development. What I find surprising is how rarely the economic connection between fighting inequality and fighting global warming is made. In reality, I think that the nexus between the possible solutions of these two problems runs deep. Let me explain why this is the case.

When people talk about inequality, more often than not they refer to the uneven distribution of wealth within a society or a country. It is not surprising that this should be the case: the sight of a homeless person huddling on the pavement a few feet away from where a Bentley is parked has a visceral impact that no statistic about different GDP per person in rich and poor countries can possibly elicit. Yet, the problem of wealth inequality between different parts of the world is every bit as important – if not more so. Every person with no more than a shred of Smith's moral sentiments[21] must hope that these disparities will be soon reduced. As I discuss in Chapter 11, however, we observe that historically improved standards of living have been associated with increased energy

---

[20] The 'Inequality' entry in its index is, by my informal reckoning, the one with more page references than any other.

[21] 'How selfish soever man may be supposed, there are evidently some principles in his nature which interest him in the fortune of others and render their happiness necessary to him though he derives nothing from it except the pleasure of seeing it.' Adam Smith, *The Theory of Human Sentiments*.

consumption (see, e.g., Ayres, 2013, 2016, 2017, Smil 2021) *and* with an increase in population. So, from the point of view of energy consumption, there is a double-whammy: if we want the economic conditions of the poorest populations to improve, the energy consumption per person must increase, and, as a result, the number of people will increase as well.[22] This raises the question of where the energy is going to 'come from'. If the developing and numerically growing countries will follow the development steps of the Western world, using old-technology fossil-fuel-based energy sources first, and only progressing to cleaner ways of producing energy at a much later stage, the emission strain on the planet will be very severe, and perhaps unbearable. Simplifying a lot, it would be as if several Chinas appeared on the emission scene all in one go. Things would look very different if the transition of the developing countries to a high-energy, high-standards-of-living condition could be achieved with low-emission sources of energy. Even in this case a cost in terms of increased emissions would have to be paid, but the transition could be managed with greater hopes to keep global warming under control.

When it comes to who should share the abatement burden, there are obvious questions of equity among nations that must be addressed. Saying that the rowdy party must be broken up because some of the guests are now drunk would justifiably strike the late-comers who had not had a sip yet as deeply unfair. Any solution to the international coordination of abatement efforts must therefore take considerations of equity into account to have any legitimacy. Economics, as an instrumental discipline, is silent about these issues. However, even agents deprived of moral sentiments can easily see that bringing all countries on board, if necessary with substantial international subsidies, is in their selfish interest – CO_2 molecules, as I have said, know no boundaries; and migrants who have to flee areas where life has become impossible because of climate change can be restrained by national boundaries with only marginally greater effectiveness.

So, the climate success of the transition ahead of developing countries hinges heavily on finding cost-effective ways of decarbonizing our energy sources. In their attempts to close the economic gap, developing coun-

---

[22] For a discussion of this important link, see Chapter 11.

tries will certainly and justifiably use the cheapest means at their disposal. We must make sure that clean energy sources, perhaps with transnational subsidies, will be their means of energy production of choice. This may seem to be a narrow technological problem, but technology is not manna from heaven – it is largely the product of what economists call 'learning by doing'. And economics has important things to say about how learning by doing can be aided by a smart regulatory framework. Conversely, modern economic analysis explains why a clumsy, even if intuitively more appealing, set of climate regulations can not only be ineffective, *but hamper technological development.* We will discuss these questions in greater depth in the body of the book (see, e.g., Chapter 16), but the three points I want to make here are, first, that even selfish agents must be in favour of making climate change actions work *across the world*; second, that economic inequality across countries makes the achievement of the common climate goal more difficult – and probably impossible without substantial help from the richer countries; and, third, that economics has a lot to say about how this can be achieved.

1.3 TWO CHEERS FOR ECONOMICS

Having just made the case for why economics is not just useful, but indispensable, to understand properly our climate-change-related choices, I can already hear some strong objections. Economics deals with, and tries to establish equivalences between, material consumption at different points in time, often enjoyed by different people.[23] In doing so, it embarks on an uncompromisingly reductionist path. In the case of the effects of climate change, this means attributing a monetary value to loss of output or capital – something that may be technically difficult, but that, to an economist, seems to make perfect sense. However, to

---

[23] It is unfair to say that the key tool of microeconomic analysis, utility, can only handle *material* consumption. In theory, aesthetic pleasure, pleasure derived from altruistic actions, or the enjoyment derived from, say, a more carefree life could be used as input to the utility function economists strive to maximize. In practice, however, the degree of subjectivity required to make these hedonistic conversions is so high and arbitrary, that most economists implicitly agree only to deal with material consumption (stuff that can be *bought or sold*), or, often crudely and at first blush almost callously, attempt to determine a monetary equivalent to the intangible they would like quantify.

handle the climate-change problem in economics terms, we have to put a price also on, say, the loss of biodiversity, on the forced migrations of populations whose lands are no longer productive, or on the loss of natural beauty. In the calculus of economics, for comparability everything must be translated into a common consumption-related unit ('utility') – a unit about which we will have a lot to say. Doing this comes at a cost of psychological hardening. There should always remain an understandable, natural and, I would say, healthy unease towards even asking questions such as: 'How much consumption should we sacrifice today to prevent the future displacement of a population whose land has been submerged?', or, even more crudely, 'How many migrants is an SUV or an exotic holiday worth?' If pushed in a corner, we may have to resort to establishing these callous equivalences in order to handle the climate-change problem without causing even more unintended damage; but we should never do so lightly.

I have a lot of sympathy for these objections, and I am the first to regard with suspicion the encroachment of economic thinking into areas where 'it does not belong'. I do not look kindly, in other words, on what has been called the 'imperialism' of economics.[24] However, in the last few years, in small part thanks to strands of research to which my research group is contributing, it has become increasingly apparent that even the strongly reductionist approach that economics employs points to very decisive and prompt abatement schedules as the most desirable course of action: we should invest in costly climate-change-abating initiatives, this modern economic research clearly says, *now and in large scale* – and we should do so even if today's sacrifices are far from small. And here is the punch line: *it is exactly because this recommendation comes from such a*

---

[24] Economic analysis, for instance, ties itself into slightly ridiculous knots when it tries to explain the 'paradox' of why citizens bother to vote. The chance that, even in the most tightly fought electoral contest, a single vote might decide its outcome, the economists' reasoning goes, is so small that no rational utility maximizer should bother to visit the polling station: her 'information costs', in economic jargon, are just too high. The fact that turn-out at elections is always in the double digits, and people often engage in the act of voting at high personal risk or discomfort, ceases to be a paradox the moment we acknowledge that the act of voting – of expressing one's *preferences* – brings to the fore key components of what we consider human worth and dignity – aspects that are simply too difficult to handle with the limited lexicon of utility analysis.

reductionist and 'heartless' approach such as the one employed by economists that we should take it seriously.

If I had been writing this book just ten years ago, I would have had to qualify strongly this bold recommendation. I would have had to say that, yes, according to some very respectable economists, acting promptly and decisively was the best course of action. But I would also have had to add that other equally respectable economists (among whom one can number Nobel-prize winners) advocated much more gradual abatement strategies. I would, in other words, have been telling yet another version of the 'on the one hand … on the other hand' story that has become a trademark joke about sitting-on-the-fence economists.[25] This is no longer the case. In the last decade or so, a substantial body of research has been developed, that points with increasing clarity towards decisive and rapid emission abatement as the optimal course of climate-change action. What has happened? We shall discuss this at length in the body of the book, but, in essence, ten or fifteen years ago the only way for economists to recommend early and steep abatement schedules was to posit an extremely high degree of altruism, understood as a high willingness to give up present consumption for the welfare of future generations. (The welfare of *future* generation is mainly at stake, of course, because we expect the most severe damage from climate change to happen well into the future.) While noble and in the abstract commendable, this degree of altruism finds little support in the way we seem willing to distribute resources in different but related areas – such as aid from developed to developing countries, or redistributive taxation. With the early analytical tools that were brought to bear on the climate-change problem, in other words, to come up with fast and rapid abatement schedules one had to assume that humans would behave very differently faced with climate-related damage (inflicted on *future* generations) than with virtually all the other aspects of life from which we can glean our degree of altruism. Needless to say, this 'observed degree of altruism' is not a given, and, arguably, could be 'improved upon'. However, the awkward question remains of why this heightened sensitivity should be

---

[25] As far as I have been able to ascertain, it was US President Harry Truman who pleaded: 'Give me a one-handed economist. All my economists say "on the one hand …", then "but on the other …".'

called 'climate-change altruism' and not, for instance, for 'developing-countries altruism'.

So, ten or so years ago, unless you assumed a rather implausible, and certainly unprecedented, degree of altruism, the main analytical tools from economics suggested that we should actually wait (until we are smarter and richer) before, say, switching to costly renewables, and that investing heavily in climate-change abating technologies now was tantamount to taxing the poor (us today) to benefit the rich (our richer great-grandchildren). This is no longer the case: as our tools of economic analysis have been sharpened, it has become clear that, let alone a saint, but even your indifferently selfish knave should go for rapid and decisive (and costly!) abatement action now. Once again: what is interesting and important is not that economics is telling us to act now and to 'act big'. It is that *even* hard-nosed, cold-hearted, reductionist economics tells us to do so.

The message is brought home with unparalleled clarity by Fig 1.1, which shows the optimal emission-abatement schedules obtained by the DICE model,[26] by the Stern (2006) approach[27] and using the modern economic models that we shall encounter in this book. We shall look in detail at what information these graphs convey in later chapters, but for the moment we just need to know that the Stern approach posited a saintly degree of altruism in economic agents; that the DICE approach tried to mimic the degree of altruism actually observed in other spheres of life; and that the modern approach does not require exceptionally altruistic agents, but fixes some of the modelling problems that plague both the DICE and the Stern approach. One can then read the various curves in Fig 1.1 as representing the trajectory of the abatement effort in three different worlds: the DICE world, the Stern

---

[26] DICE model stands for *D*ynamic *I*ntegrated *C*limate and *E*conomy model. The DICE model was first introduced in the academic literature as far back as 1993 by Nordhaus (1993), and has successively undergone many updates, the latest of which took place in 2016.

[27] The *Review of Economics on Climate Change*, to give it its full name, was launched in 2005 by Sir Nicholas Stern, Head of the British Government Economics Service and Adviser to the British Government on the economics of climate change, at the request of the then Chancellor of the Exchequer, Gordon Brown. While the academic credentials of the contributors were impeccable, it was from the start a project that saw the light in a political, rather than academic, environment.

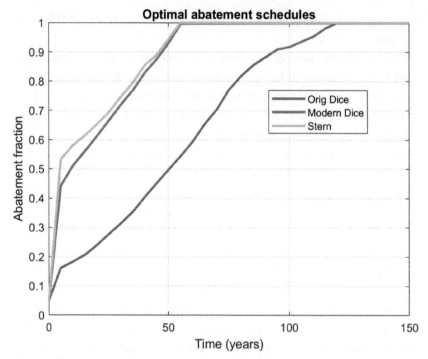

1.1 The abatement schedules obtained by the original Stern and DICE studies (curves labelled 'Stern' and 'orig DICE', respectively), and by the more modern economic models (curve labelled 'Modern DICE'). Note the similarity between the Stern and 'modern' results. These results are illustrative only, and have been obtained for a set of plausible, but not necessarily optimal, parameters for the modern version of the DICE model.

world, and the 'modern-approach' world. Note how gradual the optimal schedule recommended by the DICE model is; how much more rapid the Stern schedule is; but, above all, note how similar the 'modern' and Stern schedules are.[28]

The messages conveyed by these models are radically different: in one case, we should wait and do relatively little; in the two other cases we should act with urgency and in large scale. Why are the conclusions

---

[28] In the graph presented in Fig 1.1 the Stern and the 'modern' schedules are almost on top of each other. Let me come clean. This is coincidental and a bit tendentious, as the near-coincidence depends on a defensible, but by no means unique, choice of parameters for the modern approach. We shall discuss the robustness of these results in Chapter 12. What *is* robust is the finding that the modern abatement schedule is much steeper – implying decisive action sooner – than the DICE recommendation.

so different? How can waiting be advisable if we are facing a climate emergency? Who is right? And why is the modern version of the DICE model so radically different from the original one? How this fundamental change has come about, why we should take it seriously, and whether we are convinced of the reasonableness of these new results are some of the key themes of this book.

1.4 SHOULD WE USE MODELS AT ALL?

These developments have very important policy implications. Faced with the apparent arbitrariness of the model parameters that should reflect (among other factors) the degree of intergenerational altruism,[29] as important and influential a body as the International Panel on Climate Change (IPCC) has chosen not to make use of the linchpin of standard economic analysis of projects, cost-benefit analysis.[30] And, given the undeniable uncertainty that surrounds many key areas of the modelling, many top economists (such as Stern, Pindyck, Weitzman and Stiglitz) are either very cautious, or outright opposed to, using the output of Integrated Assessment Models for 'serious' policymaking. What they propose, instead, is that we should use optimization of means, but only after, somehow, *we have chosen our target.* In other words, we should try to attain our abatement goal as efficiently as possible (this is where the optimization bit comes in), but only after the goal has been reached in some other way.

This is indeed the rationale behind policy targets, such as limiting global warming to 1.5–2 °C, as recommended in the Paris Agreement.[31]

---

[29] *'It is extremely difficult if not impossible to meaningfully estimate discount rates for future costs and benefits'* – IPCC Chapter 1 page 76.

[30] *'Thus standard cost-benefit analyses become difficult to justify (IPCC, 2014a; Dietz et al., 2016) and are not used as an assessment tool in this report.'*

[31] So much has been said about the totemic 1.5–2 °C target, that a few important points should be made. As Knutti, Rogelj Sedlacek and Fisher (2016) point out, while the '2 °C warming target is perceived by the public as a universally accepted goal, identified by scientists as a safe limit that avoids dangerous climate change … [t]his perception is incorrect: no scientific assessment has clearly justified or defended the 2 °C target as a safe level of warming, and indeed, this is not a problem that science alone can address.' As for the more ambitious 1.5 °C target, it was added at the (almost literally) eleventh hour after surviving the gauntlet of the 2015 Paris Agreement

At first blush, this seems reasonable enough. However, even when we decide to adopt these 'exogenous' targets, cost-benefit analysis makes its way back in through the rear door. If pressed as to why we should strive to limit global warming to X degrees by the end of the century, a policy maker would probably say that, if we did not do so, there is a high chance that we will incur serious damages. For this answer to make sense one must accept that these (discounted) damages would be greater than the costs incurred to avoid them. In addition, the same policy-maker would also point out that there is a high degree of uncertainty, both in the climate outcomes and in their consequences, and this therefore calls for prudence: a very reasonable better-safe-than-sorry attitude. But, if you think about it, this is just cost-benefit-analysis-under-uncertainty by another name, and without the intellectual discipline that an 'auditable' analysis can provide. By this I mean, that, when we use a model, we can all look at the assumptions that went into it; change them as new information becomes available; and run sensitivity analysis – explore, that is, how much the results change when the uncertain inputs change. Which is a lot more than one can do with a 'commonsensical' hunch, inspired as this may be. Model-based decisions make the resulting course of action dynamic and continuously self-correcting: two features that are of key importance when we are navigating the waters of climate change.[32]

climate-change negotiations, at the request of the representatives of the Caribbean states, understandably afraid that a relatively small increase in sea levels could submerge their islands. For a good discussion of how the 1.5–2 °C target was arrived at, see www.desmog.com/2022/12/11/15-2c-history-temperature-target-climate-paris-agreement/.

[32] There is a great deal of controversy about whether the type of cost-benefit analysis that is at the heart of Integrated Assessment models is useful or misguided. As I have said, some serious economists, such as Nobel-prize winner Joseph Stiglitz or Prof Stern (2021), advocate a very different procedure: we should use models, they say, to try to minimize the costs of reaching a 'commonsensical' target, such as limiting warming to 1.5–2 °C by the end of the century, but we should not use Integrated Assessment Models to tell us what these targets should be. I have to say that some of the arguments used to make their point seem at times designed to knock down a straw man: it is emphatically not true, for instance, that all Integrated Assessment Models consider a temperature increase of 4 °C as 'optimal'; some early versions did, almost none of the new models do. And, while it is true that climate scientists appear to be more concerned about damages than economists, it is not a priori clear why their views in this particular domain should be deemed more trustworthy. For a strong and, in my view, clear rebuttal of the argument see Aldy, Kotchen, Stavins and Stock (2021), whose

This apparently common-sense-based approach may at times seem the only practical way forward, but there is little in the reasoning that led to the commonsensical conclusion that economic analysis cannot handle. If we are uncertain about outcomes, utility theory will tell us to be more prudent – the more so, the more uncertain we are. Some critics complain that the climate damages that are assumed by the economic models are too moderate. This could well be true, but, if there are scientific arguments for doing so, there is absolutely no reason why we cannot include 'tipping points', positive-feedback effects or more severe damage exponents in our economic analysis. And if the discounting (the 'writing off') of future damages just because they happen in the future seems to be so severe as to give rise to absurd recommendations, we should question whether we have modelled our preferences correctly. This is exactly what the new-generation economic models allow us to do. As a result, an important and influential body as the IPCC need not throw its hands up in despair by saying: 'Economic analysis is too incomplete to be of any use for climate change', and can endorse with new confidence targets that are no longer pulled out of a hat. Indeed, as we shall see, temperature targets very similar to the canonical '1.5–2 °C by the end of the century' can be recovered naturally as optimal by the new-generation economic models.

One last point. As I have already said, when their actions are properly modelled, modern economic analysis shows that even indifferently altruistic agents should prefer 'fast and strong' abatement schedules. However, the other blemishes of utility-based analysis (its narrow focus on material consumption and, more generally, what I have called its reductionist character) are still there. And, to make matters worse, Weitzman (2009) presented in 2009 his 'dismal theorem', according to which a standard cost-benefit analysis may break down altogether if there is a possibility of truly catastrophic outcomes (technically, if we have very slowly-decaying tails for the loss distribution).[33] If this is the case, why

position is clearly summarized as follows: 'In the context of climate change, the application of cost-benefit analysis to inform mitigation policies can help to achieve the best outcomes and avoid the worst: spending trillions of dollars but failing to get the job done.'

[33] Weitzman's argument, which I find very compelling, has not gone unchallenged. For a reply to Weitzman's challenge see, Nordhaus (2009).

should we put our faith in models whose outputs are so uncertain, and that may not be up to the task in the first place? And if somehow we added all the features our modelling leaves out, wouldn't the abatement recommendations become even stronger? Wouldn't the call for action be even more urgent?

I have little doubt that this would indeed be the case.[34] However, the course of abatement action recommended by our flawed models is already so decisive and rapid that it is resolutely hitting against the boundaries of political and practical implementability. Let me give one example. As we shall see, the 'social cost of carbon' is a key output of the economic models used to analyze the climate-change problem – roughly speaking, it can be understood as the optimal tax that should be imposed on fossil fuels to redress the externalities embedded in their use. Now, there is little point in establishing that a tax of many dollars (or euros or pounds) per litre would be 'optimal', when a modest fuel tax of a small fraction of a Euro sparked the gilet jaunes unrest of 2018 in France.[35] I could bring up many similar examples, but my point, I hope, is clear. Yes, almost certainly, if we somehow managed to bring into the economic fold considerations that are currently ill-accommodated by utility-theory analysis, even steeper abatement efforts *would* be recommended. However, between what is desirable and what is achievable there lies a hiatus that is ignored at great political cost. Bluntly put, I am interested in the policy recommendations that have a chance of being implemented – and I am painfully aware that over-ambitious targets end up playing into the hands of climate-change deniers, populist politicians and the advocates of very little change.

---

[34] For a discussion of what cost-benefit analysis leaves out, and of the prevalent biases embedded in most Integrated Assessment Models, see Stiglitz and Stern (2021).

[35] Fuel taxes in Europe range from eighty cents per litre for the Netherlands to thirty-six cents per litre for Bulgaria. In the US fuel taxes are lower, ranging from seventeen cents per litre in Pennsylvania, to three cents per litre in Alaska. Worldwide, about 20 per cent of world emissions are covered by any carbon tax at all, and less than 5 per cent attract a carbon tax as high as the lowest estimate of a reasonable social cost of carbon (Kuper, 2021). As for the *gilets jaunes* unrest of 2018, it was prompted by a proposed increase in the cost of fuel of about six cents per litre. As is well known, President Macron had to backtrack on his modest, but singularly poorly conceived, tax proposal (the fuel tax had its biggest impact on poorer suburban and rural people, who have few alternatives to switch to public transport).

CHAPTER 2

The Facts on the Ground

So physicians say of consumptive patients, that in its first phases their illness is easy to cure but difficult to diagnose, but, as time goes by, if not discovered and remedied, it becomes easy to recognize but difficult to cure.[1]

—N. Machiavelli, *The Prince*

AS I HAVE SAID, this book is aimed at an open-minded, intelligent but perplexed citizen-reader. Probably I came to the conclusion that a book such as this needed writing when, several months ago, a colleague of mine approached me at the proverbial office water cooler, and asked me a very strange question. Let me explain the setting. This colleague of mine is supremely clever, mathematically very gifted, and has published several seminal papers in the top academic journals in his field (finance). He also knows that I have a background in physics, and in nuclear engineering before that, and that is why he was asking me the question. I can't remember his exact words, but what he asked me, in rather furtive tones, was something along the following lines: '*This climate change thing – is it truly as bad as they say? Do we really know for sure? As an ex-physicist, what do you think?*'

The question, coming from him, first struck me as nothing short of extraordinary. I know for sure that he would never have asked me if something prima facie much more far-fetched (say, quantum entanglement) 'was for real'. Even if quantum mechanics is not his area of expertise, he

---

[1] '... dicono e fisici dello etico, che nel principio del suo male é facile a curare e difficile a conoscere, ma nel progresso del tempo, non l'avendo in principio conosciuta né medicata, diventa facile a conoscere e difficile a curare ...', Machiavelli (2006), page 10.

would have taken the word of the scientists in the field at face value. But, when it came to climate science, his reaction was different. What I was sensing in his question was not just a healthy scepticism, but diffidence. If the seeds of reasonable doubt have been sown in someone like him, I thought, then the information has well and truly been poisoned.

So, it is true that the main contribution of this book lies in the explanation of how economics can help us reach sound decisions about climate change. However, these decisions cannot be arrived at in a factual vacuum. Unfortunately, I cannot take for granted that the climate facts are as universally accepted as they should be. This is why in Section 2.3 of this chapter I will list the basic 'climate facts on the ground' that we can consider solidly established and that are relevant to the economic analysis that follows.

Facts, we all agree, do not speak for themselves and only acquire the power to move us to action if our cognitive reaction to them is balanced and appropriate. Unfortunately, the peddlers of climate-change doubt are at least as successful today as the sowers of tobacco-damage doubt were in the 1960s and 1970s.[2] It is therefore useful to engage first with our cognitive responses to climate facts: and one way to do so is via my parable of the dangerous burglar.

2.1 THE PARABLE OF THE DANGEROUS BURGLAR

One of the recurring objections raised against taking prompt and costly action to abate climate change goes along the following lines: 'We really don't know for sure whether the warming of the Earth is due to human activity, nor do we know how bad the consequences of this warming are going to be. But we know for sure that trying to stop climate change is going to be costly and difficult. Doesn't is make sense to wait and see?'

---

[2] A new discipline has recently emerged, that goes under the awkward name of 'agnotology'. It is the study of how false information and confusion is deliberately spread. As Cecilia Tomori (2021) points out in *Nature*, 'The strategies and patterns recur across industries: they have been documented in tobacco, fossil fuels, pharmaceuticals, food and more. This influence is so powerful that public-health researchers consider it a distinct area of study: "commercial determinants of health".' The topic is carefully examined in chapter 11 of Michaels' 2020 well-documented book, *The Triumph of Doubt*, which is insightfully reviewed in Lawrence (2020).

Like all 'tedious arguments of insidious intent', there is a superficial appeal to this line of reasoning. To argue that, no, it doesn't make sense to wait and see just because we are not certain,[3] at the start of my climate-science course I tell my students the following story. 'In your neighbourhood,' I say, 'the police has reported the presence of a dangerous and violent burglar. You can install a burglar alarm system, linked to the local police station, that, in all likelihood, will prevent the burglar from entering your house. However, the alarm system is rather expensive – say, several thousand pounds per year. The alarm system is very effective, but there is no absolute guarantee that it will stop the burglar. Of course, if you were sure that the burglar is planning to target your property you would certainly install the alarm system. But, since you cannot be sure, how confident would you have to be that you will be a future victim of the burglar for you to install the expensive alarm system?'

Most of my students put the critical probability of a break-in above which they choose to pay for the alarm system at around 30 per cent. The ones of most prudent disposition are ready to pay the installation cost if they think that the probability of break-in is greater than a few per cent. The most gung-ho, make-my-day-punk student who ever gave me an answer (let's call him Clint) put it at 50 per cent.

'If you feel this way,' I then ask, 'why do you require near-absolute certainty about the damage from climate change for you to choose to undertake costly abatement action?' The point of the parable is transparent (I hope). Yes, it is true that we are not certain about the extent of the climate-changing damages for different levels of warming – we shall discuss this point at length later in the book. But there are very reasonable scenarios in which the damage is *very* serious – I made it clear that the burglar in my story *can* be very dangerous. And, yes, we cannot be sure that the costly abatement actions we take now will indeed be effective at curbing climate change. That is why, in my story, the expensive alarm system did not give 100 per cent safety against the burglar. Yet, most reasonable people still prefer to pay the money and sleep better at

---

[3] There are different and better arguments why we should wait and see, which we will discuss in the body of the book. I will argue that, even when these arguments are taken into account, waiting and seeing is not the best option, but the parable of the dangerous burglar, presented in this section, is not enough to deal with these objections.

night. Why do so many people ask for absolute certainty of damage to countenance the idea of doing something serious about climate change, when they do not seem to be so risk tolerant in most other spheres of their lives?

I think that part of the explanation goes down to what I call the manipulation of doubt. Let me explain what I mean. When, in a previous life, I used to work as a young researcher at the X-ray synchrotron facility at Brookhaven National Laboratory, I noticed that almost all the (peer-reviewed, scientifically impeccable) papers published by a senior colleague of mine were focussed on showing the inaccuracies of Carbon-14 dating. I asked him why he found the topic so interesting. 'It's not that I find the topic particularly interesting,' he replied. 'It's just that I want to sow enough doubts in the minds of people about the dating of biological findings to make the 6,000-year-old Biblical version of creation a plausible alternative.' For the first time I realized that one can be, at the same, impeccably correct (I could not find a fault in any of his papers), yet deeply intellectually dishonest.

In the context of climate change, this selective use of evidence in order to sow doubts in reasonable people about the reality of climate change, of its anthropogenic origin, and of the likely severity of the unchecked outcomes has been turned into an art from – of which my colleague at the water cooler had been a victim. For instance, technically I would not be telling a lie if I told you that you can choose five *consecutive* segments between 1970 and 2015 in such a way that the average temperature has fallen in every single one of them. See Fig 2.1 in which the best fit in every consecutive segment shows a *decline* in temperature. Yet, I would also be profoundly misleading. There has been no 'cheating' in how each individual best fit has been carried out: each one is a proper and correct Ordinary Least Square regression – exactly as the work of my Brookhaven colleague, each piece of analysis is correct. However, Fig 2.2 shows just as clearly that presenting a graph such as the one in Fig 2.1 means playing fast and loose with the truth. Which, of course, did not stop Fox News from trumpeting in 2013: *'The planet has stopped warming up over the last 15 years, data shows'.*[4]

---

[4] Fox.News.com, 27 September 2013.

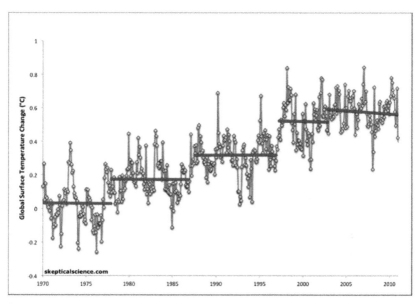

2.1 How a 'sceptic' can present temperature change. The graphic's creator is Dana Nuccitelli, Skeptical Science.

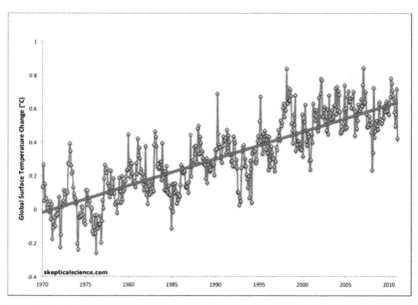

2.2 How a 'realist' sees temperature change. The graphic's creator is Dana Nuccitelli, Skeptical Science.

Don't get me wrong. A healthy dose of scepticism is always good, and I invite the reader to challenge with a sharp critical mind everything she reads (including, of course, this book) about climate change – and about anything else, for that matter. If someone is looking for certainties, science is not the place to go. It would be dishonest to say that we have *absolutely zero* doubts that the Earth's temperature is increasing; that this increase is anthropogenic; and that it can be reversed. This is not how science works. After all, the two pillars of modern physics, general relativity and quantum mechanics, have had a degree of experimental confirmation we cannot even dream of when it comes to climate science – or, probably any other science.[5] Yet, scientists harbour serious doubts that either the former, or the latter, or perhaps both, may be wrong, because in some domains there are findings that make the reconciliation of the two theories as they stand at the moment very difficult. But if scientists were only prepared to work with theories about which there is *absolute* certainty, their day at the lab would be very short indeed.

In reality, the parable of the dangerous burglar shows that, both in life and in science, we do not require *absolute* certainty to act – and, if need be, to act decisively. And, surely, we don't refuse to heed the directions of our GPS (whose proper functioning depends on general-relativistic corrections) because, who knows, the theory of general relativity could be proven wrong. A dispassionate analysis of what we know shows that there is so much scientific evidence about the reality of climate change and about its anthropogenic origin that it is intellectually dishonest to act as if we had strong doubts about this.

Admittedly, when it comes to the *consequences* of this global warming, our degree of certainty is much more limited: in physics, scientists always feel very comfortable about *inter*polating, but tend to get clammy hands when it comes to *extra*polation. And extrapolating we must, when we try to gauge what the effects of a 2-, 3- or 7-degree warming will be on the

---

[5] In quantum field theory the magnetic dipole moment of the muon has been experimentally measured to be $(g_\mu - 2)_{exp} = 0.233184600(1680) \times 10^{-11}$. The theoretical prediction of the same quantity is $(g_\mu - 2)_{exp} = 0.233183470(308) \times 10^{-11}$, with a precision of one part in a million. And as for general relativity, it has allowed us to predict the existence of objects as exotic as black holes decades before we could observe them.

ecosystem and on human societies. The Earth has been in the past much warmer than that, but *we*, by which I mean 'the human species', were not around. So, we must use rather indirect inferences to venture our best estimate of what the impact of this warming on our lives will be. However, the mere fact that we are so uncertain, as we discuss in Chapter 6, has a bearing on the choices we make: in most walks of life uncertainty makes us more prudent. Why should uncertainty make us more reluctant to take insurance action when it comes to climate change? If you are trying to undermine abatement efforts, why peddle doubt, when greater doubt should make us more prudent?

2.2 BUT IS IT REALLY SCIENCE?

Climate deniers try to stop us from taking serious abatement action by using a subtle psychological trick. They *do* realize that, if they simply overemphasized the uncertainty element, they would end up making us more willing to 'buy insurance'. So they try to convince us that the predictions we hear about climate outcomes are not just noisy, but *biased*. And, since few people would say that sciences such as, say, physics, biology or computer science are biased, they try to convince us that climate science is not 'proper science'. They have been rather successful at this, as there is an uneasy feeling among intelligent laypersons that what climate scientists do is something more akin to advocacy or political canvassing than to what 'regular' scientists do. Sadly, the most strident advocates of urgent climate action, who use the scare tactics of presenting the most catastrophic scenarios as the scientifically certain outcomes of inaction, may be effective when they preach to the choir, but, when it comes to the undecided, often end up playing into the hands of climate deniers.

Another tactic of choice to sow doubts in the minds of the undecided is claiming that climate science is still a 'young' and unsophisticated (and hence unreliable) discipline, whose practices boil down to stacking lots of empirical observations on top of one another, drawing pretty graphs – some of them perhaps hockey-stick-shaped – and interpolating in between observations. This, the objection goes, is not what 'real' science is all about. If this were truly what climate science amounted to, the critics would have a point. Indeed, we do need lots of observations, we do need to organize these observations in graphs, and we do need to interpolate between the points in the graph. However, if we want to place in climate science the same degree of confidence we put, say, on biology, or solid state physics, we need a lot more than this. Does climate science really display this 'extra bit'?

Now, I am aware that I am faced with a tricky task here, simply because nobody has come up with a watertight definition of what constitutes science and what is non-science. (Philosophers of science call this the 'demarcation problem'.) Some forty years ago Popper's falsificationism was all the rage among many practising scientists, who thought they would win philosophical brownie points by peppering their scientific papers with a smattering of falsificationist lingo. Then, as we approached a more sociologically relativistic age, Khun's 'paradigm shifts' became all the rage. After Kuhn, Imre Lakatos and his 'research programmes' garnered the interest of philosophers of science. Lakatos has never been a household name among practising scientists, but, with his *Proofs and Refutations* he became well regarded by professional philosophers of science, and so scientists began saying that they were engaged in 'research programmes'.

To make a long story short, the stack of books on the philosophy of science shelf at Blackwell's keeps on getting longer and longer, but despite, or perhaps because of, all these efforts it has become progressively clear that identifying the secret sauce that makes science 'scientific' is about as easy as getting energy from nuclear fusion. In frustration, some historians and philosophers of science took the ultimate baby-and-bath-water step, and began to argue that science did not really exist – or, rather, that it was no different from, say astrology or alchemy. (Steven Shapin arrestingly started his book *The Scientific Revolution* with the words *'There is no such thing as the Scientific Revolution, and this is a book about it'.*)

Some practising scientists (mainly physicists) got pretty much fed up with these failed attempts to give a solid philosophical grounding to what they had been doing in the lab all along (the physicists' physicist par excellence, Richard Feynman, said that 'philosophy of science is as useful to scientists as ornithology is to birds'), and today's best consensus about what constitutes science and what doesn't can be pithily, if a bit unfairly, summarized with Supreme Court Justice Potter Stewart's words:

'I know it when I see it'. (Justice Potter's words referred to pornography. You shouldn't read too much into this.)

Given this state of affairs, I will give a wide berth to the philosophical niceties of the question *'what constitutes real science?'* and take an unabashedly I-know-it-where-I-see-it attitude to the problem. So, what are the tell-tale signs that an enterprise is 'science'? What do we have to 'see' to conclude that climate science *is* science? I will take some of the tell-tale *indicia* that an activity warrants the 'science' label to be measuring, explaining, modelling and, above all, predicting. How does climate science stack up against these 'science indicators'?

First of all, there is more to climate science than collecting a lot of data and producing graphs with 'temperature curves that go up'. Science must provide a *model* to make sense of the regularities found in the data. The good news is that currently we have solid models, based on well-established concepts borrowed from physics (thermodynamics, hydrodynamics, quantum mechanics, Newtonian mechanics, etc.) that can explain why the Earth is warming, and the role played by certain gases (among which fossil fuel emissions feature importantly) in this warming. So, we understand very well why increasing the concentration of certain gases in the atmosphere would increase its temperature: we have a solid explanatory model.

However, a critic would say, good science should predict, not just explain. Now, it will come as a surprise to most readers to learn that climate change was *predicted*, and that it was predicted as long ago as the nineteenth century. Almost exactly two centuries ago (in 1824, to be precise) Fourier calculated that the Earth's temperature would be cooler without its atmosphere. Then in 1859 Tyndall showed that some gases trap infrared radiation, and worked out the implications of this for the increase in temperature of our planet.[6] But we had to wait until 1896 for Arrhenius to produce what we would today recognize as the first simple climate model – a model in which CO_2 played a key role.[7] Remarkably, until well into the twentieth century what most scientists were worried about was not global warming, but global *cooling*.

---

[6] For a discussion see Weart (2008), pages 3–5.
[7] See https://history.aip.org/climate/pdf.htm.

The reason for this was that scientists knew about the relatively recent Ice Age (we exited the last Ice Age as recently as 12,000 years ago), and they were trying to understand whether the conditions that ushered in the Ice-Age temperatures may occur in the near future. It was only in the 1960s and 1970s that the possibility of global warming began to be seriously considered.

Now, the story of how the prediction of CO_2-induced atmospheric warming evolved is not simple and linear, and is fraught with dead ends, turning points, mistakes (and corrections) – as science always is.[8] The point is that, if the evolution of climate models has been messy, it is because all science *is* messy, and proceeds by tâtonnements, revisions, mistakes and corrections. In science, however, over time a consensus explanation of the phenomenon under study tends to emerge and consolidate: and this is exactly what has happened with climate science. We may quibble about the details, but the fundamental 'physics' behind planetary climate is now very well established.[9]

Remembering her Galileo dropping stones from the top of the tower of Pisa, the sceptical reader may rebut: 'Haven't you forgotten something? Where is the carrying out of experiments in climate science? How can you say that climate science is good science when carrying out experiments is well nigh impossible?' As a matter of fact, there are areas of science – from geology, to evolutionary biology, to cosmology – where making *direct* experiments is extremely difficult. What these research programmes tend to have in common is that we try to understand what happened in a distant past that we cannot alter. We can still perform experiments of sorts (e.g., computer simulations), but the evidence we can gather from

---

[8] For a truly excellent account of how the science of climate change developed over more than one century, see Weart (2008). By analysing in detail how global warming was discovered, the author explains very well how scientific progress is far from linear, and scientific understanding is not cumulative – despite its wrong turns and dead ends, the scientific process is, nonetheless, self correcting.

[9] I say 'planetary' rather then 'Earth' because exactly the same basic model we use to explain the role played by greenhouse gases in warming the Earth is used to explain the temperature of the other planets and bodies of our solar system. (This, by the way, is why Venus is much hotter than Mercury, despite being far more distant from the Sun than the latter is.) The fact that *the same* model explains *lots* of phenomena without needing any tweaking is another indicium of good science.

this is by necessity more indirect. If you think that this is cheating, I would ask you to apply the same harsh criterion not just to the reconstruction of past climate, but also, say, to the Big Bang theory, or to the theory of evolution. Furthermore, a large number of very different pieces of evidence, analysed using different experimental methodologies, tell a coherent story about the Earth's climate in a past that we cannot directly access. Each individual source of information is often highly imprecise, but the important feature is not so much the reliability of any one source of information, but their overall congruence.[10] If we have a number of perhaps highly imperfect pieces of evidence that all lead us to reach the same conclusion, we can have more confidence in it (the conclusion is more 'robust', and demonstrably statistically more likely) than if we had to rely on a single, even if highly reliable, measurement.[11] If in a murder case many witnesses report a consistent account of what happened, it doesn't really matter if one bystander thought the murderer was wearing brown shoes and another black shoes, as long as their stories display an internal consistence. A judge or a jury will make up their minds more easily on the basis of many corroborating accounts, than if they had to rely on a single super-witness. This is what philosopher of science Wimsatt means when he says that '[t]hings are robust if they are accessible (detectable, measurable, derivable, definable, producible, or the like) in a variety of independent ways'.[12] The conclusions we can reach about the past climate of the Earth are in this sense very robust.

2.3 WHAT WE KNOW WITH CONFIDENCE

I have tried to convince my sceptical reader that climate science shares many of the key features we tend to associate with 'good science'. If this is the case, we should take what climate scientists say with the same degree of confidence (and scepticism) with which we take the

[10] When it comes to estimating past temperatures, for instance, scientists use different proxies, such as tree rings, ice cores, fossil pollen, ocean sediments, corals and many more. All these proxies have different degrees of certainty; go back into the past to different extent; have different degrees of resolution. Each source is imperfect. Taken together, they tell a coherent story.

[11] Thanks to Dr Jean Whitmore Ortega for pointing this out.

[12] Wimsatt (2007), page 196.

statements of those who work in, say, cosmology or evolutionary biology. Serious scientists also communicate the confidence they have in their pronouncements – the points in their graphs come equipped with 'error bars'. We should take the error bars of climate scientists as seriously as we take the error bars in other sciences. Especially when it comes to the consequences of climate change, these error bars are sometimes uncomfortably large. This is no accident: as in the case of Machiavelli's physician faced with a consumptive patient, climate change is a phenomenon that, when relatively easy to fix, is difficult to detect, but by the time its effects become obvious, is very difficult to tackle. We happen to be in the early, difficult-to-study phase. But this is just how most of 'normal science' works: by trying, one step at a time, to make our error bars progressively smaller. Keeping this in mind, these are climate change–related statements about which there is quasi-universal agreement, and these are the associated error bars.

First, there is virtually no doubt that the Earth has been warming over the last half century or so, and that what we are observing *is not a statistical fluctuation*. One cannot prove a statement like this just by picking a few well-chosen graphs, but the message conveyed by Figs 2.3, 2.5 and 2.6 suggests that the mountain the deniers of *this* statement have to climb is fantastically steep. Let's see what these graphs tell us.

Let's start from Fig 2.3, which is the simplest, but, at the same time, the least straightforward to interpret. It shows the annual mean temperature from 1880 to 2021. The dots are the median of the annual global temperatures; since there are considerable annual fluctuations in the temperature for a variety of random (in our context, non-climate change–related) reasons, the non-jagged yellow line shows a smooth version of the data. Finally, the upper and lower curves that surround the dots display the degree of uncertainty around the measured value. Statisticians say that, given any one measurement point, we can be 95 per cent confident that the real temperature is not outside the band itself. Note how the uncertainty band becomes thinner and thinner as we approach the present date, reflecting the greater sophistication and precision of our measurements. This is good, because we want to rule out the possibility that the effect we want to measure may be masked by measurement error.

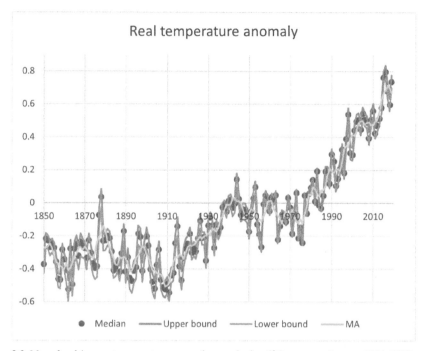

2.3 Mean land/ocean temperature anomaly over the last 170 years – reference 1961–1990. The dots show the median of the actual measurements; the upper and lower curves display the 5th and 95th percentile of the distribution of measurements; the smooth line shows a moving average of the data.

The first observation about this figure is that up until, approximately, 1980 whether the observed pattern was due to random fluctuations or to a weak trend was far from being 'optically' obvious. It is only with the 1990s that an upward trend in temperature becomes visible to the statistically untrained eye. When we look at the temperature observations for the last two decades, the upward trend appears unmistakable. Surely this should be an open-and-shut case. Or is it?

The problem is that totally random fluctuations (what in technical terms is called a 'Brownian motion') can produce trajectories into which the human eye all too easily hallucinates trends, patterns and regularities. To show the point, I show in Fig 2.4 a totally made-up path of temperature anomalies. To create these fake data, I have downloaded the real temperature data,[13] I have calculated their variability (the standard deviation),

[13] https://ourworldindata.org/grapher/temperature-anomaly. I encourage the reader to download and play around with the data the way I did.

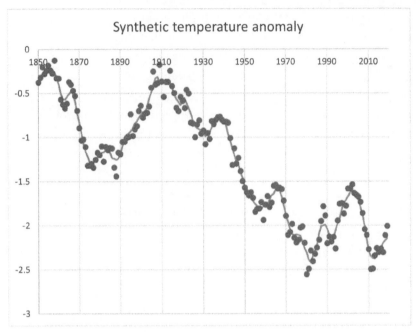

2.4 'Fake' temperature data created by calculating the variability of the true data, and using it to create a 'random walk' of temperature anomalies *with no trend*.

and simulated the evolution of the temperature anomaly over the same period of time using the same degree of variability.[14] (I have labelled the *x* axis with the same dates as in the real data to make the figures as easily comparable as possible, but the dates are irrelevant.)

The surprising (and slightly unsettling) feature from this graph is that the data appear 'trendy' (staggering up and down like a drunkard, but in a definite direction), even if each change in temperature is totally random, and independent from the previous increment. The (in this case downward) trend was purely a fluke, like flipping, say, five heads in a row. And I stress that the graph I show in Fig 2.4 was not obtained after thousands of attempts: the Excel-produced data were produced in a few seconds just by recalculating less than fifteen times the simulated

[14] For the technically inclined reader, the simulation has been carried out based on the discretized Brownian process $\Delta T = \sigma \sqrt{\Delta t} \epsilon$, with σ denoting the volatility, which I estimated from the real data to be 0.1285, $\Delta t = 1$ (in years), ϵ a draw from a $N(0,1)$ Gaussian distribution, and T the temperature.

paths. Fig 2.4 is not, in other terms, the graphical equivalent of tossing, say, twenty heads in a row. The problem is that the human eye (mind, really) 'wants' to discover patterns even where there are none – a phenomenon known in psychology as pareidolia. Whole books based on the interpretation of patterns (trends, 'resistance points', 'shoulders' and what not) in financial data have been written, bought and read. Their predictions are only marginally more accurate than those from astrology. So, one has to be very careful when drawing conclusions from a hundred-or-so points, even when they suggest an 'obvious' trend.

This does not mean that we cannot tell whether a trend is actually there. The relevant question for the readers of this book is the following: without wading deep into the statistical high grass, can we say something about whether the temperature is actually increasing that is visually more convincing than the lines in Fig 2.3? This is why I have chosen to show Figs 2.5 and 2.6. Let's start from the first. It displays the average seasonal temperature variation over the last 130 years. On the x axis the figure reports the month of the year. The first conclusion is that, yes, January is, on average, colder than February, February than March, and so on all the way to July. Few surprises here. However, this unexciting seasonal pattern has been reported for all the years from 1880 to 2019, creating a

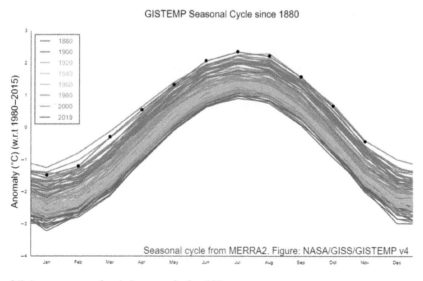

2.5 Average seasonal variation over the last 130 years.

Monthly global mean temperature 1851–2020 (compared to 1850–1900 averages)

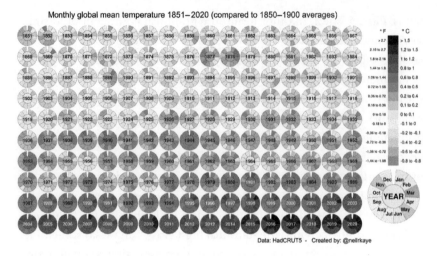

Data: HadCRUT5 - Created by: @neilrkaye

2.6 Monthly average temperatures compared to 1850–1900 average.

bundle of seasonal temperature variations. One may think that, to guide the eye, the top (hottest) lines are shown in red, and the coldest in blue. But this is not how the colours were assigned: looking at the legend in the left-hand corner of the figure one immediately sees that the blue ('cold') lines refer to the early periods (1880–1900), and the red lines to the late periods (2000–2019). It just so happens that 'late' correlates very strongly with 'hot': there are exceptions, but the relationship is very robust. A statistician would ask: 'How likely is it that this ordering may have occurred by accident?' The answer, this time, matches our optical intuition: 'So unlikely, as to be almost impossible.'

Fig 2.6 reinforces the point. It shows, again, the monthly average temperatures compared to 1850–1900 average, and it does so by associating to each year a pie with twelve sectors. Each sector of the pie represents a month, and the month sector is coloured in shades of blue or red to show whether it was hotter or colder than the 1850–1900 average temperature for the same month. Again, there are a few exceptions, but the pattern is clear: all the reddest and darkest circles are at the bottom of the graph (closer to today); most of the pale blue circles are in the top lines of the graph (the earlier measurements). Note, by the way, the asymmetry of the exceptions: there are quite a few 'hot' sectors in the top (early and 'cold') part of the graph, but there are no 'cold' slices of pie in the bottom part of the graph. Again, if a statistician were asked how likely it is that this ordering may have occurred by accident, her unequivocal answer would be: 'exceedingly low'.

Summarizing: one has to be careful drawing hasty conclusions from intriguing graphs with 'curves that go up'. However, serious statistical analysis of the available data – serious analysis of which Figs 2.5 and 2.6 are purely suggestive indicators – says unequivocally that there *is* an upward trend in temperature. More importantly, these temperature data do not exist in a vacuum. We don't just have an unexplained data pattern that we can statistically describe as a process with an upward trend. We also have a model that explains why the temperature *should* have gone up given the amount of greenhouse gases that have been injected in the atmosphere. And, as we have seen, we *predicted* that this would happen more than a century ago. More about this later – for the moment, let's continue lining up the established facts on the ground.

The second solid fact is that the warming is almost certainly due to human action (it is anthropogenic). A priori, there could have been other plausible explanations: the observed warming could be due, for instance, to changes in solar irradiance (the amount of energy emitted by the Sun), to the Milankovitch cycles,[15] to volcanic eruptions, or to other causes. All these candidate explanations have been carefully examined, and discarded. There was a decent correlation between changes in irradiance and changes in the average surface temperature until roughly the 1960s, but after that the two curves have diverged, with temperature going up, and irradiance going down. If anything, if we only looked at how much energy the Earth is receiving from the Sun, we should be observing global cooling, not global warming. And as for the Milankovitch cycles, they do help us understand some of the past fluctuations in temperature, but their predictions just do not match the

---

[15] The Earth rotates around the Sun along an ellipse whose eccentricity changes over time; the inclination of the axis of rotation also changes over time; and there is precession around this axis. Milankovitch, and many scientists after him, studied how these periodic changes in the Earth's orbit and rotation could affect the amount of radiation received – the 'energy in' part of the energy-balance equation. While these Milankovitch cycles can explain the long-term trend of past temperatures inferred from climate proxies, scientists agree that they cannot explain the recent and very rapid warming.

changes in temperature we observe today. To reproduce (with computer simulations) the current temperature changes we need other ingredients. The encouraging thing is that we understand pretty well what the missing ingredients are.

The fact is that we do not need to invoke changes in solar irradiance or Milankovitch cycles, because we have a solid explanatory model to link increased CO_2 concentrations to an increase in temperature; we have a link between human activities and increased emissions; and we have a prediction, made over a century ago, that these increased concentrations would make the Earth warmer. The overwhelming evidence therefore points to the anthropogenic origin of the warming we are observing. I do not want to give the wrong impression here. The best explanation we have of why the Earth is warming at the moment points with clarity to the increased concentration of CO_2-equivalent gases since the start of the Industrial Revolution. There is exceedingly little doubt about this. Having said that, a number of more complex phenomena, such as the feedback effect associated with the increased amount of water vapour that a warmer atmosphere can hold, are also at play, and only imperfectly understood. Feedback effects are a recurrent feature of the climate system, and are difficult to model. The thawing of the permafrost; the lower reflectivity of the Earth (albedo) as more glaciers melt; even the fact that the surface of plants seems to thicken and absorb less CO_2 as the temperature increases – these are all forms of feedback effects that we still imperfectly understand, and that play a role in global warming that is difficult to quantify. This does not change, however, the basic picture.

In sum: scientists are not quite as confident about the anthropogenic origin of the Earth's warming as about the fact that the Earth is warming, but they are still *extremely* confident that human actions are preponderantly responsible for the observed increase in temperature. This very high degree of confidence comes from linking two separate pieces of information by means of a causal model that brings together parts of physics (such as black-body radiation, or atomic physics) that were developed in completely different contexts. We are not, in other words, making up ad hoc theories to explain the temperature data: we are using extremely solid building blocks of physics that were created to explain totally different phenomena. We are not, in short, retrofitting a model to our data.

The anthropogenic origin of the current global warming, by the way, is bad, but also good news. If the warming were due, say, to a change in solar irradiance, our chances of reversing the warming trend would be much more limited, much more difficult to implement, and of much more dubious efficacy. I am referring here to geoengineering, which can be defined as the set of deliberate and large interventions to modify the Earth's climate (not weather). The most commonly proposed intervention is the alteration of the atmosphere to reflect part of the incoming solar radiation before it reaches the Earth. This can be achieved, for instance, by injecting aerosols in the atmosphere to increase the Earth's reflectivity. Since this is uncharted territory, there are obvious reservations (apart from the usual qualms about moral hazard) about the possible unintended consequences of this 'Plan B'. On the plus side there is the expectation that the strategy could bring about much faster temperature abatement than policies such as emission reduction.[16] I do not deal with geoengineering solutions to the climate-change problem in this book because I tend to regard them as 'hail-mary' options: something that is good to know we can try if everything else fails, but definitely not our first port of call.

The third piece of factual information we have to become familiar with is that what is causing the warming of the Earth is not the *emission* of gases from the burning of fossil fuels *per se*, but their permanence in the atmosphere. It is concentrations, not emissions, that matter. This is important because it brings to the fore the delicate and contentious topic of whether we should aim for zero emissions, or for zero *net* emissions – where the term 'net' takes into account the possibility of removing CO_2 from the atmosphere. When we examine the options before us from the perspective of economic analysis, the distinction between zero and net zero emissions becomes extremely important. As we shall see, this is where some of the battle lines and trenches of the climate wars have been dug.

---

[16] For an excellent comprehensive consensus 'benchmark' review, see Royal Society (2009). For a review of geoengineering approaches to limiting climate warming, see Zhang, Moore, Huisingh and Zhao (2015). For a discussion of the political and social implications, see Corry (2017).

Fourth, the permanence of CO_2 in the atmosphere of emitted greenhouse gases is very long. Suppose that we burn a piece of wood and inject some grams of CO_2 in the atmosphere. How long will it take for this excess CO_2 concentration to be brought back to zero if we rely on natural absorption mechanisms only? Or, from a different perspective, if we drastically and quickly cut emissions, how long would it take for the warming problem to 'fix itself' via natural mechanisms?

To answer these seemingly simple questions, we must understand that two different mechanisms are at play: first we must ask ourselves how much and how rapidly the CO_2 concentration will change as emissions change; then, once we have a handle on concentrations, we must model how temperature changes as a response to changes in concentration. These are two areas of climate research that have witnessed a quiet revolution in the last ten years or so.[17] Currently our best understanding is that, on the one hand, temperature rises much more quickly than previously thought in response to a change in CO_2 concentration; on the other hand, the absorption of excess CO_2 via natural mechanisms is also much faster than we thought. To get a feel for what 'fast' and 'slow' reabsorption means, let's imagine that we inject a big pulse of CO_2 today, and then we stop all other emissions. We can then ask the question: how long will it take for this CO_2 injection to fall by, say, 60 per cent?[18] According to the latest physics, the answer is about 100 years. You may think that this sounds like a long time (and, on human scales, it certainly is); however, in the 'old physics' the same level of reabsorption would only be achieved after many centuries. The very big differences in reabsorption speeds are shown in Figs 2.7 and 2.9, which show the decay over time of the current CO_2 concentration (in GtC) if we suddenly

[17] For a very good, if somewhat technical, discussion of the new and old climate modelling in the context of Integrated Assessment Models, see Folini et al. (2021), and references therein.

[18] Why did I choose 60 per cent? Because it is a non-specialist-friendly approximation to the e-folding time used by physicists in the context of exponentially decaying phenomena. The e-folding time is the time it takes for a unit concentration to fall to the level of $1/e$, with $e = 2.71828\ldots$. The exact(ish) value of $1/e$ is $0.3687\ldots$, and therefore $1 - 1/e = 0.6312\ldots \approx 60$ per cent of the original concentration has been removed.

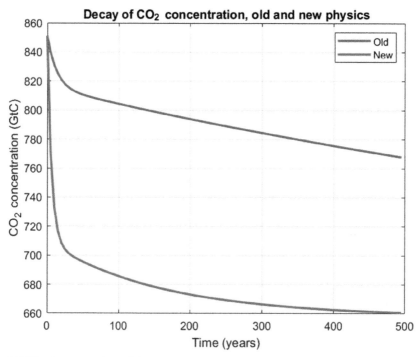

2.7 The decay over time of the current CO_2 concentration (in GtC), if all new emissions suddenly stop for the old and new physics.

stopped all emissions or, more realistically, if emissions were to follow the decay pattern shown in Fig 2.8.

This faster reabsorption speed is certainly good news. However, even these much faster reabsorption rates indicate that, if we want to limit the atmospheric warming to 1.5–2 °C by the end of the century, we cannot rely on cutting emissions alone. We must actively *remove* CO_2 from the atmosphere. And, by the way, reducing emissions (mainly CO_2 and methane) to reduce global warming should not be confused with cutting down air pollutants (mainly nitrogen oxides and microscopic nitrate particles), both because pollutants are largely local (if a city emits a lot of pollutants its inhabitants will choke in smog, but just a few dozen miles into the surrounding countryside the air can be very clean); and because pollutants tend to be absorbed or dispersed much more quickly.[19]

[19] As usual, reality is always a bit messier. Because of the COVID-related lockdowns, emissions fell by 5.4 per cent in 2020, but the amount of greenhouse gases in the

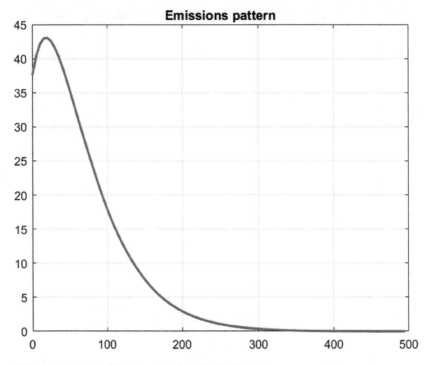

2.8 A time pattern of decaying emissions (in GtC).

The fact that cutting the emissions of greenhouse gases, important as it is, is just not enough is an 'awkward truth' that is hidden in plain sight in the footnotes and the small-font print of all the reputable literature on the topic – the UN-produced IPCC report is no exception.[20] (It is rel-

atmosphere continued to grow. This happened partly because of reduced absorption by the oceans due to the reduced CO_2 pressure in the air. However, the main reason was the reduction in nitrogen oxides (generically referred to as NOx) in the atmosphere. The reduced amount of these pollutants limited the atmosphere's ability to break down methane – a worse greenhouse gas than CO_2 – via the formation of the hydroxyl radical. In sum, the improvement in air quality associated with the 2020 lockdowns increased the lifetime of methane. So, indeed, 'efforts to reduce greenhouse gas emissions and improve air quality cannot be considered separately' (Laughner et al., 2021), but this reinforces the point that reducing pollutants is not the same as reducing atmospheric concentrations of greenhouse gases – it can even work in an antagonistic direction. For a succinct account, see Rasmussen (2021). For an in-depth analysis see Laughner et al. (2021).

[20] As one example among many of this 'asymmetry of emphasis', the *Nature News* summary of a many-page article in the prestigious *Nature* journal about what we should and should not do to achieve the ambitious target of 1.5 °C warming by the end of the

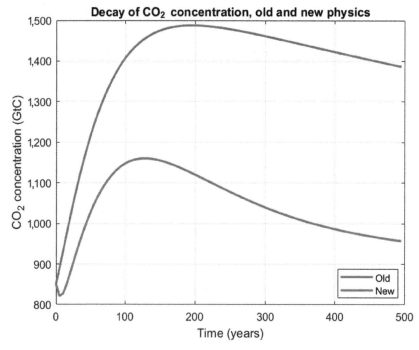

2.9 The decay over time of the current CO_2 concentration (in GtC) corresponding to the emission pattern in Fig 2.8 for the old and new physics.

egated to the fine print, by the way, because of the fear that over-reliance on removal would end up being taken as a get-out-of-jail card, and slacken our emission-cutting efforts, which remain essential.) As we shall see in Chapters 13 and 15, the important role that active CO_2 removal (the so-called *negative-emission technologies*) must play to control the temperature increase has profound consequences on the economics of the problem.

Let me move to the fifth piece of undisputed factual information: sources of renewable energy can (relatively) easily produce the *electric* energy we need. However, what we spend to produce electric energy accounts for only about 20 per cent of our total energy production.

century, devotes all of two and a half lines to the pretty essential statement: '... The model also assumes *substantial* use of carbon dioxide removal and carbon capture and storage, because if they aren't included or are included at a smaller scale, *that target is unfeasible* ...' – emphasis added, Nograndy (2021).

We can see greater uses for electric energy in the future (to move vehicles around, for instance, or for heating), and so this 20 per cent may inch up in the medium-term future, but we should not forget that using electric energy, a high-level source of energy par excellence, to cater for energy needs that could be fulfilled by low-level energy is a bit like using Chanel no 5 to light up your barbecue.[21] So, where does the remaining 80 per cent go? A good part of it (such as transportation) goes into uses for which renewables, or alternative sources of energy such as hydrogen, can play a significant role. But there remains a 'recalcitrant' 20–25 per cent of our energy usage for which it is currently very difficult to see a renewable-based solution. These are what Smil (2022) calls the 'four material pillars of modern civilization': steel, ammonia,[22] cement and plastic. The appetite for cement, in particular, seems to be inexhaustible, especially from developing countries: Smil (2022) reports that in the two pre-Covid years China alone produced roughly as much cement (4.4 billion ton) as the United States during the whole of the twentieth century.[23] The energy that goes into the making of these four material pillars accounts for only a bit less than 20 per cent of the world energy demand, and their production is responsible for 25 per cent of the current CO_2 emissions. These don't look like scary percentages, but the key problem is that currently there are no large-scale, proven ways of producing these four material pillars of modern civilization with electric energy alone (green or otherwise). Admittedly, it may be possible to find ways to decarbonize steel, cement and plastic by mid-century almost completely,[24] but the difficulty and the cost of the task should not be underestimated. This means that carbon sequestration and storage, which poses its own 'moral

---

[21] Low-level energy can be thought of as energy that has to be used 'here and now' (e.g., for heating), and that, if not used at the point and time of production is wasted. High-level energy is *versatile*.

[22] Currently, about 80 per cent of the ammonia produced in the world goes to make fertilizers. The need for fertilizers is predicted to increase dramatically if the same amount of land is to feed a significantly increasing population.

[23] Smil (2022), page 98.

[24] An observation that Smil (2022) unhelpfully relegates to the footnotes of his 448-page book.

hazard'problems,[25] will have to play an important role on the path to zero *net* emissions.

And, as the last established fact, I must mention that there is much less uncertainty about the physical effects of global warming (say, by how much temperature will rise if the CO_2 concentration reaches a given level), than about the projected economic and social impact these climate changes may give rise to. Put differently, we are much more confident in predicting what the temperature change will be as a response to a given emission pattern, than in predicting the economic and social effects of this temperature increase. As a consequence, when one looks at the economic models designed to inform our optimal climate strategy, one invariably finds that the sensitivity of the results to the assumed damage (to the so-called damage function) is high. This means that, if we model damages poorly, the results of our models can be *very* wrong. This is unfortunate for an economics-based analysis of the problem, because such an analysis rests on balancing costs and damages. Alas, there isn't much that we can do about this, short of conducting what econometricians call 'robustness analyses' – analyses, that is, of how much predictions depend on our uncertain inputs. All one can say about this is that collecting evidence about the damage function is one of the most important areas of climate research.

Having said this, it is also important to say what we *do* know about damages. The term 'existential threat' has become common parlance, but it is unfortunate, because it is, probably by design, ambiguous: if it means that, *for some populations*, a significant increase of the temperature above pre-industrial level will cause a large number of direct and indirect deaths, then the term is used correctly (but, I argue immediately below, unhelpfully). If the term is meant to imply that the human species is at risk, I am not aware of any serious scientific projection to support this

---

[25] When I speak of 'moral hazard' I refer to an over-reliance on the effectiveness, scope and feasibility of carbon sequestration and storage that may diminish our abatement efforts. The argument that we can 'simply' sequestrate-and-store our way out of the global warming problem is also often used as a glib justification for inaction. Sequestration and storage *is* feasible and should be pursued, but it is costly and logistically challenging.

claim. It is not among even the direst, lowest-confidence, predictions in the latest (2021) IPCC Special report.

Why did I say that I find the term 'existential threat' unhelpful also in its more limited meaning? Because, if we consider the consequences of several human activities, we find that many things we do cause a large number of direct and indirect deaths. If we used the term in its narrow meaning, we would therefore have to classify all of them as existential threats. For instance, 1.5 million people (mainly children) die each year of malaria – an illness which is both preventable and treatable;[26] almost 3 million people die for being overweight or obese;[27] 1.5 million people die on the roads because of car accidents,[28] and 50 million are injured; tobacco causes the death of 8 million people per year;[29] and, of course, poverty and malnutrition are the biggest preventable killers and maimers of all: about 45 per cent of deaths worldwide for children under the age of five are linked to malnutrition, 150 million children under five were estimated in 2021 to be stunted, and 45 million to be wasted.[30] So, if we want to use the term 'existential threat' in its weaker meaning, climate change is not the only such threat we are faced with, and there is no justification for using the term in the climate context and not in others.

I hope it is clear that this is not a quibble about linguistic purity: when looking at climate change, we must ask ourselves how our limited resources are best spent given *all* the threats and damages to which humanity is exposed, and their relative cost of abatement. Admittedly, one must be careful with this argument. Take malaria, for instance, for which prevention and cure are both feasible and cheap. Despite the fact that reducing drastically malaria-related mortality would appear to be a

---

[26] Medscape, 15 November, 2021.

[27] WHO, *Obesity*, June 2021.

[28] WHO, *Road Traffic Injuries*, 21 June 2021.

[29] The estimate is 7 million from direct tobacco use, and 1.2 million from 'second-hand smoke'. WHO, *Tobacco*, 26 July 2021.

[30] WHO, *Malnutrition*, 9 June 2021.

'low-hanging-fruit', for a number of reasons this within-easy-reach fruit remains unpicked. The fact that we have done relatively little to drastically reduce malaria should not be used as an excuse for not engaging in other activities (such as the control of global warming) until the malaria problem is fixed. There may be explanations, rational or otherwise, why tackling this or that 'easy' problem is *in practice* intractable. Engaging in other, perhaps more costly, abatement initiatives should therefore not be held hostage to our failure to solve a set of apparently more tractable problems. To give a concrete, if rather far-fetched, example, consider gun control in the US. Now, I am not saying that gun laws in the US constitute a weak or strong existential threat. However, there is no doubt that many lives would be saved by aligning US laws on gun control to the rules in most Western democracies, and that doing so would cost very little. Alas, there is also little doubt that, in the present political environment, the likelihood of such a piece of gun-control legislation being passed is close to zero. We should not conclude from this that we should not tackle more costly live-savings programmes until the apparently cheaper-and-easier gun-control problem has been fixed.

In sum: when climate change is referred to as an existential threat the unstated implication is that the stronger meaning should be understood – a meaning that would arguably trump all considerations of cost/effectiveness comparability with other clear and present threats. However, as I said, there is no scientific foundation to the broader meaning (a threat to the human species *as a whole*) that the term is probably meant to evoke.

One last word for my perplexed but open-minded reader: beware of individual results and conclusions about climate science even when published in peer-reviewed journals, and especially if culled by non-scientists to advance their view of the world. I strongly recommend that, when you want to find reliable facts and serious projections, you refer to the latest IPCC report (as of this writing, it is the 2021 Special Report). I recommend the IPCC reports not just because the contributors tend to be very reputable scientists in their respective areas, but because it is a *consensus* document, and, as such, it tempers the more extreme views (in either direction). It is not infallible, because good science is not infallible – but, exactly as good science, it knows that it is not.[31]

---

[31] I often quote in this book the publications of the IPCC. It is therefore important to understand the nature and reliability of this source. The Intergovernmental Panel on Climate Chnage (IPCC) was created in 1988 by the World Meteorological Organization (WMO) and United Nations Environment Programme (UNEP) to provide policymakers with the best scientific consensus about the science of climate change, and about its possible impact on societies. The reports produced by the IPCC are written and reviewed by thousands of scientists from all over the world, who are not paid by the IPCC for their work. The working of the IPCC was reviewed in 2010 at the request of the then-UN Secretary General, Mr Ban Ki-moon, with emphasis given to the management of potential conflict of interest. (As a result of this the Panel adopted in its 33rd and 34th session a *Conflict of Interest Policy.*) The IPCC policy decisions are taken at Plenary Sessions of government representatives. I note in passing that some of these governments are from oil-producing countries, and therefore will naturally try to water down the more 'radical' abatement conclusions and proposals. Therefore, if there were a bias in the recommendations – and I am not saying that there is – it should, if anything, be in a 'conservative' direction. In sum: the publications of the IPCC are *consensus* documents produced and reviewed by the most prominent experts in their fields; its policy decisions are endorsed by the representatives of many governments; and, contrary to what its critics say, it is *not* the mouthpiece of an 'activist lobby'. For the governance of the IPCC, see https://archive.ipcc.ch/organization/organization_structure.shtml.

CHAPTER 3

Deep Changes

To achieve [net zero greenhouse emissions by 2050] the whole economy will have to transform.

—HM Government, *Greening Finance: A Roadmap to Sustainable Investing*, October 2021

We can't get to net zero by flipping a green switch. We need to rewire our entire economies.

—Mark Carney, *Financial Times*, October 2021

LET ME CLARIFY SOMETHING RIGHT AT THE START. Often the terms of the climate-change problem are posed in rather Manichean terms: if we fail to act against climate change, doom and destruction will follow; but if we act promptly and decisively, all manners of things will be well, we will be richer and happier than we are now, and economic growth and social arrangements will continue evolving pretty much along the current trajectory. I think that framing the sets of climate choices ahead of us in these terms is not only highly reductive, but profoundly misleading. If someone asked me 'Given what is happening to the Earth's climate, what is your highest-conviction prediction about the way we will live in one hundred years' time?' I would venture this as an answer: that, *whatever we do about climate change*, the consequences for society as a whole are going to be huge.

To explain what I mean, let me simplify greatly for effect. If we choose not to listen to what the scientists say; if we dither and only pay lip service to our commitments to climate change abatement; if we refuse to change significantly the direction towards which we channel our consumption (e.g., if we keep preferring sun-drenched holidays to building wind turbines) – then the consequences are going to be very severe. We really don't know if, and for whom, they are going to be 'manageably bad' (whatever that means), or *really* bad, but we do know that the pain will be very unevenly spread:[1] for instance, we have good reasons to believe that it will be particularly severe (in some cases entailing large-scale forced migrations and widespread loss of life) for the populations who currently live in some large (and mainly poor) geographical areas, such as sub-Saharan Africa, or low-lying coastal regions in South-East Asia; that the damage will be still severe, but easier to manage, for other areas; and that someone (think of the sparse population of Siberia) may even end up being relatively better off.[2] But, on balance, if we choose not to act decisively to curb climate change we should brace ourselves for an acceptably-to-severely bad turn in human life on Earth. Few surprises here.

What is more surprising to most is that profound changes – albeit on balance far more benign – will unfold also if we *do* take serious action to limit climate change. How can that be? Isn't the purpose of our investment in clean energy technology to keep us living as we are living now, minus the noxious emissions? To answer these questions, let's starts from some simple facts. Keeping climate change under control means first and foremost controlling the rise in the temperature of the planet.[3] Avoiding an increase in temperature means limiting, and in the future

---

[1] 'The impacts of 1.5 °C global warming will vary in both space and time', IPCC Special Report, 2021, chapter 1.

[2] Not surprisingly, Russia is going to be the region least negatively affected by climate warming. A recent study by Kikstra et al. (2021) points out that 'mean economic output in the 'Russia+' region is 52 per cent higher with the possibility of Russia+ dominating the global economy near the end of the model horizon for high persistence level' (page 6). In addition, global warming could bring as a gift one of the most sought-after geopolitical goals of Russia/Soviet Union: year-round access to ice-free sea. Indeed, winter ice in the Bering strait is currently the lowest for the past 5,000 years, and is predicted to disappear within decades. See Page (2020).

[3] There are many aspects of climate change that we worry about, such as the increase in strength of the hurricanes, or the frequency of floods. However, most of these changes are a function of changes in temperature (gradients).

perhaps reducing, the concentration of CO_2 in the atmosphere.[4] This, in turn, means a substantial decarbonization of the economy: we have to change *radically* the way in which in the last two and a half centuries we have been extracting energy from the environment. I have no doubts that tackling seriously climate change will entail profound transformations for our economies – it will impact the production side of the economy, it will have redistributional effects and it will affect the level of employment of different parts of the workforce and economic inequality (both across and within countries). It also does not take much imagination to see that, as the world reconfigures its entire energy system, the whole geopolitical order will be redrawn.[5] But, as I will argue in the last part of this chapter, the changes may well run even deeper, and affect the very way societies function. Let me build my argument in stages, looking at the effect on our economies first.

3.1 TWO POSSIBLE FUTURE WORLDS

Let me explain better what I mean. Let's think of two possible future worlds – both compatible with a successful tackling of the climate problem. In the first, we finally find a way to harness the power of nuclear fusion – not an easy task, as we are talking here of building a mini-Sun and putting it next to a huge boiler.[6] However, if we do succeed, Fig 3.1 is a picture of how much energy we could obtain from the nuclear

---

[4] As I said, I should be speaking of 'CO_2-equivalent gases', really. For the moment, allow me to go with the flow.

[5] In 1918 Lord Curzon said that in 1918 Britain 'floated to victory upon a wave of oil'. As Bordoff and O'Sullivan (2021) point out, '[f]rom that point forward, British security depended far more on oil from Persia than it did on coal from Newcastle, as energy became a source of national power and its absence a strategic vulnerability. In the century that followed, countries blessed with oil and gas resources developed their societies and wielded outsize power in the international system, and countries where the demand for oil outpaced its production contorted their foreign policies to ensure continued access to it.'

[6] Of course, the energy we would obtain from fusion reactors could not be *directly* employed as energy source for all applications – such as aviation or to move vehicles, for instance. However, once virtually unlimited energy is available, it can be deployed in a number of ways: for instance to obtain what is called 'purple hydrogen' (where the term 'purple', to distinguish the production mode from 'brown', 'blue' and 'green', signifies that it is obtained from nuclear sources). Hydrogen could then become a very versatile

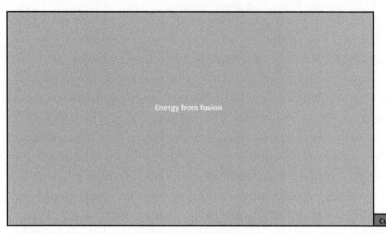

Energy from fusion

Current

3.1 The energy per person available from deuterium fusion (if and when available) *even if the world population grew to 60 billion* drawn to scale next to the current average energy utilization (per day, per person). Source: MacKay (2009).

fusion of deuterium, compared to the energy we currently consume. To put things in perspective, *even if the world population were to grow ten-fold,* the fusion of deuterium could still provide 100 times more energy per person than the current energy usage of the average US person (not the most frugal energy consumer, by the way). Why did I assume a ten-fold increase in the world population (certainly not a central scenario)? Quite simply, because otherwise the little rectangle in the bottom right corner of the figure would have been almost invisible. And obtaining clean and limitless energy from fusion would also make negligible demands on land, avoiding competition with agriculture, and with land-intensive negative-emission technologies, such as forestation. Everything we know about how changes in energy availability have altered the course of history suggests that in this fusion-energy-rich state of the world society will undergo substantial changes in the way it functions. As I said, I will come back to this towards the end of this chapter. For the moment, it is clear that the impact on our economies would be not only extremely positive, but transformative: at one stroke we would have solved the global-warming problem; and an almost limitless array of possibilities

energy source, potentially suitable for transportation and aviation. See Alverá (2021) for a good, if rather too optimistic, analysis of what hydrogen could provide.

made available by abundant, cheap energy would open up: just think, for instance, of obtaining water for irrigation via desalinization in the Sahara or Australia.

Let's now shift our attention to a different scenario – different, but still compatible with serious climate change abatement. In this scenario fusion energy keeps on remaining elusively thirty years in the making, we turn our back on nuclear fission, but we harness the power of wind and sun as effectively as possible. Now the prospects before us are more difficult to gauge. If we invest on a truly massive scale on solar and wind energy sources and, at the same time, we become far more energy-efficient; if we engage seriously in carbon sequestration and find enough room to store at a reasonable cost the sequestrated carbon; if we make substantial but not unthinkable progress in negative-emission technologies – if all these conditions are met, we should be able to keep temperature increases in check and, at the same time, cover our energy needs. We would, however, have to negotiate many constraints. We would have competition for land (with the attending impact for food prices). We would be faced with the problem of how to accommodate the energy needs of the vast parts of the world population that still have to enjoy sustained economic growth (think, for instance, of sub-Saharan Africa). We would have to increase energy efficiency dramatically. Until the population has levelled off at a presumably substantially higher level than today towards the end of the century, we would have to keep on finding new ways to squeeze more and more clean energy in more and more ingenious ways out of the intermittent renewable sources. And, as solar energy is most efficiently used relatively close to where it is generated, the geopolitics of the energy world would undergo radical shifts.

Now, all serious scientists agree that, if we want to reach net-zero in this no-fusion world, the emission-reduction part of the task will have to be taken up to a substantial extent by renewables. However, cutting emissions is not enough – we will also have to remove from the atmosphere substantial amounts of carbon. In addition, in order to supplement in an efficient way the intermittent energy supply from renewables, we will need some fossil-fuel capacity (probably with gas rather than coal) combined with sequestration and storage of the emitted CO_2. This will contribute as well to the amount of carbon that we have to store away somehow. I will discuss in some detail in Chapter 15 why relying on renewables *only* would be very inefficient, and possibly unfeasible, but let's just accept for the moment that all reasonable plans to remain within the target of 1.5–2 °C warming by the end of the century require substantial sequestration of carbon at emission, and then its storage. How big is this effort? To fulfil the necessary sequestration targets in less than thirty years a carbon storage industry will have to develop that is capable of handling two to four times as much in volume than the current global oil industry – an industry that had more than a century to develop.[7] This does not mean that the task is unattainable. It is simply another indication, from a poorly lit corner of the abatement landscape, of the scale of the necessary commitment. In reality, we will have to rethink radically many aspects of how our economies work. As ex-Governor of the Bank of England, Mark Carney, said, we cannot get to net zero just by flipping a green switch.

These two thumbnail sketches of two possible future worlds are, of course, not the only ones – and probably not the most likely ones. But, whatever serious abatement avenue we go down, the attending abatement efforts will have to be little short of a war effort – an expression to which I will return several times in this book, but which I do not use lightly.[8] As this may come as a surprise to many readers, let me expand on this point.

3.2 SIZING THE TRANSFORMATIONS

Speaking of a war effort may, at first blush, sound a bit hyperbolic. It becomes less so, when we compare the annual investment required to remain within 1.5 °C by the end of the century with other 'big-ticket items' in the world GDP tally (we can put the world GDP at $80 trillion for 2020). So, the UN Intergovernmental Panel on Climate Change

---

[7] Mac Dowell et al. (2017).

[8] I am not the only one to refer to the climate-control task as a 'war effort': see, e.g., J Randers and P Gilding (2010), *The One Degree War Plan*, Journal of Global Responsibility, www.vox.com/2016/8/18/12507810/climate-change-world-war; and www.nber.org/papers/w22590.

estimates that the financial investment necessary to meet the 1.5 °C target should be between $1.6 trillion and $3.8 trillion per annum between 2020 and 2050 just for the transformation of the energy systems alone.[9] Let's take the average and add the estimated costs for adaptation (about $200 billion per annum), and we reach a total of about $3 trillion per annum. Along similar lines, the consultancy McKinsey[10] estimates that to meet the 1.5 °C target '[c]apital spending on physical assets for energy and land-use systems will need to rise by $3.5 trillion per year, to a total of $9.2 trillion per year for the next thirty years. More than a third of this 'would have to be new spending'.[11]

How big are these figures? It is more than the world spends on military ($2 trillion); it is more than what it spends on education ($3.2 trillion); and it is about the same as the biggest spend item of them all, healthcare ($8.3 trillion). And, just to provide another yardstick for comparison, in 2020 the whole of the tax collected by the US federal government was about $3.5 trillion, and the net cash raised as US federal debt was about $4.3 trillion.[12] As for the estimated required *increase* in capital expenditure per annum, this is about half of global corporate profits.[13]

These figures should give food for thought: for instance, if we assume the public contribution to the abatement effort to be roughly 50 per cent – with the rest coming from private initiatives[14] – will this mean higher taxes, higher levels of public indebtedness, higher consumer prices, or all of the above? And yet, staggering as it is, the monetary size of the required investment only gives a very one-dimensional perception

---

[9] IPCC Report, 2018, chapter 4, *Strengthening and Implementing the Global Response*, section 4.2.1.1, page 321.

[10] *The Net-Zero Transition: What It Would Cost, What It Could Bring*, McKinsey & Company Report, January 2022.

[11] In a 2022 IMF publication (*The Great Carbon Arbitrage*) Adrian, Bolton and Kleinmijenhuis (2022) arrive at a somewhat lower estimate of $1.5 to $3.0 trillion per annum. The qualitative conclusions do not change.

[12] All Treasuries, net issuance, i.e., net of bill, note and bond retirement. US Department of the Treasury, Bureau of the Fiscal Service.

[13] McKinsey Report quoted above, page viii.

[14] B Naran et al., Global Landscape of Global Finance, 2021, Climate Policy Initiative, quoted in J Timperley (2021 October), The Broken $100-Billion Promise of Climate Finance – and How to Fix It, *Nature*, 598(7881), 400–402. doi: 10.1038/d41586-021-02846-3. PMID: 34671142.

of the scale of the required transformation – a transformation that will have to go a lot deeper than 'just' spending a lot of money. Let me explain what I mean.

To get our bearings we have to become familiar with some facts and figures.[15] Take wind energy, which has now become competitive in cost terms with fossil fuel energy *without subsidies*. Let's take an extremely aggressive deployment of shallow and deep offshore wind turbines for a country such as Britain ('blessed' both by robust winds and by an extremely long coastline). By 'aggressive' I mean that in this scenario shallow-water wind turbines are going to be located in one third of the British shallow waters (an area the size of a third of Wales), by filling the equivalent of a strip 4 km deep *all around the coastline of the UK*. To this we are going to add deep-offshore turbine installations, exploiting sea beds with depths up to 50 meters. To give an idea of the task, some of the turbines will now be located 50 km from the nearest shore.[16] Doing all of this can realistically provide 50 kWh/d per person, which is a meaningful chunk of the per-person energy needs in a country such as the UK.

Now we are approaching the punchline. To build all these turbines, we would need about 60 million tons of steel, or, roughly, one ton per person in the UK. Is that a lot or a little? Well, the world steel production *for all uses* is 0.2 tons per person. We have to be careful not to confuse stocks (total amount of steel for a given number of turbines) and flows (steel production *per year*),[17] but the size of the task is still breath-taking. Has anything similar ever been done before? From the same trusted source (MacKay, 2009) we learn that during the Second World War 2,751 *Liberty* ships were built in the USA, each requiring 7,000 tons of steel. Given the US population at the time, this means 0.1 tons of steel per American, or *one tenth of the steel needed to build the wind turbines needed to produce 50 kWd/d per person*.

What about land installations? And why not look at solar panels as well? There is no reason not to add these, and, when we do so, we see that, to make an appreciable contribution to the energy demand of a densely

---

[15] All the figures for this example are from the excellent book by MacKay (2009).

[16] We are going to leave two thirds of the waters free for shipping lanes and fishing.

[17] '*I have found out what economics is; it is the science of confusing stocks with flows*', attributed to Michal Kalechi, as cited by Joan Robinson (1982).

populated country such as the UK,[18] we will have to cover a large fraction of the available land with solar and wind farms. This usage will compete with forestation (to sequestrate carbon and limit temperature increases) and with the agricultural use of the land. Which countries will find that 'planting solar panels' is for them more profitable than planting wheat or maize? What will the implications be for the cost of food – especially for a world population that is expected to require twice as much food as today in half a century's time? (Extra food, by the way, that will have to be grown with more fertilizers whose production significantly contributes to greenhouse gas emissions.) What will the geopolitical consequences of this re-drawing of the energy and agricultural production maps of the world? We really do not know, but nothing makes me think that they will be of small significance.

The key point I am trying to make here is that, yes, the fantastic increase in efficiency of solar panels and wind turbines that has occurred over the last twenty years has made the unit cost of the energy they produce tumble. For instance, the cost per kilowatt of energy produced by solar panels has fallen by almost 50 per cent in the five short years from 2014 to 2019. And, as Professor Stock of Harvard University recently pointed out, in many parts of the USA 'building a new wind farm costs less than running an existing coal plant or building a new natural gas power station'.[19] These improvements have been faster and deeper than most could have predicted. However, we should be careful not to expect the equivalent of CPU's time 'Moore's law' for the cost of energy supply. The penetration of renewables remains limited, and we are therefore still picking the proverbial low-hanging fruits. As the 'convenient' sea-bed locations are used up, additional off-shore wind turbines will have to be located further and further out at sea, making the marginal cost of wind energy higher and higher. Today we can place solar panels relatively

---

[18] The UK is the 51st most densely populated country in the world, with a density of 280 people per square kilometre. The population density in the US is about 8 times lower (36 people per square kilometre), and in Japan some 25 per cent higher (347 people per square kilometre). As we shall see in Chapter 15, the population density of a country plays a big role in determining whether there is enough physical space for the deployment of wind and solar farms, for forestation and for agriculture.

[19] James H Stock, The Rate Debate, *Foreign Affairs*, March/April 2021, 179.

close to the point of use. Ambitious plans of 'turning the Sahara desert in a huge solar farm' have to contend with the reality that transmitting electricity over long distances (from where it is produced to where it is needed) entails substantial losses. And the welcome improvement in efficiency of solar panels of the last thirty years unfortunately means that we are getting closer to their thermodynamic efficiency limit: squeezing yet a bit more energy out of a photon from the Sun becomes harder, and more costly.

This also means that, as we approach full decarbonization, we will have to decide whether the next patch of land should be used to plant wheat, to allow methane-producing cows to graze, to increase the size of existing forests or to install a solar panel. In short: in this no-fusion scenario, if we take the decarbonization task seriously, renewables, coupled with production of 'firm' energy and with carbon sequestration, *can* provide the energy we need to sustain the economy growth the world (and the developing countries in particular) have come to expect.[20] However, we will have to make tough choices to make this happen: in a renewables-only-driven decarbonized future, almost limitless, cheap energy on tap to fuel economic growth is not on the cards.

3.3 THE WAR EFFORT AGAIN

Many estimates of the impact of the green transition on the world's gross domestic product (GDP) predict a neutral, if not positive, effect. If this is correct, isn't my description of the energy transition policies as a 'war effort' misguided? Shouldn't we look forward to a period of higher growth, rather than brace ourselves for the strictures of a war effort? Not quite, and it is important to understand why this is the case.

There are many misconceptions about what GDP measures, and what it leaves out. Valid as these points of criticism are, we can leave them to one side for the moment, and suppose that GDP does measure correctly the sum of goods and services produced in a given period of time. Even

---

[20] Many climate activists would argue that these growth expectations are neither realizable, nor desirable. I explain in Chapter 15 why I disagree on this point.

if it does, there is more (or, rather, less) to GDP than meets the eye. To explain what I mean, consider the hypothetical scenario of an epidemic foretold: suppose, that is, that some clever scientists predict that, unless we take quick action, a deadly, highly infectious disease will soon spread among the population. Taking action means developing a costly vaccine, training additional nurses and doctors, building new hospitals, procuring suitable PPE, and so on. Now, the production of vaccines and protective equipment, the building of hospitals, the recruitment of new doctors and nurses and all the other epidemic-averting actions do contribute to GDP – they are produced goods and services. But the resources to produce these goods and services are diverted from the pre-pandemic allocation of what people could spend on. Simply put, before we discovered about the pandemic, we used to spend part of our disposable income on holidays, restaurant meals, and fancy clothes. Now we have to spend the same amount of money on PPE and vaccine production, on paying the doctors and nurses, etc. In this contrived example the GDP does not change (it may even go up!) – only the allocation of resources does. But this cannot hide the fact that we would have much preferred going on holiday than buying a dose of vaccine. The vaccine becomes preferable to the holiday *only because the world has changed* – which is exactly what happens during a war, and what we fear may happen with climate change. During wars, GDP often increases because more guns have to be produced than butter. This does not change the fact that we would all have preferred a lower GDP, but the pre-war allocation of consumption.

Admittedly, the war or epidemic analogies have important limitations: both guns and vaccine can only be used for a single purpose – to divert the new clear and present danger. Re-engineering how we produce energy is different, in that it is likely to create down the line important benefits that go beyond the averting of the climate threat: for instance, cheaper energy, or less pollution. But not all of the climate-related actions are multi-purpose in the same positive way. Carbon sequestration and storage, for instance, is going to be necessary (and expensive) to limit global warming, but unlikely to produce many ancillary benefits. So, the fact remains that the reallocation of resources from the goods and services we preferred *before we became aware of climate change* to the new goods and service we now realize we need is going to be major, and, alas, only desirable in a *faute-de-miuex* sort of way.

I have sketched a picture of the changes ushered in by the decarbonization of the economy with a deliberately broad brush, and we will re-examine in much greater detail later in the book several of the points I have now only briefly touched upon. For the moment, the message I wanted to convey is simple: if we think that transitioning to a no-fossil-fuel economy implies nothing more radical than plugging our car into a road charger rather than refuelling it at a petrol station, or that we will see nothing more radical than the sprouting of lots of solar panel on our roofs, we are not being realistic. *Radical* change is inevitable, and this is going to be true whether we act decisively or we don't. In business, we currently seem to lionize the 'disruptors' who 'move fast and break things'. However, by and large humans do not much like change when the direction of travel is uncertain. Unfortunately, for better or for worse, whatever we choose to do or not to do, small variations on the *status quo* are not on the menu. This, I believe, is a reality we should all wake up to – and, as I said in the introduction, one of the key messages of this book.

3.4 THE POLITICS OF DEEP CHANGE

This brings me to one of the several neuralgic points where climate change intersects with politics. Saying '*If we do nothing, things are going to be bad; and if we act decisively, things will change radically, but in directions we cannot really predict*' is not exactly a winning political manifesto. Politicians of all stripes like to claim that they have a plan, and that things are firmly under their control. They do not like to suggest that our lives will have to change, unless they can reassure us that it will be for the better. From the perspective of a politician, 'friendly' or cosmetic changes are ok; disruption definitely is not. Telling voters that taking decisive action to control climate change will change their lives profoundly, but in difficult-to-predict ways, will not win you a lot of votes.

So, for instance, at the 2019 UK general elections all parties wanted to burnish their green credentials, but they also wanted to do so with policies that promised the least possible disruption to our lives. In this square-the-circle act, one party decided to pledge the planting of

10 million trees to 'combat climate change'. Hot on its heels, a second party quickly promised that *20* million trees would be planted. Not to be outdone, the third party, the one then headed by a boisterous leader with an unruly mop of blond hair, swiftly pledged the planting of 60 million trees.

This is a nice, family-friendly image of fighting climate change. You can almost picture it. Sixty or ten million trees roughly equates to one tree per person or one tree per family. In one's mind's eye one can see the Sunday family outing, with the little one proudly walking against the backdrop of a sheep-studded countryside landscape (no wind turbines in sight), carrying a toy spade and digging, if not for victory, at least to stop climate change. Reality is a tad different. I have asked the students of my climate-change course to work out how many trees would be required to offset a meaningful fraction of the UK emissions of CO_2. We came up with 2.5 *billion* trees. After cramming them pretty tightly, we also calculated that more than half of the whole area of Wales would have to be covered. I hope someone has told the folks in Cardiff.

To be fair, it is not just politicians who are reluctant to say clearly how much things will have to change. Activists and deniers also engage, for different reasons and probably to a different extent, in the selective choosing and culling of the available evidence – and sometimes they both seem to consider evidence a nuisance. So, when it comes to the dangers of inaction, green activists invariably pick the direst outcomes out of the plausible ones (and sometimes out of the implausible ones as well). However, when they talk about what needs doing to control climate change, they quickly become afraid to go into specifics, lest they 'put off' voters. As a result, they systematically downplay the scale of the abatement efforts required, and they rarely mention how far-reaching the consequences of decisive abatement action will have to be.

And, of course, climate-change deniers are the first to embrace with gusto the narrative that we can continue doing what we have been doing for the last fifty years, and everything will be just fine – or, actually, better.[21] In doing so, they cynically but effectively employ the same

---

[21] Yes, better. In a recurrent narrative, the dominant effect of global warming will indeed be to increase temperature, CO_2 concentration and humidity, but this will simply

techniques that were used by the tobacco-damage deniers in the 1960s and 1970s – and today they can add to the traditional tools of the trade (such as powerful and well-funded lobbying)[22] the new opportunities afforded by the internet and social media. So, it came as no little surprise to me to discover from the work by Bonnueil, Choquet and Franta (2021) in the peer-reviewed journal *Global Environmental Change* that the European oil giant, Total, 'was aware of the link between fossil fuels and rising global temperatures 50 years ago but worked with other oil majors to play down the risks for at least three decades, according to internal company documents and interviews with former executives.'[23] Faithful to the script carefully laid out by tobacco deniers a few decades earlier, Total 'personnel received warnings of the potential for catastrophic global warming from its products by 1971, became more fully informed of the issue in the 1980s, *began promoting doubt regarding the scientific basis for global warming by the late 1980s*, and ultimately settled on a position in the late 1990s of publicly accepting climate science while promoting policy delay or policies peripheral to fossil fuel control.'[24] The focus of the study is on the oil company Total, but ExxonMobil and Royal Dutch Shell are shown in the same article to have engaged in exactly the same type of conceal/deny/play-down activity.

This is not a good state of affairs. In the next few decades we will have to make decisions that will profoundly affect not just the welfare of our children and grandchildren, but the way societies will function. Apart from a not-so-tiny fraction of non-convinceable zealots (of both stripes), most reasonable people fully understand that a lot is at stake, and truly want to make sound decisions. The current cacophonous debate about climate change leaves them bewildered. In the next chapters we are going

mean that *the conditions for agricultural output will have improved*. So, the main net effect of global warming, according to this view of the world, will be positive.

[22] As an example, leaked documents reviewed in October 2021 by the BBC and Greenpeace journalist unit *Unearthed* revealed that Australia and Saudi Arabia were trying to lobby against the UN recommendations of a swift phasing out of fossil fuel burning, while Argentina and Brazil were trying to look after the interests of the beef producers by attempting to have recommendations for a more plant-based diet completely removed.

[23] Reported in *The Financial Times*, 20 October 2021.

[24] Emphasis added.

to lay out a road map to steer a reasonable course across the land of climate-change intervention. Before doing that, however, let me make the case that the changes ushered in by a radical decarbonization of our world will extend far deeper than the economic sphere, and may reach the very core of how societies function. As I say so, these claims are, of course, more speculative: I will try to convince the reader that they are not fanciful.

3.5 UNEXPECTED CHANGES

Come gather 'round people
Wherever you roam
And admit that the waters
Around you have grown [...]
And you better start swimmin'
Or you'll sink like a stone
For the times they are a-changin.

—Bob Dylan, *The Times They Are A-Changing, 1964*

If the study of 'deep history' has taught us one thing, it is that major changes in the way humans obtain the energy they need have always been correlated with similarly major changes in the way societies function. The key observation here is that, throughout history, whenever the sources and the amount of available energy have changed dramatically, deep changes in how societies function have also taken place, and these changes have always gone well beyond the narrowly technological and production aspects: they have been intertwined with changes in its most basic political arrangements. Piketty (2020) argues that even ideologies, the supposed 'engines' of history, have historically arisen as rationalizations and justifications for the inequality of wealth and power distribution – an inequality that first appeared in the history of mankind when agricultural societies were able to harness enough energy via cultivation to produce more food than needed for immediate subsistence.[25] To simplify Piketty's view almost to the point of caricature,

---

[25] See, e.g., Piketty (2020), (*On the Justification of Inequality in Ternary Societies*), page 59 and *passim.*

ideologies are *ex post* justifications for how societies happen to evolve. In turn, how a society evolves, historians such as Smil argue, is intimately linked with how the energy that society needs is obtained. And some serious historians claim that even the prevailing ethical values of a society change when the way the society gets the energy it needs changes. This, for instance, is what Morris (2015) writes: 'I call the first [set of human values] "foraging values", because it is associated with societies that support themselves primarily by gathering wild plants and hunting wild animals. Foragers tend to value equality over most kinds of hierarchy, and are quite tolerant of violence. The second system I call "farming values". [...] Farmers tend to value hierarchy over equality and are less tolerant of violence. [In] [t]he third system, which I call "fossil-fuels values", [...] fossil-fuel users tend to value equality of most kinds over hierarchy and to be very intolerant of violence.'[26]

Now, when I say that there are deep links between how societies change and where they get their energy from, you may think that I am referring to the Industrial Revolution – and, in some respects, you would not be wrong. Indeed, when a couple of centuries ago humans realized that the solar energy which had been captured via photosynthesis and stored underground for millions of years as fossil fuels could be released and used virtually 'all in one go', society changed beyond recognition. The discovery that fossil fuels could be turned into usable energy did not mean that we did the same things as before, only more efficiently or in a larger scale. For the first time in our history humanity escaped the Malthusian trap, that had made economic progress virtually non-existent from the days of ancient Greece to the eve of the Industrial Revolution. For the first time in the history of mankind, infant mortality began to fall. It was the first time that, if a child made it past the first years of her life, she could expect to live longer than thirty or forty years. Economic output per person finally began to rise, hesitantly at first, and then more consistently in the twentieth century. Urbanization accelerated as never before. Political arrangements that had lasted for centuries, if not millennia (I am thinking of monarchies and feudalism), crumbled with breathtaking speed. It is approximately during this period

[26] Page 4.

(the 'long century' between 1870 and 2010) that, as Berkley economist Bradford De Long writes, '[a]s nearly everything economic was transformed and transformed again [...] *those changes shaped and transformed nearly everything sociological, political and cultural.*'[27]

This is all true, but the Industrial Revolution was not the first time when humanity changed radically how it obtained the energy it needed to consume – and it was not the first time when social life on Earth changed dramatically as a consequence. I am referring here to the radical changes in energy intake per person made possible by the painful, fitful, yet irreversible, transformations that occurred some 10,000 years ago when a world of hunter-gatherers slowly embarked on the journey to become a world of farmers and shepherds.[28] We can think of each edible plant that farmers learnt how to grow *just where they lived* as a mini power station that converted solar energy into food and animal fodder. Each domesticated animal also became a miniature energy-transformation plant, that converted the energy produced by the plant mini power stations into different usable forms (directly into food, or to be used, say, for ploughing). From this perspective the big innovation was the discovery of how to deploy a huge number of mini power stations (plants and animals) near their point of use, and therefore to make them easy to access. Humans no longer had to chase (literally) their energy – now they could just grow it.

When this happened the changes were, if anything, even more staggering than what would occur, millennia later, with the Industrial Revolution. Let me put things in perspective. Depending on the richness of the environment, a 100 square kilometre patch of land can on average support about twenty-five hunter-gatherers.[29] Populations of

---

[27] Bradford De Long (2022), emphasis added.

[28] To be clear: there was no 'big bang' transition between foraging and farming societies. Hunter gatherers coexisted for a long time alongside early farmers, and, in the first phases of the transition, it would have been a moot point which society was better off. Farming was 'invented' in at least seven locations in three continents over the period of time from 7,000 to 3,000 BCE (Smil, 2008). Why it arose 'is perhaps the most challenging evolutionary, archaeological and anthropological puzzle that may never have a definite solution' (Smil, 2008, page 148).

[29] The estimates vary widely, ranging from less than one to a few hundreds, depending on the richness of the environment, and the estimation methodology. Smil (2018), page 28.

hunter-gatherers could not settle in one place because hunting of prey and collection of vegetables would occur at too fast a rate to allow replenishment of these resources once a given area had been 'used'. As a consequence, populations were constantly on the move, their possessions were limited to what they could easily carry with them (with obvious implication for wealth inequalities), and population densities were very low. Such low densities did not allow significant functional specialization or the creation of strong hierarchies. And 'forced labour was almost unknown within foraging societies'.[30]

Contrast this with the early farming settlements: the same amount of land could now provide sustenance for ten to a hundred times as many farmers as hunter-gatherers. And a change in the availability and source of energy did not just mean that 'there were more of us humans'. *Everything* changed. As people could now permanently settle in one place, they built lasting shelters, and began to accumulate wealth and possessions. The first large-scale projects (such as irrigation) were undertaken and had to be coordinated. Labour became much more divided than it had ever been, and slavery was 'invented'.[31] Inequality of wealth and power first arose, and then grew to previously unimaginable extents. Villages and cities developed. Empires sprang up.[32] And as a

---

[30] Morris (2015), page 64.

[31] Morris (2015) argues that horticulturalists did take slaves in raids, but these were quickly assimilated in the social structure of their captors. In contrast, the slaves of farming societies remained in a state of permanent subjugation. For a broader discussion, see Morris (2015), chapter 4, and Patterson (1982) and Watson (1980) for an Asian-African perspective.

[32] I must warn the reader that this account of the social and political effects of the transition from hunting-gathering to farming has been sketched with an extremely broad brush, and many nuances have been glossed over. For instance, the 'princely burials' and grand communal buildings of the Upper Palaeolithic period (*circa* 50,000–15,000 BC) are difficult to reconcile with the idea of an egalitarian society. See Graeber and Wengrow (2021), page 85 and *passim* in this respect. Some iconoclastically revisionist authors, among whom the same Graeber and Wengrow (2021) are prominent, argue that the 'authorized version' of the social transformations associated with the transition to farming needs to be revised and updated not just in the details, but in the substance. As these authors are in a minority, and I do not have the expertise to opine independently on the matter, I am, indeed, sticking to the mainstream 'authorized version'. For a sympathetic but strong criticism of the views by Graeber and Wengrow (2021) and of their tendency to 'make rules out of exceptions', see Scheidel (2022).

result not just of the higher energy supply, but also *of the different way in which energy was harnessed*, the body politic changed beyond recognition. Speaking of mechanical one-way cause-and-effect relationships between energy intake and these transformations is obviously very crude. But it is a fact that none of these transformations would (or could) have occurred, had not the amount and the sources of intake energy changed dramatically.

Don't get me wrong. I am not saying that these changes were inevitable, or pre-ordained, and that humans were just waiting for the additional energy from farming to unlock their manifest destiny. There was no plan, no telos to realize. However, the additional available energy, and the way in which this energy had to be extracted (by staying put, coordinating labour, investing in irrigation and food storage, etc.) dictated that similar, even if *ex ante* inconceivable, upheavals of society would occur in several locations all over the world – not simultaneously, but with remarkably similar outcomes.

The point I am making is that we routinely underestimate the impact on society of technological and energy considerations. No single invention, by itself, 'caused' the transition away from, say, feudalism. But the cumulative effect of many technological changes, each made possible by the availability of cheaper or more abundant energy sources, reaches much deeper than usually acknowledged. To pick one example among literally thousands, consider the now familiar skyscraper-studded skyline of Manhattan, or, if you prefer, Canary Wharf. An 'invention' such as the skyscraper would not have been even imaginable without the cheap energy to move, via lifts, hundreds of thousands of people to working places located tens or hundred of meters above the ground. The previously inconceivable concentration of workers made possible by the humble lift, and the advantages of co-location, have contributed to a host of deep changes in the way we live: they have profoundly altered our physical landscape; they have made daily commuting over tens of miles commonplace; they have created for the first time in history suburbia (places that are neither cities nor countryside, but sleeping and recreational quarters for the high-density workers of the skyscrapers); and they have accelerated urbanization at an unprecedented rate. Indeed, one of the countries that is currently experiencing the highest rate of urbanization is China. This means that the millions of people that previously inhabited a low-density agricultural environment now have to be squeezed into a limited working space – into a megacity. But megacities need skyscrapers, and skyscrapers need lifts. And lifts need cheap energy.[33]

Along similar lines, the availability of cheap and plentiful energy to operate mundane home appliances such as washing machines or electric irons has created the necessary conditions for half of the population (for women, that is) to contemplate for the first time in human history joining the workforce. Many other changes had to occur, of course, for this potentiality to be actualized. However, one only has to read Gordon's (2016) description of what a 'simple' task such as doing the laundry for a family in winter entailed in the nineteenth century, or Caro's (1983) account of how time-consuming and dangerous ironing was in the 1930s US south (when it required heavy slabs of metal heated on wood stoves), to realize that without the cheap-energy-fuelled home appliances such as the washing machine or the electric iron most women would still be condemned to a lifetime of house toil.

These examples, I believe, are significant because they are indicative of what I would call a historical regularity (I say 'regularity' because, when it comes to history, 'law' is too redolent of Marxist determinism): over and over again, greater energy availability and different sources of energy have been associated with deep changes in the way societies organize themselves; power between different sections of a society shifted; opportunities for parts of the populations opened up (women joining the workforce) or closed down (the 'invention' of slavery); some vast geographical areas gained or lost influence (the countries of oil-rich Middle East are beginning to realize that, unless they 'reinvent' themselves,

---

[33] Prof Barr of Rutgers University (Barr, 2018) has created a simple (regression) model to account for the rise in number (and height) of skyscrapers worldwide; the two explanatory variables are GDP and urbanization rate. Taken together the two variables have a strong explanatory power, which, roughly speaking, means 'Tell me how rich a country is, and how far urbanization has progressed in this country, and I will tell you how many skyscrapers there are.' The model by Prof Barr points to the economic advantages of clustering people in central cities. Economists refer to economic indivisibilities and transport costs to explain why it makes sense to have workers clustered together.

their influence on the global scene is destined to fade away);[34] and what an individual person can expect from life (starting from how long she can expect to live) has changed dramatically. Again, I don't want to be misunderstood: 'more energy' did not 'cause', say, slavery. However, without the functional specialization made possible by the availability of much more energy delivered by agriculture in an extremely localized manner, the conditions – such as the accumulation of wealth – that ultimately led to slavery would not have existed.

What has this to do with the current efforts to limit the effects of climate change? A lot, really. *If* we do the responsible thing and embark seriously on the journey to decarbonization, where we get the energy from, and how much energy we will be able to 'afford', will have to change dramatically. The change will be much more rapid than the similar changes that have happened in human history. As a consequence, the timescale for adaptation will be enormously compressed. As I said, there is no simple law, no deterministic link, and no preordained telos between energy and social arrangements. The association between how much energy is available, how the energy is obtained, and how a society structures itself around these 'boundary conditions' is, however, undeniable, and there are no reasons to believe that 'this time it will be different'.

3.6 ADAPTATION

One of the key points I have tried to make in this chapter is that, irrespective of how successful we are in tackling climate change, society will change radically, and in difficult-to-predict ways. These changes will unfold over very different timescales, but some may occur unexpectedly quickly. There are other changes in our ways of life which are more predictable, less disruptive, and potentially very rapid: they go under the rubric of 'adaptation'.

The key observation here is that, even if we take prompt and decisive abatement action, by sheer thermal inertia substantial changes in climate

---

[34] As Bordoff and O'Sullivan (2021) point out, this decline may be far from linear, as 'dependence on the dominant suppliers of fossil fuels, such as Russia and Saudi Arabia, will most likely rise before it falls'.

are inevitable. Human societies adjust to changing conditions by adapt-ing. Therefore it is inevitable that we shall have to adapt to a warmer climate – even if we don't know yet exactly how much warmer. And, yes, as humans have always done, adapt we will. In itself, this is almost a truism. Several aspects of the climate-change adaptation debate are, however, not trivial. Let me spell out a few.

First of all, adaptation is sometimes touted as a get-out-of-jail card. Even if the world were to become warmer, things are not going to be *that* bad, this narrative goes, because we will adapt. Or, in a related strand of argument, some people say that we should pause before diverting resources to emission abatement, because, again, we can adapt and adaptation will be cheaper and less disruptive (say, fewer jobs lost in the oil industry). The unstated assumption behind these arguments is that adaptation is always cheap, close-to-painless and easy – that it is the equivalent, writ large, of putting on a hat on a sunny day. In reality it is anything but. Let's look a bit more in detail at what climate-change adaptation can potentially mean.

The Chinese mountain tree known (to botanists, at least) as Qilian juniper, can survive harsh environments for over a thousand years. Paleobotanists have looked at its rings, and deduced from their spacings how arid a particular summer many centuries ago happened to be. Scientists have carried out this temperature reconstruction exercise for Qilian junipers that grew in north-central China (the Qinghai-Tibetan Plateau), and have found indications of several multi-decadal droughts between roughly 350 and 500 AD (see, Cook, 2013, and, especially, Wang, Yang and Ljungqvist, 2019). This is just the period when the Huns and the Avars began their Western migrations – the migrations that, by displacing the populations in their westward path, first threatened and then dealt a fatal blow to the Roman Empire. Now, as many historians have noticed, this is an interesting coincidence. We cannot be sure whether the Huns and Avars began moving and displacing populations because of these megadroughts[35] (the debate of whether they did has been going on since 1907, when Huntington first proposed the idea). However, if they did, this would be a text-book example of adaptation to climate change, and

---

[35] See on this Cook (2013).

of the unpredictable reach of its effects. And it is a textbook example of how painful and wealth-destroying 'adaptation' can be. Moving from the times of the fall of the Roman Empire to the present days, in a 3 °C warming scenario the 150 million people of sub-Saharan Africa may be forced to 'adapt' by migrating because of the likely desertification of the Sahel.[36] We can only hope that, as a result of this, Europe (currently struggling to cope with the migration of one to two million immigrants per year)[37] will not go the way of the Roman Empire.

Of course, not all adaptation has to be so painful. In general, climate adaptation is any action taken to mitigate or counteract the effects of climate change. Using a more heat-resistant crop; building a dam to prevent flooding; installing an air conditioner to sleep better at night; making one's home more energy efficient; and, yes, if no other options are available, even migrating to cooler regions – these are all forms of adaptation. What these different forms of adaptation have in common is that almost invariably they are costly and/or painful: after all, we would already be using the heat-resistant crop if it yielded more than the variety we are using now; we wouldn't be building a dam if we were not afraid of being flooded; and we would not migrate if our environmental conditions were not dire. And a second recurring feature of adaptation is that it often requires energy: energy to run the air conditioner a few extra hours; to build a new dam; to produce the fertilizers for the less-yielding crop; etc.

Admittedly, not *all* forms of adaptation require energy or are costly and painful. So, for instance, in their important work on climate change, mortality and adaptation, Deschenes and Greenstone (2011) mention 'substituting indoor exercise for outdoor exercise or changing the time of day when one is outside' as forms of adaptation.[38] But, in general,

---

[36] See, e.g., Lynas (2020), page 136 and *passim*, and references therein.

[37] Eurostat, Statistics Explained, https://ec.europa.eu/eurostat/statistics-explained/index.php?title=Migration_and_migrant_population_statistics.

[38] Deschenes and Greenstone (2007) took a first look at adaptation in their well-known, and controversial, paper on the effect of climate change on the US agricultural sector. (It was controversial because it concluded that 'climate change will lead to a $1.1 billion (2002$) or 3.4 per cent increase in annual profits' for the US agricultural sector.) I do not want to enter this debate, but I would note that it was unfortunate that in the title of their Yale working paper and of the *American Economic Review* paper that followed (*The Economic Impacts of Climate Change: Evidence from Agricultural Profits and Random Fluctuations in Weather*) the three-word qualifier 'in the USA' was missing, as

we do things the way we do not by chance, but because this is the most efficient way of doing them that we have come up with. Yes, changing the time of day when one is outside is easy if we are choosing when to go for a stroll; less so if we earn our living as a farmer in India. At the end of the day, one cannot escape that 'adapting' means making the best of a situation that, for some reason, has become worse.[39]

How much will adaptation cost? It is very difficult to say. In a perfectly functioning market economy, and from the perspective of an omniscient benevolent social planner,[40] at any point in time the *marginal* cost of emission abatement, carbon removal and adaptation should be almost the same. In the previous sentence 'marginal' is the important word: the idea being that what is equalized is the cost of the last unit of each climate-damage-reducing activity.[41] This is good news. For almost any good or service, its marginal cost increases with the amount of the good or service required. So, having an extra arrow (adaptation) in our quiver will make the total cost of damage reduction smaller, because we will not be forced to climb up the marginal cost curves of emission abatement

the article was taken, often disingenuously, to imply conclusions about the effects of climate change on the *world* agriculture that it was not meant to convey.

[39] The recent book by UCLA Professor of Geography Jared Diamond (Diamond, 2019) is in essence a study in adaptation – tellingly, its title is *Upheaval – How Nations Cope with Crisis and Change*. It adds an interesting dimension to the adaptation debate, because it doesn't take adaptation for granted, but analyzes what makes societies able to withstand dramatic changes. It is, if you want, the positive side of the story told in *Collapse* (Diamond, 2011), which traces the fate of societies that failed to adapt successfully. Interestingly, the subtitle of this latter book mentions societies that *chose* to fail or succeed.

[40] We shall see in Chapter 12, that the 'fiction' of the omniscient benevolent social planner is necessary to circumvent the free-riding problem.

[41] The idea that it is not the average cost, but the cost of the last unit, that determines the price can be counterintuitive. For a non-technical but correct discussion of the marginalist ideas, see Wasserman (2019), pages 26–29 and *passim*. For those readers interested in a quantitative, yet relatively simple, treatment of price theory, I strongly recommend Jaffe, Minton, Mulligan and Murphy (2019), who present the currently prevailing view of how prices are arrived at. From a history-of-ideas perspective, the so-called marginal revolution was truly a watershed, that turned on their heads the conceptions that had prevailed since Adam Smith of what constitutes the price of a good: it is not the cost of production that determines value, the marginalists said, but the satisfaction of the wants of the consumers. For a very good discussion of what 'value' means in economics, See Mazzucato (2018).

and carbon removal when these become too steep. In simple terms, if I want to deploy thirty *extra* units of climate reduction (whatever that means), I can achieve this reduction more cheaply if I can deploy ten units of abatement, ten units of carbon removal and ten units of emission reduction, than if I had to use fifteen units of abatement and fifteen units of removal.

This is what Economic 101 tells us. In reality, things are more complex, especially in the case of climate change. To begin with, the equalization of costs at the margin is only efficient for established production technologies. However, when we buy the (possibly expensive) products of a nascent technology (such as, say, direct carbon removal) we also lower its future production costs because of economies of scale, increased efficiency, innovations in how to produce the stuff better, etc. – this is what economists call 'learning by doing'. This means that, in making our choices about how to spend our global-warming-fighting dollar, we should not just look at the marginal costs today.[42] But, of course, we cannot know for sure how much a given technology will become cheaper, or how effective an adaptation will turn out to be. This means than in a field as rapidly changing as that of climate-control technologies, even a rational resource allocator is currently groping in the dark more than economic textbooks like to admit.

When it comes to abatement, there is another fly in the ointment of the equal-marginal-cost argument. Let's remind ourselves of the idea: an omniscient benevolent social planner would make sure that the last bit of abatement, or of removal, or of adaptation should cost the same (for the same effect). Why? Because if it did not, we should immediately go for the cheaper option and do more of it. Since the low-hanging fruits have all been picked, as we do more of it, its cost creeps up, until the cheaper option is cheaper no more. It sounds simple enough. However, the omniscient benevolent social planner does not really exist, and it is still an open question how the free-rider problem can be tackled. Now, when it comes to climate change, adaptation is (usually) paid for and benefitted from locally, but the problem is global. This is different from abatement or carbon removal, where the costs are local, but the benefits

---

[42] The field of finance called 'real option theory' looks exactly at these aspects.

global, diluted and conditional on other parties, over whom we have no control, 'playing ball'.

Let me explain why this difference is important with an example. Suppose (this is just a parable, not a proper analysis) that the inhabitants of Manhattan want to work out whether building a dam to protect their island against rising seas (a textbook example of adaptation) would be cheaper than abating CO_2 emissions. What degree of abatement are we talking about? Clearly, we cannot expect the city of New York to curb its emissions so much (or, actually, to remove from the atmosphere enough CO_2) to affect the global climate to such an extent, as to prevent the rise in sea level that would threaten Manhattan. Whether building the dam is worth the money or not, depends on what other states and countries are doing. If these other states and countries are not engaging seriously in abatement and removal, then the people of Manhattan should certainly build their dam. If, instead, there is a serious international effort to curb CO_2 emissions, then building the dam would not be the best use of money. But the New Yorkers cannot count on this and – this is the key point – resources are limited: what is spent on abatement cannot be spent on adaptation. (Remember: economics is the science of scarcity.) So, given their finite resources, for them it is a much safer option to go for adaptation than for abatement.

The point here is that, since the benefits of adaptation are felt where the money is spent *and do not depend on anyone else 'doing their bit'*, the temptation to go for the adaptation rather than the abatement option is very strong. The reader by now knows where this reasoning is going to lead: since every Manhattan in the world makes the same considerations, local adaptation with sure benefits is always preferred to 'diffuse' abatement with conditional benefits, and the global warming problem grows worse and worse – perhaps to the point that adaptation becomes extremely difficult, costly, or outright impossible.[43]

---

[43] The example, stylized in the extreme, is not totally fanciful. In 2019 New York's mayor, Bill de Blasio announced that '[w]e don't debate global warming in New York City […] any more. The only question is where to build the barriers to protect us from rising seas […] and how fast we can build them. […] When we complete the coastal extensions, which could cost $10 billion, Lower Manhattan will be secure from the rising seas through 2100.' (Quoted in Lynas (2020), page 130.) Clearly, the $10 billion spent by the City of New York on the barriers cannot be spent on abatement. (By the

These considerations are important because human ability to adapt is sometimes presented as a reason not to worry too much about climate change: the clever primate called *Homo Sapiens*, the argument goes, has always found ways to adapt to changing conditions from its early savannah days, and it will find ways to cope with a different, warmer climate as well. This is true, in the sense that humans, as a species, *will* survive climate change; but nothing in this story implies that the adaptation will be painless, or that we will have the luxury to adapt at a leisurely pace: in the case of global warming the adaptation window of opportunity may be shorter by orders of magnitude than for other events our species has had to contend with. And, as usual in the case of climate change, the most vulnerable populations are just those with the scarcer (technological, economic) means to adapt.

To conclude: yes, by adapting, when possible, we will reduce some of the pain and damage of global warming; and, yes, adaptation is certainly an important option to consider when choosing how best to cope with the change in climate. However, we must accept that in most of the cases that really matter adaptation will be costly, energetically expensive and unpleasant.

way, the $10 billion price tag may be on the optimistic side. After Hurricane Katrina the programme of dykes and sea improvements around New Orleans cost about $15 billion, but it is not designed to keep New Orleans dry to the end of the century.)

CHAPTER 4

How Economists Think about Climate Change

The last temptation is the greatest treason
To do the right deed for the wrong reason

—T. S. Eliot, *Murder in the Cathedral, 1935*

4.1 TWO WAYS TO LOOK AT CLIMATE POLICY

Taking serious abatement action is costly, and, as I already said in the opening chapter, doing so on a meaningful scale calls for investments little short of a war effort. This means that the trade-offs between certain sacrifices today and possible/plausible/probable benefits in the future must be weighed carefully: if it is true that we don't have the luxury of waiting and seeing, it is also true that we do not have the opposite luxury of acting hastily and inefficiently. Both economists and, in their moments of more honest disposition, policy-makers are well aware of how daunting the abatement task ahead is. They tend to look at the problem, however, from rather different perspectives. Politicians tend to favour hard limits, often expressed in terms of the 'maximum affordable' CO_2 concentration or temperature by some magic date (say, the end of the century – what happens after that, by the way?).[1] While having clearly established, measurable and 'one-number' targets has a lot of superficial appeal when one is setting policy, the approach has a certain ad-hockery

---

[1] For instance, in 2009 a degree limit was adopted both by the Major Economies Forum and by the G8 group of developed countries. The Copenhagen and the Cancún agreements of 2009 and 2010, respectively, then adopted the 2 °C limit as the goal of the United Nations negotiations.

about it: why 2 °C rather than 3 or 1.25 °C? Faced with the same problem, economists take a different perspective: they prefer to weigh the trade-offs between costs and benefits of various abatement policies, and to arrive at the optimal courses of action as the output of their optimizing analysis. So, some of the questions of most relevance for economists are when to act, how to act, in what scale to intervene and how large the carbon tax should be (today and in the future). Not surprisingly, this is the area where there has been ample room for principled disagreement among very serious economists (say, Stern, Weitzman and Cline on the one hand, and Nordhaus, Toll and Gollier on the other).[2]

This disagreement has not been yet another bun fight in the Senior Common Room of an Oxbridge college. How much we should invest today in controlling climate change; which abatement initiatives it makes sense to back now and which would be a waste of resources; how much we should tax carbon or subsidize renewables – from the perspective of economics, finding the correct answers to these near-existential questions boils down to choosing a quantity economists call the *social discount rate*. Alas, true to their reputation, economists have strongly disagreed about what the correct value of this quantity should be – and, historically, this has been one of the reasons why policy-makers have gravitated towards fast-and-frugal rules of thumb. And, not surprisingly, faced with this disagreement among top economists, even very intelligent commentators (I am referring to Nobel-prize winners in physics) have thrown their hands up in despair, and said, '*It is hopeless: just pick a number for the social discount rate, and you get the answer you want*'. If this were truly the case, and since so much seems to depend on the 'right' choice, what is the intelligent reader to do?

Much has been made of this disagreement. Ultimately, at the root of the disagreement there lurks this arcane-sounding quantity, the social discount rate. It may have an ugly name, but I am exaggerating only a

---

[2] Some economists, such as Pindyck (2013), have argued that economists should *not* calculate trade-offs, because our ignorance about how climate change will unfold is just too big. My view on this is that in the economist's tool kit there are solid and useful instruments to deal with imperfect knowledge – and that these ignorance-informed analyses produce answers skewed in the prudent direction one would expect from intuition.

bit when I say that, if the question of choosing the appropriate social discount rate could be settled, many important problems about the optimal abatement strategy would be solved as well. Fortunately, despite the forbidding name, this quantity is actually not arcane at all, and a key goal of this book is to explain what it is, *and how we can use it to help our decision-making*. At first blush, the fact that Nobel-prize winners have found the task of finding the 'right' social discount rate difficult does not inspire a lot of confidence in my enterprise. I am more optimistic. I intend to show that, leaving technicalities aside, the choice of the *appropriate* (not the *right*) social discount factor is something about which every intelligent person can have a well-reasoned view.

4.2 THE SPACE BETWEEN ETHICS AND 'FACTS OF NATURE'

How can this be? How can an intelligent, but not-Nobel-prize-winner reader (and writer, for that matter!) hope to say something useful about a concept that so far has seemed so intractable? Because I intend to show that this elusive quantity, the social discount factor, is made up of four components: the first is 'almost factual'; the other three are linked to how 'impatient' we are; to our dislike for taking risk; and to our dislike for 'feast and famine' (which can be translated in how big a role our dislike for uneven consumption is allowed to play in arriving at our abatement decisions). There is, of course, more to the economic analysis of climate change debate than this, but these four building blocks can provide the simplest and clearest way to organize our thoughts in a logically coherent way on such a complex topic.

So, yes, thinking about climate change is so difficult because it inhabits the uneasy space between ethics and facts of nature. But it is exactly because three of the key components of the social discount factor have an *ethical* dimension that, with Socrates, I believe that any intellectually honest person can have opinions as valid and defensible as those of the cleverest scientist. The intelligent layperson should trust the climate scientists when they say that the Earth is warming, or that today's warming is almost certainly anthropogenic. She should also trust the physicists and engineers when they work out the feasibility and cost-effectiveness of the various abatement options. But the same intelligent layperson does not have to trust anyone about the 'correct' social discount factor, because, when it comes to such an exquisitely ethical choice, she can make up her mind as validly and correctly as anyone else.

Philosopher Bernard Williams makes a closely related point when he questions the links between ethics (how we should *live*) and philosophy (that he defines as a set of highly specialized and tightly argued statements): 'How could it be that a *subject*, something one studies in universities (...), something for which there is a large technical literature, could deliver what one could recognize as an answer to the basic questions of life?'[3] The way he replies to this question has a direct bearing on the answers an informed citizen can arrive at about climate-change choices: 'It is hard to see how this could be so,' Williams continues, '*unless, as Socrates believed, the answer were one that the reader would recognize as one he might have given himself.*'[4] It is the ethical dimension of climate change choices that makes the problem complex; that makes it interesting; and that makes it within the reach of the human-all-too-human citizen.

How does one go from the social discount rate to choosing whether we should act quickly and decisively, or wait until we are smarter and richer (but the climate problem certainly more intractable)? And how does one translate how much one cares about future generations into a number? How, in sum, does one turn a number into a course of action? Some analytical tools, called Integrated Assessment Models, have recently been developed to answer these questions. They are anything if not ambitious. They provide a simplified, but, hopefully, realistic description of the physics *and* economics of climate change for the whole planet. They take as inputs our best guess about future economic growth (the quasi-factual quantity I was talking about), our understanding of the climate system, and our preferences (about how much we value smooth consumption, how much we care about the welfare of future generations, how much we dislike risk). Given these *facts and preferences* they tell us what the best course of action should be – where by 'course of action' I mean how much of current consumption we should sacrifice to limit climate change, which abatement initiatives make sense and which would be a

---

[3] B Williams, *Ethics and the Limits of Philosophy*, page 1–2, emphasis in the original.
[4] Ibid., page 2, emphasis added.

waste of resources, how quickly we should tackle the abatement effort, how large a carbon tax should be.

Do these Integrated Assessment Models hold all the answers? Of course they don't. First of all, the description of the physics of climate change is coarse and very simplified – they make ample use of what scientists call reduced-form models, which, in plain English, can be roughly translated as using a short-cut when the fully-fledged *ab initio* model is too difficult or computationally expensive. And, as for their handling of preferences, until recently technical (computational) difficulties made treatment by Integrated Assessment Models of our preferences very unsatisfactory. Take, for instance, our two basic 'types of' preference, our dislike for risk, and our dislike for feast and famine (uneven consumption over time). With the early Integrated Assessment Models these two basic preferences were on a collision course: the more we cared about risk, the more the early models forced us to say that we should leave the future and richer generations to fend for themselves; and the more intergenerationally altruistic we said we were, the more the models required us not to care about risk. As a result, the early Integrated Assessment Models put their users in a straightjacket, and were strongly criticized both from outside and from within economic circles.

To be sure, economists knew *in principle* how to get around these strictures, but, given the extremely long horizons of the models (centuries), and their ambition (modelling the 'utility of humanity'), the computational difficulties were just too big to allow anything other than extremely simplified approaches – which, not surprisingly, produced rather puzzling results. The more these models were perceived as simplistic and the results as puzzling, the less believability Integrated Assessment Models commanded. After the initial enthusiasm (that led to the granting of the Nobel Prize for Economics to Prof Nordhaus for his work linked to his best known economy/climate model, the DICE model), Integrated Assessment Models seemed to be headed for an impasse.

In the last few years, these technical difficulties have begun to be surmounted (and I like to think that my research group has made a small contribution towards making their output more useful and realistic). From these efforts a new consensus is beginning to form: as I mentioned in the opening chapter, we neither have to assume that *Homo Economicus* is a selfish agent, callously indifferent to the fate of anybody apart from his most direct offsprings, nor do we have to assume that he has the moral disposition of Mother Theresa of Calcutta. We just have to model his aversion to risk *and* his dislike for uneven consumption without pitting one set of preferences against the other. When we do so, the advisability of prompt and decisive abatement action naturally follows. In this sense, Integrated Assessment Models are witnessing a new dawn.

Why should we care so much about what Integrated Assessment Models say? Because they provide a way to organize our thoughts in a logically coherent manner. If we use Integrated Assessment Models, a target of 1.5–2 °C for the acceptable warming by the end of the century, for instance, no longer has to be plucked out of thin air, but can be derived, criticized and, if needed, revised *in either direction*. As all models, Integrated Assessment Models need improvement, and, indeed, my main research efforts at the moment are exactly in this direction. But having a half-decent model is already a powerful starting point. If we find a model assumption too crude, we can try to see how much the model predictions depend on this dodgy assumption. If not so much, we can live with the model. If the dependence is strong, then there is more work to do, and we must refine our modelling assumptions. This is just the way all of science works.

Even better: when the results the model produces run against our intuition – when, that is, the model spits out an answer at odds with what we had expected it to say – this is exactly when we learn a lot. Perhaps the modelling was wrong, in which case we now know that we have to fix it, and where to look for the faulty bit. But perhaps it was our intuition (read 'prejudice') that was wrong, in which case we have truly learnt something useful. Integrated Assessment Models are powerful, not when they confirm what we thought we knew, but when they challenge our pre-conceived ideas. If we dismiss the uncomfortable results, or if we tweak and torture the model until it gives the answers we wanted it to give in the first place, then we are just wasting good CPU time (an activity that, by the way, contributes to climate warming).[5] This is why part of this book

---

[5] When it comes to CPU time used for climate research, my remark about its environmental impact is tongue-in-cheek. It is a very serious concern, however, when it

(Chapters 8–12) is devoted to explaining what Integrated Assessment Models have to say about our best course of action, to what extent we can trust their answers, and, if we don't, what else we could do.

4.3 THE LAST TEMPTATION

This brings me to what I call 'the last temptation'. Integrated Assessment Models have become both influential and heavily criticized in policy-making circles. The origin of the criticism is easy to understand: the early incarnations of one of the best known models (Nobel-prize-winner Professor Nordhaus' DICE model) gave puzzling and counterintuitive answers. These early versions of the DICE model suggested that, definitely, we should take climate change seriously, and that we should act to control it. But, according to these early versions of the DICE model, the best way to control climate change is not to invest heavily today in abatement initiatives, but to research and develop more efficient technological solutions. The very gradual pace of abatement these early versions of the DICE model recommended dismayed many commentators, who had hoped for a 'call to arms' as urgent and robust as the one delivered by the Stern (2006) report.

Understanding *why* the early versions of the DICE model gave such gradualist recommendations is very important – and we will look at this aspect in detail in future chapters. Once we have understood the origin of its gradualist recommendations, we can understand which of the DICE model assumptions are both questionable and of far-reaching import. By doing so, we can improve the modelling. Prof Nordhaus, the author of the DICE model, has been exemplary in this respect, by making his code public, and justifying at length and accurately every single one of the parameters and of the modelling assumptions that enter the model. This is exactly how good science should work.

Despite the scientific openness of its creator,[6] the DICE model has been reviled, not only by climate-change activists, but also by some

comes to CPU-intensive activities such as the 'mining' of cryptocurrencies, especially if these were to become widespread.

[6] From the very start, the code for the DICE model has been made publicly available both in spreadsheet and in code form, and copious documentation and justification for all

economists, as 'dangerous', 'wrong-headed' and sometimes little short of evil.[7] The Stern report, which appeared shortly before the DICE model, and that advocated much more decisive abatement action, was immediately far more popular, as it seemed to chime much better with the expectations of 'progressive' commentators – it seemed, that is, to give the answers one wanted to hear. Yet those who decried the recommendations of the DICE model and enthusiastically endorsed the conclusions of the Stern report generally failed to grasp that the latter uses *exactly* the same conceptual framework (based on cost-benefit analysis) as the former.[8] The conclusions reached by the two models were so different because one key input was different (yes, you guessed correctly, it was the social discount rate). However, as we shall see, the Stern report yielded recommendations more similar to the course of action suggested by the new-generation models not because it managed to model the climate problem better: in the modelling implied by the Stern report risk aversion and dislike for feast and famine are still squarely on the same collision course as in the DICE model. The Stern report results appear more appealing because the same oversimplified modelling approach it shares with the DICE model – an approach *any* economist would agree is poor – was patched with a very contentious choice. This is a choice that very few economists consider defensible for one of its inputs – what economists call the utility discount rate – that is, in simple terms, by how much we should reduce the value of a future

---

the parameters has been provided. The building, several years ago, of my own first version of DICE was immensely helped by this scientific openness.

[7] I have recently published a non-technical article on the importance of negative emission technologies in *The Conversation* (see https://theconversation.com/forget-net-zero-to-halt-global-heating-aim-for-net-negative-195484), in which I mentioned that I had obtained the results *using a 'much modified' version* of the DICE model – similar to the one that I discuss in this book. Despite explaining that I was changing the DICE model in important ways, I was attacked for even touching the model of a 'climate criminal' (Prof Nordhaus).

[8] To be clear: Prof Nordhaus's recommendations are best read as directing our efforts against climate-change more towards research and development than towards immediate implementation: 'It should be emphasized that the primary requirement is support for *research and development*, not production. Developing new low-carbon technologies and energy sources is much more important than subsidizing the current generation of low-carbon equipment in cars, houses, and industry.' Nordhaus (2021), emphasis in the original.

benefit or loss simply because it is in the future. When the future covers generations to come, the utility discount rate approximately reflects our degree of 'generational altruism'. See Chapter 9 for a discussion of this point.

The debatable choice for this quantity made in the Stern report reflected, in my view, a desire to 'encourage' the model to give the answers we thought we knew all along and wanted to hear. This, I believe, *is* the last temptation: to (try to) do the right deed, but for the wrong reason. Yes, the Stern review did approximate more closely what today we recognize as the 'right answer', but arrived at the right conclusion for what I believe are the 'wrong reasons' (or, at least, weak reasons).

Does all of this matter, if in the end the policy recommendations from the latest economic modelling are so similar to the Stern ones? It does, because poor modelling is sterile, in the sense that it does not lead us anywhere. Using tortured model inputs to obtain the results we thought we knew already is an expensive exercise in bias confirmation, not in discovery. I do research to be surprised. What we want to understand is whether it is possible to get to Stern-like policy results using the most convincing economic modelling, *and assumptions about human nature that do not require people to behave in an implausibly altruistic manner*. The exciting news is that this seems to be indeed the case. In the next chapters we shall gather the tools to test this contention.

CHAPTER 5

How Economists Look at Choice

5.1 HOW TO BUILD A MODEL OF HOW WE CHOOSE

In Chapter 1 I made the case that looking at climate change through the lens of economic analysis is profitable – let's call my justification for this claim the *credo-quia-absurdum* argument: we should listen to the urgent calls for abatement action that economic analysis makes exactly because, even in its most-up-to-date incarnations, it is still forced to neglect many aspects of reality – *and because these aspects, if somehow included, would make the case for strong and decisive abatement action even stronger.*

What am I referring to? What are these important missing features? To name just a few, our dislike for inequality (perhaps modest, but certainly not zero) is neglected in most models; we do not quantify in any way what would suffer from loss of biodiversity or of natural beauty, nor would we know how to translate these losses into an equivalent 'loss of consumption';[1] and when very poor populations suffer extreme climate-related damages, the economic-loss needle for the world as a whole barely moves, exactly because these populations are so poor, and therefore affect the model optimal solutions disproportionately little. We feel that the severity of this human suffering should greatly affect our response to climate change, but we don't know how to quantify and model it.

Different as they are, all these missing ingredients have something in common: the fact that, if somehow captured, they would almost

---

[1] There are attempts to handle these aspects in a utility-maximization framework. In my opinion, the best treatment of the economics of biodiversity is the magisterial Dasgupta Review (2021), commissioned by the UK HM Treasury. At 610 pages, it is not easy bed-time reading, but it is extremely rewarding and, as technical material goes, very clear and 'as simple as possible, but not more than that'.

invariably suggest prompter and more decisive abatement action. This then means that the output of Integrated Assessment Models – even the 'best' ones – should be taken as a *lower bound* of how quickly and in what scale we should act to limit climate damage. Lower bounds tend to be uninteresting because they often have little 'bite'. In the case of climate change, the lower bounds we find are extremely useful because the speed and scale of the recommended climate action are such that they are already hitting hard against the boundaries of practical implementability and political acceptability. *Theoretically*, it may be interesting to find that we should act even more decisively. *In practice*, I would gladly sign today on the proverbial dotted line if someone told me that we will follow the optimal abatement policies of the very-imperfect modern Integrated Assessment Models.

So, in this and the following chapters I will no longer engage in apologetics, and assume that the reader is willing to embark on this exploration and has on open mind about the findings. I must now provide this willing, but probably still hesitant, reader with the essential building blocks to understand the analysis to follow. This is what I intend to do in this chapter.

To get started, the first thing to is to introduce the three psychological reactions humans display when faced with (possibly uncertain) out-comes, and to explain how these reactions are captured by the workhorse of (micro)economic analysis, utility theory. Above all, I need to show how these psychological reactions, and the way we choose to model them, have a direct effect on the choices we make about how to keep climate change under control.

The distinction I have drawn (between the psychological drivers and how we model them) is extremely important: our modelling of the psy-chological reactions to uncertainty may be debatable, but the reactions themselves are much more 'robust' and universal. Indeed, to a very large extent, those who arrive at different conclusions about what should be done about climate change, ultimately do so because they have different psychological reactions to climate outcomes.[2] This remains true whether

---

[2] This is not strictly true: outright deniers – i.e., people who ignore evidence and prefer narratives based on pseudo facts or fanciful theories – display some other psychological features that cannot be modelled using the three building blocks I introduce in this

or not they use economic analysis. For instance, the policy preferences of a climate activist who strongly dislikes the gradual approach taken, and the conclusions reached, by the original DICE model, and who advocates a much more decisive abatement investment, can be described as having a greater concern for the welfare of future generations, than what is implicitly modelled in the DICE model. Her psychological drivers are different from those assumed by Prof Nordhaus. Conversely, the abatement choice of someone who thinks that not using cheap coal today is a bad idea, even if doing so increases the concentration of CO_2 in the atmosphere, can be understood in terms of low regard for the welfare of future generations, and/or a high tolerance for risk. (This assumes that both the climate activist and the coal supporter broadly accept the mainstream scientific evidence and are willing to update their beliefs as new evidence becomes available – see again footnote 2.) The important point here is that the psychological engines behind our climate choices have a much greater generality, reach and validity than the specific ways in which economics tries to model them: some may find the treatment of these psychological motivators by utility theory too crude to be of much use, but this does not mean that the underlying drivers are not at play.

I described above the choices of the activist by saying that her psychological drivers were different from those assumed by Prof Nordhaus. Does this mean that we have to accept that the all-important conclusions about climate intervention are ultimately purely subjective? Not really. All economists who come up with some values for the parameters that are supposed to describe these psychological drivers do not do so in a vacuum. They would typically observe people's behaviour in other areas (such as the chosen level of redistributive taxation, or the aid paid by rich to poor countries) and argue: 'Since you have made choice X in this setting, I can deduce that the parameter that describes the psychological driver at play (say, risk aversion, or dislike for inequality in consumption) must have value x. *I will then use the parameter value x also when it comes to describing the same psychological driver in the context of climate-change choices.*' Economists, in short, will typically try to ensure not that choices are

---

chapter. I am not aware of any systematic way of modelling quantitatively the decision-making process of conspiracy theorists and fact deniers.

intrinsically right, but that they are consistent. They will not argue that you should donate more or less to developing countries, or that you should accept a higher or lower level of taxation, but that, given that this is the way you feel about foreign aid and income inequality, then, to be consistent, you should care this much about the welfare of 'others' also when it comes to climate change.

Economists will also often employ a different line of analysis. They will say, for instance: 'When it comes to climate-change you say that we should care about the welfare of future generations exactly as much as we care about ours. Fair enough. But do you realize that, if you really believe in this lofty statement, then logically you should accept this and that consequence?' If the logical consequences of our high-minded statement seem absurd, then the economists may point out to us that we were actually grandstanding, not expressing thoughtful preferences.[3] Similarly, the same economist may say 'If you really do not care a jot about future generations, why are you setting money aside for your children (why, in economist-speak, when it comes to your children, do you seem to have a "bequest motive"?)'. The economist, I stress again, is agnostic as to whether you should look after the welfare of your descendants (or of future generations), but would like you to be consistent in your choices. If we are really happy to live with the logical consequences of our stated choices, then the economist has nothing to add or rebut. Philosophers, of course, take a much more sanguine approach to all of this, and are more willing to make prescriptive statements. The distinction between preferences and ethical prescriptions is clear enough in theory. As we shall see, in climate-change-related issues there is a finer line between consistency in preferences and ethical choices than is usually recognized – and, in part, this is what makes the topic so fascinating.

5.2 STRONGER THAN PREFERENCES

Before we turn our attention to how our preferences can be modelled, we must look at a principle that is stronger than any preference: in

---

[3] We shall see in Chapter 9 one such important argument in the 'wrinkle in time' thought experiment.

economics it is called the principle of no-arbitrage. (To be precise, one preference still must hold for the principle of no-arbitrage to make sense: the fact that we prefer more to less. I don't think that this is very contentious.) In the absence of uncertainty, absence of arbitrage is probably *the* single most important principle to guide our choices about climate-change abatement. And even when we add uncertainty, and the 'bite' of this principle is weakened, we must always keep in mind the message that underpins the idea of no-arbitrage.[4] Why is it so important? And how can something be more important than one's preferences?

The text-book definition of arbitrage is precise, but not very intuitive. I will therefore introduce the concept by way of an example. Suppose that I know for sure that, if I do nothing, in ten years' time I will suffer a damage of $100 (this may come from climate change, for instance, but the reasoning is much more general). I have $80 today, with which I can do two things: either invest them in a technology that I know will reduce for sure the future damage; or ignore the future damage, and invest my money in the productive technologies of the economy – the technologies, that is, that produce goods to consume. Finally, let's suppose that if I invest all my money in the damage-abating technology the future damage will be reduced from $100 to $10 – again, without any uncertainty. What should I do?

Well, the answer clearly depends on the rate of return on the productive technologies of the economy. Suppose that this rate of return is 5 per cent. If I invest all my money in producing more goods (and I do nothing about the certain future damage), then in ten years' time my investment will yield $80 \times (1+0.05)^{10} = \$130.31$, I will then take on the chin my loss of $100, and I will be left with $30.31. If instead I had devoted my initial capital to damage limitation (if I had fully invested in the damage-abating technology, that is), my future damage will be reduced to $10, but I will have nothing to show on the good-production side of the equation. So, I have to choose between a strategy that in ten years' time will make me richer by $30.31 or poorer by $10. *No matter what my preferences are*, I will definitely choose to invest all my money in the productive technologies of the economy, and accept the future damage when it comes.

---

[4] For a good discussion see Gollier (2013), chapter 1.

However, if the rate of return on the good-producing technologies had been 1 per cent, then my initial $80 would have only grown to $88.37. After suffering the certain damage of $100, I would be nursing a loss of $11.6, *greater than the loss of $10 that I would have suffered if I had invested everything in the damage-abating technology*. Just as certainly, and no matter what my preferences are, in this case I should put all my money in avoiding the future damage.

If all of this sounds very obvious it is because, in a certain way, it is. What is the relevance of all of this for climate change, and its abatement? The important point is that, when we consider investing in (diverting resources to) emission-abatement initiatives, we must always keep in mind what else we could do with the same money, *and whether the return on the alternative investment opportunities is higher*. Clearly, all of this maps rather imprecisely to the real-world climate-change problem. To begin with, we do not know for sure what the damage will be, and therefore our preferences – our attitude to risk – must play a big part in the decision. Furthermore, the climate risk problem is not static (a fixed amount in the future), but it gets worse the more we wait to take action. Therefore the rate of increase in the damage if we do nothing may well be higher than the rate of growth of the economy. Having made all these qualifications, the principle behind the no-arbitrage principle remains valid: whenever we consider diverting some of our investment capabilities to the abatement of emissions we must always ask what else we could do with the same capital, and whether these alternative uses could make us better off. Since our resources are limited (remember that I defined economics as the science of scarcity), this is the essence of the choices we have to make about how to tackle the emission-abatement problem.

To give some concreteness to the principle, allow me to go back to the case discussed in Chapter 1 of the falling cost of solar panels – a cost that, as we saw, fell by almost a factor of ten in less than a decade. The principle of no-arbitrage tells us that, if the rate of fall in the price of solar panels is higher than the rate of growth of the economy, then I should wait. If prices have fallen by a factor of ten in ten years, the rate of fall has been about 23 per cent per annum, which is certainly much higher than the rate of growth in the economy. Had we rushed to install the early solar panels, we would now be saddled with inefficient and expensive devices. Not a good way to use *limited* resources. So, if the future climate damage were fixed in magnitude, and we could have predicted the price fall, we should definitely have waited to invest. The problem, of course, is that in this ten years the climate damage has not remained fixed at $100, but it has grown. How does the rate of growth of the damage compare with the rate of fall in prices of solar panels and the rate of growth in the economy? The real-life problem is more complex because the very act of investing in consumption technologies makes the climate damage worse (via increased emissions); conversely, the act of investing in a today-perhaps-uncompetitive abatement technology makes its cost go down (this is what economists call 'learning by doing'). The key advantage of Integrated Assessment Models is that they can, in principle, handle both these feedback loops. The problem is clearly difficult (and this is where Integrated Assessment Models provide a good analytic tool). The underlying principle, however, is simple.

As I said, the moment outcomes are no longer certain the no-arbitrage principle loses much of its bite. Indeed, Merton, Black and Scholes won the Nobel prize in Economics for their work on the pricing of derivatives (and much else) using the no-arbitrage principle by turning a super-risky situation (the trading of options) into one with no risk at all. This is because, to use the no-arbitrage principle, they had to reduce the problem at hand to a certainty setting – and since they were dealing with some of the riskiest instrument that markets have invented, this was no mean feat. This is why their solution to the problem is so elegant and, once the uncertainty has been exorcised, so simple.

We can tame uncertainty, however, only in very special cases – and climate change is certainly not one of these. When outcomes are uncertain, just saying that we prefer more to less does not take us very far. At the very least, we must also specify how impatient we are, how much we dislike static risk, and how we feel about uneven consumption patterns. So, when it comes to the choices we have to make about how to tackle climate change, it remains true, of course, that we still prefer more to less, but other, subtler psychological drivers of our choice-making take centre stage. To handle the decisions about what to do with the climate problem in a consistent manner, we must understand what these choice motivators are.

5.3 THE PSYCHOLOGICAL DRIVERS

So, if they are so important, what are these psychological drivers? Much as I believe that bullet points do not belong in books but in PowerPoint presentations, I will make an exception here and enumerate the three essential reactions to consumption choices as follows

- impatience
- aversion to static risk
- aversion to feast and famine.

Having succumbed to the bullet-point temptation, I immediately have to backtrack a bit, and confess that I am cutting some corners here: the three psychological drivers of our choice process listed above are arguably the most important in the context of climate change (I will explain why this is the case), but the way we make decisions is affected by a number of subtler decisional nuances. I will discuss some of these later in the chapter, and I will explain why I think that they play a secondary role in the decisions about climate change. However, there is at least one other psychological driver of decisions that may play a significant role when we make decisions about climate change, and that I should therefore mention now: ambiguity aversion. What is this? Suppose that you are told that in the canonical two urns of probability problems there are red and blue balls, and that if you draw a red ball you win $1,000. You are also told that in the urn to the right the fraction of red balls is 50–50, while the fraction of red balls in the left urn is unknown. From which urn would you prefer to draw your ball? (Please pause for a moment to consider from which urn *you* would prefer to draw the ball.)

Most people choose the right urn (the one with a *known* 50–50 fraction of red balls), despite the fact that, given the information available, they will not be more likely to win the $1,000 prize with this choice. This preference for settings that are still uncertain, but for which the probabilities are better known, is called *ambiguity aversion*. Now, ambiguity aversion certainly plays a role in the choices we make about what to do about climate change: after all, deep uncertainties abound in virtually every aspect of climate modelling and of the damages climate change may produce, and people would surely feel better if they knew with greater certainty at least the likelihood of the various climate outcomes before them. This also means that we are likely to prefer courses of action in which we are less exposed to ambiguity. This is certainly true. However, for reasons that will become clearer in what follows, I believe that ambiguity aversion is a less important driver of our climate choices than the three features listed in the bullet points above, and therefore, for the sake of simplicity, I have decided to ignore it in the account I give in this chapter.[5]

5.4 IMPATIENCE

So, let's start from the first item in the list above: impatience. This feature reflects our preference for experiencing the same enjoyment from consumption earlier rather than later. If only one holiday is to be had, given a choice between jumping on a plane tomorrow or in a year's time, most of us would prefer packing our trolley bags straight away, not in twelve month's time. As we shall see, a common way of reflecting this preference is by 'making equivalent' immediate and future happiness (utility) by 'discounting' (reducing in magnitude) the later happiness. So, perhaps I would be just indifferent between when to take the holiday (now or in one years' time) if the future holiday could be four days longer: the pleasure from a four-days-longer holiday starting *today* is, of course, greater still, but the pleasure from the longer-but-later holiday may become just equal to the pleasure from the shorter-and-immediate holiday when the future pleasure is reduced (discounted) because of its remoteness. The important point is that, *ceteris paribus*, future happiness appears to be considered less valuable – appreciated less – by most people *simply by virtue of being future*.

Many philosophers (and several economists in their more philosophical moments) find this preference difficult to justify. It is not difficult to see why. Suppose you are choosing how much to save for your retirement. Saving means foregoing consumption today in the hope of greater

---

[5] Incidentally, ambiguity aversion is one of the extra features that the modern economic treatment allows us to capture. So, I will not discuss it in detail in this book, but it plays a significant (if not centre-stage) part in the climate-modelling approach I advocate.

consumption in the future. So, you are comparing a privation now (what you give up if you save) with a future privation (what you will suffer if you *don't* save).[6] Saying that you are impatient means that a given privation later in your life should be considered less important in your comparison of happinesses than the same privation today *just because it is in the future.* Your future self may well be unhappy with your choice today, but has no way to change the decision-making process of you-today. Note that this does not necessarily imply any time inconsistency: if your impatience (and your full preference set) do not change, you will still make the same investment decision at any time between now and your retirement. Despite this 'conflict of interests' between you-today and you-in-retirement, (most) economists just stand by and let you make your investment choice today as you please. The important underlying idea is that, since your self is considered unitary,[7] nobody is better placed than you to make choices that only affect your unitary self.

Giving less value to the identical consumption simply because it is in the future may at first blush seem 'irrational', but I do not think it is very profitable to use the rationality label when it comes to preferences. One can, after all, construct a passably believable evolutionary story of why we may have evolved to value consumption here and now more than the identical consumption in the future. In a textbook example we can stipulate as part of the rules of the game that the future consumption is certain. However, such absolute certainty is never available in real life – in the actual context, that is, where our evolutionarily tuned preferences have been formed. The textbook-identical slice of cake in a month's time may in reality not be truly identical, or may not materialize at all; or, perhaps, in a month's time I may have a stomach upset; worse of all, in a month's time I may be dead – and, if this sounds unnecessarily morbid and melodramatic, our possible non-existence because of, say, an asteroid falling on Earth is the one and only reason why Prof Stern

[6] When I say 'privation' I am actually referring to loss of 'utility'. If we want to remain for the moment model-free, we should perhaps say 'loss of happiness'.

[7] Libertarian paternalists would disagree about this, and talk about externalities imposed by your present upon your future self. I have a lot to say about this – so much that I have written the best part of a book about the problem of 'internalities' (if you are interested, see Rebonato 2012, 2014) – but the topic would take us too much off the main track.

allows a tiny bit of impatience to enter his climate-change calculations. We shall have a lot more to say about this. So, discriminating between identical consumption simply because it occurs at different times, and preferring the earlier consumption to the later, may well have conferred our ancestors an evolutionary advantage in the uncertain world in which our species evolved: a bird in the hand, in other words, may be preferable not only to two birds in the bush, but also to two birds tomorrow.

Whatever the origin of our impatience, matters become a lot more complex when the trade-off between happiness or loss thereof involves different generations. Now the argument 'nobody knows better than I do which trade-off is acceptable for *me*' obviously no longer applies. With their philosophical hat on many economists have therefore taken a very strong stance about using the concept of impatience when we are dealing with the welfare of future generations. As far back as 1928 Ramsey wrote that giving a smaller weight the unhappiness of future generations is 'ethically indefensible and arises merely from the weakness of the imagination'. And in his 1948 book that effectively started the study of economic development, Harrod 'doubled down' by calling the practice of discounting for impatience a 'polite expression for rapacity and the conquest of reason by passion'. Closer to us, Solow (1974) only partially tempered these strong pronouncements when he wrote, 'In solemn conclave assembled, so to speak, we ought to act as if the [discount rate on future well-being] were zero.'[8]

The relevance of this for climate change decisions is clear: if we really believe that we should weigh the happiness of future generations exactly the same as our own happiness now (despite the fact that we do not seem to consider even our own future happiness equivalent to our present happiness), then we should accept heavy sacrifices today to improve the climate outcomes of our descendants. There is something starkly deontological (and – I don't mean it as a slur – a bit Kantian) in this position, as it is definitely not derived from observing our preferences, but from an a priori principle. This impartiality principle tells us how we should, if not feel, certainly behave, and finds a moral fault in us if we act differently.

[8] Partha Dasgupta, *Ramsey and Intergenerational Welfare Economics*, The Stanford Encyclopedia of Philosophy (Summer 2020 Edition), Edward N Zalta (ed.), https://plato.stanford.edu/archives/sum2020/entries/ramsey-economics/.

As we shall see in Chapter 9, matters about intergenerational welfare are a tad more nuanced than these Sunday-pulpit pronouncements seem to imply. But, without wading into deep philosophical waters, we can at least apply the economist's favourite tool, the consistency check. If we take this approach, we can ask what exactly makes future generations different from us. In essence, the fact that they do not exist 'here and now'.[9] So, the question is 'Which trade-offs of happiness are we prepared to make for people that are not "here and now"?' We can have a decent approximation to 'future people' by looking at people who live in other countries (these people are 'now', but not 'here'). The approximation is far from perfect, because, when we talk about future generations our mind immediately latches onto *our* children, and *their* children, and *their* children. However, as these degrees of kinship get diluted, we can try to mix the two aspects of remoteness (spatial and temporal).

When we do so, the observed fraction of GDP allocated by rich economies to improve the conditions of developing countries does not seem to imply a great degree of concern for people who are significantly removed from us.[10] If geographical remoteness is a good proxy for temporal separation, this raises the consistency question of why we should be 'infinitely altruistic'[11] when it comes to the damage our CO_2 emissions will inflict on future generations, when we display rather little altruism vis-à-vis the welfare of today's world poor. It is exactly for this reason that many economists argue that we would get a much bigger

---

[9] Future generations may also be different from us because they will be richer. If they are, the same loss of consumption will hurt them less. See in this respect the discussion in Chapter 10. However, this is taken care of by looking at equal 'happiness', not consumption, now and in the future. This is why pure impatience is modelled by discounting utility ('happiness'), not consumption ('money').

[10] In percentage terms, the most generous countries are Sweden, the UAE and Norway, who in 2015 devoted 1.14 per cent, 1.09 per cent and 1.05 per cent of their national product to their overseas development assistance. In the same year, the tenth most generous country (Switzerland) eartagged 0.52 per cent of its national product to foreign aid. The percentage for other rich countries falls off rather quickly. (The USA, by the way, is top in absolute size of aid, but, in percentage terms, does not make the top ten. World Economic Forum (2015), *Foreign Aid: These Countries Are the Most Generous.* www.weforum.org/agenda/2016/08/foreign-aid-these-countries-are-the-most-generous/.)

[11] The expression 'infinitely altruistic' can be misleading: what I mean here is treating the welfare of 'distant others' exactly on the same footing as our own welfare.

bang for our welfare buck if we ensured that, say, malaria is eradicated or that clean water is available to everyone today than if we spent the same resources on the more expensive emission-abatement projects. Of course, consistency arguments are double-edged swords: perhaps, given the degree of altruism about future generations revealed by the abatement commitment we seem to be ready to undertake, it is the fraction of GDP that we devote to foreign aid that we should revise.

We will have a lot more to say about impatience discounting when we look at how to model this psychological feature within the framework of utility theory (see also the discussion in Chapter 9 on this point). For the moment, we can already say that handling impatience is tricky enough when the same person is at the receiving end of the time-separated sacrifices and benefits, and *much* more problematic when the 'happiness trade-offs' straddle different generations. In a rather wishy-washy way, many economists like to say that the rate of discounting of happiness (the rate at which future happiness becomes smaller just because it happens to be in the future) should be 'small but not too small' (whatever that means). This, of course, is hardly satisfactory, especially because early economic modelling of climate choices seemed to indicate that this was *the* parameter that made all the difference in producing a fast or slow abatement schedule. Indeed, the Stern/Nordhaus unnecessarily strident controversy revolved exactly on the 'correct' choice for this impatience rate. Lord Stern reluctantly brought himself to allow for a tiny 0.10 per cent impatience discount rate not because he conceded that we should regard the interests of our descendants even a tiny bit differently from ours, but because he thought that humanity might after all disappear for causes other than global warming. In those pre-Covid days, the example he adduced to justify our untimely demise was the probability (estimated at 0.10 per cent per annum) of our civilization going the way of the dinosaurs because of a rogue asteroid hitting our planet: the let's-dance-while-the-*Titanic*-is-sinking logic here being, apparently, that it would after all be a pity to make sacrifices today if we are all going to disappear anyhow tomorrow.

As we shall discuss later in the book, I am no fan of the zero-impatience assumption. If the case for prompt and large investment in abatement initiatives rested only on the shoulder of this almost-infinite altruism, I would find the case uncomfortably weak. However, as I said in Chapter 1, when we employ a more satisfactory economic modelling of our other psychological drivers of choice than it was possible to do with early DICE models, we no longer need a near-infinite degree of altruism to endorse fast and large-scale investment in abatement efforts today. Indeed, as I show in Chapter 12, roughly the same abatement recommendations as in the Stern report can now be recovered even with the relatively 'callous' degree of impatience assumed in the DICE model, as long as other important decisional drivers, which we discuss below, are better described than in the Stern and DICE models. I find this very important, because most social and political programmes whose success is predicated on people being significantly more saintly than they are usually observed to be seldom boast a good track record of success.

5.5 AVERSION TO RISK

We have looked at impatience. Let's move to the next important driver of our decisions in our list: risk aversion. Aversion to risk is arguably the most readily understood of the psychological drivers of our choices. Most people, when asked whether they would like to play a 50–50 coin toss depending on the results of which they can win or lose with equal probability, say, $100,000, would decline to play. Or, alternatively, they would need an *inducement* (say, $30,000) to accept to play the game.[12] Indeed, the observed empirical observation that most people refuse a zero-expected-gain gamble is one of the many definitions of risk aversion. The greater the compensation required to enter the gamble, the more the person is said to be risk averse.[13]

---

[12] 'Small' gambles that are entered into for the *frisson* provided by the act of gambling in itself are not described by risk aversion. In this case we derive enough enjoyment from playing the lottery game to compensate us for the 'disutility' of accepting a zero-expected-gain gamble – or even a slightly negative-expected-gain gamble, as all casino games and lotteries are.

[13] There are, of course, limits to how much compensation one can ask to enter a gamble: if, to enter the $100,000-gamble above, one were to require a $110,000 compensation, it would literally be a 'heads I win, tails you lose' situation. Normally we don't have to worry about these so-called no-arbitrage bounds.

It is important to stress from the outset that there is nothing 'rational' about being risk averse. Our dislike for 'gambling for no compensation' may perhaps have a biological, evolutionary explanation, but this does not make it rational in any accepted sense of the word. In this sense, it is no different from the other psychological driver we have looked at so far, impatience. Risk aversion is just one of the recurring features humans tend to display when faced with uncertain outcomes.[14]

As we shall see in detail in Chapter 7, the same monetary gain or loss can be disliked to a very different extent by different people. This can be because they are intrinsically more or less prudent, but it can also depend on how rich they are. It is clear that a $1,000 gamble will be perceived as vastly more risky, and therefore disliked a lot more, by someone on unemployment benefits than by Bill Gates. A more reasonable description of our aversion to risk is to say that Bill Gates and the person on unemployment benefits would equally dislike to lose the *same fraction* of their total wealth. There is no tight logical argument to show that this should be the case, and the empirical evidence about whether proportional risk aversion describes well how people accept or turn down gambles is mixed. However, positing that poor and rich people have an identical dislike for the same *percentage* loss is a step in the right direction (it is better, that is, than considering as relevant the absolute monetary value of the gamble).

---

[14] A short but important digression: I consider the expression 'rational choice theory' (the capacious tent under which utility-maximization-based decision theory can be accommodated) strongly misleading. 'Consistent choice theory' would be a better description. The way 'rational' choice theory works is by *observing* first a number of recurrent psychological features (preferences): such as the fact that we dislike large risk bets; that we dislike uneven consumption; and that we prefer more to less. These are preferences, and there is nothing intrinsically 'rational' in holding them. Then a model is created and calibrated to reflect these *observed* preferences: the model, that is, says that our preferences are accounted for *as if* we behaved as the model assumes (say, as if we maximized expected utility). Finally – and only here is where the rational/consistent bit comes in – we observe choices in decisional settings other than those used to formulate (calibrate) our utility model, and we assess whether these *new* choices are *consistent* with what the calibrated model says. If they are not, it may be a reason for arguing that we are being inconsistent. (This is the approach I take in Chapter 8.) Or, perhaps, our calibrated model was poor, in the sense that is was not useful for extrapolating beyond the 'primary' observations we have used to build it.

Both risk aversion in general, and its quasi-proportional nature, matter a lot for the decisions we make about climate change. The first obvious reason is that uncertainty is ubiquitous and very large in every area of climate modelling, and in the estimation of the damages it may produce. So, let's assume that you were ready to pay X to avert a *certain* future climate-related damage of magnitude Y. If now I told you that Y is not the certain value for this damage, but only its *expected value*, and that this damage might actually be much greater or much smaller, your risk aversion will make you accept an outlay today greater than X to defray (with certainty) this now-uncertain damage. Note that, in this example, the damage is now uncertain, but your best estimate for its expected value (Y) has not changed. It is only the uncertainty I have introduced that, because of your risk aversion, makes you willing to make a greater sacrifice today to defray the damage. The difference between the outlay you were prepared to make when you thought the magnitude of the climate damage was certain (X), and the higher outlay you willingly make in the case of uncertainty is exactly the equivalent of the $30,000 compensation you required to enter the $100,000 bet: it is the *cost of uncertainty*. So, the more uncertain the climate outcomes are, the more we should be willing to invest to abate its effects.[15] This matters, because the original version of the DICE model (and, for that matter, the Stern report) assumed a world with no uncertainty whatsoever. So, the neglect of this psychological feature in the DICE model obviously skewed its recommendations in a less prudent direction. We shall discuss this in detail in Chapter 7.

The fact that, at least as first approximation, people of different wealth seem to dislike to a similar extent losing the same fraction of their wealth matters a lot for climate-change policies. We shall look at this aspect in detail in Chapters 7 and 10, but we can already give a taste of the argument. Saying that someone is risk averse just means that the increase in happiness for a given gain is smaller than the pain for the same-magnitude loss (this, after all, is why a fair bet is rejected in the first place). Now, we do remain risk averse for any level of wealth; however,

---

[15] Here I am not being strictly correct: whether uncertainty in income gives rise to an increase in saving (and hence investment), depends on the sign of *relative prudence*. Explaining this concept properly would entail too long a detour.

as our wealth increases, our loss of happiness becomes more similar in magnitude to our increased enjoyment for the same-size loss or gain. If this is the case, and if we are sure that we will be richer in the future, we are more ready (we can ask for less compensation today) to enter a *future* lottery than a lottery here-and-now. In climate-change terms, this also means that, if we are much poorer today than we shall be by the end of the century, then a sacrifice today to defray a future damage may be unjustified even if the future damage is larger in absolute terms than the sacrifice today: if we are confident that we are really going to be that much richer in the future, then the loss of happiness for today's investment (cancelled consumption) can be bigger than the loss of happiness for the future climate-related loss, even if this is bigger in monetary terms. And this remains true even if we display no impatience (impatience reinforces the effect). This is a direct consequence of the wealth-dependence of the level of pain for a given loss.

Note that the key point of this argument is that we should not focus on the magnitude of gains or losses, but on the attending changes in happiness. It is changes in happiness (projected, discounted, compared) that determine our choices. Economics attempts – perhaps clumsily, but with a touchingly ambitious reach – to model and quantify exactly these changes in happiness. We could discuss at length whether the attempt to quantify and compare happiness is audacious or foolhardy, or perhaps even distasteful. Certainly it is reductionist, in the sense that very many features of what makes us happy have to fall by the wayside. But, once again, the answers about the climate-change problem that economics comes up with are interesting exactly because they are obtained from such a reductionist framework.

5.6 DISLIKE OF FEAST AND FAMINE

We now come to an extremely (and perhaps the most) important psychological driver of choice in the context of climate change: the technical term for this feature is the elasticity of intertemporal substitution, which is quite a mouthful, and not terribly transparent. I will therefore accept the need to pay a price in lack of precision, and refer to it simply as our dislike for feast and famine. What do I mean by this?

Suppose that you can decide how to allocate a certain consumption stream over time. To make the argument clearer, suppose that you display no impatience. And, remembering Einstein's dictum that matters should be made as simple as possible, but not any simpler,[16] let's suppose that you have to decide your consumption allocations over just two dates, today and tomorrow. How would you choose your consumption schedule? Since we have assumed that you are not impatient, and all the cashflows are certain, the only psychological feature at play is your intrinsic dislike for uneven consumption. When the problem is presented in these terms, most people choose to split their consumption evenly: fifty today and fifty tomorrow. This choice simply reflects the observation that for most people living in a mansion for one year may be nice, but, if this means living under a bridge for a year, they would prefer a run-of-the-mill comfortable terraced house for two years. So far, so unexciting.

To make things interesting, let's introduce now a twist: what you do not consume today, you can invest, and it will produce *for sure* $1 + r$ units of consumption 'tomorrow'. Now your choice is more difficult. You still dislike feast and famine, but the investment opportunity makes some degree of unevenness in consumption more acceptable: we have seen that you would turn down a 45-55 split (that adds up to 100), but you may well accept a 45-60 allocation (that sums up to 105). So, the rate of return on investment that you accept is closely linked to your dislike for feast and famine: the greater this dislike is, the higher the return required for you to decrease consumption at some point in time in order to increase it at other times. The key point is that the existence of investment opportunities, and the fact that you *are* impatient, makes your preference calculus more complex, but does not change the fundamental dislike for jumps in consumption.

---

[16] The attribution of the dictum to Einstein is actually rather flimsy. According to the reliable *The Ultimate Quotable Einstein* (2010) '[t]his quotation prompts the most queries; it appeared in Reader's Digest in July 1977, with no documentation.' Since quoting Einstein sounds a bit better than quoting Reader's Digest, I will stick with the traditional attribution. Other contenders stretch all the way back to William of Ockham.

We should also note that return on investment and impatience pull in the opposite direction: the more impatient you are, the more you want to consume today; the higher the certain return on your investment, the more you are willing to make a sacrifice to enjoy a higher consumption tomorrow. And I should stress again that this has nothing to do with risk aversion: in our choice about how to spread our consumption over two dates nothing at all was uncertain, and therefore our aversion to risk cannot play a part in our choices. Dislike for feast and famine is an altogether distinct psychological feature from risk aversion, that should be modelled independently of our dislike for risk. Why do I harp on this point? Because the early Integrated Assessment Models used to analyze the economics of climate change were forced, for computational reasons, to create an artificial link between these two psychological features – more than that, they were setting risk aversion and dislike for risk and famine on a collision course. We shall look at this in what follows, but the policy consequences of this unholy alliance were deep and disturbing.

What has this got to do with climate change? A lot, really. Of all the psychological features of our choice process this is probably the most important when it comes to deciding how much we should invest in abatement technologies today. It is certainly more important than our aversion to risk. And exactly because it is so important, we have to look at it a bit more carefully. When I have referred above to dislike for uneven consumption, I was implicitly referring to my own consumption. However, with decisions relating to climate change future generations are immediately brought into play. Saying that I don't like uneven consumption in this context means, for instance, that I may choose not to pay $1,000 today to eliminate a future damage cost of $1,300, if this damage will be borne by considerably richer descendants: simply because, if they are rich enough, their loss of happiness for a loss of $1,300 may well be smaller than my loss of happiness for parting with $1,000 today – and this may remain true even if I do not discount their losses because they occur in the future (the 'impatience' bit). I must stress that this has nothing to do with being 'envious' (*'they are so rich, let them pay for the problem'*): it is a matter of spreading evenly (fairly?) pain and pleasure from consumption or lack thereof.

This may seem reasonable, but brings to the fore an important question: who decides what is a 'fair' trade-off? Let's suppose that we know for sure that our descendants will be richer than we are.[17] What is the level of loss for the future richer generations that gives rise to the same level of loss *of happiness* from our losing $1,000, $1,100, $1,500 or $2,000? What if someone (who?) were to say $10,000? Who gets to decide on this acceptable-for-them level of pain? There are some elements of similarity in this with redistributive (progressive) taxation, but there is also an important difference: in democratic societies, both rich and poor (and the well-off, and the comfortably well-off, and the not-quite-poor-but-struggling) get to vote on the acceptable level of taxation. But our future generations have absolutely no say in what *we* deem to be a desirable (fair?) 'trade-off of intergenerational pain' – and whatever *our* preferences are, they will play a big role in determining how much we should invest today to abate emissions.

Economists try (with ingenuity only matched by the difficulty of the task) to estimate what our dislike for feast and famine is from a variety of indirect sources. This is all well and good, but it only tells us (if it tells us anything)[18] about our own choices. When *we* decide about how even we would like *our* consumption stream to be, nobody can question our choice, as this choice is made by our unitary self, that will suffer or enjoy the consequences.[19] But the situation in the case of climate change is radically different. The only principled way to approach this problem, I think, is to explore how uncertainty in the appropriate degree of dislike for feast and famine will affect our abatement choices. We shall revisit these conclusions in what follows.

---

[17] See Chapter 10 for the degree of confidence we can place in this important assumption.

[18] Estimates among macroeconomists and econometricians of the elasticity of intertemporal substitution vary wildly, from 0.2 to more than 2. Either choice of a value for this parameter above or below 1 is routinely caveated in academic circles as being 'contentious'.

[19] A paternalist, libertarian or otherwise, may argue that human beings are systematically plagued by decisional biases, and that therefore there is a case for intervening with the trade-off an individual may make about her own consumption stream: hence, for instance, compulsory pension contributions.

5.7 IS THAT ALL?

We have looked at pure impatience, at our dislike for risk and at our preference for smooth consumption over time. Is that it? Are these the only psychological features of decision-making that a good economic theory of choice should capture? Of course not. Our reactions to risk and preferences over distribution of consumption (over time and among people) are subtle and complex, and any model, *qua* model, can only hope to capture them in a very approximate manner. For instance, we dislike and worry a lot about inequality of consumption among different people at the same time – so much so that a pretty dry, 650-page scholarly tome about inequality (Piketty's *Capital in the XXI Century*) became a most unlikely international best-seller in 2018. Can utility theory model this psychological feature (our dislike for inequality, that is, not our liking for Prof Piketty's work)? It certainly can, but at the cost of making the analysis more complex (a single representative agent or a homogeneous population will obviously no longer do), and of introducing more parameters in the utility function. Are the additional complications worth the extra effort? Now, on the one hand, accounting for this psychological driver could make a big difference in the modelling of our responses to climate change, since climate damages are likely disproportionately to affect some of the poorest populations.[20] On the other hand, dislike for inequality appears to be very unevenly spread around the globe (with Scandinavian voters willingly accepting levels of redistributive taxation that would probably cause a revolution in the USA), and this 'cultural' aspect makes economic modelling of what is a *global* phenomenon particularly tricky (should we use, for instance, Sweden's or American's dislike for inequality?) In any case, we can confidently assert that, if inequality dislike were incorporated in the economic modelling of climate change, it would make the optimal abatement efforts even larger and more urgent. Therefore the conclusions of the argument of this book would be, if anything, reinforced.

---

[20] '[M]any of the impacts of warming up to and beyond 1.5 °C, and some potential impacts of mitigation actions required to limit warming to 1.5 °C, fall disproportionately on the poor and vulnerable', IPCC Special Report (2021), chapter 1.

Apart from this important psychological driver (which could be incorporated in mainstream economic modelling), there certainly are many other features of decision-making, broadly and imprecisely covered under the umbrella of decisional biases, that are not accommodated by standard utility theory. A whole area of economics and asset pricing that goes under the imprecise but suggestive rubric of *behavioural economics* has blossomed in the last thirty years. Again, the immense popularity amongst the general public of books such as Nobel-Prize winner Kahneman's *Thinking Fast and Slow* can be taken as an indication that this different description of how we make choices strikes a deep chord. What are the essential differences between 'classical' and 'behavioural' economics? In a (small) nutshell, classic utility theory assumes an (instrumentally) rational behaviour on the part of the decision-maker; behavioural economics places the emphasis instead on the irrationalities that supposedly plague our decision-making, and makes the case that these deviations from what rational choice theory assumes are not small corrections, but often take central stage.

The debate between behavioural and 'classical' economists has spawned tens of thousands of articles, and I cannot possibly do justice here to the different sides of the argument. However, when it comes to the choices about what to do about climate change, governments and big organizations are the main actors. Since many of the psychological drivers that underpin behavioural choice theory supposedly stem from our irrational (System-1) cognitive mechanism hijacking our deliberative and rational (System-2) mechanism, one should hope that the decisions about climate change – which will affect us and our future generations for decades and centuries – are not taken on the hop, and are made after deliberation of a sufficiently careful nature to bring our System-2 (rational) decision-making to the fore.[21] Therefore, for all of the allure of behavioural economics, it seems to me that *rational* choice theory provides a more appropriate lens through which the problem of climate change can be analyzed. I am not the only one to feel this way, as the literature about rational choice theory applied to climate change is

---

[21] I would have a lot to say about the System-1/System-2 construct, and about how 'irrational' our choices really are. The interested reader can see my thoughts on the matter in Rebonato (2012, 2014).

huge, but the papers that apply behavioural economics to decide how we should tackle climate change are relatively few and far between.[22] So, for the rest of this book, we shall look at how rational choice theory models the psychological drivers of choice I have described in this chapter, and at how this affects the choices we can make about what climate action we should take.

---

[22] I should mention here the book by Santa Clara University Prof Hersh Shefrin, Shefrin (2023).

CHAPTER 6

How Utility Theory Works

Now it would be very remarkable if any system existing in the real world could be exactly represented by any simple model. However, cunningly chosen parsimonious models often do provide remarkably useful approximations.

—Box (1979).

6.1 WHAT UTILITY THEORY TRIES TO ACHIEVE

In the previous chapter we have sketched with a broad brush the more salient and relevant psychological drivers of choice – relevant, that is, to the problem of climate change. In this chapter I intend to show how economic theory tries to capture the psychological features that drive our choices with a construct (utility theory) that is amenable to quantitative analysis. The attentive reader will have noticed how the previous chapter was 'psychologically descriptive', by which I mean that I have focussed on how people are *observed to behave* when faced with choices about uncertain outcomes. So the plan for this and the next chapter is now to pour this rich psychological material into the funny-shaped vessel provided by a mathematical theory. It is then for the reader to decide whether utility theory does an acceptable job at capturing the essence of how we make choices.

The utility construct is anything if not ambitious: in economic theory, it should describe how human beings, endowed with the psychological features we have discussed in the previous chapter, make decisions consistent with these preferences. The task is obviously dauntingly difficult, and, unsurprisingly, utility theory did not spring Athena-like fully formed in its present form from Zeus' head. In reality, if one looks at how the concept of utility evolved, one can't help noticing that there is more than a small element of serendipity, or at least of path-dependence, in how utility theory assumed its present form.[1] In particular, if nineteenth-century utilitarianism had not sown the seeds that enabled a very special way of looking at 'happiness' to prevail, modern utility theory would have probably never seen the light of day, at least in its present form. This is simply to stress that we should not consider utility theory as the discovery of a 'fact of nature', but as the product of a historical process. The interesting task is to see whether, despite its contingent character, it can provide us with a useful analytical tool – in our case, to tackle the problem of climate change.

6.2 THE ORIGINS OF UTILITY THEORY

Herodotus would not have liked utility theory. In his *Histories* he tells the story of the Athenian law-giver Solon – a wise man par excellence. Herodotus writes that Solon was goaded by the proverbially rich Croesus to say who in his opinion was the happiest man who ever lived – Croesus, no doubt, was counting on Solon confirming that he, Croesus, the richest man on earth, was also the happiest.

But according to Herodotus this is not what Solon replies. 'I cannot tell,' he says, 'because I do not know yet how your life, Croesus, will end'. The implication here is that if in his last days Croesus were to be disgraced, or to realize that he had been deceived about what he cherished most in his life, or to suffer any other devastating blow, then no amount of previous happiness could compensate for this final reversal: 'You seem to me to be very rich and the monarch of many people, but I couldn't say anything about this question you keep asking me [who the happiest man on earth is] until I find out *that you have finished your life well* ....'[2] This feeling that true happiness can only be reckoned 'in the end' is common in the classical world. So, for instance, along very similar lines the Chorus of Sophocles' *Oedipus Rex* pronounces: 'Do not call

---

[1] A very good book on the evolution of the ideas of pleasure is Wootton's (2018).

[2] Herodotus (1991), *Histories: Norton Critical Edition*, Walter Blanco transl., page 13.

mortal man happy, before he has crossed the final limit of his life without suffering pain.'

Despite the 2000-plus year gap, we generally find that this way of looking at our 'total happiness' still makes a lot of sense. After all, when, after reading about the tribulations of the Princess Bride and her suitor or any such characters (from Odysseus and Penelope, to Elizabeth Bennet and Mr Darcy, to Renzo and Lucia), we learn that they lived happily ever after, we do not ask whether all the travails (the 'disutility') that preceded the happy denouement were actually worth the bliss that followed. They lived happily ever after, and that, we feel, is good enough.

That is not at all the way modern choice theory looks at happiness – or, to use the technical term, at utility. Expected utility theory, to give it its full name, was invented by von Neumann and Morgenstern in the immediate aftermath of the Second World War.[3] It gave a rigorous mathematical foundation to a set of ideas that had been brewing in the intellectual ether at least since the Bernoulli cousins in the eighteenth century. Bentham and the utilitarians of the nineteenth century came even closer to something resembling the modern incarnation of utility theory, but the mathematical foundations were shaky at best.

So, what was von Neumann and Morgenstern's big idea? First they showed that, if a number of pretty reasonable conditions are satisfied, you can come up with a function that works as follows. You can think of function as a black box into which you feed something – your choices, in this case – and that spits out *a number*. Given a choice between a set of alternatives, the black box (the function) returns a higher number the more you like an alternative. So, if you prefer going to the beach to reading this book, the function may return 3 when you feed into it

---

[3] The seminal book that introduced expected utility theory in its modern form was von Neumann and Morgenstern (1944). As it presented game theory alongside expected utility theory, the book was truly a child of its troubled post-war, early-cold-war times. It quickly became very influential not only in policy and strategic circles, but also in the cultural world at large. Stanley Kubrick's 1964 film *Dr Strangelove: How I Learned to Stop Worrying and Love the Bomb* neatly captured the *Zeitgeist* and is loosely inspired by the application of game theory to the problem of nuclear deterrence.

'reading this book', and 10 when you input 'going to the beach'. And so on for any possible alternative. So far, so unexciting.

Utility theory gets more bite when you are faced with *uncertain* outcomes. Then von Neumann and Morgenstern show that, faced with uncertain outcomes,[4] you 'should' make your choices in the following way (I'll explain in a moment why you *should*). First you work out the probabilities of each possible outcome. Then you feed each outcome into the utility black box in your head, and receive back the number that describes how much you like that outcome *if it were to happen for sure*. Next, you give each outcome a weight equal to its probability of occurrence (that you had worked out before) and you multiply each weight by the corresponding utility (how much you liked that outcome). Finally you sum up all these products. In mathematical terms you have calculated the expected utility for that set of outcomes – or, as economists say, for that *lottery*.

What good is this? Suppose that you have two distinct sets of uncertain outcomes – two distinct lotteries, that is. In set one you win $100 with a 40 per cent probability and you lose $10 with a 60 per cent probability. In set two you win $1,000 with a 10 per cent probability but you lose $20 with a 90 per cent probability. Then expected utility theory says that you should calculate the expected utility (as we just described above) for both lotteries, *and choose the one with the highest expected utility.*

Again, why *should* you? One stock answer is because that is the 'rational' thing to do. For a host of reasons we won't go into, I really don't like this answer.[5] A somewhat better answer is that this way you will be making 'consistent' choices. This is a bit more satisfactory, but not something to get overly excited about. A more compelling answer is that, if the choices are about matters financial and you make your choices following the procedure that Messrs von Neumann and Morgenstern recommend, that you cannot be taken for a ride – or, as economists say, you cannot be

---

[4] The outcomes can be uncertain, but with known probability of occurrence.

[5] People often like to talk of *rational* choice theory. After the discussion of the previous chapter it should be clear why I dislike the adjective 'rational': there is nothing more rational about preferring more to less, disliking even bets or preferring even consumption than about preferring chocolate to spinach. More humbly, what we *can* hope is that our choices should display *consistency*.

used as a money pump: nobody can hope to make money out of you for sure by presenting you with a series of cleverly constructed lotteries, and hoping that you will 'trip up'.

One more interesting twist. Suppose that the set of possible outcomes that make up a lottery are not all at the same time: you may have to choose between a fifty-fifty chance of $\pm 1,000$ dollars today, or 50 per cent chance of losing \$500 today versus a 50 per cent chance of winning \$600 in a year's time. How can you handle that? This is where the big split (between time-separable and non-time separable utility functions) appears. In one case (the simple one) the theory says 'Put the consumption at the different times into the utility box, obtain the associated utility number and then apply to this number a *discount factor.*' We will have a lot more to say about discount factors, but you can think of them as devices to translate utility at future points in time into utility right here, right now.[6] Once you have done this, we can just add up all the (discounted, expected) utilities, and choose the 'lottery' that produces the highest number.

For non-time-separable utility functions discount factors are still there, but the (big) complication is that I can no longer say that the overall happiness (utility) today is just the sum of the individual discounted 'pieces of future happiness'. My happiness now becomes some more complex function of, in principle, all the happinesses I can expect to receive: the pleasure from a large consumption today, for instance, may get spoiled by my expectation of a lower future happiness. But also in this more complex case the general idea remains valid: to make consistent, non-gameable choices, modern utility theory says, you should calculate the discounted expected utility of all the different lotteries, and choose the one with the biggest number attached to it.

Now, utility theory is not without its critics, both from within the economics profession, and from the outside. Expected utility theory

---

[6] Note carefully that I am discounting – bringing back to today – utility, not money (consumption). There are discount factors that bring back to today consumption/money, but these are more complicated. Why so? For one thing, it makes a difference whether you receive a given amount of money in the future when you expect to be rich or poor: you will value this same amount of money very differently. We won't go into this, but this is where the *stochastic discount factor* comes to the fore.

has not won many friends by being applied to aspects of life (such as having children, getting married, or protecting the environment) where it only manages to capture a tiny fraction of what really matters. And the encroachment of the use of utility's first-born child, cost-benefit analysis, in all sorts of social policy matters where it really has little of much use to say constitutes what has been dubbed the 'imperialism of economics'. As I said in Chapter 1, despite my reservations about using economic analysis 'where it does not belong', I still think that looking at climate change through the lens of expected discounted utility makes a lot of sense – and I do so exactly *because* it is so crude and it leaves so much out of the analysis. Once again: if Tertullian said *Credo quia absurdum*,[7] so I rejoin that, when it comes to climate change, we should listen to utility theory *because* it is so crude and reductionist. So, let's try to understand a bit better how it works.

6.3 BETTING WITH THE BERNOULLIS: UTILITY AND DIMINISHING PLEASURE

We have seen that the idea of 'adding up' pleasure and pain is relatively novel, and that it comes with a heavy philosophical baggage of assumptions about what makes us happy. But even if we accept that maximizing pleasure over pain is a reasonable thing to do, how are we going to go about it?

In order to get some useful results, just saying that we want to maximize utility ('happiness') is not enough. We have to specify how our happiness changes as our level of consumption increases or decreases – in layperson's terms, when we feel rich or poor. Of course, we all feel happier if we consume more – so we all agree that utility should 'go up' with consumption. But we cannot go very far with this rather banal observation. All useful forms of utility theory contain in some form an additional – subtler, yet very fundamental – insight about human nature: the fact that we suffer more for a given loss than we gain pleasure for a same-magnitude gain. It took time for this insight to gain hold, but without it modern utility theory would have been stillborn.

---

[7] I believe because it is absurd.

In order to understand a bit better what this asymmetric way of feeling about gains and losses entails, and by way of preparing the ground, let me introduce you to a question that was first submitted by Nicholas Bernoulli in 1713 to the mathematician de Montmort, and was given an answer twenty-five years later by Nicholas' brother, Daniel.[8] The reasoning is so clear and so modern, that it is worth going through Daniel Bernoulli's arguments and his (translated) words carefully. Early in his paper devoted to this problem, he says:

> [C]onsider the following example: somehow a very poor fellow obtains a lottery ticket that will yield with equal probability either nothing or twenty thousand ducats.[9] [...] Would he be not ill-advised to sell this lottery ticket for nine thousand ducats? To me it seems that the answer is in the negative.

A small pause here to navigate the sea of double and treble negatives – the original was in Latin, which can handle rhetorical negatives more deftly than the English language. Daniel Bernoulli here is saying that the poor fellow is *not* ill-advised to sell his ticket, and, that, therefore he should sell it. So, Daniel Bernoulli suggests that the poor fellow should not accept the gamble, but accept *for sure* a bit less than the expected value of the gamble (which is, of course, 10,000 ducats). Let's continue.

> On the other hand I am inclined to believe that a rich man would be ill-advised to refuse to buy the lottery ticket for nine thousand ducats. *If I am not wrong, then it seems clear to me that all men cannot use the same rule to evaluate the gamble.*[10]

So, different men, faced with the same prospect, 'would be well-advised' to choose differently. But in which respect do the poor fellow and the rich man differ? By the way the situation has been set up (we know nothing

---

[8] A Swiss mathematician, Gabriel Cramer, found a very similar solution ten years earlier, in 1728. As in the Darwin/Wallace case, not always does the race go to the swift.

[9] A ducat was a coin containing 3.5 grams of gold. A gram of gold, as of this writing, is worth £35.2. Twenty thousand ducats are therefore approximately worth £700,000 in today's money. This matters because we are talking about wins and losses that *make a difference*, and this is the domain where utility theory makes sense. In other words, don't try to use utility theory to explain why you buy or don't buy a ticket in the National Lottery.

[10] Emphasis added.

about one being more saturnine, phlegmatic, bilious or choleric than the other), they only differ in how much wealth they have. And here is Bernoulli's conclusion: to make the choice procedure universally valid

> … the determination of the *value* of an item must not be based on its price, but on the *utility* it yields. […] [T]his utility is dependent on the particular circumstances of the person making the estimate. Thus there is no doubt that the gain of one thousand ducats is more significant to a pauper than to a rich man though both gain the same amount …

So, purely based on their wealth (and not on their character), different individuals behave differently faced with a risky prospect because losing one ducat hurts a lot more if you are a poor rather than a rich fellow, and because you are less happy if you gain a ducat than you are sad for the loss of the same amount. Bernoulli's explanation of why 'the gain of one thousand ducats is more significant to a pauper than to a rich man' handsomely stands the test of time: it is because, according to Bernoulli, 'any increase in wealth, no matter how insignificant, will always result in an increase of utility which is inversely proportionate to the amount of goods already possessed'. Today we may quibble as to whether it is exactly inversely proportional, but the intuition is clear, and remains correct to this day.

The importance of this vision was to underpin the work of Bentham and successors, who so broadly extended the concept of expected utility as to build a whole system of political philosophy on it, aptly named 'utilitarianism'. The mathematical *i*'s and *t*'s still had to be, respectively, dotted and crossed (as I said, this came with von Neumann and Morgenstern as late as the mid 1940s), but the promise of utility theory has remained with us ever since. In order to solve questions in moral philosophy Leibniz had said 'just calculate', as if rationality on its own could give us the 'moral' answers we are looking for.[11] Daniel Bernoulli

---

[11] Lest you find the reach of modern utility theory too ambitious, let's not forget that Leibniz 'presented his project as being the world's most powerful instrument, an end to all argument, one of humanity's most wonderful inventions […]; the ultimate source of answers to some of the world's most complex and difficult theological, moral, legal, or scientific questions; and a foolproof means to converting people to Christianity and propagating the faith, amongst other things'. See in this respect the delightful article by Jonathan Gray (2016), *'Let us Calculate!' Leibniz, Llull, and the Computational*

realized that, when it comes to describing how we choose, mathematics by itself can only do half the job – that, *pace* Descartes, we cannot pull ourselves up by our logical, deductive bootstraps alone. With his utility theory we see a first marriage of mathematics and psychology.

6.4 FROM PARLOUR GAMES TO CLIMATE CHANGE

Bernoulli used this insight about the wealth-dependence of our risk choices to solve a parlour game that goes under the name of St Petersburg Paradox. Interesting as this is, discussing it would take too long a detour. What we are really interested in is the connection between Bernoulli's insight and climate change policies. To understand this connection, let me remind the reader that in standard economic modelling the assumption is normally made that the world output will continue to grow in the decades and centuries to come. We shall discuss in Chapter 10 how much we can trust this assumption, but, for the moment, let's accept it at face value: in the future we expect to be richer. Keeping this in mind, let's go back to Bernoulli's 'very poor fellow' – that is to say, to us, compared to our great-great-grandchildren (who are the 'rich man' in Bernoulli's story). Suppose that, in order to curb the change in climate a significant sacrifice has to be made. The *same* sacrifice will hurt a lot more the poor fellow (us) than the rich man (our great-great-grandchild) – it will cause a greater loss of utility for us than for them. Therefore it seems to make sense to delay the sacrifice until we are better able to shoulder it. From this perspective, choosing a fast and costly abatement schedule now is like imposing a tax on the present poor to subsidize the future rich.

Now, as we shall discuss in Chapter 8, the original DICE model was fully deterministic, that is, it assumed to know for sure both the rate of technological growth,[12] and the rate of increase of damages with temperature – and to know the behaviour of both these quantities all the way down to year 2600 or thereabouts. This is part of the reason why

Imagination, The Public Domain Review, available at https://publicdomainreview.org/essay/let-us-calculate-leibniz-llull-and-the-computational-imagination.

[12] To be more precise, the DICE model assumes a deterministic path for the Total Factor of Production: this is the all-important quantity that determines, for given input of labour and capital, how much the economy will produce.

the abatement schedule recommended by the original DICE model was so gradual: if we really knew that we were going to be so much richer in the future – the DICE model assumes that by the end of the century we will be between five and ten times richer than we are today – and that climate damages were not going to get out of hand, then, yes, it would indeed be wise to wait, and pass the (somewhat larger) climate bill to our rich great-great-grandchildren.

There is a fly in the ointment: in the discussion so far we have implicitly assumed that the sacrifice made now or in the richer future remains of the same magnitude. However, the more we wait, the more intractable the climate problem becomes, and the more resources we will have to throw at its solution. For all we know, there may even be 'tipping points', that is, thresholds in climate warming beyond which the increase in temperature, and the accompanying damages, get out of hand. So, whether we should wait or not depends on a horse race between how fast we are going to become richer, and how fast the climate problem becomes more difficult to control. As we know very little about either of these quantities (the very-long-term rate of growth of the economy and the rate of increase of damages with temperature) it seems foolhardy to rely on the output of a model that has to make bold assumptions about both. What are we to do?

We could of course, put into the model a more severe 'damage function', or a lower rate of growth in the economy, and we will, indeed get a different answer. But, by doing so, we have just substituted for a pair of quantities we know very little about two different values about which we are just as uncertain. Recall what I wrote about the 'last temptation' in Section 4.3: if we change the parameters of a fancy model so as to give us the results that our preconceived ideas wanted us to obtain, we are just wasting good CPU time. So, choosing more 'pessimistic' values for the damage function or the future economic growth is rather arbitrary: how much more pessimistic should we make them? It is partly because of this apparent arbitrariness that, after seeing the first results of the original DICE model, many serious commentators began to doubt whether Integrated Assessment Models really were going to be of much help in the making of our climate choices.

Should we throw our hands up in despair, then? Should we abandon utility theory altogether? Not all. One of the key insights of utility theory is that our degree of ignorance changes our choices, *and does so in the direction of us becoming more conservative the more uncertain we are.* Financial economists play a neat trick, whereby they model risk aversion by pretending that risk-averse economic agents are risk-neutral (don't care about risk), but apply probabilities to the various possible outcomes that are different from the 'real ones'. We won't go into how this works, but the key point is that this shuffling around of probabilities is done by giving more weight to the bad outcomes – the more so, the more the choosing agent is risk averse. The new, 'fake' probabilities are therefore *pessimistic* probabilities. So, understanding that the possible outcomes for the problem at hand are very uncertain, and quantifying this degree of uncertainty is exactly what utility theory needs to suggest a more prudent course of action – how much more prudent, of course, will depend on how uncertain the outcomes are, and how risk averse we are. A lot of information can be extracted from (partial) ignorance. The next chapter will give a feel for how all of this works in practice.

CHAPTER 7

From Choice to Utility

And if someone really claimed that nothing can be known,
he would also not know whether we can know at all,
if he really claims to know nothing.[1]

—Lucretius, *De Rerum Natura*, IV, 469–470

I F WE ACCEPT THAT UTILITY MAXIMIZATION provides a useful conceptual framework for reaching decisions, the next question is: how can we set up a quantitative model that can have a sporting chance of making reasonable recommendations? As I said in the previous chapter, with utility theory one makes use of a *function*, a black box, that is, that takes in some inputs, and spits out a number. The inputs are supposed to describe the outcomes of different choices, and the *numerical* output the attending 'happiness' (utility) – with a bigger number signifying more happiness.

Can we say something more about the description of the different outcomes? In principle, this input to the black box could be very complex, and need not be numeric – it could be a statement such as 'going to the beach tomorrow'. To make things tractable and simple, we normally use consumption as the input to the utility black box, and we implicitly assume, perhaps rather crassly, that we can always find a consumption equivalent to non-consumption outcomes (such as increase or loss of

---

[1] This is my own, slightly tendentious, translation of a passage of Lucretius' *De Rerum Natura*. To see if, and how much, I have twisted Lucretius' words, here is the original: 'Denique nil sciri siquis putat, id quoque nescit an sciri possit, quoniam nil scire fatetur.'

natural beauty, biodiversity, etc.). So, *pace* Oscar Wilde, a utility theorist is supposed to know the price, *and hence the value,* of everything.[2]

This is where the psychological drivers discussed in the previous chapter come to the fore. First of all, the function we want to set up to describe our degree of happiness should account for the fact that humans seem to prefer more to less. To reflect this, the function that describes our happiness (utility) as a function of consumption should 'go up': more consumption, more happiness.

How steeply should this function go up? And, should it go up at the same rate for all levels of consumption? Now, the next slice of cake – or, if you are an oligarch, the next billion – never quite tastes as good as the first. So, the utility function should, yes, keep on increasing, but at a slower and slower rate. If inputting a $1,000 in the utility black box when your total wealth is $10,000 returns an increase in happiness of 10 (in some units), then inputting the same amount when you are $1,000,000 rich should produce a number smaller than 10 – how much smaller, depends on how quickly you get satiated.

Next, we have seen that people do not appear to like risk,[3] or, equivalently, that they need to be rewarded to assume risk to which they were not exposed. The fact that people seem to be happy to pay insurance premia *even when the premia are actuarially unfair* is another indication that we seem to be risk averse. So, as an entry-level reasonableness check, we should test that our utility engine should choose among different courses of action with the same average outcome those that entail the least risk – we call this feature risk aversion, or to be more precise, aversion to *static* risk. The willingness of humans to pay for insurance and peace of mind should also be recovered by the utility mathematical engine.

As we have seen, there is something else humans do not like: to be exposed to big variations of consumption *over time.* As I said, most of us would prefer to live twenty years in a decent terraced house, than ten years under a bridge and ten years in a mansion. So, how much

---

[2] Making these equivalences is crass indeed, but sometimes we can glean a monetary value for non-consumption pleasures by observing how much we require to be compensated for their subtraction, or how much we are willing to pay for their preservation.

[3] As I already said, I am not talking about gambling, normally engaged in for relatively small sums, and for which the thrill of playing provides 'pleasure' in itself.

of today's consumption we are willing to give up (invest) in order to produce a more even consumption stream in part depends on our dislike for feast and famine. A half-decent utility theory should be able to recover this recurrent observed preference as well – by which I mean, it should recommend courses of action that reflect this basic dislike for wild fluctuations in consumption over time.

Note that when I am looking at the dislike for feast and famine I am comparing consumption at different times. When consumption happens at different times, impatience also plays an important role. As we discussed at length in the previous chapter, empirically, we observe that for people willingly to postpone consumption they have to be promised a larger consumption in the future. Our utility function should therefore spit out a smaller 'happiness number' if the same consumption occurs later.

Let's try to get a feel for how this set-up might work. Consider a run-of-the-mill utility function, and let's consider a bet here and now. As we have seen, a key feature of any reasonable utility function is that it should go up (as a function of consumption): this simply means that we never get satiated, and more consumption always brings at least a tiny bit more pleasure. You can check from Fig 7.1 that your happiness does keep on increasing as your wealth increases. But the really interesting feature of any utility function worth its salt is that it should be concave, as also shown in Fig 7.1 – with the concavity reflecting our diminishing pleasure for the same additional consumption.

The concavity of the utility function is its single most important feature. By construction, it reflects our satiation, but it does a lot more. Consider risk aversion first. Risk aversion is defined as our dislike for a zero-expected-gain fair lottery. Suppose that your initial level of wealth is W. A fair lottery is a situation where your wealth goes from W to $W + \delta$ or $W - \delta$ with equal probability. What is the expected utility from entering this lottery? It is just the average of the utilities corresponding to the levels of wealth $W + \delta$ and $W - \delta$. But, since the utility function we have chosen is concave (goes up less steeply than a straight line), the average must be below the utility corresponding to the initial wealth. So, the concave function we have chosen describes our risk aversion. The more concave the function is, the more there is an asymmetry from the win and lose utilities, the more risk averse we are. Just by using a concave utility function, we have managed to model our first psychological driver of choice!

What about our dislike for feast and famine? To see the problem clearly, let's suppose for the moment that we are not impatient. Suppose then that we have a certain wealth, $2 \times W$, that we want to spread over two dates. Clearly, since the total wealth we can play with is fixed, our possible distributions are described by allocations $W - \delta$ at time 1 and $W + \delta$ at time 2: the more we consume on one date, the less we consume on the other. But the concavity of the utility function ensures that the sum of the utilities associated with any δ different from zero (with any uneven distribution of our consumption) is lower than the utility of same-consumption allocation, where we consume W at time 1 and W at time 2. This is just because the increase in utility from adding δ to W is smaller than the decrease in utility from subtracting δ from W. So, with the same feature of the utility function (its concavity) we kill three birds with one stone: we describe the fact that we like extra consumption less and less as we become richer; our risk aversion; and our dislike for uneven consumption. Not bad for a curve as simple as the one shown in Fig 7.1.

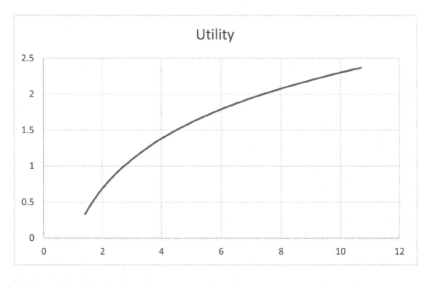

7.1 A typical utility function. Consumption (in arbitrary units) is on the x axis.

This sounds promising, but herein lies the problem: if you think about it, your aversion to risk is something psychologically quite different from your dislike of uneven consumption (after all, the latter preference remains even if there is no uncertainty whatsoever in the wealth you will receive – so it must be distinct from risk aversion, which only kicks in for uncertain outcomes). However, with the simple, entry-level utility functions shown in Fig 7.1 (the utility functions the original DICE model used), these two drivers of choice are joined at the hip: as the same degree of curvature controls both our aversion to static risk and our dislike for feast and famine, as we increase risk aversion, we are forced to say that our dislike for uneven consumption rises *exactly by the same amount*. As we shall see, this puts risk aversion and dislike for feast and famine on a collision course, and this forced marriage is at the root of the biggest problems with the original formulation of the DICE model. To understand why this is the case, we shall have to look in more detail at how Integrated Assessment Models work. This we do in Chapter 8.

7.1 BEYOND ENTRY-LEVEL UTILITY FUNCTIONS

We have made the case that, for a utility function to pass 'the laugh test', it should be able to account in a half-decent way for all the main entry-level psychological features of the choice process that we discussed in Chapter 6 – and we have seen that even very simple utility functions clear this obstacle. However, the process of choice is far richer than this, and more complex features than impatience and dislike for feast and famine play an important role in how we make decisions – features that are at the core of the differences between the early and the new-generation utility-based analyses of climate change. What am I referring to?

Let's forget about impatience for a moment. Even if we are not impatient it is not obvious that the 'happiness' from consumption over two dates can be neatly split into the sum of the happiness over the first and the second date. Perhaps our happiness on time 2 also depends on our consumption at time 1: we may be very happy at time 2 living in a terraced house if we had been living at time 1 under a bridge, or very miserable if we had been living in a mansion. So, how we feel today depends not only on what we consume now (something that time-separable utility function can handle easily), but also on what we grew accustomed to consume in our past (economists call this feature 'habit formation'). With great psychological insight, in *Paradise Lost* Milton captures exactly this psychological feature when he reminds us that great part of Lucifer/Satan's pain after landing in Hell at the end of his nine-day fall stems from remembering the exalted position from which he fell:[4] an economist would say that his utility function (Satan's, that is, not Milton's) appears to be definitely 'non-time-separable'.

Leaving the regrets of the Prince of Darkness to one side, another important component of our happiness appears to be relational: it does not depend just on what *we* can consume, but also on what everyone else around us appears to be able to consume. A holiday to Brighton may feel great if most of the people around us don't get to go on holiday at all, but distinctly underwhelming if most of our neighbours seem to be jetting off to the Seychelles. With a transparent metaphor, economists refer to this feature as 'keeping up with the Joneses'. So, keeping up with the Joneses makes our happiness also depend on what *other people at the same time* consume; habit formation introduces a dependence on what *we were able to consume in the past.* Neither of these psychological features can be accommodated by expressing our happiness (utility) today as the sum of separate and independent 'pieces of (discounted) happiness' occurring in the future. In econo-speak these more complex utility functions are called 'non-time-separable'.

Habit formation and keeping up with the Joneses (as these two psychological features are called in economics) are not the only aspects of choice-making that are difficult to reconcile with the simple and easy-to-work-with time-separable utility functions. Not surprisingly, there are many other fine features of the process of choice that simple utility functions cannot capture. Nonetheless, if we want to try and see whether choice-making can be modelled at all, we have to start somewhere. As mathematician Tegmark reminds us, if we have a difficult problem that

---

[4] In Heaven, Lucifer drank 'rubied Nectar', ate 'Angels' Food' (*Paradise Lost*, V.633), and lived in meadow lands covered with flowers and 'delicious Vines, the growth of Heav'n' (V.635). After the fall '... the thought/ Both of lost happiness and lasting pain / Torments him; round he throws his baleful eyes / That witness'd huge affliction and dismay / Mixt with obdurate pride and steadfast hate' (I.54–58).

we don't know how to solve, we should try our hand at an easy problem that we don't know how to solve.[5] So, time-separable utility functions should be regarded as our first stab at modelling our choice process in a quantitative, rather than descriptive, way: they are our first line of attack to the problem we don't know how to solve.

As I said, working with utility functions that can be neatly decomposed into the sum of (perhaps discounted) utilities over different times is very easy and leads to highly tractable analyses, but has no good economic justification. Simplicity, however, is never to be sneered at and, in general, I need a pound of extra modelling realism to trade off an ounce of simplicity. So, the relevant question is, 'How much do we miss if we choose to use these entry-level tools?' More to the point, if we want to tackle the problem of climate change, how good a job do the standard, time-separable utility functions do? Is the extra complication that comes with employing complex utility functions always worth the trouble?

For problems other than climate change, the answer to the trade-off question is 'It depends'. However, when it comes to the study of global warming, the answer can only be a resounding 'Yes'. It is not difficult to see why this is the case. Climate change is a problem that unavoidably involves trade-offs in consumption over extremely long time horizons. Now, when the nice time-separable utility functions are used to account for basic facts in asset pricing that bring the time dimension into play in an important way, they fail miserably: they cannot even get close to explaining, for instance, the observed returns on the stock market;[6] nor do they explain the observed level of interest rates.[7] And the most troubling feature is that, if we try to fix one problem (say, the 'too high' observed compensation for taking equity risk), we are making the other problem (the 'too low' observed interest rates) even worse.

---

[5] 'My dad used to say: "If you have a tough question that you can't answer, first tackle a simple question that you can't answer".' Tegmark (2015), page 18.

[6] If we take into account how risky equities are, the return reaped by investing in stock market over the next century cannot be explained using time-separable utility functions. Mehra and Prescott (1985) call this the equity premium puzzle. For a good non-technical account of the equity premium puzzle, see Cornell (1999).

[7] If we use simple and nice-to-work-with utility functions, we arrive at an equilibrium interest rate which is much higher than what we have observed during the last century – let alone in the last twenty years. Weil (1989) calls this the 'risk-free-rate puzzle'.

The proverbial blanket appears to be, not just too short, but of the wrong shape.

Non-time-separable utility functions do a much better job at explaining at a semi-quantitative level these basic facts in asset pricing, and therefore give us hope that they can perform adequately well also when used to study the trade-offs brought in by our emission-abatement choices. The conceptual complexities these fancier functions introduce, however, are not trivial, the technical difficulties not indifferent, and the computational burden *very* demanding[8] – and this is why the early modelling approaches (both by Nordhaus and by Stern) made use of the easy, time-separable utility function. It takes, however, a heroic leap of faith to trust an approach that cannot explain the most basic facts in finance to give us guidance about what we should do about climate change – one of the most important decisions our generation is called upon to make. Non-time-separable utility functions are definitely worth all the effort, because the answers they produce are *qualitatively* different from the early answers – or, when similar, only so by accident.

7.2 THE FINE PRINT

Let me only say that what econometrics – aided by electronic computers – can do, is only to push forward by leaps and bounds the line of demarcation from where we have to rely on our intuition and sense of smell.

—Ragnar Frish, Nobel Prize Lecture, June 1970.

I have to come clean on one point. (The present section is a bit more technical than the rest of the treatment, but for honesty and full disclosure it is essential.) The more complex non-separable utility functions used in state-of-the-art climate modelling produce really 'steep and fast' recommendations for emission abatement only if parametrized with a modest dislike for feast and famine – in technical terms, with an elasticity of intertemporal substitution (EIS) greater than 1. This parameter choice has recently become popular among economists, but is far from

---

[8] For some state-of-the-art climate-change calculations using non-time-separable utility functions this means using the most powerful computers currently available for days of non-stop computing.

universal. Estimates based on micro behaviour tend to produce estimates of this key quantity smaller than 1.[9] However, empirical estimates based on different methodologies bring out results for EIS greater than 1. See, for example, Hansen and Singleton (1982). So, whatever choice one makes for EIS (greater or smaller than 1) some economists will look at it with suspicion. I tend to look at the question of whether the EIS should be greater than 1 from the modelling rather than the econometric-estimation perspective. What I mean by this is that an economy where EIS is greater than 1 displays many important features found in real markets, and in how investors behave. For instance, one important advantage of choosing an EIS greater than 1 is that, by so doing, we can satisfactorily account for a number of puzzles in asset pricing, such as the equity-premium puzzle (see Mehra and Prescott, 1985) or the interest-rate puzzle (see Weil, 1989), already alluded to in footnotes 6 and 7. See the work by Bansal and Yaron (2004) in this respect. More generally, in the economy Bansal and Yaron model with EIS greater than 1, an increase in the uncertainty about economic growth *increases* the compensation that investors demand for taking risk. This makes sense, but an EIS smaller than 1 would produce the opposite effect. In the same EIS-greater-than-1 economy an increase in volatility also induces investors to invest *less* in risky assets (this also sounds plausible). And in the same economy a higher expected rate of return on investment induces investors to buy more risky assets – also something that makes a lot of sense to me.

Should we be impressed by these successes? Why do I think that all these features, which have to do with investments and asset prices, are relevant to the climate-change problem at hand? Because deciding when and how to invest in abatement initiatives is exactly an investment decision – a decision, that is, about how we should compare and evaluate the different uses to which our resources can be put. So, I do accept that the model by Bansal and Yaron, parametrized with an EIS greater than 1, may not fully account for how economic agents behave in all contexts. But I think that it does a very acceptable job at accounting for investment behaviour, *and this is what matters most for the task at hand.*

[9] Havranek (2015) examined more than 2,700 estimates of this quantity, and finds that for micro estimates the average reported value is around 0.3–0.4, with values above 0.8 improbable.

7.2.1 REDUCED-FORM MODELS. Another way to look at the choice of the 'right' value for this important parameter is to recognize that utility theory is a *phenomenological* attempt towards describing our choice process. What does this mean? In physics phenomenological models (also called 'reduced-form' models) are not obtained from first principles, but are reasonable descriptions of how some phenomena work. For instance, if I wanted to explain the properties of a spring, I could try to model all its atoms using quantum mechanics and electrodynamics. Or I could simply express my commonsensical, empirical observations about how springs behave by saying that the force they exert is equal in magnitude to the displacement from equilibrium, times a constant that is specific to each material.[10] The full-Monty, quantum-mechanics-plus-electrodynamics treatment of the problem would allow us to calculate the material-specific constant from first principles (this is the hallmark of a fundamental model). But, as I sketch in footnote 10, I could also use a set of weights, measure how much springs of different materials stretch, derive the proportionality constant, and write the results on a piece of paper (this is how the phenomenological approach works). The advantages of the rough-and-ready approach are too obvious to state. The drawbacks are subtler: first, the parameter we have estimated cannot be transferred from one material to another: from knowing what the spring constant is for iron we cannot *deduce* what it should be for copper. Second, we cannot know the range of validity of our law: how much can I stretch the spring, for instance, for the nice simple relationship in footnote 10 between displacement and force to remain valid? I have no way of telling, short of measuring.

Now, utility theory is a fully phenomenological description of choice-making, and therefore it comes with lots of free parameters, and just as many health warnings: how much can we stretch the utility spring from where I have observed how we make choices, and still hope that the behaviour I have observed will still hold? Coming back to our vexed EIS parameter: given the nature of utility theory (even in its fanciest forms),

---

[10] The equation is one of the simplest in physics: $F = -kx$, where F is the force, x the displacement (how much the spring has been stretched), and k is called the spring constant. If I apply a known weight, I know what force it exerts, I can measure how much the spring gets stretched, and deduce the spring constant *for that material.*

I do not find it disturbing that different parameters should be used for different applications – any more than I find disturbing that I should use different spring constants for different materials. The important thing is that I should use a parameter that works well for applications *similar to one I am interested in*. For the reasons I have outlined, explaining the price of investments seems to me very important for deciding what to do about climate change. Therefore I find it reasonable and appropriate to use parameter values that account for these particular empirical facts well – for sure, I would be the first to use a smaller-than-one EIS if the problem at hand warranted such a choice. And I would feel no worse for doing so, than if I had to switch from the spring constant for iron to the spring constant for copper.

So, to summarize: the results reported in this book have been obtained with a value for the EIS of 1.45, which is right in the middle of the range of the EIS-greater-than-1 literature – see Jensen and Traeger (2014) in particular. I stress that, if the value for the EIS were chosen to be smaller than 1 (say 0.65), the same conclusions of a faster and steeper abatement schedule than the original DICE schedule would still hold, but the difference would be less pronounced.

What I have sketched so far is, of course, just a 30,000-foot view of how the utility framework may be used to account for our key psychological drivers, but it is enough to give us an understanding of how economists think about climate-change policies. We are therefore ready to examine in some detail their analytical tool of choice – Integrated Assessment models. This we do in the next chapter.

CHAPTER 8

What Are Integrated Assessment Models?

There's no model that describes the whole economy, the point of a model is to simplify a certain aspect of the world, so you can get your head around it and learn something about it; it provides enormous illumination about things that you can use to think about the actual world and, in many ways, the most useful models are the ones which are most unrealistic because they may tell you something which really changes the way you think ... [Economic] [m]odels are devices to ensure that you can't get away with sloppy arguments or a lack of rigour. It's imposing rigour on the arguments.

—Lord Mervyn King, transcript of his address on Central Banking for the Markus' Academy, Princeton University, 28 February 2022.

A S WE DISCUSSED IN THE PREVIOUS CHAPTERS, when economists try to tackle the climate-change problem their analytical tools of choice are the so-called Integrated Assessment Models. So, in order to get our bearings around the debate we will look in some detail at what are arguably the most famous (and most hotly debated) of the Integrated Assessment Models: the DICE and Prof Stern's models. Why am I focussing on these two models, since, if one counts the various versions and variations, there are literally dozens of Integrated Assessment Models?[1] I have chosen to discuss and contrast the policy recommendations from these two models because they can be taken as representative instances of two very different abatement policies: the 'slow-and-gradual' (the DICE model), and the 'fast-and-aggressive'

---

[1] For an early review of Integrated Assessment Models, see Parson and Fisher-Vanden (1997). For a comparative discussion of a key element of Integrated Assessment Models, the damage function, see Tol and Frankhauser (1998).

(the Stern model). This makes for a simple discussion, but I don't want to leave the reader under the impression that Nordhaus' and Stern's models are the only games in town.

Why am I bothering with models? Why do we need models to decide how much it is efficient to invest in emission abatement, but we don't use models to work out how many shoes or mobile phones the economy should produce? Because there are market prices for shoes and mobile phones. Prices are powerful signals, that embed in a remarkably efficient way information about costs of production, demand and supply. It is thanks to the price signal that there are no shelves full of shoes nobody wants, and no queues to buy a mobile phone. When it comes to climate change, the problem is that the price of some goods (say, petrol) is distorted, in the sense that it does not contain the full information – the damage inflicted on future generations does not make its way into today's price (these are the 'externalities' we discussed in Section 1.1.2). And some 'services' (such as the finite carbon-storing capacity of oceans) are not priced at all. When price signals are absent, we must work out what the missing 'shadow prices' would be if all the benefits and costs were taken into account. We must fix, in other words, the market failure. To do so, we need models. And when it comes to climate change, the models in question are called Integrated Assessment Models.

So, our goal in this chapter is to gain a broad understanding of how Integrated Assessment Models work, of what they try to achieve, and of whether we should trust their answers. This is what we do in this chapter. Before we get started, however, it is essential to understand that Integrated Assessment Models are not (or not just) clever academic toys. The recommendations they produce have significant policy implications. The results of the DICE model, for instance, in the USA inform the assessment of the so-called social cost of carbon by the Interagency Working Group on Social Cost of Carbon. The social cost of carbon, roughly speaking, is the optimal tax that we should apply to emissions, and that should fund the abatement investments.[2] It doesn't take much to see that a lot

---

[2] In practice, the ability of governments that face re-election to levy taxes on the voters' consumption of fuels anywhere close to the social optimum has proven in the Western democracies to be very limited. Politically, it has therefore proven easier to move the regulatory burden to emitting companies. This is but one of the many.

is at stake, and that getting this quantity right is key to tackling climate change successfully. It is also important to understand why European policy-makers have turned their backs on Integrated Assessment Models à la DICE, and whether this position should be reversed.

Integrated Assessment Models are anything if not ambitious. They try to combine in one fell swoop the physics of planetary climate, and the macroeconomics of the world as a whole. The reason for their breath-taking scope is that the two aspects, the economic growth and the climate of the planet, are closely interlinked, and neither can therefore be considered in isolation. In a thumb-nail sketch, the link between the two aspects, the physics and the economy, goes as follows. Let's assume first that no action to curb climate change is taken. Then, as we increase industrial production, global output increases, but so do CO_2 emissions. As CO_2 emissions increase, they contribute to global warming, and this, in turn, causes damages that reduce the economic output.[3] As economic agents understand that this is the case, they decide to divert some of the capital that, absent the climate problem, would normally be devoted to the production of consumable goods and services, to reduce emissions – and therefore, ultimately, global warming and output reduction. The details are obviously complex, but it is already clear from this description that there should be an *optimal* level of investment in the abatement technology: invest too little, and the reduction in economic output is more severe than it could have been; invest too much, and the improvement in output is not compensated by the cost of abatement. So, Integrated Assessment Models are *optimization devices* – that it to say, models that find the 'sweet spot' between abating too little and abating too much.

Fig 8.1 shows the interlinked structure of an Integrated Assessment Model such as DICE in a bit more detail.[4] Let's try to read this picture. There are two grey 'blobs', one associated with the physics and the other with the economics of the problem. Crucially, these two blobs

---

climate-change-related examples where economics intersects, or perhaps collides, with politics.

[3] Climate damage could directly affect capital, which is one of the inputs to economic output. This is not the way climate damages are modelled in the DICE model.

[4] A very good introduction to the DICE model is given in Schubert (2019).

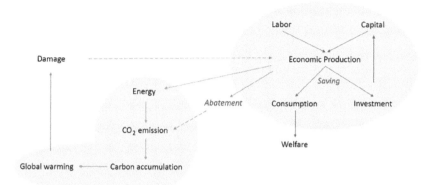

8.1 A schematic view of the structure of the DICE model. Reproduced from Melin (2020).

are connected by three arrows, labelled 'Damage', 'Abatement' and 'Energy' – we shall come to these in a moment. If we neglect the arrows, the economics blob (the one on the right) is totally standard in macroeconomic modelling: there is a production function that takes in two factors of production (capital and labour), and yields the economic output.[5] This output is then split into what we decide to invest for future production, and what we decide to consume. It is only how much we consume (now and in the future) that increases our welfare (utility): we make the sacrifice of investing today simply in the hope of obtaining more consumption tomorrow.

Let's move to the second grey blob, the one to the left, that describes the physics of the climate system. Economic output requires energy, and this is in part produced by fossil fuels, which contribute to the CO_2 concentration in the atmosphere. These emissions persist in the atmosphere for a period of time linked to the effectiveness of the natural absorption mechanisms, such as the absorption of CO_2 by the

[5] For the economically minded reader, the production function is as standard as it gets in economic modelling (Cobb-Douglas) and is given by $Y_t = TFP_t \times K^\gamma \times L^{1-\gamma}$, where Y_t is gross output at time t, and K_t and L_t denote time-t capital and labour, respectively. As for the term TFP (the Total Factor of Production) it is the magic sauce (technological innovation, solid property rights, stable laws and political systems) that has allowed humanity to escape the Malthusian trap. (By the way, in the DICE economy everybody works, and therefore the labour force is equal to the population. The exponent γ, chosen in the DICE model to be 0.3 can be interpreted as the fraction of production that goes to the providers of capital.)

oceans. (As we saw in Section 2.3, the natural reabsorption rate of CO_2 is *very* low, and this is one of the many reasons why solving the climate-change problem is hard.) Emissions add to what in the figure is labelled as 'Carbon accumulation'. It is this carbon accumulation that gives rise to global warming, which, in the DICE modelling, is simply described as an increase in temperature.[6] The place holder representing global warming is within the physics blob (as it should be), but it is linked to the 'Damage' inflicted on the economy. Note that 'Damage' belongs to neither blob: it lives 'by itself' because, strictly speaking, it is neither a physics-related quantity (it depends on the production technologies we use, for instance), nor is it part of the canonical economics modelling of production. In reality, it constitutes one of the two links between the two systems (blobs), as signified by the dashed red line. (The other link is signified by 'Abatement', which we discuss below.)

As explained, economic agents are not the passive recipients of this damage, but they decide how much to invest in consumption-producing technologies[7] and how much of the available output to devote to their abatement efforts. ('Abatement', again, is placed outside the two blobs, as it strictly belongs to neither.) The key observation is that how much we decide to devote to abatement affects the level of emissions, the CO_2 concentration, the carbon accumulation, the temperature increase, and, ultimately, the economic damage: and this concludes (one pass of) the cycle.

So, economic agents have two levers at their disposal: how much to invest in consumption-producing technologies, and how much to devote to abatement.[8] These two levers are called 'control variables' and, in

---

[6] This is not as bad as it sounds, as many types of damages are mediated by a temperature increase, and the important thing is that we model acceptably well the damage function – the function, that is, that links the temperature increase to damages. For instance, the weather (by which I mean the severity of hurricanes, floods, droughts, etc.) is linked in complex ways to the temperature gradient across different latitudes, and this gradient, in turn, depends on the temperature.

[7] For a closed economy, one can say that savings must equal investment. Since we are dealing with the planet as a whole, the economy is by definition closed.

[8] Investment in 'consumption-producing technologies' is an ugly term, which I use to denote that part of investment devoted to produce stuff that we want to consume and that, by being consumed, increases our utility. If we did not have to worry about climate

Fig 8.1, are shown in red. It is extremely important to understand that the decision of how much should be invested in consumption-producing technologies and how much in damage abatement is not made once, but at every point in time (in the DICE model time is discretized in 100 five-year steps, but this is just a technical detail). So, savings and abatement are actually (control) functions of time. The outputs of the DICE model are therefore the optimal savings and abatement schedules (functions). How do we obtain them?

The answer may sound a bit embarrassing, but, really, we find the all-important sweet spot by a glorified process of trial and error: we start from a reasonable guess, and, using some clever numerical tricks, we keep adjusting our initial guess until we find an optimal solution. We know that the solution is optimal because we cannot find another schedule of savings and abatement that produces a greater welfare today for humanity.[9] Welfare, of course, is what is returned by the chosen utility function: as discussed in Chapter 7, this is a function that takes only (present and future) consumption as input and returns our level of 'happiness' *today* for a given schedule of consumption. I must stress that only today's welfare is maximized, but, if we are to some extent altruistic and care about future generations (see in this respect the discussion in Chapter 9), a component of our happiness today also comes from knowing that our grandchildren will not face a dire climate future – and our utility function 'knows' about how altruistic we are.

One more important feature of the original DICE model is worth discussing. As Fig 8.2 shows, there are three types of variables in the DICE model: the control variables (as we have seen, the savings rate and the abatement schedule); the output variables (the welfare returned by the utility function); and a number of exogenous variables, that describe the mechanics of the physical system, of its interaction with the economy,

---

damage all investment would be devoted to consumption-producing technologies. When the damage to output from climate change appears, it makes sense to divert some investment from the usual consumption-producing technologies to damage abatement.

[9] Saying 'cannot find' is weaker than saying 'there isn't': people who engage in complex optimizations live with the constant fear that a better, undiscovered, solution may lurk somewhere.

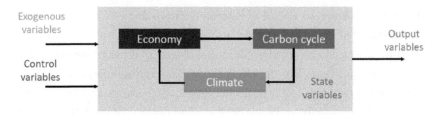

8.2 The types of variables in the DICE model. Reproduced from Melin (2020).

and of the economy itself.[10] In its original version, the DICE model assumes that the economic agents who make their choices know perfectly everything about how the world works, even in the presence of climate change. So the agents in the model know exactly the rate of growth of the population; how much the economy will grow for centuries to come; the damage function (which translates a future temperature increase into an economic damage); how effective our abatement technology will be at reducing emissions and the temperature increase; and many other things. Nothing in the original DICE model was uncertain (stochastic).

Making such a bold omniscience assumption may seem outlandish (and it is), but, admittedly, this is staple fare for the economic literature devoted to understanding economic growth.[11] However, the perfect omniscience assumption, never very palatable, can become particularly indigestible once we begin to look at the effects of climate change on the economy (about which the original growth models were obviously silent). As human society may be about to face climate conditions not encountered since the transition from hunting-gathering to agriculture, we really know very poorly how well we may be able to adapt to the new conditions and how severe the damage will be. Given this background of deep uncertainty, the original DICE model tried to set for the supposedly perfectly known parameters values right in the middle of our current best estimates: however, as we shall see, the welfare obtained with the 'average parameters' can be very different from the average of the welfares

---

[10] 'Exogenous' simply means that they are assigned from 'outside' the model, on the basis of our expert knowledge of how the world works. They are not the product of the optimization process – as, for instance, the level of output would be.

[11] The classic Ramsey, Koopman and Solow models all make this assumption, and many more.

associated with different possible values of the same parameters. In plainer English, even if we have no reason to change our *central* estimate, the very fact that we are uncertain about its true value changes our decisions. As I said in Chapter 7, 2,000 years ago Lucretius understood very well that the realization that we don't know something is a (very useful) piece of information in our decision-making: if we say that we don't know, we at least know *that*. We have discussed this feature at length in Chapter 7, but it is so important that we have to look at it again in Section 8.1.

8.1 THE KEY FEATURES OF THE DICE MODEL

Analyzing all the bells and whistles of the DICE model (even in its pared-down original formulation) would take us on a long detour, and would not necessarily help our qualitative understanding substantially. For our purposes, we can profitably concentrate on three key features of the model: the choice for the damage function; the assumption that we shall be much richer in the future; and what I have called in the previous section the omniscience assumption, thanks to which all surprises are banished. Let's look at each of these features in turn.

8.1.1 THE DAMAGE FUNCTION. In the original DICE model, the damage function – the function, that is, that translates a temperature increase into economic damage – is given a quadratic form: if the temperature anomaly[12] doubles, the economic damage increases by a factor of four. This behaviour is shown as the bottom line in Fig 8.3.

Saying that the damages increase by a factor of four for a doubling of the temperature anomaly sounds quite a lot. In reality, as the same Fig 8.3

---

[12] For very good reasons, in climate science temperature changes are expressed in terms of *temperature anomalies*. A temperature anomaly is the difference between the temperature at a given point and a given time and the temperature at the same point and a chosen reference time. Speaking of temperature anomalies rather than absolute temperature is very convenient: even if, say, the temperature in a city is considerably higher than the temperature in the surrounding countryside, if the city's temperature increases by, say, 1 °C, the *change* in temperature in the countryside will be very close to 1 °C as well. So, we need much fewer records of temperature anomalies to get a fair picture of what is happening to the temperature of the whole world.

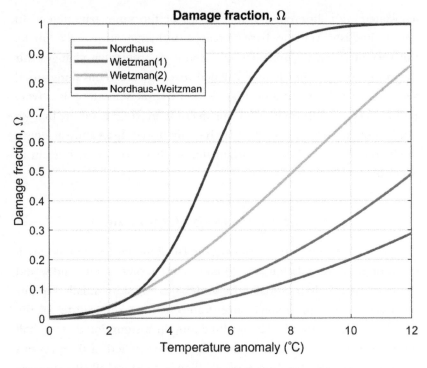

8.3 Different damage functions and the associated fraction of output lost, Ω.

shows, a quadratic damage is among the tamest of the damage functions that have been proposed, especially for severe temperature increases. For a temperature increase of 8 °C, the DICE function predicts a percentage loss of output of little more than 10 per cent; the Nordhaus-Weitzman function in the same graph predicts an output loss of about 90 per cent. Who is right?

It is difficult to say, and perhaps the question is not even well-posed.[13] The point is that we did not arrive at this damage function a priori using some well-understood model of how the climate interacts with the economy. Rather, the damage function has been painfully esti-mated using observed climate-related damages and relating them to the

---

[13] The question may not be well-posed because damages are not only a function of the climate (proxied by temperature), but also of the degree of adaptation. The same increase of the sea level can be devastating or manageable for a city depending on whether a dam has been built or not. See the discussion in Section 3.6.

comparatively very modest temperature increases we have observed so far.[14] The problem is that (unfortunately for statisticians but luckily for humanity) we can currently observe only the behaviour of this function relatively close to the origin, that is, very close to small temperature increases, and hope that we can extrapolate to regimes of much higher temperature increases. To understand how this extrapolation procedure may fail badly, think of a doctor who scrupulously records the body temperature and the physical discomfort of a patient when her body temperature is around 37 °C (say, between 37 and 37.5 °C). If the doctor used this temperature/discomfort graph, which may well display a quadratic increase of discomfort as the temperature climbs from 37 to 37.5, in order to predict how the patient may feel at 42.5, she would confidently conclude that the patient will be experiencing very severe pain, and would be well advised to lie in bed. In reality, the patient would be dead.

Now, the tame damage function assumed in the DICE model is at the root of one of its more hotly discussed conclusions: if the economic damage is truly only quadratic in temperature, we can 'afford' quite a considerable temperature increase – more precisely, the costs associated with avoiding very severe temperature rises (say 3–5 °C by the end of the century) would not be justified *because the damage is so relatively small*: it would cost us more to abate than taking the limited climate damage on the chin. The conclusion is both disturbing and logically inescapable: if we accept the DICE damage function, and the logic of all Integrated Assessment Models only modest abatement efforts are worth the money. You can immediately see how much hangs on using the 'right' exponent for the damage function. Indeed, most studies of the sensitivity of the output of the DICE model on its many parameters clearly show that, if you want to get *one* physical parameter right, it better be this elusive damage exponent.[15] And this is why the damage function used in the DICE model has been so savagely attacked: use one of the more 'severe' damage functions, and, all of a sudden, much of the gradualism of the

---

[14] For the interested reader, statistical regressions have been the analytical tool of choice.

[15] See, e.g., Rebonato, Ronzani and Melin (2023), and Barnett, Brock and Hansen (2021): 'The solution to the decision problem we pose shows some initial caution until future damage possibilities are more fully revealed …'.

DICE-model approach disappears, and the case for prompt and decisive action becomes much stronger.[16]

Which brings us back to the same question: who is right? Which curve should we use: the bottom or the top one in Fig 8.3? The problem, of course, is that, given the very limited information we have today, hard evidence for the more severe damage functions is hardly more compelling than evidence for the tame ones. It is easy to imagine conditions of abrupt climate change and tipping points, in which case the more severe damage functions could be justified. But perhaps we are underestimating the adaptation abilities of the human species, in which case an even milder damage function would be more appropriate. As I said, currently we simply do not know. Now, it is true that present empirical evidence helps us little in choosing the right number for the exponent; and it is also true that, given the relatively modest damages observed so far, there is little evidence for a change in curvature of the damage function for higher temperatures.[17] However, we know that we don't know, and we know that the range of our reasonable uncertainty is huge. As we have seen in Chapter 7, choice theory tells us that in itself this uncertainty should radically change our optimal abatement schedule, even if our central estimate for the exponent does not change. This means that the change in abatement schedule as we move from the omniscience to the uncertainty case is important and skewed towards prudence *even if our uncertainty about the exponent of 2 is symmetric around the DICE estimate.* Indeed, as already mentioned, one of the key results of financial economics is that we can model the effects of uncertainty by pretending that risk-averse agents are risk-neutral (do not care about risk), but skew the probabilities of different outcomes *in a pessimistic direction.*

---

[16] Recall what I said in Chapter 1 about the 'last temptation': if we simply use a severe damage function in order to obtain the answer we wanted to get in the first place, we are wasting good CPU time. With as many levers (degrees of freedom) at your disposal as those offered by the DICE model, if you are hell-bent on it, and have few scruples, you can obtain virtually any answer you want.

[17] see W D Nordhaus and A Moffat (August 2017), A Survey of Global Impacts of Climate Change: Replication, Survey Methods, and a Statistical Analysis, NBER Working Paper Series, 23646.

8.1.2 EVER RICHER?. So much for the damage function. The other key assumption in the DICE model is that we will be (much) richer in the future. Why does this matter so much? By playing some parlour games with the Bernoullis we have learnt that how rich we are can substantially change how much a given loss will hurt us – and therefore the choices we should make faced with the *same* gamble depend on the level of our wealth. But (present and future) wealth also matters when we have to decide how to 'spread' consumption over time. As we have seen, we can describe this 'driver of decisions' in terms of our dislike for feast and famine (or, as economists prefer to say, in terms of our aversion to intertemporal substitution). If we have a strong dislike of uneven consumption, we are likely to look with an envious eye at our rich grandchildren, and we are ill-disposed to make sacrifices today (say, forego holidays to build wind turbines) if the benefits are mainly to be enjoyed by future richer generations. If, on the other hand, our aversion to inequality of consumption is not so strong, the reduction in the consumption of future generations due to climate damage will play a bigger role in our abatement decisions.

Since this point is really important (and at the heart of the conclusions reached by the DICE model), let me expand on it a bit. To make things (much) simpler, suppose that we are not dealing with future generations, and that it is only your present and future consumption that motivates your choices today. Let us also suppose that you do not care a bit about having a relatively even stream of consumption. Finally, let's suppose that you are told that you will face a damage (loss of consumption) in the future for sure, but that you can limit this damage by investing (forgoing some consumption) today. Then your decision of how much to invest today will depend on balancing the loss of utility from not consuming today with the (impatience-discounted) loss in utility due to the future damage. However, given your total indifference to uneven consumption, this trade-off will not be influenced *by whether in the future you will be richer or poorer than today.*

Now, this result was obtained with zero dislike for uneven consumption, but this is not very realistic. Let's switch on, then, *some* dislike for feast and famine. Once this psychological feature of choice-making is allowed to come into play, how you behave immediately depends on whether in the future you expect to be richer or poorer than you are now. If you think that you will be richer, you immediately behave in a less generous way towards your future richer self, and this reduction in generosity will be more pronounced, the more you are unhappy about uneven consumption.[18]

Here is another useful way to look at your aversion to feast and famine. Even if, all else being equal, you dislike uneven consumption, you would still accept to part with *some* of your wealth today, if it could be very profitably invested so as to give you *a lot more* consumption tomorrow. By doing so, you do create a more uneven consumption flow, but you are more than compensated for this by the fact that you will consume a lot more in the future – after all, you still prefer more to less. Indeed, one can prove that the willingness to accept uneven consumption is a measure of your willingness to substitute consumption over time in response to a change in the rate of growth of your investment: the more your sacrifice will pay off, the more you accept feast and famine (or, perhaps, one should say famine and then feast). Obviously this matters a lot for the optimal investment in emission-abatement initiatives. The more effective we think these initiatives will be, the more we will invest in them – this is pretty obvious. But, and here is the crux of the argument, the more tolerant we are of uneven consumption, the more we are willing to accept sacrifices today to defray future damages. This is why our aversion to feast and famine plays such a big role in our optimal abatement policy.

Now, here is one big problem with the original DICE model. We have seen that, given the huge uncertainties that plague our understanding of climate damages, risk aversion should play a big role in our decision-making: knowing that we don't know matters. However, with the simple utility functions the original DICE models employs, a high degree of risk aversion by necessity implies a high aversion to feast and famine. So in the original DICE model the increase in abatement efforts today due to a more prudent disposition is negated by our greater reluctance to make sacrifices for our richer future beneficiaries. And conversely, if we say that we are relatively tolerant about inequality of consumption over time, then

---

[18] Needless to say, if the future 'person' is not you, but a future human being, things are even more complex.

the DICE model forces us to say that we care very little about static risk – despite the fact that we are facing one of the most uncertain events in recent human history. This is why economic growth assumptions matter so much with DICE's entangled preferences: because risk aversion and acceptance of uneven consumption are on a collision course.

8.1.3 THE OMNISCIENCE ASSUMPTION. Which brings us to the third big assumption of the DICE model: that we 'know everything'. There is no stochasticity in the DICE model, as the rate of growth of the economy and of the population, the damage produced by a certain degree of warming, the cost of future abatement technologies – everything, in short – is perfectly known today.[19] Since human civilization in general, and the post-industrial world in particular, have never experienced the degree of global warming we fear we may soon face, saying that we know for sure what the damages will be will strike most readers as little short of outlandish. Why has the DICE model gone down this route?

For once, the computational burden of running a fully stochastic simulation (running, that is the DICE model for several values of the uncertain parameters, and averaging the associated utilities) is not to blame. Indeed, most economists who approach the DICE model with a view to improving it, guess that avoiding the omniscience assumption is the lowest-hanging fruit to pick, and try to make the DICE model more 'realistic' by adding stochasticity (uncertainty) to its key variables. But when they do so, they generally find that just adding uncertainty changes the key DICE conclusions (the gradual abatement schedule we have discussed at length) surprisingly little. What is going on? How can we be risk averse and, at the same time, decide to act as if the huge degree of uncertainty we are facing with climate change hardly mattered? We have discussed this already in Chapter 5, but the key point is that, for the reasons just discussed, to get a barely acceptable degree of tolerance to uneven consumption, the DICE model is 'forced' to assume that the economic actors in its universe display very little risk aversion. Why so? The problem, again, is that for the class of utility functions used in the

---

[19] As a technical aside, since there is no stochasticity in the DICE model, what is accomplished is not really maximization of the discounted *expected* utility, but just of the discounted utility.

DICE model, the degree of risk aversion is inextricably linked to another key feature of our psychological decision-making process: our aversion for what I have called 'feast and famine'. As we discussed, if we play around with the inputs of the original DICE model so as to imply a greater degree of risk aversion, we are forced to say that we strongly dislike huge variations in consumption over time – and, as we shall see, *this has a much bigger effect on the optimal allocation*: what is gained in terms of higher abatement investment by recognizing that we are reasonably risk averse is more than lost by being forced to imply that we care so much about fluctuations in consumption.

There is no way to get around this problem with the (popular) class of utility functions used in the DICE model. Indeed, as we shall see, what distinguishes what I call in this book the 'modern' economics modelling of climate change from the traditional approaches is exactly the breakage of this unholy, and counter-intuitive, link between risk aversion and dislike for feast and famine. Once this forced connection is broken, we can model both a reasonable degree of risk aversion (which will call for steeper abatement schedules) *and* a modest dislike for uneven consumption (which will generate even steeper abatement interventions).

Why wasn't this done straight away? Why did we muddle along with patently inadequate utility functions for so long? Because the 'modern' approach is conceptually much more appealing, but the attending computational costs can be prohibitive. If one wanted to attack the problem by sheer brute force, one would have to carry out about $2^{100} = 1.2 \times 10^{30}$ calculations (as a reminder, 10^{30} means a 1 followed by 30 zeros). If each calculation could be carried out in a tenth of a millisecond, there wouldn't have been enough time since the start of the universe to finish one single run. Therefore, throwing computing power to the problem was, for once, not an option, and it has taken the discovery of some very clever numerical tricks to turn the problem from utterly impossible to still-daunting-but-at-least-feasible.[20]

---

[20] With the most state-of-art numerical tricks it still takes a few days for a single run to complete.

8.2 WHERE HAS THE SOCIAL DISCOUNT RATE GONE?

I made the case in Chapter 1 that the social discount rate plays an absolutely key role in making our choices about climate change. I said, perhaps with some hyperbole, that, once we agree on the social discount rate, everything else is almost a footnote, at least on the economics side of the problem. After such fanfare, the social discount rate seems to have disappeared. Did I forget about it? If we have managed not to mention it so far, is it really so important?

No, I did not forget about the social discount rate, and, no, it has not lost its importance in the few chapters between the introduction and here. Even if we have not mentioned it by name, the social discount rate has been with us all along. To see how it was hidden in plain sight, let me make an important point. In economics the process of discounting (the process, that is, of bringing 'something' from the future to now, so that we can compare this something with similar-type quantities) is ubiquitous. But we have to be very careful about what this 'something' is. If the something is directly utility ('happiness'), we already know how to bring back to today – by using the impatience discount rate that we have discussed as the first of our psychological drivers. However, money (or, to be more precise, consumption) is not the same as utility – this is what the Bernoulli cousins have taught us. Therefore we have to discount future consumption differently. For instance, it makes a difference in terms of our utility today whether we receive the same future amount of money (we enjoy the same future consumption) when we are rich or poor. We attribute a lot of value to consumption ('money') that arrives when we feel poor, and relatively less if we get the same amount of 'money' when we are feeling rich – this is, after all, why we are happy to pay actuarially unfair premia to insure our house against fire: because the insurance company pays up exactly if and when we are feeling *very* poor. So, to make it comparable with our utility from consumption today, we have to discount future consumption differently depending on the future state in which it is received.

The social discount rate knows about this, and adjusts accordingly the value of future consumption. We can see this clearly by using a one-line formula. If we use the simple (time-separable) class of utility functions, we can write the social discount rate, r as

$$r = \delta + \gamma \times g. \qquad (8.1)$$

In this equation δ is the rate of utility discounting – our 'impatience' –, g is the rate of growth of the economy, and γ can be interpreted as our dislike for uneven consumption.[21] (In the case of the more complex utility functions, there are additional terms in Equation 8.1, but the intuition does not change, so we can stay with the simpler case.) This is the rate at which we should discount future *money*. Now, even if they are not explicitly combined into an expression such as Equation 8.1, all the ingredients on the right-hand side of the equation that make up the stochastic discount rate are still there in the equations of all Integrated Assessment Models, and can be used more flexibly than if they were combined in one single number.[22] Therefore, the social discount rate is still with us, but it has been decomposed into its constituents for greater flexibility. And, apart from the rate of growth of the economy, these constituents are nothing but the psychological drivers of choice that we have discussed at length in Chapter 5 – so, nothing could be more important on the economics side of the equation. In Integrated Assessment Models the stochastic discount factor has been taken apart in its constituent bits and hidden away, but has lost none of its potency.

---

[21] The correct name for the quantity γ is the inverse of the elasticity of intertemporal substitution. In the case of time-separable utility function, one could also say that γ is the coefficient of static risk aversion. I don't terribly like this interpretation, because the social discount rate, r, differs from the impatience rate, δ, even in an economy with no uncertainty – and this is so even when aversion to static risk cannot be the reason why r is greater than δ.

[22] For instance, the social discount rate is obtained by imposing that we are at equilibrium, and therefore in the neighbourhood of a maximum. Every well-behaved function is almost flat at its maximum – that is why a ball thrown straight up in the air 'stops' before falling down –, and we can make use of this observation (we can impose the 'first-order condition') to obtain the function behaviour for small deviations around the maximum. However, all functions are flat(ish) around their maximum only for small deviations. In reality, the investments required to tackle climate change are anything but 'small', and therefore the use of the observation that all functions are flat(ish) around their maxima to derive the combination of factors into the social discount rate is of dubious validity.

CHAPTER 9

How Much Should We Care about Future Generations?

OW MUCH SHOULD WE CARE ABOUT future generations? From the discussion in Chapter 8, we can readily appreciate why this is one of the most important questions when it comes to deciding how to tackle climate change – the only other 'preferences' of similar importance being our dislike for uneven consumption, and our dislike for risk. Important as the question may be, it is patently obvious that it has no clear-cut right-or-wrong answer. This does not mean, however, that we are left without any guidance whatsoever. Decisional consistency, for instance, may be overrated, but, *faute de mieux*, can still give us some terms of reference for the problem. What I mean by this is that, if we find similarities between climate-change-related altruism and other forms of altruism with which we are more familiar, we can compare our choices in one domain with the choices we want to make in the other. If there are significant differences, we may then ask ourselves whether these differences are justified.

As a psychological sanity check, consistency is one tool at our disposal, but not the only one. We can also explore the ultimate logical consequences of sticking with any choice criterion we may want to employ when this is pushed to some limiting cases. Using a mixture of introspection and consistency, we can then see whether we are comfortable with what we find. This is what we try to do in this chapter. A warning, however, before we get started. The topic of this chapter would easily deserve a whole book, and a hefty one at that – and I would certainly not be the best qualified author to write it. I therefore offer my thoughts on the ethical aspects of the matter as the non-technical reflections on what is a philosophically very technical field. For the reader who wanted to start delving more deeply into the topic, I strongly recommend Jollimore (2021) and Dasgupta (2008, 2020).

9.1 A WRINKLE IN CLIMATE

We have seen that the Stern report adopts an almost zero discount rate for utility.[1] Stern believes, in other terms, that we should care about future people exactly as much as we care about ourselves. This view tends to be associated with classical utilitarianism, of which Sidgwick (1907) is in this respect an eloquent proponent:

> It seems [...] clear that the time at which a man exists cannot affect the value of his happiness from the universal point of view; and that the interests of posterity must concern a Utilitarian as much as those of his contemporaries, except in so far as the effect of his actions on posterity – *and even the existence of human beings to be affected* – must necessarily be more uncertain.[2]

I note in passing that, in line with the sentence that I have italicized in the quote, the tiny utility discount rate used by Stern in his work (0.1 per cent) is exactly *and only* justified by the possibility that humanity may not exist in the future. Apart from this small 'concession', assigning a different weight to the welfare of future beings than to ours has therefore been dubbed morally callous by classical utilitarians – see, in this respect, the various pulpit quotes in Section 5.4.[3] Saying that we should care about future generations no less than we care about ourselves sounds

---

[1] For an excellent and balanced discussion of Ramsey's views on intergenerational discounting in general, see Dasgupta (2020). For an application of these ideas to the context of climate change, see Dasgupta (2007). Both papers are somewhat technical, but highly worth the effort.

[2] Emphasis added, page 414.

[3] I often refer to Prof Stern as the standard-bearer of this extremely altruistic position, but the view is shared by a number of economists. Dietz, Hope, Stern and Zhengelis (2007), for instance, claim that a non-aggressive ramp-up of abatement initiatives can only by justified by those who deny the anthropogenic origin of climate change; by those who stress the adaptability of the human species; and by 'those who accept the science of climate change and the likelihood that it will inflict heavy costs, *but simply do not care much for what happens in the future beyond the next few decades*' – emphasis added.

noble and commendable. However, what would the logical consequences be of adopting a near-zero rate to discount future utility in some rather extreme cases? Nordhaus (2007) presents a nice thought experiment to throw light on this question. Let me quote in full.

> Suppose that scientists discover a wrinkle in the climate system that will cause damages equal to 0.1 percent of net consumption starting in 2200 and continuing at that rate forever after. How large a one-time investment would be justified today to remove the wrinkle that starts only after two centuries? Using the methodology of the [Stern] Review, the answer is that we should pay up to 56 percent of one year's world consumption today to remove the wrinkle. In other words, it is worth a one-time consumption hit of approximately $30,000 billion today to fix a tiny problem that begins in 2200.

Big numbers always sound impressive, but can be difficult to relate to. We can translate these big numbers, as Prof Nordhaus does, in the more manageable terms of average consumption. A quick calculation then shows that, in the case of 'wrinkle in climate' thought experiment above, the choice of discount rate in the Stern review would justify reducing per-person consumption today from $6,600 to less than half of that ($2,900), in order to avoid a reduction in consumption from $87,000 to $86,900 in two centuries' time, and continuing at that rate ever after. Would *you* be willing to make this sacrifice today?

Answering the question is deceptively simple (most people would probably say 'no'), but we should not forget that, by the way the thought experiment is set up, we are mixing a stock (the monetary sacrifice today) and a flow (the future damage that continues forever after at a known *rate*): this is usually a mistake, or at least an inconsistency, first-year economics students are warned against. Having said that, the real-life abatement-initiatives problem is exactly posed in terms that mix stocks and flows: how big a sacrifice should we accept today, in order to reduce the on-going damage that will result from climate change? The powerful point that the wrinkle-in-climate thought experiment brings home is that, when it comes to how much we should care for future generations, there is a temptation to engage in grandstanding. However, if these 'in-solemn-conclave-assembled' pronouncements are to be taken seriously, they should at least withstand a bit of introspection: which is what Prof Nordhaus' example provides. As Koopmans said:[4]

> [T]he problem of optimal growth is too complicated, or at least too unfamiliar, for one to feel comfortable in making an entirely a priori choice of [a utility discount rate] before one knows the implications of alternative choices.

Of course, in itself the thought experiment does not *prove* anything. Perhaps it is our clear intuition that we should not accept a cut in consumption of more than 50 per cent that is at fault. (How would you *prove* that, by the way?) However, the experiment does suggest that, as Koopmans wrote, in these settings entirely a priori choices are difficult – and dangerous! – to make.

Do we have other tools, apart from introspection, to validate, or correct, our pronouncements about how big a sacrifice we should make for the benefit of our distant descendants? To some extent we do, at least if we are ready mentally to substitute distance in time with distance in space or in economic conditions. What I mean by this is that the case of global warming is rather unique, in that climate damage will be mainly inflicted on people who are distant from us both in time and, if we live in the West, in space. Can we do some consistency checks here? To some extent, we can. We can try, that is, to 'calibrate our generosity' by seeing how generous we feel about people who are separated from us either in space or in time.

Now, redistributive taxation and a non-flat taxation rate, for instance, are made possible by our willingness to part with some of our wealth, if we are better off than most, in order to improve the lot of those less fortunate than we are, *and who live close to us* (taxes are levied at national level). Pay-as-you-go pension arrangements also benefit 'spatially nearby' people, but these will mainly live in the future. And the amount of foreign aid paid to developing countries can give us an indication of our degree of altruism, but for geographically distant people today. So, all these cases are different but relevant, because we can observe behaviours that

---

[4] Koopmans (1965), 1–75.

reflect how big a sacrifice we are willing to make to benefit the 'distant other'. Neither proxy is perfect, of course. First of all, both in the case of taxation and of foreign aid, the sacrifices are made by the better off in order to help the poorer; in the case of climate change, economists expect our grandchildren to be richer, and perhaps *much* richer, than we are. In the case of today's emission-abatement initiatives wealth therefore seems to be redistributed from today's poor to tomorrow's rich. Having said that, the future populations that stand to lose most from climate change will inhabit some of what are now among the poorest areas of the planet (think, for instance, of the Sahel): I hope to be wrong, but these populations strike me as unlikely representatives of our richer descendants.

Second, both taxation and foreign aid are also related to our dislike for inequality – a 'psychological driver' that seems to me to be related to, but distinct from, altruism. If we gloss over this difference, we can perhaps justify a 'generous' level of taxation by deliberating behind a Rawlsian veil of ignorance.[5] However, even if we assume that the democratically chosen levels of taxation were picked behind a Rawlsian veil of ignorance, it is difficult to draw stable conclusions, applicable over decades if not centuries, from what citizens of different countries have considered as 'acceptable' taxes over the last fifty years or so. If we take a snapshot of European countries as of 2019 (where we can assume that the tax rates have been democratically accepted by the voters) we find values for the top marginal rate of tax ranging from 76 per cent (Sweden) to 29 per cent (Bulgaria).[6] And even if we look at a country such as Sweden whose voters seem to have high tolerance for steep levels of income taxation, we find that in the relatively short period from 1995 to 2020 the top rate varied between 61.4 per cent (in 1996) and almost half as much (32.3 per cent in 2020). And as for the proportion of GDP devoted to foreign

[5] According to Rawls (1971–1999), to ensure our impartiality, we are to reach ethical decisions as if all knowledge about our social status, our personal characteristics, and even our historical circumstances were hidden from us: behind, as it were, a 'veil of ignorance'. For a very good article-length discussion see Freeman (2019).

[6] https://taxfoundation.org/taxing-high-income-2019/. The calculation refers to the 'effective marginal tax rate', that takes into account income tax, consumption tax, payroll tax and employee's social contributions.

aid, the variation is, if anything, even larger, with values ranging between 0.03 per cent (Russia), to more than 1 per cent (interestingly, one of the most generous countries, Turkey, with 1.15 per cent, is far from being one of the richest).[7] All of this simply suggests that, if we want to extract a 'universal' value of altruism from observed freely chosen behaviour, we seem to observe much greater variations (both over time and across different countries) than we would like to for a parameter we need to apply with confidence over several centuries. The huge difference between marginal rate of taxation (which is directed to contemporary beneficiaries in the same country where the tax is levied) and the level of foreign aid does suggest one thing, however: that some notion of 'psychological distance' matters greatly when it comes to how altruistic we feel. Let's explore this aspect a bit further.

9.2 DISTANCE AND ALTRUISM

I would gladly give up my life for two brothers or eight cousins.

—J B S Haldane, attributed

Can the notion of 'distance' be made a bit more precise? When we say that the intergenerational discount rate should be close to zero, we are effectively saying that 'distance' (in time, in geographical location, or in both) between people should not matter at all in our decisions.[8] Now, perhaps all of our moral intuitions are flawed, but the fact remains that, when we *actually* decide what sacrifices we are willing to make for other people, how 'distant' these beneficiaries are from us seems to make a huge difference. One may declare that we should not feel this way, and that distance is not a relevant attribute in parcelling

---

[7] Wikipedia (2020), https://en.wikipedia.org/wiki/List_of_development_aid_country_donors.

[8] Australian philosopher Peter Singer makes use of the concept of spatial distance to evaluate the ethical obligations we may have towards people who live far away from us. The notion has been recently extended by MacAskill (2022), who argues that distance in time should not give rise to a different evaluation. I hasten to add that the conclusions both Singer and MacAskill reach using the restricted or enlarged concept of distance are in important respects different from mine – an observation that does fill me with some apprehension.

out our generosity. One may arrive at such a statement by taking an extreme utilitarian approach, or perhaps following a deontological route (a route, that is, that attempts to arrive at what we should do from a priori rational principles). Given the patchy-at-best success record of deontological approaches to ethics, personally I tend to regard with suspicion ethical pronouncements arrived at in an a priori manner, and to take our observed, real-life moral choices seriously. As I said, I am well aware that I am stepping over a very technical, specialized and complex field. However, I offer to my reader the observation that abstract moral principles that in important respects do not resonate with the way we actually feel should at the very least face a strong uphill justificatory battle. I have a lot of sympathy in this respect for the observation of Cambridge moral philosopher Bernard Williams when he said that the litmus test of the relevance of all our highly technical and specialized philosophical conclusions is that the answer they provide should be one 'that the reader would recognize as one he might have given himself'. If they do not display this 'deep resonance', ethical prescriptions, no matter how noble-sounding, appear to me at least suspicious. And, if someone in the western world asserts that *complete* intergenerational impartiality is a self-evident truth that can only be concealed by our greed or 'rapaciousness', yet the same person fails to donate a very large part of her wealth and income to third-world aid, it is difficult to repress the doubt that the noble-sounding pronouncement is actually rather similar to what game theorists call 'cheap talk'.[9]

And, after all, if we really believe that no form of 'distance' should matter and that no kinship or proximity should sway our deliberations (as a near-zero discount rate implies), we may well ask ourselves what are the features of these 'distant and alien' people that we find relevant in reaching our conclusion. In crude terms, what makes them worthy of our altruism? If we answer that *the* relevant feature is their ability to experience pain and pleasure as much as we do (as a utilitarian would probably say),[10] then it is difficult to see why we should exclude *any*

---

[9] A definition of cheap talk is communication between the parties of a strategic interaction *that does not affect the payoff of the game.*

[10] Of course, the utilitarian answer is probably the most common, but not the only possible justification.

sentient beings, such as animals, from this calculus (this is, indeed, the position taken by some philosophers such as Singer).[11] To push the reasoning one step further: if we discovered that our fossil emissions greatly affect the welfare of the (sentient and intelligent) inhabitants of planet Zorg in a far, far away galaxy, how much would we be willing to curtail our economic well-being to improve their lot? Going back to philosopher Bernard Williams again, he made what I understand to be a similar point when he said that, if two children, one of which is your daughter, are at risk of drowning, and you ponder for five seconds about which child you should try to save, you have pondered for five seconds too many.[12] Defending the claim that 'distance' is irrelevant in making ethical choices may not be impossible, but is certainly not easy.

In the last decades a lot of philosophical work has also begun to look at morality as an evolutionary construct – a construct, that is, that has evolved to allow the more efficient spreading of the genes of a species as highly social as ours. When biologist Haldane made the tongue-in-cheek remark that he would lay down his life for two brothers, or for eight cousins, he was trying to explain (via the mechanism of kin selection) how altruism can develop in a biological world driven by the selfish gene (even if the term 'selfish gene' had not been coined yet). However, his statement can also imply that our moral intuitions – in particular, about what degree of generosity is appropriate *towards whom* – may have evolved as a mechanism better to spread our genes.[13] The topic is very contentious, but, if there is a kernel of truth in this evolutionary view of morality, the importance of what I have called 'distance' in reaching our

---

[11] See, e.g., Singer (1979–1993). For a discussion, see, e.g., Gruen (2021).

[12] I remember this example from my reading of Bernard Williams' work, but I have not been able to locate the exact source: it has just been filed in the highly imperfect storage system provided by my overloaded neurons. I would be grateful if a reader could point me in the right direction, and correct my probably imprecise, but hopefully serviceable, quotation.

[13] Related, but different, views are expressed in Wilson (1975, 1978). Wilson's *On Human Nature* (1978), is particularly rewarding for the non-technical reader – indeed, E O Wilson was awarded the Pulitzer prize for the book. The more recent *The Social Conquest of the Earth* (Wilson, 2013), touches on related themes at a level accessible to the non-specialist. Needless to say, some of the views of sociobiology are highly controversial, with Stephen Jay Gould and Lewontin among the most vociferous critics.

moral choices, and the weakening of our moral regards as the distance increases, follows very naturally.

In short: saying that kinship, national proximity and temporal separation should have *no* weight in our wealth-allocation decisions seems to be profoundly at odds with the way we, as humans, universally appear, not just to behave, but to feel. When we choose a near-zero value for the discount rate to use in problems such as climate-change abatement, the consequences and the ethical resonance of our choice become opaque, as several steps separate the highly technical choice of a model parameter, the utility discount rate, from its ethical implications. However, noble prescriptions that imply choices we do not recognize as 'our own' seem to me of no greater relevance and usefulness to us as human beings than similar intimations of centuries past – such as, that all earthly pleasures are to be ignored, if not positively avoided.

When it comes to our climate-change choices, finding a broad-church agreement about the optimal course of action is absolutely vital – I elaborate on this point in Chapter 17. And if we want to find agreement among potentially very differently disposed individuals, it is important that we should *not* have to ask them to be infinitely altruistic, for them to agree that we should act now and in large scale to tackle the climate-change problem. So, what I regard the most important feature of the modern economic treatment of the climate change problem is that we do not require a saintly degree of altruism (as the original Stern-report approach did) in order to choose very urgent and very large commitments to the abatement task. Even if we feel that the timber of humanity is more crooked than we perhaps wish it were, we can still reach the conclusion that we should engage in decisive abatement initiatives right now, and in large scale. I cannot overemphasize how important this observation is, as it provides even indifferently selfish human beings with an extremely powerful justification for decisive and urgent climate action.

CHAPTER 10

Growth

10.1 WHY GROWTH MATTERS SO MUCH

Expectations about economic growth play a key role in determining the optimal course of abatement action. To understand why, suppose for a moment that we are confident that humanity will be much richer in the future – the DICE model certainly is, since it assumes that, even in the absence of climate mitigation, the generations alive by the end of the century will be five to ten times as rich as we are today. As we have discussed, if we have a strong dislike for uneven consumption over time, we would be hard-pressed to justify a high level of investment (of sacrifice) inflicted on the present 'poor' generations to benefit our much richer grandchildren. The way economists put it, it would be tantamount to a tax levied on the present poor to help the future rich.[1] The argument, however, rests on our expectations of continued (and strong) economic growth (and on our strong dislike for uneven consumption). This prompts an obvious question: if expectations about growth are so important and so much rests on them, how confident can we be about them? What can history teach us about expected growth? How confident can we be that we will be as rich as our economic models project?

---

[1] As I have said, this argument also rests on the assumption that future climate damage will be evenly spread across the globe. As it happens, it appears very likely that the greatest climate damage may be suffered by populations that will be among the poorest also in the future. I have touched on the inequality issue, and on its relationship to climate change, in Chapter 1. In this chapter I am assuming that the damage from global warming will be inflicted evenly around the global and on a 'representative agent'.

10.2 WHAT DO WE KNOW ABOUT GROWTH?

Ask a layperson what she thinks a healthy but 'normal' rate of growth for the Western economy should be, and you are likely to hear an answer between 2 and 3 per cent per annum. Anything less is considered sluggish, and a growth below 1 per cent positively anaemic. And as for mentioning a negative growth rate, this is the stuff, not dreams, but early-ending political careers are made on.

Nobody knows for sure, of course, what the future rate of growth of the economy will be. What history does tell us, however, is that taking 2–3 per cent as the norm for growth is a bit like taking your best ever record as a batsman as a good indication of how well you expect to be batting for the rest of your cricket life. As a rule, the world economy has *not* grown at 3 per cent – to be more precise, until very recently the world economy had hardly been growing at all. Let's get some numbers to put things in perspective.

Measuring today's economic growth is difficult enough, so you can only imagine how difficult it is to gauge whether the economy was growing in Rome at the time of Octavianus Augustus or in China during the Ming dynasty. However, we can pole-vault over the methodological difficulties, and present some consensus figures – consensus figures that become more and more reliable as we approach the present times. First of all, the almost unchallenged consensus among economists is that from the dawn of civilization to roughly the 1500s there is almost no economic growth to speak of. How do we know? We cannot know the details, of course, but some simple reasoning can give us some pretty useful clues. The simple reasoning goes as follows.

These are three things we *do* know: first, the minimum level of subsistence; second, the broad demographic growth in the Common Era (roughly no net population growth in the period to 1500); and, third, the approximate size of the economy at the start of the sixteenth century. Now, suppose that the economy had grown from the year 0 at the rate of 1 per cent. Since in 1500 the vast majority of the population was not that much above subsistence level, if the size of the population had remained roughly constant in the period to 1500, then at the time of the Roman Empire the economic conditions would have had to be impossibly below subsistence.

161

To give an idea of the implied growth, just think that if the economy had on average grown, not at 1 per cent, but at a quarter of a per cent from the year 0 to 1700, and if the average person could survive on 1,000 calories per day, then in the late days of the Roman republic the amount of daily calories available per person would have been less than 25. A *Mars* bar is 228 calories: try and make it last for twenty days while waging Caesar's *maximis itineribus* campaigns.

What if the size of the population had grown substantially (thereby increasing the size of the economy even if production per head did not change)? The same reasoning in reverse shows that the size of the population at the time of Augustus would have had to be absolutely tiny. So, some broad-brush information, and a bit of logic lead us to conclude that economic growth up to the beginning of the capitalist era must have been close to zero.

The next question is: Did capitalism make a big difference in the growth of the economy? We can trace the birth of the first proto-capitalist institutions around 1500. From 1500 to 1820, early capitalist institutions in the West barely made a difference to growth: developmental economists put economic growth for the period 1000–1500 to 0.12 per cent, and growth for the 1500–1820 period to 0.14 per cent per annum. Confronted with such precision, the ex-physicist in me shouts for some error bars, and, when these are taken into account, we can safely say that, up to 1820, there was no discernible difference in the growth rate of the economy before or after 1500. These figures refer to the whole of Western Europe. In the Netherlands and in Britain economic growth during the 1500–1820 period was discernibly higher (around 0.28 per cent), and economic historians still debate exactly why higher growth occurred in these two countries. Remarkable as this growth was in this early capitalist phase, it is still very low compared with what we consider today a 'normal' rate of growth.

Let's agree on 1820 as a reasonable date for the start of the Industrial revolution. Surely the economy began growing at dizzying speed at this point? It all depends on what you call 'dizzying speed'. In the 1820–1870 period average incomes grew in Western Europe by 1 per cent per annum. Dizzying indeed, if compared to what had happened in human history up to that point; but, as economist Ha-Joon Chang points out,[2] no better than the rate of growth in Japan during the so-called lost decade of the 1990s.

Between 1870 and the First World War, we have the so-called Belle Epoque of capitalism. And, sure enough, economic growth in Western Europe did accelerate – but, again, probably less than you might have guessed: from 1.0 per cent for the 1820–1870 period to 1.3 per cent from 1870 to the start of the First World War.

The staggering human costs of the First World War caused the first reversal in economic growth since the early 1800s, but one can consider this as an aberration – one would use the term 'statistical blip' if the underlying events were not so tragic. And, of course, ten years after the end of the war the West experienced the Great Recession (when production in the USA fell by a staggering 30 per cent between 1929 and 1932). But, economic progressivists say, this was just another aberration, made worse than it should have been by the worst possible monetary and economic policies from the central banks, and, therefore 'it doesn't really count' either. So let's fast forward to the period after the Second World War.

Finally we *do* get some impressive rates of growth. Between 1950 and 1970 incomes grew in Western Europe at a 4.0 per cent pace, in the United States at 2.5 per cent, in West Germany at 5.0 per cent and in Japan at 8.0 per cent. (Of course, growth was stronger in those countries that had been most severely ravaged by the war: when you start from a very low level, any growth at all can give an impressively high *percentage* increase.) This turbocharged growth began to sputter between 1971 and 1979, after the suspension of the $/gold convertibility, the oil price shock, and the attending rampant inflation. After that, economic growth has resumed in the West, but with marked regional variations, and with nothing like the élan of the 1950–1970 period.

We have now exited the aftermaths of the 2008 Great Recession, and rates of growth in the West show large variations (with the USA currently posting the most robust and Italy the weakest growth among the G7 countries). The COVID pandemic, the economic rebound as the world unevenly began to exit its grip, and the energy crisis caused by

[2] Chang (2014).

the 2022 Russian invasion of Ukraine, of course, scrambled any growth signal very severely. But there is a generalized perception that something is 'temporarily' wrong with the state of the world economy, that we should fix this something, and that somehow we should get back, if not to the 4–8 per cent growth, at least to the 'normal' 3 per cent growth.

As long as we can achieve this without inflicting too much damage on our planet, I could not hope for anything different. And, since hoping is free, allow me even to hope for (why not?) 6 per cent, or even 8 per cent! However, one thing is hoping, and another thing is having expectations grounded on reasonable premises. Unless for some reason we think that the 1950–1970 period was the norm and the rest of human history (or at least of capitalist history) an aberration, we are likely to be sorely disappointed.

10.3 ABSOLUTE GROWTH AND GROWTH PER PERSON

There are some further worrying considerations that should temper our optimism about future economy growth. When politicians talk about economic growth they normally refer to the total growth in the economy. Over short time scales (e.g., if we are comparing one quarter with another, or one year with the next) this makes perfect sense. But in the long term, it can be profoundly misleading.

If we are interested in a jingoistic tally of growth numbers (a bit like counting gold medals at the Olympics), looking at the total growth in a country's economy can do. However, for most applications what matters – that is, what gives an indication of whether the average person is living a more comfortable life – is economic growth *per person*, not total growth. Now, since 1700 the growth in the world population has been staggering. This implies that, if instead of focussing on total growth we look at growth per person, we get a very different, and much more sombre, message, shown in Table 10.1. In the West, during no century has the rate of growth in the economy been above 1.7 per cent, and the average for the West since 1700 has been 1.1 per cent. Higher growth rates (about 3–4 per cent) have only been experienced by countries in an economic catch-up phase – a phase that, by definition, stops when the catch-up is completed.

Table 10.1 Growth per person for different historical periods from the year 0 to 2012.

Period	World	Europe	America	Africa	Asia
0–1700	0.00%	0.00%	0.00%	0.00%	0.00%
1700–2012	0.80%	1.00%	1.10%	0.50%	0.70%
1700–1820	0.10%	0.10%	0.40%	0.00%	0.00%
1820–1913	0.90%	1.00%	1.50%	0.40%	0.20%
1913–2012	1.60%	0.40%	1.70%	1.10%	2.00%

Source: piketty.pse.ens.fr/capital21c.

And, needless to say, not all the world can be catching up (with whom can *everybody* be catching up? With Mars?).

So, one of the key questions (and perhaps *the* key question) for development economists is why economic growth changed so dramatically in the last two centuries. It is not just that early economists did not predict this would happen. They positively thought that GDP growth per person would be impossible: I am referring, of course, to Malthus and his dismal (but, in his days, very justifiable) view of the human economic predicament. His key starting point was that labourers had zero bargaining power, and would therefore be paid just enough to keep them alive (not a bad assumption in the pre- and early-industrialization periods, when the supply of cheap labour was virtually unlimited). Apart from labour, what else do we need to produce stuff? In Malthus' agricultural days, mainly land, and, at any point in time, it is reasonable to assume that the best land has already been taken and put to work. So, the *marginal* productivity of both land and labour could be both safely assumed to be declining: if we add one labourer, she will produce less than the average of the existing labour force; and the next acre of land will be less productive than the currently used farmland.

Now, suppose that we have a lucky year, with a particularly plentiful crop. The subsistence-level labourers will temporarily be better off, and will have more children. In a favourable environment, population grows exponentially, as the scourge of imported rabbits in Australia readily shows. However, moving back from Australian rabbits to Malthusian workers, the resources to feed an exponentially growing population don't even grow linearly (this is where the diminishing productivity of labour and capital come in). The next year's 'normal' crop will therefore not be enough to feed the larger number of mouths, and famine will follow the short feast: as a result, the population will be back to the pre-good-crop level – and still live at subsistence level. (The equilibrium, by the way, will be re-established via a painful increase in infant mortality and in a deferral of the procreation age.)

What if we had a technological break-through? What if someone found a way to plough the land, or irrigate fields, or rotate crops much more efficiently? Would that make the lot of the labourers better? In Malthus' days unfortunately not. The key point here is that in his view (and, in his days, in reality) the wage labourers earned was basically what was needed to keep them alive. So, in his days the greater productivity of the land would support a slightly larger population, but each individual labourer would remain, on average, at subsistence level. After the technological innovation, society would be made up by a larger number of equally miserable individuals.

So, why did things change? Because of two reasons, essentially: first, *continuous* technological innovation; second, the no-longer-unlimited supply of cheap labour. Continuous technological innovation simply means that we keep on inventing new ways to squeeze more productivity out of processes, resources and people. And, when the supply of cheap labour is no longer effectively infinite, the industrialist will be ready to bid more for the services of labour than what is needed to keep them (barely) alive. How much? Exactly up to the point where the extra cost in labour (and capital) equals the last bit of profit for the capitalist from whatever the firm produces.

This 'new' way of looking at costs and profits from the perspective of the last little bit of cost or profit has been called the 'marginalist revolution' – where the name indicates that we look at costs and profits 'at the margin'. But the results of the marginalist analysis only become interesting if there is the continuous technological innovation. Never-stopping innovation is the only engine that lifts overall living standards: this is the key result of the workhorse of development economics, the Solow model of economic growth.[3] Can we expect this continuous innovation to go on forever?

[3] The Solow model can be enriched in many directions. To start with, in the Solow world, people invest a fixed percentage of their income: they do not choose the optimal level of saving and investment. Second, technological innovation rains on earth from the

Unfortunately, when it comes to explaining why an exceptional growth rate prevailed after the industrial revolution, and an even more exceptional rate of growth materialized during the *Trente Glorieuses*, current economic theory is not at its explanatory best. In cosmology, in order to explain the expansion or otherwise of the universe, one has to introduce dark energy and dark matter. These vaguely Star-War-reminiscent terms are not small corrections: our best current estimates give roughly 68 per cent of the universe to dark energy, 27 per cent to dark matter, and the remaining paltry 5 per cent to the 'normal' stuff that we can touch and feel (say, the Earth, the galaxies, this book, etc.). The inconvenient problem is that we don't really know what this dark stuff is: in physics we need these two terms to explain some pretty fundamental observations about the universe, but we have no clue as to what they actually 'are' (or, even, if the question of what they 'are' makes sense).

When it comes to explaining economic growth things are not a million miles apart: we do know that, as more capital (think of it, for instance, as extra machinery) is put into production, the economy produces more. We also know that as we put more labour (more workers) to a project, the output will increase. No surprises here: capital and labour are the equivalent of the stuff we understand: of 'regular mass' in cosmological explanations. Unfortunately, they fall similarly short of the mark when we try to explain where growth comes from: our best guesstimates of how much capital and labour contribute to extra production come up, in percentage terms, with numbers in the mid to low teens. Which means that the economic growth cannot really be explained by the things that we can more or less readily measure and understand, capital and labour input.

Now, economists are no less resourceful than cosmologists, so they have come up with their own equivalent of dark matter and dark energy: the *total factor productivity*. The name is fancier and more serious-sounding than 'dark matter' and 'dark energy', but, again, 'total factor productivity' simply stands for a placeholder to signify what we are left with once we have accounted for the stuff that we can measure. Not for nothing, Nobel-prize winner Robert Solow famously called the total

sky – or, rather, from outside the model. There are fancier models that fix both these shortcomings, but their conclusions, and their emphasis on the rate of technological change, do not change.

factor productivity 'a measure of our ignorance'. And in econometric circles, the total factor productivity is referred to as 'the residual' – ask any econometrics 101 student, and she will tell you that the residual is whatever is left in a regression after we subtract what we *can* explain: in other words, the unexplained bit. This is unsettling to say the least: on the one hand, we observe with the start of the Industrial Revolution an unprecedented shift in economic growth – a truly exceptional historical one-off. On the other hand, we can explain with quantities (labour and capital) that we can understand and measure a smallish portion of this exceptional growth. All the action, economists agree, has come from an unprecedented increase in the total factor productivity. Annoyingly, we really don't know what this 'thing' is. Quoting Nobel Prize laureate Michael Spence from memory (and therefore probably imprecisely – apologies here), he once said that, when it comes to development, we know some of the ingredients, but not the recipe.[4]

Since we don't know what it is, we cannot really predict whether it is here to stay (nor why, for some reason, it wasn't with us before); whether it may depart as suddenly as it appeared on the scene; or whether it may have taken its leave from planet Earth already, but we haven't noticed yet. One of the best-known economists who believes that recent (last century's) growth is probably unrepeatable – that is, that increase in the total factor productivity was a one-off – is probably Robert Gordon. Here is what he says about future expected growth[5]

> My book adopts the 'special century' approach to economic growth, holding that economic growth witness a singular interval of rapid growth that will not be repeated ... Our first order of business is to identify those aspects of the post-1870 industrial revolution that made it *unique and impossible to repeat.*[6]... The flood of inventions that followed the Civil War utterly transformed life ... What makes the period 1870–1970 so special *is that these inventions cannot be repeated.*[7]

[4] Again from memory, he said these words, or similar ones, at one of the quarterly PIMCO strategic sessions. I believe that he was rephrasing what he had written on the topic in other fora.

[5] Gordon writes about the US economy. His arguments are transferable to the developed world, but clearly not to developing countries.

[6] Emphasis added.

[7] Gordon (2016), page 16.

Gordon's point (and his justification for the 'impossibility' of growth similar to that witnessed in the 'special century') is that most of the really life-transforming inventions have already taken place. We wax ecstatic at every new app that can be downloaded on our Android phone ('Look, with this app I can monitor whether my pet dog is exercising enough: isn't this amazing ...!'), but we tend to forget that in 1870 'urban working-class family members bathed in a large tub in the kitchen, often the only heated room in the house, after carrying cold water in pails from the outside and warming it over the open hearth-fireplace'.[8]

To appreciate how uniquely transformative the innovations of the early twentieth century have been, just think of electricity. Everybody understands that electricity made the business of getting light where it would otherwise be dark much easier. What is less obvious is that electricity completely changed our urban landscape, by allowing the 'invention' of skyscrapers: just try to imagine the Manhattan skyline if people had to climb stairs to their homes and offices. Similarly, as late as the end of the nineteenth century, something which today is as simple as doing the laundry was, especially in winter, a time- and resource-consuming activity, that would take a significant part of the domestic working day. As women were carrying out these household chores, they simply could not conceive of taking on an outside job. And a century and a half ago, the ice to make sorbets in the summer for the English Embassy in Venice had to be carried down from the ice-fields of the not-so-near Dolomites, and stored in shaded underground vaults during the hot summer months.[9] By the 1950s, most households in the States could freeze foods at *sub-zero* temperatures. Transportation, communication and entertainment witnessed similar quality-of-life-changing transformations.

In the 1970s we all thought that, somehow, our lives would keep on changing for the better at the same pace, but facile extrapolations into the future of last century's changes have disappointed us. All science fiction movies of thirty-to-forty years ago (from *Blade Runner*, to *Back to the Future* to the early *Star Wars*) featured flying cars buzzing around in the urban skies as common as bicycles during rush hour in Beijing. That is

---

[8] Ibid., page 3.

[9] The building is no longer an embassy, but a hotel overlooking the lagoon. The underground vault is still open to the guests, and is worth a visit.

not what happened. As Peter Thiel said in his now-famous address at the Yale School of Management 'We wanted flying cars, instead we got 140 characters.'

Gordon distinguishes three Industrial Revolutions. We have all heard about the first. In the second, that roughly spanned the 1870–1940 period, with benefits spilling over to the 1970s, output per hour, output per person and total factor productivity (the best available measure of innovation and technological change) all grew more rapidly than ever before or since. During the third Industrial Revolution, associated with computers and digitalization, the rate of growth in this metrics of production has been far slower, with the ten-year average annual growth in TFP of almost 3.5 per cent in the 1950s, but hovering between 0.25 and 0.75 per cent from the 1980s to date.

There are many reasons why productivity growth has not kept the dizzying pace of the 1950s. One important difference between the economy of the 1950s and today's economy is the fraction of services over goods in the GDP tally. In the United States in 1870 26 per cent of the population worked in the service sector, a staggering 50 per cent in agriculture, and about a quarter of the working population in manufacturing broadly construed. Move to the late 1980s, and 63 per cent of the workforce is employed in the service sector, 31 per cent in manufacturing, and a puny 6 per cent in agriculture.[10] Give or take a few percentage points and the same picture holds for Japan or West Germany.

There is nothing intrinsically 'bad' in the move from producing 'stuff' to rendering services. However, it is relatively easy to improve the efficiency of a gadget-producing machine, of an agricultural practice or of a process. Give the profit incentive, and in this respect human ingenuity seems to be almost limitless. But when it comes to services, efficiency improvements are far more difficult to come by, and, sometimes, even difficult to imagine. In the rich West, we seem to spend more and more money on restaurant meals, holidays, grooming, and entertainment, and, if this is what we want, there is nothing wrong with that. However, to the extent the national GDP becomes more and more skewed towards

---

[10] Data from McKinsey and Company (October 1992), Service-Sector Productivity and International Competitiveness.

services, we cannot expect the same efficiency gains that have driven the improvement of, say, television sets, cars or phones. Can a barber really learn how to cut hair much more efficiently? Looking into my CD collection, I have discovered that Glenn Gould's 1955 recording of the Goldberg's variations lasted thirty-five minutes and twenty-three seconds; in 1981 he performed the same piece in fifty-one minutes and eleven seconds. Does this mean that he became less efficient? So, if the shift in what the economy produces from goods to services is a permanent feature – and, if anything, I would think that in the West the trend will accelerate in the near future: just think of who will take care of an ageing population – it is difficult to see much improvement in total factor productivity.

Something else 'happened just once': after the Second World War an unprecedentedly large fraction of women joined the work force. In the late 1800s the fraction of working women in the West ranged from 15 to 35 per cent (and were mainly employed in low-efficiency jobs such as maids, house cleaners, etc.). Today 61 per cent of women work in Canada, with participation rates for the UK, the USA, Germany and France ranging from 58 to 52 per cent.[11] Now, when women worked at home, their labour, back-breaking as it might have been, was not recorded in the GDP statistics. As they joined the 'official' work force, their now-transparent contributions to the GDP became visible. It was a double 'whammy': first, a previously unaccounted-for ghost workforce appeared in the records; second, their efforts became progressively directed towards activities for which productivity growth is much easier to come by – as, say, doing brain surgery rather than raising children. (Don't get me wrong: as a parent I know that raising children is probably as demanding as brain surgery, and perhaps more. It is the efficiency gains that are, at best, elusive, as I discover almost every day when I repeat with my teenage child all the mistakes parents have been making for generations.)

We could go on. If the reader is interested, the book by Gordon is unparalleled in breadth and scope (even if very US-centric). To present a balanced picture I must point out that, among economists, Gordon

---

[11] https://ourworldindata.org/female-labor-force-participation-key-facts.

is definitely on the pessimistic side. The fact remains, however, that counting on a continuation of the rate of economic growth we have seen in the last century is definitely optimistic. I don't know whether 1, 0 or 1.5 per cent will turn out to be the right prediction for the next fifty years. But I am ready to take a very large bet with any reader that it will not be 3 per cent. (Warning: I would be very surprised if I will be around to collect or pay on the bet, and that is why I am making it rather light-heartedly.)

10.4 THE LINKS BETWEEN GROWTH AND CLIMATE CONTROL

The reason why I devote so much attention to the long-term expected growth of the world economy is because our optimal emission-abatement strategy depends very strongly on how rich we are going to be in the future. Nordhaus goes as far as saying that it is *the* single most important quantity in deciding how fast, and how deeply we should decarbonize. Why is this the case?

As we have discussed in Chapter 5, people display aversion to uneven consumption, and, all else being equal, tend to arrange as smooth a consumption pattern over time as possible. Now, investing today means consuming less today in the hope of increasing our future consumption. The greater the expected rate of return from my investment, the more I will be willing to make a sacrifice today. However, the increase in happiness because of the greater future consumption is diminished the richer we will be in the future: formally, this is reflected in the decreasing steepness of the utility curve; but this is simply a representation of the psychological feature first identified by Bernoulli when discussing the desirability of the same bet for the poor fellow or the rich man of his tale. So, for sure, $1,000 will make me happier if I am poor than if I am rich. But perhaps I may prefer the same $1,000 paid to my poor self today than $1,200 or $1,500 received by my future rich self *even neglecting impatience*.

Keeping these considerations in mind, let's look at investing $1,000,000 today to reduce emissions – an obvious sacrifice – in order to negate a future climate damage. How big the reduction in the future damage has to be for today's sacrifice to be acceptable depends (among other things) on how rich the beneficiaries of the abatement will be. For a given fix dislike for uneven consumption, the richer our descendent will be, the more we may feel that they should 'take care of themselves'. So, all else being equal, the more we expect future generations to be rich, the less we are inclined to invest in climate initiatives today. This is the 'tax on the poor' argument again. And, of course if for any reason we thought that our great-grandchildren will be *poorer* than we, then the same logic works in reverse: we may choose to invest the $1,000,000 today to reduce emissions even if the benefit for the future generation were only, say, $900,000 because their associated loss of happiness may well be higher than our loss of happiness for the monetarily greater privation (whether this is truly the case, depends on how much poorer they will be, and on how much we care about uneven consumption.)

In sum: our expectations about economic growth in the distant future have a big impact on the optimal abatement strategy. And whether growth will indeed continue, and at what pace, seems to me highly uncertain. Yet, for such an important variable, *no scenario in the mainstream economic projection models envisages a zero – let alone negative! – economic growth over the next 50 or 100 or even 200 years.* And this is despite the fact that the projections produced by these models are expected to cover a wide range of possible future events for all kind of variables: the plausible variations in global warming often examined, for instance, spans the 1.5–4.5 °C range. Apparently, zero economic growth – what we have observed for most of human history – is considered less likely than a 4.5 °C warming (that could have pretty catastrophic consequences for our planet, with possible increases in the sea level measured in feet, not in inches). This, I think, is a blind spot that economic analysis of climate change must address. We shall see what the abatement consequences of deep growth uncertainty are in Chapter 12.

CHAPTER 11

Population

11.1 POPULATION DYNAMICS

How much energy we will consume in the near- to medium-term future will clearly depend on the growth of the world population. This is true, but also oversimplified. It is not very helpful to talk of the growth of the world population as a whole: rather, we should look at the projected population growth for different regions of the world, and at the different energy requirements arising from populations in different stages of economic growth. There are currently very different levels of economic welfare in different parts of the world, and – strongly correlated with this –, there are very different rates of infant mortality and very different life expectancies. Despite the wide spread of demographic outcomes, some strong regularities can be discerned: as we look at synchronous populations across geographies we see that we can correlate fertility and infant mortality with economic conditions in a very structured manner. (See Figs 11.4 and 11.5 later in the chapter, and the accompanying discussion.) And when we look across time, we also see that, as economic conditions have changed, different regions of the world have followed similar trajectories of economic development and demographics.[1] What are these regularities, and how can we explain them?

A good place to start is, once again, the Malthusian view of the world – ironically, the model of population dynamics that he presented in his 1798 book, *An Essay on the Principle of Population*, and that accounts pretty well for the world demographics from the settlement of the first

---

[1] Modern models of demographic development trace their origin back to Notenstein (2015). The simple model discussed in this chapter is a version of the Notenstein model.

agricultural societies to his days, had already just begun to break down in an unexpected and unprecedented way, even if few were aware of the momentous changes the Industrial Revolution was ushering in. So, Malthus' intellectual breakthrough happened just when the conditions for its validity were about to change – perhaps forever. (Conventional dates for the start of the Industrial Revolution range between 1760 and 1785.)

Let's remind ourselves of Malthus' simple idea. First, he noticed that, in his day, economic output grew less than one-for-one with the size of the labour force or of the land employed: the last piece of land is less productive than the first, and the last labourer hired not as efficient as the first. The second ingredient for his model was the equally plausible assumption that, if, for any reason, output increases (say, because of a year with particularly favourable weather and plentiful crops), then the population would increase as well. Unfortunately, it is exactly this population increase that sows the seeds for the next downturn: as there are more mouths to feed, as the land productivity returns to normal, and as the extra labour is less productive than the existing one, malnutrition ensues, with an increase in infant mortality. So, in the long run a dismal equilibrium is re-established, in which the income level is just enough to allow subsistence.

What happens in Malthus' world if, instead of a bumper harvest, we have a technological innovation (say, a new system of irrigation) that *permanently* increases the productivity of the land? As we have discussed, in this case, yes, the population level would increase, but not the standard of living, as everyone would still remain at near-subsistence level. We would simply have a larger number of similarly miserably poor individuals. For reasons that are to this day not fully understood, the magic of the Industrial Revolution has been that humans, for the first time in their history, have found ways to grow output more rapidly than the population – that is, to increase *output per person*.[2] And this growth in living conditions per person that began with the Industrial Revolution has been mirrored in a similar increase in energy utilization per person

---

[2] A very good non-technical account of the Malthus model is given in CoreEcon (2017), pages 73–75.

– in the early phases, of course, the extra energy came almost exclusively from the burning of fossil fuels.

For the purpose of the current discussion the important observation is that, where (or when) the economic conditions are close to subsistence (virtually Malthusian), we observe high fertility (often close to the maximum birth rate of 40–50 live births per 1,000 people), high infant mortality, and little or no population growth. Infant mortality in this stage is staggering: in pre-modern societies more than 300 out of every 1,000 newborns would die before their first birthday.[3] Even in Europe (the first continent to experience sustained, post-Malthusian growth), the improvements in infant mortality with material conditions were painfully slow: by the end of the nineteenth century the infant mortality rate was still between 20 and 25 per cent for Germany, Austria and Russia.[4]

It is only if and when the economic conditions begin to improve – or, to be more precise, when output begins to grow more rapidly than the population – that a way out of the Malthusian trap is found. When this happens, first we observe a decline in infant mortality, but little variation in fertility. This is the period associated with an explosive growth in the population – and, for once, the adjective 'exponential' is correctly used. After this phase, if favourable economic conditions persist and the standard of living stabilizes at a high level, infant mortality remains low, but fertility also declines – sometimes to a point where the rate of new births is below the replacement level: this is what we are already experiencing in very rich regions with relatively low immigration, such as Japan and some parts of Europe. This gives rise to the population pattern schematically shown in Figs 11.1 and 11.2.[5]

Let's look at these figures in some detail. In Fig 11.1 we assume that at time zero the population (shown by the blue line) has a starting level

---

[3] Sadly, infant mortality is currently only half as much for a country such as Afghanistan. See Fig 11.4.

[4] Smil (2021), page 27.

[5] The picture I am painting is overly stylized, and some demographers have vigorously challenged the validity of the broad patterns depicted in Fig 11.1. See Smil (2021), page 25 and *passim* for a discussion and references of dissenting voices. Note, however, the qualitatively striking similarities between the population growth obtained with the baby model in Fig 11.2 and the actual behaviour of the rate of growth of the world population since 1675 shown in fig 2.2 of Smil (2021), page 28.

Economic growth and population

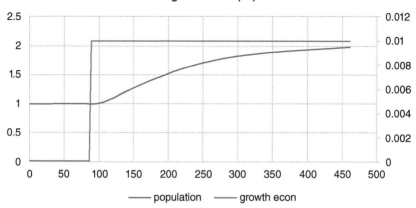

11.1 The population of a region that transitions from a period of no economic growth to state of constant positive economic growth. The right y-axis refers to the growth in the economy (red line).

Economic and population growth

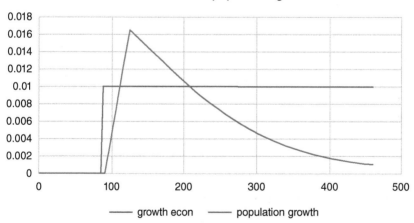

11.2 The rate of growth of population in a region that transitions from a period of no economic growth to state of constant positive economic growth (blue curve).

of 1 (the units both of time and of population are arbitrary). The red line then shows the rate of growth of the economy. The figure shows that for the first 90 time units there is no economic growth, and the *level* of wealth per person is such that the population is at subsistence level, and mortality and fertility rates balance each other. As a result, the population level is low and stable, as shown by the initial flat segment of the blue curve. Apart from fluctuations (not shown in the figure), we are at steady state (in a condition of dynamic equilibrium). We then assume that after 90 time units for some exogenous reason the economic growth rate jumps from 0 to 1 per cent. This sudden change in the growth rate of the economy is shown as the step increase in the red curve in Fig 11.1. As economic conditions improve, this immediately brings about a reduction in infant mortality. However, fertility remains high, because the country is not rich yet (the new-found economic growth has not increased the level of wealth per person enough). The decline in fertility, that is (inversely) proportional to the level of wealth per person kicks in with a lag (also arbitrarily set at 90 time units). The two curves in Fig 11.1 bring home two very important points. The first is that both fertility and mortality depend on how rich the society is, not on the rate of economic growth (which in our example remains constant after the initial step increase). Second, that the population does increase very rapidly when people begin to become richer, but then levels off, and stabilizes at a new level.

The same message, but from a slightly different perspective, is conveyed in Fig 11.2, which shows not the population, but the population *growth*. Notice how, after the initial increase, the growth in population reverts down to zero (as fertility declines), bringing about the stabilization of the population at a higher level, as shown in Fig 11.1. As the quip goes, a car in the garage and a TV set in the living room are the most effective forms of contraceptive that humanity has discovered.

Another way to look at these changing reproductive patterns is to note that when economic conditions undergo a permanent change, there occurs within a human population a switch between the two polar reproductive strategies observed across many animal species: high number of offsprings in a high-mortality environment in the hope that some will reach the reproductive stage (as in, say, rabbits); and low number of offsprings, and high 'investment' in them to ensure that they reach the age of reproduction (as in, say, elephants).[6] What is amazing is that, in

---

[6] In biology, there is the related concept of r-selection versus k-selection, where the 'r' and 'k' labels come from the symbols for growth (r) and environment support capacity (with 'k' for Kapazitätsgrenze: literally, boundaries of capacity) in the so-called Verhulst model of population dynamics. As far as I have been able to ascertain, it is rare for the same species to switch reproductive mode with changing environmental conditions.

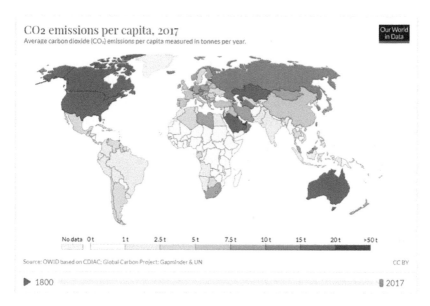

11.3 CO_2 emissions per capita (courtesy of *Our World in Data*).

the case of the human species, the collective switch from one mode to the other occurs despite the fact that, in principle, every couple can, to some extent, make an individual choice as to how many children to have. This model of population growth is extremely schematic, and, indeed, has been recently criticized (more harshly, I would say, than it deserves). But, while the details may be too coarse for a professional demographer, the basic picture is good enough for our discussion.

To develop my argument, let us now take a look at Fig 11.3, which shows the CO_2 emissions per capita in 2017. The most striking observation is how little the whole of sub-Saharan Africa is currently contributing to global emissions (a graph of the *cumulative* CO_2 emissions to date would show a similar picture, and even starker disparities in total emissions between rich and poor countries). Now, as we discuss in Chapter 15, economic growth has historically been strongly associated with an increased use of energy. In the West, this increase in the use of energy has been made possible by the discovery of how to release the energy contained in fossil fuels, which have a much greater energy density than biomass such as wood.[7] Of course, higher energy availability is a necessary, but by no

[7] See Ayres (2013, 2016, 2017).

means sufficient, condition for economic growth to ensue (and societies to change). We still imperfectly understand why, but this enabling factor (the availability of plentiful cheap energy) ignited in the nineteenth century an unprecedented economic growth in the West. Other parts of the world followed suit, with different time lags – but some large areas still have to enjoy sustained and robust economic growth.

Which brings us back to sub-Saharan Africa, as a prototypical example of a region which is today extremely poor, that has historically contributed little to global emissions, and that is still to embark on a stable development trajectory. Two paths of economic development seem possible for these regions. One, which we all hope will not materialize, is that for the foreseeable future they will remain much poorer than the West and some developing South-East Asian countries. If this happens, fertility and infant mortality will remain high, population will experience modest growth, energy consumption per capita will remain low, and so will emissions. This is not an outcome anybody can hope for, but it cannot be ruled out.

The other main scenario – a scenario that personally I consider more likely – is that economic growth similar to what is currently experienced by India, if not by China, will materialize in sub-Saharan Africa and other currently very poor areas in the next decades. In this case there are two possibilities. In the first, these now-poor areas will retrace the steps historically followed by Western countries of fossil-fuel-led growth, relying on the cheapest and dirtiest energy sources first (such as coal), and then progressively transitioning to cleaner energy. If this happens, the medium-term demographic implications would be a sharp increase in the population (as infant mortality falls), and a large increase of CO_2 emissions from dirty energy sources. If the experience of other countries that have made the demographic transition associated with sustained economic growth is anything to go by, it would then be several decades before the population could stabilize at considerably higher levels than today. During this long transition period the level of CO_2 emissions would be high, and growing. Emission reductions in other parts of the world could be largely negated along this path of economic development.

Some back-of-the-envelope calculations can provide a scale of the problem. It is extremely difficult to predict if and when regions that are showing no sign of economic growth will exit this period of stagnation. However, currently there are several emerging-market or developing countries that seem poised to make a transition out of poverty. Of these, thirteen strongly rely on coal as their cheapest source of energy;[8] and six further countries rely for their growth on oil, the second worst polluter after coal.[9] None of these countries by itself can be a 'new China' – if for no other reason than their populations are much smaller. However, if these countries continue along their current development path, they could easily produce in the decades to come cumulative carbon emissions similar to or greater than what China emitted between 2000 and 2020. And Gallagher (2022) calculates that if just four of these countries (Indonesia, Iran, Nigeria and Saudi Arabia) were to keep on growing as they were before the pre-COVID pandemic they would emit about as much as China did in the first twenty years of the new century.

It does not have to happen this way, though. We have already seen examples where the historical path of economic development followed by the West has been short-circuited in developing countries. The most obvious example is telecommunications, where many African countries have largely by-passed the phase of the land-line installations, and leap-frogged directly to mobile phones. Another example could be traditional retail banking, where the 'local branch' for the young African saver has often become her mobile phone. To some extent, one can therefore hope that the huge energy needs of the economically and numerically growing populations of the still-to-develop countries could be met in large part by modern, clean sources of energy. (Solar power, for instance, has obvious advantages in the African continent, since one of the main determinants of the effectiveness of photovoltaic cells is the angle of incidence of the sun light.) In this to-be-hoped-for scenario a growing African population would still generate increased emissions, but on a more manageable scale.

---

[8] In alphabetical order, these are Bangladesh, Congo, Egypt, Ethiopia, Indonesia, Pakistan, the Philippines, South Africa, Tanzania, Thailand, Turkey, Uganda and Vietnam. Gallagher (2022).

[9] These are, again in alphabetical order, Algeria, Brazil, Iran, Kazakhstan, Mexico, Nigeria and Saudi Arabia.

Having said this, there are limits to how much and how quickly these economies can grow without relying on fossil fuels. The first requirement of any growing population is to find the extra food. Now, we have become extremely efficient at squeezing more foodstuff out of an acre of land: as recently as in 1950 agriculture could feed (on a poorer diet than today) 2.5 billion people; in 2019 a much smaller fraction of farmers was able to provide food for almost 8 billion mouths.[10] There is no reason to believe that we have reached an efficiency plateau in food production. However, these staggering improvements have come at a cost: the energy from the Sun that fuels the process of photosynthesis has had to be 'subsidized' by an ever-increasing fraction of non-Sun energy (mainly in the form of fertilizers). The problem is that the production of these fertilizers is energy intensive, and it is difficult to produce this energy via electricity. Also, the large-scale machines needed in agriculture (from tractors to combine harvesters) are not as easily powered by batteries (that could be charged via renewables) as cars can be. As a consequence, given the demographic pressure that we can expect from countries that begin to attain comfortable standards of living, we can at most hope for a partial decarbonization along the development path of the currently poorest nations. This means that, to keep emissions under check, carbon sequestration (technologically well established, but still expensive) will have to play a major role in this development history.

How likely is it that a 'relatively clean-growth' scenario will materialize? How likely is it, that is, that at least those parts of energy production that can be provided by renewables will indeed be produced with limited recourse to fossil fuels? The most obvious problem is that most of these still-to-develop countries are very familiar with coal and oil technologies, and often have abundant supplies of fossil fuels (of very-dirty coal more than of medium-dirty oil). From their perspective, the very understandable temptation is therefore to embark on the path of least resistance and to fossil-burn their way out of poverty – exactly as China did in the first phase of its economic expansion. Understandable as the taking of this path of least resistance may be, the consequences for CO_2 emissions – and hence global warming – would be dire.

___

[10] Smil (2022), page 46.

Another problem is that renewables, such as solar and wind, have very low marginal costs compared to fossil fuels (sun and wind are free), but require high capital outlay upfront. Unfortunately, African countries are far from being rich in capital. Therefore, apart from any consideration of equity and fairness, it would be in the interest of the rich West to facilitate and subsidize the funding of these large-scale projects.[11] As ex-governor of the Bank of England, Mark Carney, points out, to make a difference this would mean 'mobilizing trillions of dollars of capital to finance decarbonization in emerging and developing countries – a hitherto unimaginable number *but without which real sustainability is not possible*'.[12] The political instability of many African states and their poor governance structure, with high levels of corruption and the syphoning offshore of wealth by rapacious political élites, pose additional challenges. Unfortunately, these are not the only ones.

11.2 CHALLENGES

There can be numerous obstacles to the realization of the doubly positive outcome (robust economic growth fuelled by clean energy), and some of these obstacles can be traced back to climate change again. For instance, some of the regions of the world at greatest risk from even modest temperature increases are the countries of the Sahel – the strip of nations (Mauritania, Mali, Niger, Burkina Faso and Chad, and parts of Senegal and Sudan) that border the south of the Sahara.[13] The

---

[11] For a nice, non-technical discussion of the climate-infrastructure financing options for developing countries see Gallagher (2022). For a good discussion of the geopolitical implications of the transition see Bordoff and O'Sullivan (2022).

[12] Carney (2021), page 13, emphasis added.

[13] 'Sahel' means 'shore' in Arabic – the 'sea' implied be the word 'shore' being in this case the Sahara desert. One 3third of the droughts occurring in the world are in the Sahel (Kemoe, Okou, Pitra and Unsal, 2022). The Sahel countries have GDP per capita ranging from $926 to $3,500 (PPP 2011), infant mortality five to ten times as high as countries such as France or the USA, life expectancy as low as fifty-three years (Chad), and averaging around sixty years. The Shael is home to more than one tenth of the full population of Africa. See, e.g., Eizenga (2019) for a discussion of the economic and geopolitical characteristics of the area. For a good discussion for the general reader of the constraints imposed by geography on this region, see Marshall (2015), chapter 5 in particular, with the warning that the eloquent and well-argued link between geography and global politics presented in the book is, at times, a bit too 'deterministic': the

economies of these countries are strongly based on a subsistence-level agriculture, carried out on what is already marginal farming and grazing land. It is not difficult to imagine a scenario where a modest temperature increase could turn these regions into a southern extension of the Sahara, depriving their populations of their already meagre means of survival.[14] The present already extremely harsh living conditions of these countries make the whole territory politically unstable, riven by conflict, and fertile ground for terrorist organizations. The worsening of these conditions could create mass forced migrations, much of which could be directed towards European shores. The tensions created in Europe by the current migrations, in all likelihood smaller in scale than what Southern Europe would experience if the Sahel population were forced to leave, should give the West food for thought. As Reuveny (2007) points out 'LDCs [Less Developed Countries] will experience more climate change-induced migration and conflict than DCs [Developed Countries]. However, the political fallout may extend beyond LDCs. The inevitable feeling of hostility may foster a fertile atmosphere for global terrorism recruitment, which may already be underway. For example, British and Italian authorities have recently identified Eritrea, Ethiopia, and Somalia as fertile recruiting grounds for terrorists'.[15] Again, just from a purely selfish point of view, this is another important reason why the rich nations of the developed world should strive to prevent even those temperature increases that the rich West may be able to adjust to with relatively little difficulty, but that could prove disruptive for poorer and more vulnerable populations. And, needless to say, these complex but important political considerations cannot be handled by the economic models I describe in this book: this does not mean, however, that they should be forgotten.

11.3 IS NO GROWTH AN OPTION?

Stepping back from the specific case of the sub-Saharan countries, the link between economic growth and population growth of those countries

---

subtitle – 'Ten maps that tell you *everything* you need to know about global politics' – (my emphasis) is symptomatic of the occasional geo-deterministic overreach.

[14] See on this point, Xu et al. (2021).

[15] Page 669.

that still have to undergo strong economic development will be a key determinant of the future emission outcomes for the whole world. (Let's just think for a moment about the huge difference that the welcome economic growth of China during the post-Mao era has made to the world emissions.) Since Africa up to now has contributed next to nothing to global emissions, we rarely think of this continent as a contributor to carbon emissions when we talk about climate change. Yet, geographical areas, exactly such as Africa, where substantial improvements in economic conditions are long overdue, may well hold, via the demographic channel, the key to the success of worldwide emission control. Under conditions of stable and sustained growth it would not be difficult to imagine an African population of over 2.25 billion by 2050 – little less than present-day China and India combined. Economic growth would stimulate an increase in population via the usual channel of decreased infant mortality. This young population growing in numbers and prosperity would require a lot more energy. Whether this huge energy requirement would then be met with low- or high-emission sources could therefore make a substantial difference to the success of the world decarbonization efforts. This is the reason why a serious discussion of emission policies does not make sense without giving due consideration to the world demographics – and demographics cannot be reduced to saying that 'on average population will grow and then stabilize'.

Calls for halting economic growth, based on the claim that 'we are already rich enough, we just have to redistribute wealth fairly' are parochially focussed on the conditions of the richest parts of the West (and, I would argue, are not necessarily valid even for the rich West).[16] And the huge inequality among different wealth percentiles of the population of rich western countries pales into insignificance compared with the inequalities across countries. Even the poorest people in the UK, for instance, have access to free health care (through the NHS) and to free education up to the age of eighteen for their children: in many parts of the world both these services are still unattainable luxuries.

---

[16] When I consider, for instance, the twin problems of the ageing populations of rich countries (with fewer and fewer members of the workforce having to sustain a larger and larger population of retirees) and escalating costs for health care in old age, I do not see other solutions than robust economic growth even in the West.

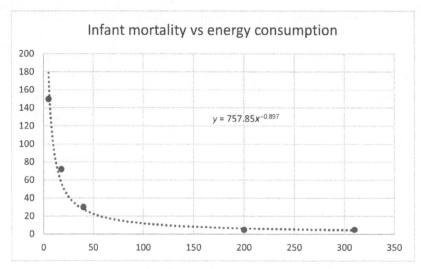

11.4 Infant mortality (deaths/1,000 births) against energy consumption (GJ/annum) for a few countries – from left to right: Afghanistan, India, China, Japan, USA.

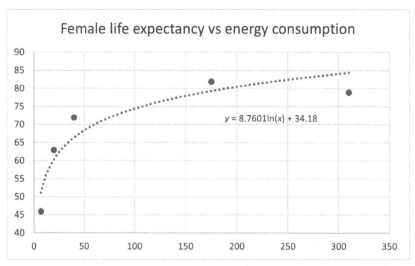

11.5 Female life expectancy at birth (years) against energy consumption (GJ/annum) for a few countries – from left to right: Afghanistan, India, China, Japan, USA.

To bring the point home, let's pause for a second to look at Figs 11.4 and 11.5, which show infant mortality and female life expectancy at birth against energy consumption for a few countries (the broad pattern is broadly confirmed as we add more countries to the picture).[17] It is clear that these most absolutely basic indicators of well-being (not for nothing they are referred to as the 'survival' indicators) are to this day intimately linked to the amount of energy available for the population. We are therefore faced with two wishes (that regions such as Africa may soon enjoy sustained development and that this may be accomplished without a major increase in fossil-fuel emissions) whose realization appears to be on a collision course.

Some social philosophers and a number of climate activists have tried to escape the poverty-emissions dilemma by envisaging a world in which today's poor nations are 'allowed' to attain a level of wealth per person similar to what Europe enjoyed in the mid 1950s, and in which, at the same time, the West is steered along a path of robust *negative* growth, so as to converge around the same standard of living.[18] I cannot imagine Western voters willingly choosing to embark on a path of severe degrowth – and this observation by itself raises the question of which political changes in the West would be required to bring about this piece of social engineering. But let's assume for a moment that, by choice or compulsion, the West reduces its economic output to mid-1950s levels. In the 1950s the wealth per person in the West was high enough to reduce substantially infant mortality, but not so high that fertility had already spontaneously declined – indeed, the European population was robustly growing in the 1950s and 1960s, *without significant immigration*. But, as we have seen, there is a strong link between

---

[17] Data adapted from Smil (2008).

[18] To my knowledge, the term 'degrowth' was first used in 1972 by the social philosopher André Gorz. The best known modern proponent of degrowth is probably French economist Serge Latouche. I should also add that the term 'degrowth' is sometimes also used (e.g., by University of London Prof Jason Hickel) not to mean reducing GDP, 'but rather as reducing [energy and resource] throughput'. Much as I find this usage of the term confusing, I have no problem with this specific part of Prof Hickel's position, which is presented in Hickel (2021). Where we differ is that Prof Hickel does not think that a reduction in energy usage 'can be accomplished while continuing to pursue economic growth at the same time'. I think that it is not only possible, but, in Europe at least, it is already happening. Increasing the pace of decarbonization of the economy seems to me a much safer option than embarking on the path of social engineering that real degrowth entails.

fertility levels and GDP per person. Therefore, to keep population from growing (after all, it is total output, not output per person that matters for emissions) some type of one-and-a-half-child policy would have to be imposed.

On top of this, we should not forget that the current population in the West is currently higher than it was in the 1950s.[19] This means that, if we want to go back to a level of *emissions* similar to what we had in the mid 1950s, the energy *per person* would have to be considerably lower than they were at the start of the Trente Glorieuses. Given the close link between energy consumption and well-being that I explore in Section 15.1, this would not bode well for the Western populations that would have to experience degrowth. And I cannot even imagine what the consequences of these transformations for unemployment and for the provision of social services would be – revenues from taxation, after all, would fall dramatically (as they have fallen, in the USA, in the aftermath of all recent economic slow-downs, such as the bursting of the 2001 dot.com bubble, after the 2008 financial crisis, and, of course, after COVID).

Let's nonetheless assume that somehow the West goes back to the level of output it had in the mid 1950s: let's assume, that is, that we have found a socially acceptable way of 'de-growing' the West. Now the Global South has to grow. The question of how the poor regions of the world should now achieve the standard of living of Europe in the 1950s or 1960s remains as unanswered as it is today. It's economic illiteracy to assume that there is a 'fixed amount of growth to go around', and that, just because one region of the world is de-growing, another will automatically take up the slack. In reality, every single developing country that has escaped the clutches of poverty has done so via export-led economic growth (coupled with initial protection of the fledging national industries). Not even China, that has undisputedly become an economic juggernaut, has managed yet to find a way to grow its economy through domestic demand. And the net exports of the countries that

[19] There were 540 million people in Eurpe in 1950. By the end of the twentieth century there were 725 million. Our World in Data, https://ourworldindata.org/world-population-growth-population-growth-by-world-region.

have developed, of course, have been towards the West.[20] Which brings me to the punchline: to whom are the developing countries going to export, if at the same time the West is de-growing?

This is why I believe that economic growth, fuelled by energy availability, is the only route humanity has so far discovered to escape the Malthusian poverty trap. Only once in the history of mankind we seem to have stumbled upon the magic sauce to produce a steady improvement in material conditions per person, and this has been through sustained economic growth. Turning our backs on this unprecedented engine of improvement in the material conditions of living seems to me an extremely dangerous experiment. Perhaps I don't have quite as Panglossian a view of humanity's current condition as Steven Pinker's,[21] but if, behind the proverbial Rawlsian veil of ignorance, I had to choose in which century to be born, I would only have a thirty-second hesitation to choose the twenty-first. And if I were a woman, the time to reach my decision would probably go down to five seconds. Above all, I hope that my grandchildren will choose the twenty-second century as their best 'blind choice'.

Am I looking at reality through rose-tinted glasses? Haven't we been facing in the last decades a period of slowing growth and increasing inequality? Hasn't our standard of living already taken a turn for the worse? Has economic growth, with the attending undeniable costs, stopped lifting the global standards of living and is it just concentrating

---

[20] Things are more nuanced: early-stage development countries may export raw materials to more-developed countries, that then export the finished products to the West. So, some more advanced developing countries may import a lot. After the intermediate flows are cancelled out, however, the big picture does not change: as recently as the 1970s, developing countries were still mainly exporting raw products, to be turned into manufactured goods in the West. By the beginning of the twenty-first century almost 70 per cent of exports from developing countries were manufactures. Krugman and Obstfeld (2004).

[21] I am referring here to Pinker (2018). As for calling Prof Pinker Panglossian, perhaps I am being unfair. In his *Candide*, with the figure of Prof Pangloss Voltaire was not taking aim at the promise of progress that the Enlightenment was offering, but at the religious justification for suffering that goes under the name of theodicy. Prof Pinker is a neo-enlightenment person, not an advocate of theodicy.

wealth in the hands of a small fraction of the population? In the rich West, we may get a perception of economic stagnation, but, if we take a global perspective, the last twenty years have been an impressive success story. The consultancy McKinsey has produced a very interesting study of the improvement in material conditions over the last twenty years, and has taken the analysis to an unusually granular level.[22] The opening sentence of their report sets the tone: 'By 2019 3.5 billion people, close to half of the world's population, lived in microregions with living standards equivalent to the top 21 percent in 2000.' The report then shows the robustness and near-universality of the (positive) relationship between life expectancy and real GDP per capita, and that both these basic indicators of well-being have grown in the vast majority of microregions. At an aggregate level, in the year 2000 the median GDP per capita was $3,728 and the median life expectancy 69.8 years; by 2019 the same quantities were $9,511 and 73.7 years: four extra years of life and almost three times as much income. In the year 2000, 30 per cent of the population lived on $2,400 per year or less and could only expect to live sixty-five years. By 2019 the fraction of the population in the same income/life expectancy bracket had shrunk to 5 per cent. At the opposite end of the spectrum, the same combination of life expectancy and GDP per capita enjoyed in the year 2000 by the top 1 per cent of the population was by 2019 achieved by 6 per cent of the population. On a global scale, the last twenty years have been 'a miracle of widespread growth' in health and income.[23]

Having said this, it cannot be denied that this prolonged growth has already caused significant stresses on our planet, and that these stresses seem very likely to increase greatly.[24] The most pressing question

---

[22] Bradley et al. (2022).

[23] This generalized increase in material well-being is, in principle, compatible with a growth in inequality: each microregion could be getting richer, but the wealth in each could be more and more unevenly distributed. To what extent this is the case, and in which parts of the world this happened, is the main research concern of an economist such as Piketty – see Piketty(2014, 2020).

[24] Are the stresses associated with continuous growth sustainable in the long run? See in this respect the discussion in Section 17.4.

is therefore how economic growth can be achieved without inflicting irreparable collateral damage on the planet, and in the most cost-efficient way. It is to this all-important question that we begin to turn in the next chapter, where we look at what 'modern' economic modelling has to say on the matter.

CHAPTER 12

So, What Should We Do?

[P]rudent archers [...] set their aim much farther than the place they intend to reach [...] not to attain such height with the strength of their arrows, but to be able with the aid of so high an aim to reach their goal.[1]

—N. Machiavelli, *The Prince*

WE ARE FINALLY COMING TO WHAT IS, arguably, one of the most important chapters of the book: the chapter where we compare and contrast the policy recommendations of the original DICE model, and the recommendations that we obtain when a more satisfactory treatment of our psychological drivers of choice is employed. (For simplicity I will call in this chapter the two modelling approaches the 'original' and the 'modern' version of the DICE model.)[2] I stress again that, when I speak of a more satisfactory treatment of our psychological drivers, I don't mean that a certain degree of aversion to uneven consumption is self-evidently more psychologically plausible than another. I simply mean a treatment of preferences that recovers stylized facts about investment returns – the returns, that is, against which the investment in abatement has to be pitted.

For obvious reasons of familiarity and ease of access, I will report in this chapter the results obtained by my research team using what I have called the modern approach. In part these are obtained using our own models,

---

[1] 'E fare come gli arceri prudenti, e quali prendono el loco dove disegnano ferire troppo lontono e conoscendo fino a quanto va la virtú del loro arco, pongono la mira assai piú alta che il loco destinato, non per raggiungere con la loro freccia tanta altezza, ma per poter con l'aiuto di sí alta mira pervenire al disegno loro...', Machaivelli, 2006, page 18.
[2] Henceforth, modern; no scare quotes.

and in part reproducing results presented in the literature. A precise comparison of the results obtained by different versions of the modern models would entail too detailed a discussion. However, the qualitative conclusions presented in what follows are shared by all the studies that have used non-time-separable (modern) utility functions, as long as the same preference parameters and the same climate models are used.[3]

As we shall see, the results we obtain using the modern approach are very different from the results of the original DICE model. I must stress once again, however, that the reason for these differences is *not* that we have changed the original DICE model assumptions about how the world works. It would have come as little surprise, for instance, if we had made the damage function more severe, and found that, as a consequence of this, we should abate more. This would not have been very surprising, and is not what we have done. Instead in the studies we have carried out using the modern approach, the 'central locations' of the original parameter values in the DICE model – the values, that is, that have sometimes been so robustly challenged by its critics – have not been shifted with respect to the original version: they have simply been replaced by distributions of values centred around the same expectation.[4] So, for instance, Fig 12.1 shows that, if the DICE model assumed a value of 2 for the damage exponent (shown in the figure by a vertical line), in the modern version we have not used a higher value, but we have simply acknowledged that, given our present state of knowledge, its true value could plausibly have the distribution of values shown by the continuous line – a distribution that implies that the most likely values lie somewhere between 1.25 and 2.75.

As I said, despite the fact that we have not changed the central estimates for any of the DICE parameters, we obtain very different

---

[3] See, e.g., Jensen and Traeger (2014), Bansal, Kiku and Ochoa (2019), Rudik (2020), Daniel, Litterman and Wagner (2019), and references therein. The biggest variations among studies are in the social cost of carbon, which is very sensitive to input parameters and numerically delicate to calculate.

[4] This does not mean that we believe that the central estimates of the original DICE model are perfect – and, we are sure, neither does Prof Nordhaus. We simply want to distinguish between different policy recommendations stemming from better modelling of the 'physics' of the problem – an on-going task – and different policies coming from a better modelling of our preferences.

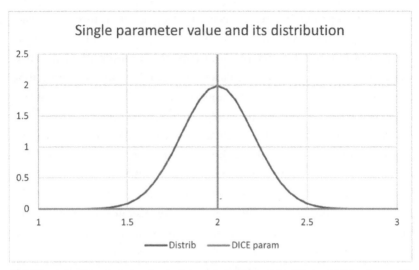

12.1 How a single parameter value in the original DICE model (the vertical line for $x = 2$) is replaced by a full possible distribution of values (the bell-shaped line) *still centred around 2*. In the modern version thousands of values for the parameter are sampled, each with a probability proportional to the height of the bell curve. The spread of the bell curve, and the shape of the bell curve itself, are purely indicative, and the actual model uses a more sophisticated statistical approach.

results. How can this happen? Because we are now able to describe in a much more convincing way our preferences, and preferences acquire a lot more 'bite' when there is uncertainty. This improved modelling then produces different results through two channels: first, given the empirically defensible degree of uncertainty we have introduced, our aversion to static risk can finally kick in (risk aversion can play no role in the original DICE model, because everything is assumed to be known with certainty). And, since we can now disentangle risk aversion from dislike for uneven consumption, we can use a realistically high degree of risk aversion – a degree of risk aversion, that is, that can account for such basic facts in asset pricing as the return from equities – without implying that we have an extremely high aversion to unequal consumption. I have explained why being able to do so is important.

It is important to pause briefly on this point. In his very good book on adaptation to climate change, MIT Prof Robert Pindyck stresses how little we know about the damage function – the function, that is, that translates a given degree of warming into economic damage. First he makes the very valid point that '[t]here is no economic (or other) theory that can tell us what the loss function [..] should look like'.[5] He also despairs that empirical analysis can tell us much about economic damages for temperatures much higher than what we have experienced to date. I am a tad more optimistic, but the analogy I presented in Section 8.1 about the doctor who tries to extrapolate how her patient will feel with a raging fever by observing how much worse he feels today, when his temperature has climbed to 37.5 °C, makes the same point. He also adds that '[i]t may well turn out that over the coming decades climate change and its impact will be mild to moderate. [...] But we are not certain that the outcome will be so favorable. There is a possibility of an extremely unfavorable outcome, one that we would call *catastrophic*.'[6] I fully agree with this as well. From this, however, he concludes that '[t]he IAMs [Integrated Assessment Models] and related models that have been used to estimate the Social Cost of Carbon have little or nothing to tell us about such outcomes.'[7]

It is on this point that I have a different perspective. Perhaps Prof Pindyck's irrelevance claim may have been valid for the early-generation models, such as the first incarnations of the DICE model, in which there was no room for uncertainty, everything was deterministic, *and risk aversion was therefore not allowed to play any role*. But we have come a very long way from these early modelling efforts. Today we can model both the fact that we know so little about damages, *and* that we really do not like being so uncertain about something so important. The very fact that we are so uncertain can substantially change our optimal policy and the social cost of carbon. Not for nothing, after all, one of the key economic quantities that determine how much we should invest in the face of uncertainty goes under the name of 'prudence', which mixes dislike for static risk and for uneven consumption. With the DICE model, Prof Nordhaus did not try to give us the final answer to an extremely difficult question, but showed the modelling direction following which more satisfactory answers can be arrived at.

---

[5] Pindyck (2022), page 70.
[6] Pindyck (2022), page 71. Emphasis in the original.
[7] Ibid. Similar views are articulated in Pindyck (2022).

In itself, modelling properly the radical uncertainty about damages and our aversion to this uncertainty is certainly important. Being able to do so is a great advantage of the new-generation models. However, it is our degree of aversion to feast and famine that does most of the heavy lifting in shifting the abatement burden back towards today. If we don't 'mind that much' that our grandchildren will probably be so much richer than we are, we will accept a greater abatement burden today. And, again, we can only use a low aversion to feast and famine *and* a high degree of risk aversion thanks to the flexibility (and empirical realism) of the modern approach. Taken together, these two features give rise to the radically different policy recommendations presented in what follows.

12.1 HOW MUCH AND HOW QUICKLY SHOULD WE ABATE?

Before presenting more detailed results, an important qualification is in order. The goal of any Integrated Assessment Model is to produce an optimal course of action to tackle the climate-change problem. Suppose for a moment that we can put to one side all the reservations about the optimality of this policy. How should it be implemented? Who, in particular, would have the power to enforce it? Now, we have already discussed the free-rider situation that plagues the climate-change problem: as we have seen, everybody finds that it is rationally optimal not to abate in the hope that everyone else will – and, as a result, nobody does. When the rational choices of each agent fail to bring about the best solution (and the agents understand that this is the case), very often the rational agents themselves invoke the intervention of a co-ordinator – say, the state, or a regulator.[8] The problem with climate change is that, because of the *local* cost of abatement but of the *global* effects of a rise in temperature, the co-ordinator would have to have supranational powers, and one such

[8] As an interesting example, in the run-up to the 2008 subprime crisis, Citigroup CEO, Chuck Prince, asked his regulator to do something to stop him (and his competitors) from pursuing the subprime business model. He understood full well that it was all going to end in tears, but he also understood that if his firm, single-handedly, had stopped engaging in the subprime business, however toxic, Citgroup would have suffered, and its competitors (briefly) benefitted. Asking for a co-ordinator to step in and curb his actions (and those of his competitors) was the rational thing to do. Alas, his pleas went unheeded.

entity is nowhere close to having been found. Therefore, the 'optimal' policies that we shall discuss are those that an omniscient, benevolent and all-powerful social planner would enact. The problem of how an approximation to this social planner can be found is different, and its solution really difficult – we shall park this problem for the moment.

Keeping this proviso in mind, let's get started. A key quantity returned by Integrated Assessment Models is the optimal fraction of economic output produced without CO_2 emissions. I shall often refer to this fraction as the abatement schedule, and denote it by the symbol μ. A fraction close to 1 means that the economy is almost fully decarbonized. A value for the abatement function of, say, 0.4 means that, along the optimal path, we should cut 40 per cent of the emissions that we would produce if we did not have to worry about climate change. So, the curves in Figs 12.2 and 12.3 are really key to understanding the results.[9] Let's look at them in some detail.

Let's start from the first figure. The two curves in Fig 12.2 show the 'gradualist' (and much criticized) pace of abatement recommended by the original DICE model (bottom curve) and the much more aggressive schedule recommended by the modern approach (the upper curve). According to the original version of the DICE model, we would be better off waiting until the end of the century to be 80 per cent decarbonized. The modern approach recommends that 80 per cent decarbonization should occur in less than forty years' time. The difference is dramatic, and the abatement schedule recommended as optimal by the modern approach is at least as aggressive as the most ambitious current abatement pledges (remember that we are talking of the decarbonization of the *whole* economy, not just of the easy bits, such as electricity provision).

What about the abatement schedule suggested in the Stern review – an abatement schedule that, as we have seen, required a 'saintly' degree of intergenerational altruism? The results obtained with original DICE, the modern DICE and the Stern model are shown in Fig 12.3. Admittedly, the Stern model recommends a more aggressive abatement schedule, especially in the early years, but the big differences are between the

---

[9] To be precise, the industrial emissions, e_{ind} are modelled in DICE as
$e_{ind} = \sigma \times y_{gross} \times (1 - \mu)$, where σ is the carbon intensity, y_{gross} is the pre-damage, pre-abatement output, and μ is the abatement fraction.

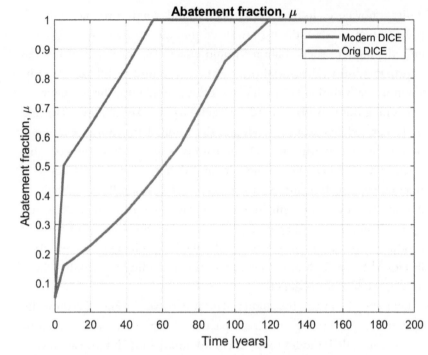

12.2 The abatement schedules suggested by the original DICE model (bottom line, labelled 'Orig DICE'), and by the modern approach (top line, labelled 'Modern DICE'). Time in years on the x axis.

schedule recommended by the original DICE model and the top two lines. After the first five to ten years, the differences between the Stern and the modern DICE curves are of the same order of magnitude as the model uncertainty. So, in essence, the Stern and the modern DICE approaches convey a similar qualitative message: abate as much and as fast as you can practically and politically achieve.

What happens to emissions with the original and the modern DICE models? The curves labelled 'Orig DICE' and 'Modern DICE' tell the story (we shall examine the third curve separately). With the original DICE model emissions only start falling in some forty years' time, and do so at a rather leisurely pace (remember that this is not a prediction, it is a recommendation). The modern version of the DICE model tells a very different story: it recommends very prompt abatement action with emissions falling in five years' time from the current 38 Gt/year to little

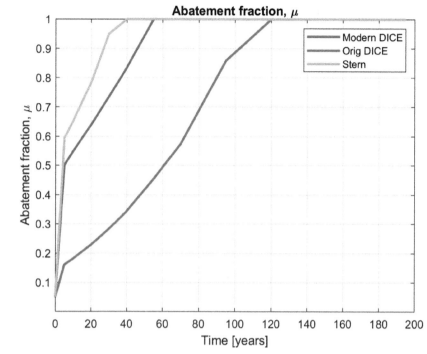

12.3 The abatement schedules suggested by the original DICE model (bottom line, labelled 'Orig DICE'), by the modern approach (middle line, labelled 'Modern DICE'), and with the degree of impatience implied by the Stern report (top line, labelled 'Stern'). Time in years on the x axis.

more than 20 Gt/year. Again, this is derived as an optimal policy, not as a prediction. The problem is that, while it may be technologically possible to achieve such drastic cuts in emissions, it is difficult to project such an inversion of current trends (emissions, recall, after the short COVID-induced blip, are still going up). This means that, as we move from the theoretical recommendations of an economics model to what we can actually do, we find ourselves in a policy tight spot: the original DICE policy looks more plausible as a prediction, but it implies a worryingly high rise in temperature; the modern DICE gives much more desirable climate outcomes, but, as a prediction looks definitely implausible – how implausible, is shown in Fig 12.4, which displays the historical pattern of emissions up to 2021, and the emissions consistent with the recommendations of the modern DICE. We shall revisit this point when we look at optimal policies with negative emissions.

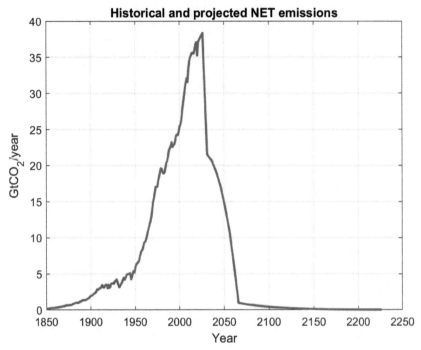

12.4 The historical CO_2 emissions up to 2021 and the emission schedule recommended as optimal by the modern DICE model.

Let's park these reservations to one side, and let's continue with our analysis of what the old and modern DICE models recommend we should do. Another very important observation is that the optimal temperature increase that we can 'afford' is very different in the original DICE model and in its modern version, *despite the fact that the expectation of the temperature exponent that translates temperature increases into damages – 2 in the DICE model – has remained the same.* As Fig 12.5 shows, with original DICE model we should be willing to tolerate temperature increases by the end of the century as high as 3 °C. Depending on the exact calibration, the modern approach can easily suggest for the optimal allowable temperature increase by the end of the century a value just a shade lower than 2 °C, and therefore (just) within the the IPCC target of 1.5–2 °C by the end of the century.[10] For comparison, the Stern model produces a temperature

[10] The exact value depends on the precise choice of parameters, but it is always considerably lower than the temperature increase by end of the century predicted by the original DICE model.

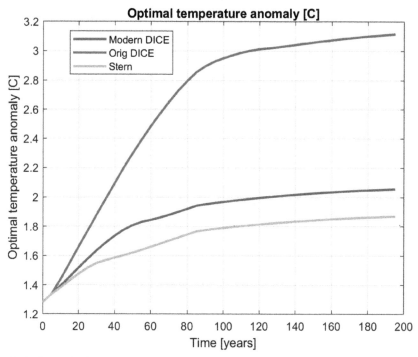

12.5 The optimal temperature anomaly as obtained using the original DICE model (bottom line, labelled 'Orig DICE'), the modern approach (middle line, labelled 'Modern DICE'), and with the degree of impatience implied by the Stern report (top line, labelled 'Stern'). Time in years on the *x* axis.

profile just slightly below the modern approach (again, well within model error). This means that we do not need to make the damage exponent on average more severe than it is in the DICE model,[11] nor do we have to assume an extreme degree of intergenerational altruism, in order to

---

[11] Howard and Sterner (2017) have recently proposed a damage function that still retains the quadratic dependence on temperature found in the DICE model, and still recovers roughly the same damages for the temperature increases observed so far, but estimates a slightly different proportionality coefficient (the parameter a_2 in the formula *damages* $= a_2 T^{a_3}$). The methodology they use to estimate these parameters is in essence the same as the one used by Nordhaus in the original calibration of the DICE model. Horner and Sterner have simply availed themselves of more recent and more plentiful data. In the results we report, we centre the damage exponent around the DICE (and Horner and Sterner) value of 2, but we use the slightly more severe proportionality coefficient estimated by Horner and Sterner. We stress that we do *not* use the much more severe damage function that Horner and Sterner calibrate to mimic the effect of tipping points.

obtain a much lower optimal temperature increase: we mainly have to disentangle risk aversion and dislike for feast and famine.

This is important. The 1.5–2 °C temperature target is not just any target, but it is the target that was enshrined in the Paris Accord, and that has since assumed almost talismanic value. Does it really matter whether this target can be shown to be, not just aspirational, but optimal? On the one hand, every scientist agrees that this target is not some hard limit, buttressed by precise scientific calculations. As Harvard's Dr Schrag points out, as far as we currently know, there is no cliff either side of the 1.5–2 °C interval. In his words, '1.5 °C is not safe and 2.2 °C is not the end of the world'. What we *do* know is that 1.6 is safer than 1.7, and 2.2 safer than 2.3.[12] And, in any case, I would be willing to bet a considerable amount of money that most politicians would be hard-pressed to answer the question: '1.5–2 °C exactly above what?' Answering this question is not straightforward, because, as my colleague Kainth (2021) writes, indeed, the 2015 'Paris COP21 Agreement (United Nations 2015) makes reference to "pre-industrial levels". However, there is no formal definition of what is meant by "pre-industrial" in the UNFCCC / Paris Agreement.' Kainth (2022) then adds: 'Rather confusingly, in the definition of the Equilibrium Climate Sensitivity (ECS) the radiative forcing in 1750 is used as a zero-forcing baseline. Ideally, 'pre-industrial period' should represent the mean climate state just before human activities started to demonstrably change the climate through combustion of fossil fuels. Practically speaking, combined global land and ocean data is only available since 1850 as part of the HadCRUT5 dataset. Hence, the IPCC AR5 made a pragmatic choice to reference global temperature to the mean of 1850–1900 period when assessing the time at which particular temperature levels would be crossed.'

All of this may well be true, and an uncompromising rationalist may conclude that obsessing on this round-number target as if it were the be-all and end-all of climate control does not make a lot of sense. The fact, however, remains that the 1.5–2 °C target *has* become a universally recognized policy reference point, and that it *has* become part of the political

---

[12] Quoted in *The Economist* (December 2022, www.economist.com/interactive/briefing/2022/11/05/the-world-is-going-to-miss-the-totemic-1-5c-climate-target).

discourse. This has value in itself. Clear and simple targets, especially if expressible in numbers, and even more especially if in round numbers, *do* serve a useful role. If we tell ourselves that we want to do 100 push-ups per day, we are much more likely to succeed than if we just decide that push-ups are good for us, and we should do lots of them – the more the better. It is therefore important that the results which we obtain using the modern approach give a solid model justification for the Paris Agreement target, which at the time had been roundly criticized by economists for being 'arbitrary' and 'pulled out of a hat'. This is no mean feat, because it may encourage European policymakers to re-engage with DICE-like Integrated Assessment Models, on which they had turned their backs when they were giving optimal end-of-century temperature targets of 3 or 4 °C.

12.2 OPTIMAL POLICIES WITH NEGATIVE EMISSIONS

So far we have only looked at optimal policies when the main lever at our disposal was how much to abate – in practice, how much of the required energy should be produced without emitting CO_2 in the atmosphere. How would these policies change if we allowed direct removal of CO_2? We shall look at technological and political aspects of negative emissions in some detail in the next chapter. We shall have a lot to say (in favour and against) about their desirability, but, for the moment, let's just look at the policy implications of adding carbon removal to our toolbox from the perspective of a rational and politically unencumbered policymaker.

Fig 12.6 shows three curves: the optimal abatement schedule obtained with the original DICE approach (bottom line, labelled 'Orig DICE'), with modern approach coupled with negative emissions (middle line, labelled 'Negem') and with the modern DICE model (top line, labelled 'Modern DICE') without negative emissions. So, the first observation is that, when removal of CO_2 is allowed, the rate of abatement is indeed faster than that suggested by the original DICE model, but considerably slower than what the modern DICE version without negative emissions recommends. Yet, as Fig 12.7 shows, the optimal temperature path with negative emissions still remains within the 1.5–2 °C target by the end of the century, *and then significantly declines*, back to values marginally below today's warming. How is this possible?

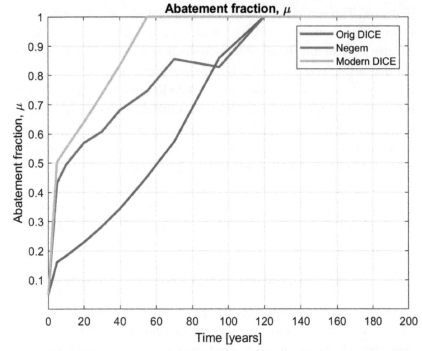

12.6 The optimal abatement schedule obtained with the 'original' DICE approach (bottom line, labelled 'Orig DICE'), with modern approach coupled with negative emissions (middle line, labelled 'Negem') and with the modern DICE model (top line, labelled 'Modern DICE') for the number of years from today shown on the x axis.

Fig 12.8 tells the story: the line labelled 'Modern DICE' shows the optimal emissions if we can only abate – note that the reduction is very fast, because there is nothing else that we can do to control climate-induced damages. The line labelled 'Negem DICE' then shows the optimal emissions if we can both abate and remove carbon. The initial abatement is somewhat slower, because the policymaker knows that she can make up for the slower pace of abatement by removing carbon in the near-to-medium future. (In the real world, this is not without dangers. We shall look at the important considerations of moral hazard in the next chapter.)

Another important observation is that, as Fig 12.8 shows, by the end of the century we should be removing very large amounts of CO_2 – not much less than we are emitting now. These recommendations have been obtained using the best available estimates of present and future

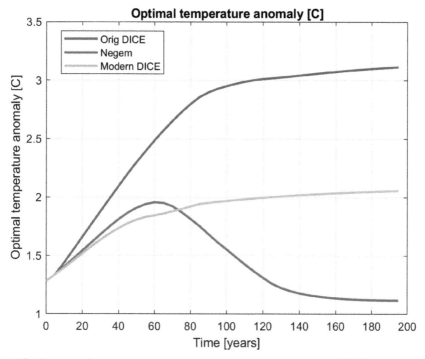

12.7 The optimal temperature anomaly as obtained using the 'original' DICE approach (bottom line, labelled 'Orig DICE'), the modern approach coupled with negative emissions (middle line, labelled 'Negem') and the modern DICE model (top line, labelled 'Modern DICE') for the number of years from today shown on the x axis.

marginal costs of abatement and removal – so these large removed amount make good economic sense from the perspective of a cost-benefit analysis. Our models do not know, however, about practical considerations such as 'Where shall we put the stuff?' We must therefore discuss in Chapter 13 both the technological and logistical (storage) challenges that this entails.

Looking at Fig 12.9, which shows the pace of carbon removal, we also notice that carbon removal starts very slowly, and really takes off after mid-century. Why this delay? If carbon removal is so effective, why is it not starting right away? It all boils down to the relative *marginal* costs of removal and abatement. A *marginal* cots, as we have discussed, is the cost of removing or not emitting the last ton of CO_2. As we shall see in Chapter 13, only two negative emission technologies (afforestation and bioenergy with carbon sequestration and storage) are currently deployable in scale

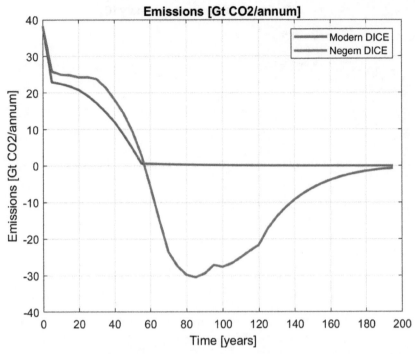

12.8 The optimal emissions (in Gt CO_2/annum) with abatement only (curve labelled 'Modern DICE') and with abatement and negative emissions (curve labelled 'Negem DICE'), for the number of years from today shown on the x axis.

at a reasonable cost. Unfortunately, they both strongly compete for land, and therefore have hard implementation limits. If we try to plant too many trees or to grow too much biomass for burning, the opportunity costs of these carbon-removal technologies (what else we could do with the land – such as growing edible stuff) quickly increase. With serious land competition, food prices soon begin to increase rapidly. And as for the other negative emission technologies that have been proposed, they are somewhere between an early deployment stage and the drawing board. We count (don't forget the magic of the increasing total factor of production) on their costs to fall, but this is expected to be some considerable time in the future.

This is why for the best part of the twenty-first century the marginal cost curve for carbon removal is above the same curve for abatement. This does not mean, however, that we should only focus on reducing emissions. After the low- and middle-hanging abatement fruits have been

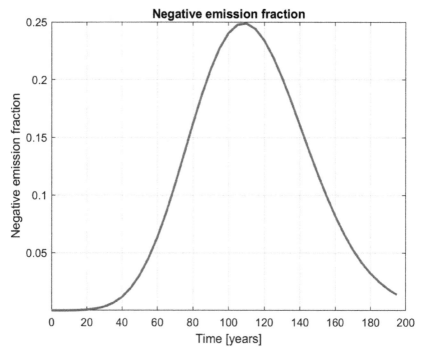

12.9 The pace of carbon removal, as illustrated by the negative-emission fraction. Time in years on the x axis.

picked, the abatement costs climb rapidly, and it can become more convenient to deal with the next ton of CO_2 by removing it. For details on how the modern model has been calibrated to the IPCC marginal costs, see Rebonato, Kainth, Melin and O'Kane (2023).

And, to conclude, devoting a significant part of our resources not just to abating emissions, but also to removing carbon, can ease the stresses inevitably associated with changing rapidly the way our whole economy is structured. See, in this respect, the discussion in Section 12.2. These positive features must be weighed against the risks of moral hazard – of relying, that is, on future removal too much, and slackening our abatement effort. This is why it has been argued that we should have separate accounting targets for emission reduction and negative emissions.[13] Yes, it is true that, from the theoretical standpoint of an

---

[13] See, for instance, the policy brief article by *Frontiers*, available at www.frontiersin.org/articles/10.3389/fclim.2019.00004/full. While I agree with the review that a separate

economic model populated by rational agents, a ton of CO_2 removed is exactly equivalent to a ton not emitted. This equivalence, however, ceases to be true in our sub-lunar world. For a non-technical discussion of these topics, see my article in https://theconversation.com/forget-net-zero-to-halt-global-heating-aim-for-net-negative-195484.

12.3 THE SOCIAL COST OF CARBON

What about the social cost of carbon – the compensation, that is, for the unpaid climate damage inflicted on future generations? An intuitive way to think about emission externalities is to think of a 'carbon tax' paid by us and our children as a tool to redress the damage inflicted on third parties (later generations) by our carbon emissions. Once again, the tax is not meant to 'punish' anybody (as the commonly used term 'sin tax' suggests): for better or for worse, there is no moralism in economics. The tax simply distributes effectively across generations economic pain – a pain that takes into account, among other things, how rich, and hence able to shoulder the levy, the successive future generations are expected to be. So, in principle, the size of the optimal carbon tax is one of the most important quantities to be derived from economic analysis – indeed, if you read the academic literature on the subject, you sometimes get the impression that it is the only quantity that matters.

Now, if the idea of a carbon tax may well be loved by economists, it does not enjoy a similar popularity amongst voters (and hence politicians). In the eloquent words of Robinson Meyer (2021)

> [t]he carbon tax aimed to reduce carbon-dioxide pollution [...] by apply-ing a commonsense idea: If you don't want people to do something, charge them money for it. [...] Such a cost would have percolated through the economy, raising gasoline and jet-fuel prices, closing coal-fired power plants, and encouraging consumers and companies to adopt cleaner forms of energy. It was a straightforward, perhaps even beautiful, idea – a bid to apply the economic precepts of the 19th century to one of the great prob-lems of the 21st. Its poise was matched by its elite support. The carbon tax

accounting for emissions and removal can make good political and psychological sense, I hasten to add that I do not concur with many of the points there raised.

won acclaim from self-described socialists and red-blooded libertarians, Democratic senators and Republican secretaries of state, Elon Musk and Janet Yellen. It was a particular favorite of the economics profession. Some 3,589 economists once declared it 'the most cost-effective lever to reduce carbon emissions'; in 2018, it helped William Nordhaus, a Yale professor and the author of several books about the policy, win the Nobel Prize in Economics.

We will come back to the political fortunes of this perhaps-even-beautiful idea. For the moment, let's just recall that the social cost of carbon recommended by the original DICE approach was of the order of $40 per ton, rising sharply to well over $500 per ton in 150 years' time. This is the line labelled 'DICE orig' in Fig 12.10.[14] Contrast this with the social cost of carbon obtained with the modern version of the DICE model, as shown in the curve labelled 'DICE modern'. The optimal carbon tax *today* is always higher (considerably so, in a range centred around $150), but it peaks much earlier than for the original version of the model, and then declines.[15] The reason why the modern version of the DICE model obtains a much earlier maximum for the carbon tax is that, thanks to its much more robust abatement schedule, by the end of the century the economy has been fully decarbonized, the temperature has stopped rising, and the climate-change problem is under control. A high carbon tax is therefore no longer needed.

All models agree that our children should pay a higher tax than we do – simply because they are expected to be richer, and therefore better able to foot the bill. However, as we have seen, the simplistic utility function used in the original DICE model is forced to imply a very high degree of

[14] As a side remark, the DICE model has been criticized for suggesting too low a social cost of carbon. This may well be true. However, let's not forget that the 'low' DICE social cost of carbon is way higher that the carbon taxes that have been applied to date. Similarly, as my friend Prof Shefrin points out in his recent *Unsettling Behaviors: The Behavioral Economics and Politics of Global Warming*, the optimal abatement schedule suggested by the DICE model more than fifteen years ago may be lower than the recommendations given by the modern approach. However, if we had started heeding its 'over-moderate' prescriptions back in the mid-1980s, we would be in a much better place than we find ourselves now.

[15] The traditional DICE social cost of carbon eventually declines as well, but the decline starts much later, and is not visible over the time scale displayed in the graph.

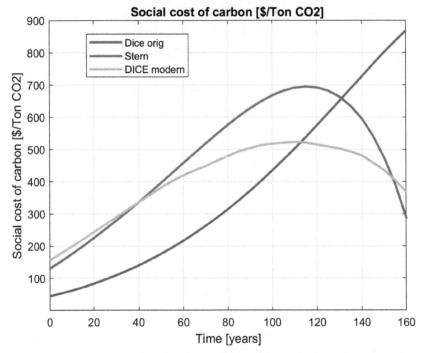

12.10 The social cost of carbon (in $ per ton of CO_2 emissions) for different times (in years) from 'today' recommended by different versions of the DICE model – see the text for a discussion. The curve labelled 'DICE orig' shows the social cost of carbon obtained with the original (deterministic) DICE model. The curve labelled 'Stern' shows the same quantity obtained with a version of the DICE model calibrated to be roughly equivalent to the Stern model. The curve labelled 'DICE modern' shows the social cost of carbon recommended by the modern version of the DICE model.

aversion to uneven consumption for a reasonable degree of risk aversion, and therefore puts a much greater burden on the shoulders of our richer descendants. As a consequence, the current carbon tax recommended by the old approach is much lower than that obtained when risk aversion is disentangled from aversion to uneven consumption, as the modern DICE models can do.

It is also very interesting to look at the social cost of carbon recommended by a Stern-like modelling approach. As one can see, it is reasonably similar to the carbon tax obtained with the modern DICE approach. However, as I have pointed out many times, it is 'right for the wrong reasons': because it makes very debatable modelling choices about preferences whose effects serendipitously almost cancel each other out. As we know well by now, these choices are that, on the one hand, the Stern modelling implies a high aversion to uneven consumption (a dislike that makes the observed market prices of equities and bonds a mystery); on the other hand it says that we should have an extremely high degree of altruism (so high, that, barring the possibility of extinction, we should consider the welfare of human beings many centuries in the future *exactly* as relevant to our decisions as our own welfare). Do these blemishes matter, if the answer is in the end in the right ballpark? Yes, they do, because if the modelling assumptions are difficult to defend, then the whole approach becomes a dead end: we have to 'sit tight' with the results that we have 'accidentally' obtained (and that can only be corroborated by using a more satisfactory approach), but we cannot ask the model to answer other questions, for which the lucky cancellation of errors may no longer occur.

I stress that the curve I have labelled 'DICE modern' is actually an average of the curves obtained with different model assumptions (such as the degree of uncertainty in the the Total Factor of Production or in the damage exponent). As Fig 12.11 clearly shows, there are significant variations among these model versions, but the qualitative behaviour remains the same: the social cost of carbon today is always (much) higher than for the original DICE model, and peaks much earlier. It is then a good exam question for my course on the economics of climate change to ask for an explanation of the detailed behaviour of the various curves. For our purposes, we don't have to go into this level of detail. The important message is that the much higher cost of carbon obtained with the modern approach implies that there now are many more abatement initiatives that make economic sense *today*: these are those that would cost more then \$40 per ton of CO_2 removed (the carbon tax obtained with the original DICE model), but less than approximately \$150.[16] The difference in the recommended carbon tax is very significant, and it explains why the original DICE model basically said 'Don't rush into abatement now, you would be wasting a lot of money', while the modern

---

[16] In an efficient market, an emitter faced with a tax of X dollars per ton of CO_2 emitted would consider all options (such as using carbon sequestration and storage or switching to a different energy source) that cost up to $X - \epsilon$ dollars before emitting the same ton of CO_2.

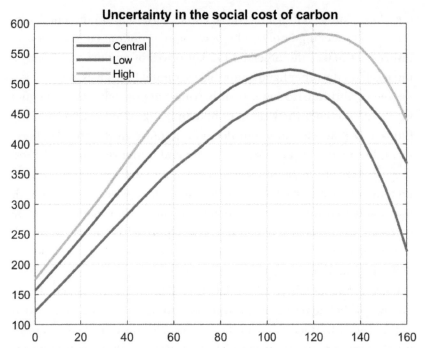

12.11 The dispersion of the social cost of carbon (in $ per ton of CO_2 emissions) for different times (in years) from 'today' recommended by different versions of the modern DICE model. The curves labelled 'High' and 'Low' show the highest and lowest estimates over different choices of how uncertain we are about the Total Factor of Production and in the damage exponent. The curve labelled 'Central' shows the equally weighted average over all these different estimates.

approach makes a case for immediate action. Note that, at around $150/ton, even some *removal* options are worth the cost *today*. Which means that, whether we like it or not, if the time is out of joint, it is up to us and to our children (not their grandchildren) to set it right.

12.3.1 ARE ESTIMATES OF THE CARBON TAX TOO IMPRECISE TO BE OF USE?. A recurring objection to these estimates of the social cost of carbon is that they are very sensitive to the choice of parameters (Fig 12.11 shows that these critics do have a point) and, as a consequence, too imprecise to be of practical use. We may all agree, these critics say, that the carbon tax should be higher than that suggested by the early DICE model; but how much higher?

Given the range of values suggested by the modern approach, my pragmatic answer is 'As high as the electorate can bear': given political constraints, the danger of overshooting (of applying, that is, too high a carbon tax) is, for all intents and purposes, zero.

Let me be clear: no abatement initiatives with a cost anywhere close to $150 per ton of carbon removed are currently undertaken. Perhaps the estimates produced by (our version) of the DICE model are too high. But all researchers who have worked with the modern version of DICE-like models agree that the carbon tax should be considerably higher than what the original DICE model recommends – and, in any case, there currently are many abatement options with a cost of less than even the original DICE $40 per ton that are not actively undertaken. We can therefore begin worrying whether we are abating too much when we reach the grey area approximately spanned by the three curves in Fig 12.11. As the saying goes, that would be a nice problem to have, and we have a long way to go before we encounter it.

12.3.2 How Important Is the Social Cost of Carbon?. How important is determining the 'right' social cost of carbon? Normatively, extremely so. If we lived in a world populated by rational and well informed human beings it would perhaps be the single most important quantity an Integrated Assessment Model can return. To make sure we get the solution 'just right', we could then argue about the precise details of the modelling approach (of the physics and of our preferences). However, in a rational world, we would all agree that this is *the* quantity we would want to nail down. Alas, this is where rational and well-informed human beings collide with political reality. As I have already discussed, levying petrol taxes a small fraction of their optimal value has proven extremely difficult, and sometimes politically suicidal.[17] It will therefore

---

[17] A carbon tax is the solution favoured by economists (and has been backed by environmentalists and scientists), but has been deeply unpopular with the electorate. As Robinson Meyer recently wrote in *The Atlantic*, a carbon tax 'could not overcome its enduring unpopularity with the American public, [and] died last month at its home in Washington, D.C. It was 47. The death was confirmed by President Joe Biden's utter lack of interest in passing it. [...] The American carbon tax leaves behind dozens of supportive think-tank employees, thousands of politically engaged and idealistic Americans, and 3,589 dejected economists.'

come to little surprise for the politically astute reader to learn that the global average tax on carbon is \$3 per ton.[18] In reality, politicians have realized that they have to shift the cost of paying for the abatement from the voting-poll-visiting consumers onto agents who cannot kick them out of office as easily – such as the emitting corporations.[19] Whether this is the most efficient way of levying the carbon tax could be debated at length, but it doesn't change the size of the optimal tax – which is what the social cost of carbon calculation tells us. And the two practical messages are clear: first, that the level of taxation should be high enough to create a serious disincentive to using fossil fuels; second, that, if a direct carbon tax levied on consumers is unworkable, subsidies and production taxes are the next-best tools. Let's look at some of these topics.

12.4 CARBON TAXES AND CARBON SUBSIDIES

In an ideal world, populated by rational and homogeneously wealthy individuals that would approve of a carbon tax, there is little doubt that governments should impose substantial taxes on fossil fuels – this is what the social cost of carbon is all about. In reality, the use of fossil fuel is currently heavily *subsidized*, with subsidies taking the form of production subsidies (to reduce the cost of producing coal, oil or gas), or consumption subsidies. Fig 12.12 shows the global consumption subsidies between 2010 and 2021 – note, incidentally, the sharp increase in the aftermath of the COVID crisis.

Since the production of fossil-fuel-generated energy should be taxed, not subsidized, the half-a-trillion dollars spent globally to reduce the cost of fossil fuels at the point of consumption sounds like murder most foul. And, indeed, we are not short of pledges by the G7 and G20 countries that fossil-fuel subsidies should be removed as a matter of priority. However, the subsidy problem is actually complex, and far from painless to address. Now, it is true that the persistence of the subsidy problem *is* in part due

---

[18] Parry (2021). There are local exceptions to this: Canada, for instance, has announced that its emission price will climb to CAN\$170/ton by 2030. (*Ibid*).

[19] The lobbying power of some industry sectors, and the clout they have in the legislative process, should by no means be underestimated. There are no 'easy targets' for the abatement-minded politicians. See also the comments in footnote 22 of Chapter 3.

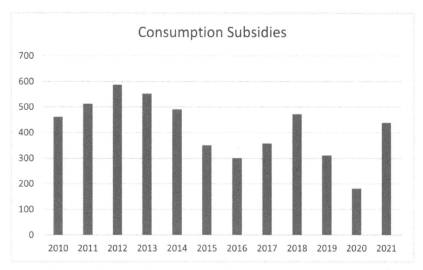

12.12 The worldwide fossil fuel consumption subsidies between 2010 and 2021 (in $bln). Data: International Energy Agency, 2021.

to the political pressure from fossil-fuel companies, that are powerful lobbyists. And, in part, it is also true that governments pursue energy-cost control policies out of fear that high energy prices can depress economic growth and stoke inflation. However, production subsidies also protect jobs in very vulnerable sections of the workforce. As we have discussed, even if, overall, new jobs would be created in the production of cleaner energy, the pain and the social tensions on the transformation path should not be underestimated. As for removing consumption subsidies, we must remember that high energy prices tend to inflict a disproportionate pain on the poorest sections of the population. Even in a country as rich as the UK, an increase in energy bills of £600 would mean that the poorest 10 per cent of households would see their energy spend rise from 8.5 per cent to 12 per cent of their total household budget. An increase of the average energy bill by £1,200 per household would amount, according to the Resolution Foundation, to a 'living standard catastrophe' – in concrete terms, this would effectively force the poorest sections of the population to face the choice between putting food on the table or heating their homes.[20]

---

[20] 'Industry and consumer estimates have suggested that the annual amount paid by the typical customer could go up from the current level of £1,277 to between £1,890 and

This simply points to the fact that tackling the climate-change problem is always more complex than any silver-bullet analysis may suggest. Economic models at their prescriptive best can tell us what we should aim for – say, a carbon tax of X dollars. This information is indeed useful. Economics can also help us by suggesting efficient ways to 'get there' (see the discussion in Chapter 16). And the 3,589 dejected economists whom we met in footnote 17 understandably bemoan the fact that we are turning down a tool (carbon taxes) that in principle makes so much sense. But, as we have seen in this section, the further we stray from the lands inhabited by *Homo Economicus*, the more ethical and political considerations become intertwined with the 'technocratic' solutions. As Italians say, 'Tra il dire e il fare c'e' di mezzo il mare' – which, with some liberty, could be translated to mean that a gulf as wide as the sea yawns between what theory tells us to do and how we can actually do it without creating too much unintended damage.

12.5 HOW TO MAKE UP YOUR OWN MIND

I said in the opening chapters of this book that, arcane as the term 'social discount rate' may sound, and difficult as its precise value may be to pin down precisely, expressing a view on whether it should be 'large' or 'small' is not beyond the grasp of the intelligent layperson. It is time for me to make good on my promise. How can the reader make up her mind as to whether the old or the modern DICE recommendations should be heeded?

Remember, first, that using a high social discount rate means that we are going to reduce today's value of future costs and benefits – the more so, the greater the social discount rate and the more distant the costs and benefits are. So a low social discount rate is associated with fast and aggressive abatement, a high social cost of carbon, and, in general, greater sacrifices today to reduce the future damages inflicted by climate change; and vice versa. Keep this in mind as your compass to show the direction of travel (more or less abatement is associated with a lower or higher social discount rate), and let's look at its individual components.

£2,240 in 2022.' *Rising energy costs: the impact on households, pensioners and those on low incomes*, House of Lords Library, 31 December 2021.

The first component of the social discount rate is your 'impatience', that is, how much you prefer to have something earlier rather than later. In intergenerational terms, this translates into how much weight you think it is fair to give to the welfare of future generations with respect to ours. I cannot answer this question for you, and neither can the best economist in the world. The higher your concern for the welfare of future people, the greater the sacrifice you should be willing to make today, and the lower the social discount rate. Answering this question is far from easy, and that is why thought experiments such as the wrinkle-in-time situation discussed in Chapter 9 can be of help. The only thing I would add about this is that, if you really conclude (as we have seen, in illustrious company) that we owe future generations exactly the same duty of care we grant ourselves, then you should ask yourself if you want to extend the same duty of care to today's poor people separated from you in space rather than in time. If not, you should ask yourself why. Again, only you can answer these questions – but, I would argue, you should probably strive to be consistent in your choices. We have discussed this in Chapter 9, and there is no need to go over this again.

The second question you should ask yourself is how much you dislike uneven consumption.[21] Again, you must take an intergenerational perspective, and you should ask yourself how much you think that our richer future descendant should shoulder more of the abatement burden *simply because they will (probably) be richer*. How would *you* spread the abatement burden, if someone told you that the future generations will be richer, and perhaps *much* richer, than ours? Perhaps tomorrow's poor will be as well off as today's middle classes (this is exactly what has happened in the West in the last 150 years). Would this change your response? If you don't feel that the likely future richness of your grandchildren matters that much when it comes to who should shoulder the greatest sacrifices, again you should choose a low social discount rate – which means that you should go for decisive abatement (and big sacrifices) today.

---

[21] A technical aside: in the classical expression for the rate of social discounting one normally interprets one of the coefficients as risk aversion rather dislike for uneven consumption. In the simple setting in which this formula is derived (time-separable utility functions) the two quantities are the same. In the case of climate change, aversion to uneven consumption (or its reciprocal, the elasticity of intertemporal substitution) has a greater impact on the optimal policy.

Answering this question is far from easy. If we are prepared to replace dislike for uneven consumption over time with dislike for uneven consumption across space (same-time wealth inequality) you can consider the following thought experiment. (See Chapter 9 for a discussion of the substitutability of 'distance in time' with 'distance in space'.) Imagine a society where half the population has a wealth per person of W and the other half a wealth per person of $W/2$. In layperson's terms, one half of society is twice as rich as the other half. I assume that you dislike inequality and that you want to organize wealth transfers between the two halves so as to maximize the total happiness. You can organize for a member of the rich half of society to give up $1, and for every member of poor to gain $$X < 1$. What value of $X would you choose? Clearly, if you strongly dislike inequality you will require the sacrifice of one dollar even for a very small increase in the wealth of the poor. Conversely, if you care very little about inequality, you will want the poor to become richer by close to the sacrifice of the rich to organize the swap. Probably, you are somewhere in between these two extremes. To see where exactly you stand, please pause for one second to consider by how much *you* would like the poor to improve their lot for the rich to part with $1. When you have done this, please repeat the same exercise for the case where the ratio of the wealth of the rich to the wealth of the poor is no longer 2 but 5. (The inequality is much greater now, so you will require a dollar sacrifice to produce a lower minimum increase in the wealth of the poor.) Once you have completed both thought exercises, please take a look at Table 12.1.[22] To give a last (Rawlsian) twist to the story, you should imagine the social planner either to be a Martian, or not to know whether, after the choice, she will end up in the rich or poor half of society.

This is how you can read the table. The column on the left gives you the increase in wealth of the poor that you, the social planner, deem appropriate for a $1 sacrifice of the rich. The central and right column correspond to the case where the wealth ratio of rich to poor is 2:1 and 5:1, respectively, and report the inverse of your dislike for uneven consumption. The smaller the number in the column, the more you

---

[22] This thought experiment is adapted from Gollier (2013), chapter 2, page 35.

Table 12.1. The column on the right gives you the increase in wealth of the poor that you, the social planner, deem appropriate for a $1 sacrifice of the rich. The central and right column correspond to the case where the wealth ratio of rich to poor is 2:1 and 5:1, respectively, and report the inverse of your dislike for uneven consumption.

$\Delta W(poor)$	Wealth ratio = 2	Wealth ratio = 5
0.1	0.30	0.70
0.2	0.43	1.00
0.3	0.58	1.34
0.4	0.76	1.76
0.5	1.00	2.32
0.6	1.36	3.15
0.7	1.94	4.51

dislike inequality, and (after swapping distance in space for distance in time) the more you care for uneven consumption. And this is the punchline: consider first the case when the rich/poor wealth ratio is 2. If you have chosen as the minimum increase in wealth for the poor of about $0.35 to justify a $1 sacrifice from the rich, then you agree with parameter choice of the original DICE approach. If you required an increase in wealth for the poor of about $0.6, then you agree with parameter choice of the modern DICE approach. To check the robustness of your introspection, you can look at the case when the wealth inequality was 5:1. Now your parameter choice is consistent with the original DICE parameters if you required an increase of $0.1 for the poor; it is consistent with the modern DICE parameters if you required an increase of $0.3. By the way, if you (as my son did) chose a value of $0.5 for the case of a 2:1 wealth ratio (which corresponds to a coefficient of 1, and to a logarithmic utility function), you have implicitly decided that you wanted to equalize the *percentage* change in wealth for the rich and the poor.

A last consistency check to conclude (or, rather, a check that you are not grandstanding): there is currently large wealth inequality across the globe. If you have chosen an original-DICE-like coefficient (which implies that you really dislike inequality), what fraction of GDP do you think it is fair to give as international aid? Last time you went to the ballot box, was your political choice consistent with this?

Let's move to a different component of the social discount rate. If it is the *uncertainty* associated with the possible outcomes of climate change that keeps you awake at night, and, especially, if the spread of respectable expert opinion on what possible climate outcomes should be makes you uncomfortable – if you have what economists call 'ambiguity aversion' and you would prefer the climate uncertainty to be resolved as early as possible – then your social discount rate is low, and you should be prepared to shoulder substantial sacrifices today for peace of mind.

Finally, recall that in this chapter we have shown that, as long as you dislike ambiguity, are reasonably averse to risk and do not terribly mind uneven consumption, you don't have to be Mother-Theresa-of-Calcutta-altruistic for your social discount rate to be low. If these preference conditions are met, even if you do not care about the welfare of future generations almost exactly as our own welfare, a fast and aggressive abatement schedule today remains your preferred course of action.

So much for your preferences. The other important component of the social discount rate is what I called in the introduction the 'quasi-factual' piece of information, the expected growth of the economy. If you think that the world will be much richer in the future (as most, but not all, economists believe) it means that the rate of return on production investment is very high. If that is the case, you should think twice before diverting too many resources towards emission abatement, because you are paying a high cost for this. But this is predicated on your being confident that we *will* be much richer in the future. Perhaps we will not, and perhaps we will not be *exactly because of climate change.* If economic growth were to stutter, and even to go in reverse, than *we* should definitely be shouldering the bigger share of the abatement effort. The aversion to intergenerational unevenness in wealth now works in reverse: in a world that becomes progressively poorer, the more you dislike uneven consumption the more you should choose to abate now. From this perspective, abating early can be seen as an insurance policy against our being unable to afford much abatement in the future.

Depending on how you answered the preference-related questions above, and depending on your beliefs (not hopes!) about future growth, you can then determine if you are a high- or low-social-discount rate person: you can determine, that is, whether you *think and feel* that high sacrifices today to keep climate damage in check are justified. Personally, I do, but that's just me. If you reach different conclusions, you are not a freak or an evil person: a Nobel-prize winning economist (Prof Nordhaus) shares your gradualist views and recommends that today we should devote proportionally more resources to R&D than to immediate abatement. Our richer and smarter grandchildren, in his view, will tackle the problem more effectively and with smaller reduction in welfare.

Whatever your choice, once you have made it, the factual information that I present in the rest of the book about what works and what does not work in climate-change control can help you decide which political party offers an instrumentally effective and honest plan to realize your stated goals. You will not be spoiled for choice.

CHAPTER 13

Taking the Dirty Stuff Out

I N THE PREVIOUS CHAPTER WE HAVE SEEN what an important role economic models assign to the removal of carbon in our attempts to limit the damages of climate change. We have barely looked, however, at the technological, social and political implications of negative emission technologies. This is what we do in this chapter.

After all the attending economic costs are taken into account, Integrated Assessment Models consider a molecule of CO_2 not emitted exactly equivalent to one molecule removed from the atmosphere. (This is where the focus of *net* zero emissions comes from.) At first blush it seems as simple as $2-2 = 0$, but, in reality, the issues linked with Negative Emission Technologies – the active *removal* of CO_2 from the atmosphere – are both poorly appreciated and complex. That is unfortunate, because grasping the importance of Negative Emission Technologies is key to solving the global-warming problem – and to ensuring that the transition to a decarbonized world is as painless as possible. Everybody's attention is understandably focussed on reducing emissions. However, it would be extremely difficult to keep the damages from global warming under control just by emitting less. And we should not close our eyes to the fact that a sudden reduction in size of the fossil fuel industries would cause severe social and economic pain among some very poor sections of the workforce (think, for instance, of coal miners), and in some very poor part of the world (think of oil-exporting Central Africa).[1] I will return to this point in the last section of this chapter.

---

[1] Oil is the main export from the Central African countries to the European Union, making up in 2021 41 per cent of its total exports. The balance of trade for these

Don't get me wrong: reducing emissions is essential and, from the narrow perspective of limiting temperature increases, the stronger the reduction in emissions, the better. However, there are exceedingly few realistic abatement-only paths consistent with keeping the warming of the planet by the end of the century within the 1.5–2 °C target. The IPCC, and every serious climate scientist, are very clear about this: all the practical and politically plausible strategies consistent with staying within the chosen target involve substantial removal of CO$_2$ from the atmosphere. As a reference point of the scale of the endeavour, Yale Professor Stephen Pacala has estimated that to stay within the same 1.5–2 °C limit by the end of the century, we need to remove 20 per cent of current emissions by mid-century, and 40 per cent by the end of the century.[2] Experts may quibble about the exact percentages, but there is no serious disagreement on this. Yet this 'inconvenient truth' (to use a by-now-hackneyed expression) is usually relegated to the footnotes and the fine print. When it is not, it is fiercely challenged. We must understand why.

13.1 THE PERSISTENCE OF CO$_2$ IN THE ATMOSPHERE

Let's start with the bad news. As we have seen in Chapter 2, once we have injected a molecule of CO$_2$ in the atmosphere, it will take a very long time before it is reabsorbed. There are several natural reabsorption mechanisms at play, of which the absorption by the oceans is the most important, but they all operate over very long timescales. To make things worse, as the fastest absorption mechanisms take up more and more CO$_2$, they become less and less efficient at doing so (oceans, for instance, acidify, and acidification makes the absorption slower). To quantify the speed of natural reabsorption climate scientists like to use the concept of *e*-folding time. This is a fancy word to express the time it will take for

countries is slightly negative, but the oil exports go a long way towards balancing the essential imports that are made up of mechanical equipment, vehicles, foodstuff and pharmaceutical products. European Commission, 28 April 2021, available at https://ec.europa.eu/trade/policy/countries-and-regions/regions/central-africa/index_en.htm.
[2] Stephen Pacala interview, https://e360.yale.edu/features/negative-emissions-is-it-feasible-to-remove-CO\$_2\$-from-the-air.

a given excess concentration to be reduced by a factor of approximately 3.[3] Now, as we discussed in Chapter 2, the latest, most up-to-date estimates suggest that, as far as the removal of excess CO_2 concentration is concerned, the *e*-folding time should be of the order of a century. This means that it should take around a century for approximately 60 per cent of a given excess amount of CO_2 to be reabsorbed via natural mechanisms. You may think that this is a *very* long time, but it is actually relatively good news, because old estimates used to suggest that it would take an extremely long time (much longer than the end of the century) to revert back to pre-industrial concentration levels even if we stopped emissions 'cold turkey'. So, let's take the relatively optimistic estimate of reabsorption as our benchmark. What is the relevance of this?

We have by now become familiar with schemes to reduce atmospheric pollution, and, at least in the West, these have been very successful. Therefore, we naturally tend to think that we are faced with a similar problem when faced with the control of climate change. Unfortunately, the nature of the climate-change problem is radically different, and, because of the long persistence of CO_2, much more intractable. As a reminder of why reducing pollution and abating CO_2 concentrations are so different, remember that, during the 2020 months of worldwide COVID-induced lock-downs, pollution in large cities dropped significantly and quickly. However, in the same period, despite a modest drop in emissions, CO_2 concentrations in the atmosphere kept on increasing at almost the same rate.[4] So, if we stop polluting, the pollution level goes down quickly and *locally* – by which I mean, close to the point of

[3] To be more precise, by a factor of e, with $e = 2.71828\ldots$. The concept of e-folding time was originally introduced in chemical kinetics, to describe the decay of one chemical compound into another. When the rate of decay depends linearly on the concentration of the reactant, chemists say that we are in a *linear kinetics* regime. There has been much discussion of whether linear kinetics apply to the removal of CO_2 from the atmosphere, and currently the general consensus is that it does not.

[4] National Oceanic and Atmospheric Administration: 'Levels of the two most important anthropogenic greenhouse gases, carbon dioxide and methane, continued their unrelenting rise in 2020 despite the economic slowdown caused by the coronavirus pandemic response…The atmospheric burden of CO_2 is now comparable to where it was during the Mid-Pliocene Warm Period around 3.6 million years ago, when concentrations of carbon dioxide ranged from about 380 to 450 parts per million.', NOAA Research News, April 7th, 2021.

reduction. If we stop emitting greenhouse gases, there is a significant thermal inertia, and the effects of local emission cuts are diluted because the CO_2 concentration is global: this, after all, is why we have a free-rider problem in the first place.[5]

To bring the point home, in Fig 13.1 I show what a rather optimistic model of CO_2 absorption implies about temperature changes with a very 'aggressive' abatement schedule. Note that the abatement schedule is aggressive indeed: as the figure shows, in this scenario *all* emissions (not just emissions associated with the production of electricity) fall to almost nothing by the end of the century, and to less than 10 per cent of the current level within fifty years. I would gladly sign on the proverbial dotted line if someone could guarantee that this pace of abatement of *all* emissions (not just those associated with the production of electricity) will indeed be achieved, especially for the period between now and mid-century. The same figure also shows the behaviour of the average temperature anomaly, which keeps on increasing, albeit at a lower and lower rate, until the end of the century, and reaches a value of 2.25 °C. Bottom line: as the temperature follows the concentrations (not the emissions!) with a lag, by the end of the present century the temperature would still be rising even with this aggressive reduction in emissions.[6] Are there abatement-only paths consistent with staying within 1.5–2 °C by the end of the century? Yes, as Fig 13.1 shows, there are, but they are extremely – and, I would argue, unrealistically – aggressive. Compare

---

[5] In some cases, reducing pollution can have a negative effect on global warming. In India, for instance, wet-bulb temperature has increased over the last thirty years (because of the increase in humidity), but maximum temperatures have not. Scientists think that this is because the concentration of air pollutants (atmospheric aerosols) *has increased* during the same period, and this has allowed more of the incoming solar radiation to be reflected, thereby cooling the affected regions. See in this respect Geert Jan van Oldenborgh et al. (2018), Extreme heat in India and Anthropogenic Climate Change, *Natural Hazards and Earth System Sciences*, 18 (1), quoted in McKinsey Global Institute Case Study, 'Will India Get Too Hot To Work?', November 2020. (By the way, the wet-bulb temperature is the lowest temperature to which air can be cooled by the evaporation of water into the air at a constant pressure. Increasing humidity therefore increases wet-bulb temperature.)

[6] These calculations have been carried out using the 'new physics' results mapped to the three-box model used in the DICE IAM. The 'new physics' results predict a much faster reabsorption than the earlier version of the climate model. With the original DICE modelling the reabsorption times would have been at least twice as long.

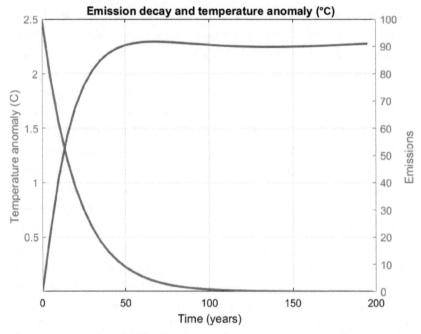

13.1 A very aggressive schedule of emission reduction (orange curve, right-hand *y* axis), and the associated atmospheric temperature anomaly (blue curve, left-hand *y* axis). Time from 'today' in years on the *x* axis.

again the realized and needed emission schedule shown in Fig 12.4. In brief: the inertia of the climate system is long indeed, and we cannot *realistically* count on emission cuts alone to stay within the 1.5–2 °C target.

So, yes, we certainly must reduce emissions, and, yes, we must do this promptly. Renewable-energy technologies are by now mature and cost-efficient. Let's deploy them aggressively. However, over the medium term the main effect of this aggressive abatement will largely be to avoid the problem getting worse and worse. Realistic emission reductions by themselves will not keep temperatures from rising for a very long time, and will not allow us to remain within the 1.5–2 °C target by the end of the century. Negative Emission Technologies are the only means to achieve deep reductions in concentrations, beyond what natural sinks can provide (where 'deep' means more than 100 parts per million). They can also reduce the transition pain on the way to decarbonization. However, they also present some clear dangers. Let's examine both pros and cons.

13.2 NEGATIVE EMISSION AND SEQUESTRATION TECHNOLOGIES

What can we do, then? This is where negative emission and sequestration technologies come to the fore. As we have seen, the key idea to keep in mind is that, as far as climate change goes, it is only *concentrations*, not emissions, that matter. Therefore if we could remove more CO_2 molecules than we inject, we would be moving in the right direction. How can we do that? There are basically two routes: one is by encouraging and enhancing natural absorption processes; the second is by devising new 'synthetic' removal mechanisms. Neither is without drawbacks. Let's understand why.

When people think about removal of CO_2 from the atmosphere the first thing that comes to mind (if *anything* come to mind) is often sequestration and capture. It is important to understand, however, that capture and sequestration is not necessarily the same as net removal. Capture and sequestration are the processes by means of which CO_2 emissions are captured at the point of emission (typically in the exhaust flue of a conventional gas or coal plant), and then safely stored underground 'forever'. Both processes are technologically mature (forms of carbon capture have been around since the 1930s), and, for some forms of emissions,[7] very effective. However, they are rather expensive. The lack of incentives or subsidies has kept the technology from developing or from becoming more price-competitive, but this is an area where large improvements and cost reductions are likely to be achieved.

Once captured, the CO_2 must be safely stored away, effectively, forever. This is also doable, but as I shall discuss, it entails non-trivial logistical problems (in simple terms: where are we going to store the huge amounts of captured CO_2?). However, even if we leave cost and storage problems to one side, we would still be a long way from solving the *concentration* problem. This is simply because, if the CO_2 captured is generated by burning fossil fuels, the whole cycle is *at best* carbon neutral – in practice, given the inevitable 'frictions',[8] it still contributes to emissions, albeit at

[7] Capture works well for large-scale, locally concentrated emissions, such as are found in the exhaust flues of a power plant.

[8] Examples of 'friction' are the energy used to transport the fossil fuel, the energy that goes into the building of the 'scrubbers', the energy needed to store safely the captured carbon, etc.

a much reduced rate. So, this cycle of activities still does not constitute a *negative* emission technology.

Things are different if the captured CO_2 comes from the burning of biomass (wood pellets, or other specially produced organic fuel). Why are things different now? Isn't a CO_2 molecule emitted when burning biomass just as bad as a molecule emitted burning coal? Not really, because when we burn biomass the CO_2 that is emitted was taken out from the atmosphere a few years or decades ago (the time it took for the tree or the plant that we burn to grow). Therefore, when we burn biomass, the steps in the cycle are: take out CO_2 (as the plant grows), emit CO_2 (as the biomass is burnt), immediately take CO_2 out again (as the emissions are captured). On top of this, we have also obtained energy. Which means that, even after allowing for some 'frictions' (see footnote 8), we have subtracted some CO_2 from the atmosphere, and we have obtained energy. It sounds too good to be true: why don't we do more – *much* more – of this?

There are many reasons. In part, it is because biomass burning and sequestration can only cater for some of our energy needs: biomass works well for domestic heating, for instance, but sequestration at the domestic level is not economical; and we can't use biomass and sequestration, say, for aviation, or for high-intensity energy production: fossil fuels have a huge energy density, and, together with their low cost, this is one of the key reasons they are so handy to use. The fact that costs of producing energy from biomass are still relatively high, of course, does not help (but costs normally come down once we begin investing in, and experimenting with, any technology). But there are other problems: while storing carbon does not pose anywhere close to the technological challenges associated with storing nuclear waste, it is *much more* space-consuming. Currently, we have identified sites (such as oil and gas reservoirs, or unmineable coal seams) that can provide the storage capacity needed for the period to 2050, and possibly to the end of the century.[9] However, whenever one tries to use a stock solution (large but finite storage facilities) to tackle a flow problem (continuous emissions) sooner

---

[9] This refers to an aggressive sequestration programme of *all* sources of emission, not just of emissions from the burning of biomass. These calculations clearly depend on the rate of emission abatement.

or later one is likely to run into problems. So, yes, carbon sequestration and storage is a useful, and, arguably, essential, stop-gap measure while we wean ourselves off carbon burning. But, if we continue emitting in large volumes, it is difficult to see where the vast *and ever-growing* volume of sequestrated carbon could be stored.

Storage is one problem that stands in the way of 'going big' with biomass carbon sequestration and storage. However, the biggest problem with growing biomass for burning is that the whole process strongly competes for land – land that we need for crops (especially with a growing world population), to grow new forests, for farms of solar panels and for large-scale wind-turbine installations. We will look at these constraints in detail in Chapter 15 (are they binding? If so, in which parts of the world?), but we already see the first occurrence of what will be a recurrent theme: even leaving cost considerations to one side, every carbon removal solution hits against some form of constraint. There is no silver bullet and no 'killer app': when it comes to controlling global warming we must rely on a portfolio of solutions, each tailored to the specific geographical conditions, and each with idiosyncratic, locality-specific advantages and drawbacks – as the case of afforestation, to which we turn next, clearly shows.

13.3 AFFORESTATION

If carbon sequestration and storage has its limits, what about reforestation instead?[10] The idea is deceptively simple. Algae and terrestrial green plants (trees, grasses, crops, etc.) convert CO_2 into biomass by using the energy from the Sun (CO_2 and water are transformed into carbohydrates via photosynthesis). Effectively, organic carbon sequestration is the net transformation ('fixation') of inorganic carbon (CO_2) from the atmosphere into organic carbon in green plants. Now, both animals and plants breathe (respiration). For plants, respiration means using the sugars produced during photosynthesis and oxygen to produce energy to grow: respiration is to some extent photosynthesis in reverse. In this

---

[10] A note on terminology: '*re*forestation is the recreation of forests in areas that had forests before. *Af*forestation is the creation of forests in areas that were not covered by forests before.

process plants release back into the atmosphere some of the CO_2 they absorbed during photosynthesis. While the tree is growing, some of the carbon that has been fixated goes into organic material, such as the trunk, the roots, the leaves, etc. In addition, as plants and various organic material die, they decompose and release part of the carbon back into the atmosphere. Some of the carbon becomes part of the topsoil, and some goes into sedimentary rock, where it can become fossil fuel. If we burn this fossil fuel, we release CO_2 (and water) back in the atmosphere.

So, the first observation is that forests *store* a huge amount of carbon, but only *growing* forests remove a substantial amount of carbon. Even if we look at the Amazon forest, it stores an enormous amount of CO_2, but, at steady state, removes hardly any. Yes, any new sapling will capture and store CO_2 as it grows. But, if the forest is at steady state (is not growing in size any more), some trees will at the same time be dying, and releasing back into the atmosphere via decomposition the carbon they had captured during their lifetime. Indeed, for a dense habitat such as the Amazonian forest, a new tree will only be able to grow when an old one dies and makes the physical growing space available. So, if we want to increase the amount of CO_2 captured we must increase the size of the forest.

Things, as usual, are not quite as simple. Roughly speaking, CO_2 is 'food' for plants. Therefore there has been speculation that, as the concentration of CO_2 in the atmosphere increases because of anthropogenic emissions, even mature forests may grow more, and, by so doing, may sequestrate additional CO_2. (The process is called CO_2 fertilization.) The latest scientific evidence suggests that this may be wishful thinking: the conclusions of a recent *Nature* paper are that, although a 38 per cent increase in CO_2 concentration did induce a 12 per cent 'increase in carbon uptake through gross primary production, this additional carbon uptake did not lead to increased carbon sequestration at the ecosystem level. Instead, the majority of the extra carbon was emitted back into the atmosphere via several respiratory fluxes [...]. Our results call into question the predominant thinking that the capacity of forests to act as carbon sinks will be generally enhanced under eCO2...'[11]

---

[11] Jiang et al., The Fate of Carbon in a Mature Forest under Carbon Dioxide Enrichment, *Nature*, 8 April 2020, www.nature.com/articles/s41586-020-2128-9.

The next consideration is that, if we are ultimately concerned with temperature changes (and care about CO_2 concentrations only insofar as they influence temperature changes) we have to take *albedo* into account. Albedo is the proportion of solar radiation reflected back into space. The more energy is reflected, the less 'energy in' is radiated back by the Earth acting as a black body, and the less the resulting warming. So, to a first approximation, albedo is 'good' for controlling global warming.[12] Now, forests have better CO_2 sequestration properties than grassland, but a much lower albedo (10–20 per cent compared to 40–50 per cent for crop- and grasslands). And, for comparison, snow-covered land has an albedo of about 80 per cent (which, by the way, is why one can get easily sun-burnt while skiing). So, the effectiveness of forests for temperature reduction depends on where the forests are grown: in cold regions, substituting snow-covered land with forests can actually *increase* the temperature by lowering the albedo of the land now covered in trees. [13]

The third consideration is probably the most important one: planting new forests takes up a lot of land. I mentioned in Chapter 1 that the green pledges of the three main UK parties in the run-up to the 2019 general elections: to plant 10, 20 or 60 million trees to offset carbon emissions. As we have seen, when we calculate how many trees would be needed to offset as little as 15 per cent of the UK emissions we come up with an estimate of about 2 *billion* trees, which would cover an area about as large as half of Wales. But the key problem is that when we look at forests, that cannot be grown to infinite size, we are trying to solve a flow problem (the *continuous* emissions of CO_2) with what is effectively a stock solution (a possibly increasable, but very finite amount, of land that can be covered by forests). Which means, that, once the half of Wales we have covered in new forests has absorbed its 15 per cent of emissions over a

---

[12] As usual with climate physics, the effects of albedo on the temperature are complex. Since changes in albedo change the Earth's temperature, they also change the amount of water vapour that the atmosphere holds at equilibrium (the warmer the atmosphere, the higher the H20 concentration). Now, water vapour is a very powerful greenhouse gas, and an increase in its equilibrium concentration means an increase in temperature. In addition, a higher equilibrium concentration of water vapour also means greater cloudiness; this, in turn, reduces the Earth's albedo – it is a classic feedback cycle.

[13] Eliasch Review (2008), page 26.

period of time, we have to find another half Wales to absorb the next emissions, and then another half after that, and so on.

When we keep this in mind, we see that forests, despite being touted as the greenest of green solutions, are not a panacea for removal of CO_2.[14] After correcting for albedo, their net ability to remove CO_2 is more limited than usually appreciated, but, more importantly, a *continuous* offset of emissions requires an ever-increasing area devoted to forests. You can think about it this way: removal of CO_2 always implies storing the stuff somewhere – if at all possible, in a very space-efficient manner.[15] In the case of forestation, the somewhere is in the body of the trees that grow on land that could be used for crops (or for wind farms, or for solar installations). And whenever land competition becomes an issue – and, apart from the case of nuclear energy, it almost always does – the impact on food prices, and hence on the poorest populations, must be kept in mind.

13.4 DIRECT AIR CAPTURE

If removing CO_2 from the atmosphere we must, and land competition keeps on reappearing as a constraint, what other alternatives are there? There are (currently expensive) proposals that go under the name of Direct Air Capture. With Direct Air Capture the idea is to suck carbon dioxide out of the atmosphere by using fans to blow air over chemical compounds that capture CO_2 as they come into contact with it. When these compounds are later exposed to heat and chemical reactions, they release the CO_2, which can then be captured, compressed, and stored ('sequestrated') underground. From the point of view of CO_2 concentrations, Direct Air Capture is a fully negative technology, and removal plants can be placed anywhere – not necessarily in the proximity of CO_2 production. Unfortunately it is expensive, both in monetary and in energy terms. In dollar terms, the costs started at around \$600/Ton, but they have fallen to between \$100 and \$200/Ton. Thanks to the magic

---

[14] Admittedly, forests bring other advantages, such as increase in biodiversity, erosion control, etc. I am focussing here only on their CO_2-removal credentials.

[15] In this respect, the storage density afforded by trees is poor: by volume, it takes a lot more trees to store a given amount of CO_2 than if stored underground.

of learning by doing, costs will certainly come down if we begin installing Direct Air Capture plants in size, but the blowing of the fans, the chemical reactions, the compression and the storage will still require a lot of energy. This could in principle be provided by renewable energy sources when the wind blows harder or the sun shines brighter than needed by the demand for electricity. However, there are many competing uses for this 'surplus clean energy',[16] and wind and solar installations also require land (or sea-beds). We have circled back, once again, to the problem of competition for land – a problem so important that I deal with it in a chapter of its own (Chapter 15).

In sum: some form of CO_2 removal is certainly going to be necessary to remain within the 1.5–2 °C target of temperature increase. As I said, a portfolio of solutions, rather than any single silver bullet, will provide the most successful removal strategy. However, an additional big problem remains with negative emission technologies – a problem whose nature is non-technical, but political. We have to look into this.

13.5 WHY CARBON REMOVAL IS NECESSARY

I am sure all my readers have heard of renewable energy. How many, however, have heard of negative emission technology? Much fewer, I think. Perhaps some readers have encountered the concept for the first time in their lives in the pages they have just read. Yet, as we have seen, removing is as important as not emitting. Why don't we hear more about the removal part of the equation?

One reason why green activists do not like to talk about carbon removal is because of the fear of a moral hazard problem.[17] If we tell people that CO_2 can be sequestrated and stored, the argument goes, this will slacken their emission-reduction commitment, and we will continue

---

[16] 'Green hydrogen' is also high on the list of possible uses for the 'surplus energy' generated at times of low demand by renewables. The list, alas, keeps getting longer.

[17] In economics moral hazard arises when an entity has no incentive to reduce a risky activity because the entity does not bear the full cost of its consequences. So, if you buy insurance on the contents of your house, you may lock the door less assiduously than if you hadn't bought insurance. Or, perhaps, you will not install a burglar alarm. You have become more risk tolerant because you no longer bear the full cost of a theft. Property insurance providers lose a lot of sleep over moral hazard.

burning fossil fuels with abandon. I am not a great fan of 'informational paternalism' – by which I mean that I do not like being economical with the truth even if it is for a 'good reason'. In the specific case of global warming I find that fighting disinformation from deniers with doctored and 'managed' accounts of the climate situation is particularly bad – not least because it can backfire, and give ammunitions to the deniers.[18] So, the moral hazard problem with carbon removal is real. However, this does not mean that we should therefore avoid talking about carbon sequestration and storage in one form or another (I include forests among the sequestration and storage devices).

Another reason why negative emission technologies and carbon sequestration are not popular is because of the no-growth, anti-industrialization agenda of many climate activists. In these circles, fossil fuels *cannot* be seen as part of the solution, and the only sensible thing we can do with them is to leave them all in the ground – the transition and adaptation timescale for total decarbonization that these activists offer is, in effect, yesterday. Furthermore, since the energy from renewables alone cannot provide at the same time the energy that a growing world economy requires *and* foot the energy bill that comes with many carbon-capture solutions (as we have said, all serious scientists, and the IPCC *in primis* agree on this), the conclusion is that we must stop growing. Now, I am the first to say that the rich West is currently unconscionably wasteful in its use of energy. However, increased efficiency and energy frugality will not allow the world (including its currently poorest parts) to grow anywhere as much as we must all hope it will. I cannot see how a substantial improvement in the living conditions of the currently poorest

---

[18] Climate deniers are extremely efficient at amplifying, taking out of context and, in general, 'spinning' the slightest imprecision or awkwardly phrased statement of climate scientists. The well-known case of 'climategate' (where poorly phrased emails by scientists at the University of East Anglia were hacked, hand-picked and disseminated on sceptics' blogs) is probably the best known, but not the only, example. In the end, the names of the East Anglia University scientists were fully cleared, and the integrity of their research confirmed. By then, unfortunately, the episode had become 'the hack that changed the world', and the belated apologies from one of the hackers (who eventually reproduced the results from the scientists) did little to restore the confidence of the public. See for further details www.bbc.co.uk/news/uk-england-norfolk-59176497.

portions of the world can be achieved without significant additional energy expenditure. As I show in Chapter 15, the link between living standards and energy expenditure is as close to a clear and robust relationship as you can expect to find in the whole field of economics. (See, for instance, Fig 15.3.) I am the first to recognize that there can be principled disagreement about how much, and what type of, growth can be desirable. However, as I have argued in Section 11.3, embracing an unreflective no-growth approach to climate change effectively means denying the currently poorest parts of the world any reasonable chance to reach comfortable standards of living. Humanity has never found a way to improve living conditions without greater energy expenditure. I see no reason why 'this time should be different'. I have covered these points, and there is no reason to go over them again.

There is a third argument against relying on carbon removal in our climate-change strategies. The current proven technologies (afforestation and bioenergy with carbon sequestration and storage), the critics say, present serious problems if deployed in large scale (competition for land, loss of biodiversity, etc.). I fully agree on this point. In our carbon-removal plans we must therefore rely on technologies (such as direct carbon capture) that have so far not been deployed in any significant scale and that need substantial improvement and reduction in cost of production. But if we decide to go down this route, the critics say, we have to rely on a possible, but by no means sure, technological development of efficient and scalable removal technologies. Doing so, they argue, is too much of a gamble, and we must focus, cost what may, on what we know to work for sure – that is, abatement.

Now, it is true that currently non-biomass, non-afforestation-based negative emission technologies have a long way to go in terms of effectiveness and cost reductions. But forty years ago the same arguments could have been made about solar panels. When I took my first lessons in Solid State Physics, my professor taught us (correctly at the time) that it took more energy to build a solar panel than what it would produce in its lifetime. Should a climate-concerned citizen at the time have concluded that banking on solar panels and wind turbines to tackle climate risk was too risky, and that we should focus instead on proven and available adaptation solutions? Yes, we cannot know for sure that the cost and effectiveness of removal technologies will come down – exactly as we could not have known for sure a few decades ago that the cost and effectiveness of televisions, mobile phones, personal computers, cars, and everything else would have improved so dramatically. Yet every technology into which significant investments have been made has improved literally by orders of magnitude in any measurable metric. My mobile phone today has more computing power (and a vastly greater range of applications) than the department computer I was using in my Oxford lab in the late 1980s. And I don't need a university grant to buy a new model. The reverse of the argument is also true. There *is* a foolproof way to keep removal technologies expensive and inefficient: it is to starve them of investments and subsidies. Then their ineffectiveness becomes a self-fulfilling prophecy.

The general point I am making here is that the problem of global warming is too far-reaching for *any* political and ideological view to be allowed to hijack the climate-control agenda. (This, of course, applies not just to no-growthers, but to the market fundamentalists as well, who believe that only the unfettered dynamism of private initiative fuelled by the hope of private profit can tackle the problem.) If we want to find a solution to global warming, this solution must therefore be recognized as acceptable by both the market zealots and by the no-growthers. It is exactly because the task ahead is as demanding as a war effort, that we must find broad church policies behind whose banner very different views of the political and social good (from communist China to the capitalist United States) can gather and act.

As we accept the need for rapid and large-scale cuts in emissions, these wide-consensus policies must take into account the significant dislocations that the decarbonization process will entail. Economic models such as DICE (both in its original and it its modern incarnations) see the labour force as instantaneously re-deployable in the highest-return initiatives: in the world according to DICE, the coal miners who lose their jobs down the coal pit will immediately find new jobs installing solar panels, or building wind turbines. This simplistic narrative of a painless transition is then reinforced, when serious institutions such as the International Renewable Energy Agency (IRENA) predict, probably correctly, that by 2050 twice as many jobs will be created in the renewables sector as will be lost in the fossil fuel industries.[19] This may well be correct, but these statistics should not be taken to imply that the *same people* who lose a fossil-fuel-related job will find a job in the renewable industry. A recent report by the consultancy McKinsey[20] projects 'a gain of about 200 million and a loss of about 185 million direct and indirect jobs globally by 2050' in a 1.5 °C-by-end-of-the-century scenario. It would be close to miraculous if all the transition-related job vacancies were filled by those who have been displaced. In reality, there will be winners and losers, both among countries and among differently skilled groups of the same national population.[21] As usual, the poorest – the poorest countries and, within a country, the poorest sectors of the population – will often fare worst. Central African countries, for instance, which are high exporters of oil, will suffer more than most.[22] And, in all countries, coal miners have historically proven to be among the most difficult groups of workers to re-employ in different sectors of the economy. The World Bank has produced a very thoughtful account (*Global Perspective on Coal Jobs and Managing Labor Transition out of Coal*, World Bank Publications, April 5, 2022) of the job implications of transitioning out of coal. The key observation is that, yes, the number of workers employed in coal mines is relatively modest (less than 5 million worldwide), but the coal industry generates many more jobs in related sectors of the economy. Closing coal mines 'negatively affects workers along the coal value chain, hurts local economies reliant on mine workers' earnings, fragments community well-being and social capital, and squeezes public finances'. And '[i]n

---

[19] *Global Energy Transformation: A Roadmap to 2050*, IRENA, 2018.

[20] *The Net-Zero Transition: What It Would Cost, What It Could Bring*, McKinsey & Company Report, January 2022, page viii.

[21] One also has to be very careful reading deceptively simple accounts of jobs lost and jobs gained. For instance, a recent report by the IEA World Energy Outlook finds far more jobs gained than lost in the energy transition to 2030 if the pledged commitments to reduce coal usage are fulfilled. However, it seems to count only *direct* job losses for coal (which it sets at 2.1 million out of the almost 5 million currently employed), but includes large gains in ancillary clean-energy activities, such as increase in efficiency (which has the greatest job gain, at 3.3 million). Even leaving any 'redeployment issues' to one side, it is essential to consider gains and losses all the way down the value chain both for coal and for renewables.

[22] *Global Perspective on Coal Jobs and Managing Labor Transition out of Coal*, World Bank Publications, April 5, 2022, page 61.

some communities, closing mines can create a persistent, destabilizing demand shock as displaced workers struggle to transition to new jobs, because few alternatives are available or workers are unwilling to accept lower-paying options or move to regions with greater labor demand'. Which all points to the conclusion that it is inevitable that many painful bumps will be encountered along the decarbonization path.

To smooth the pain of this transition period, aiming in the medium term for a *net*-zero emission policy, rather than an *absolute*-zero policy, can therefore make a big difference, at least in the initial transition phase. This transition phase may be longer than anticipated, or hoped: yes, we are finally weaning ourselves off the fossil-fuel dependence for the production of electric energy. However electricity only accounts for about 20 per cent of our total energy consumption. What Smil (2022) calls the 'four pillars' of the modern world – namely: cement, steel, plastic and ammonia – account for a significant part (about 15–20 per cent) of the remaining 80 per cent of the energy requirement, but, as we discussed, they are not easy to produce with renewables. Decarbonizing the electricity production is (relatively) easy; decarbonizing the whole economy vastly more difficult.

This means that, in an optimistic but realistic scenario, we should prepare ourselves to live in a *net*-zero (and perhaps a net-negative) world in which renewable sources of energy operate for longer than we may have wished alongside carbon removal and fossil-fuel plants equipped with carbon-sequestration-and-storage facilities. To avoid large climate damage we must reduce emissions aggressively; however, we must also remove and/or capture and store emitted CO_2 in large scale. Yes, it is true, the technologies to directly remove or capture-and-store vast amounts of CO_2 are at the moment at best partial solutions because of the problems (competition for land, storage space, high energy costs) mentioned above. However, we cannot put all the burden of the decarbonization of the economy on the shoulders of the renewable sector alone. Carbon-sequestration-and-storage and negative-emission technologies are needed to reach *net*-zero, and, if possible, *net-negative*, emissions. They can also make an important contribution towards achieving our final climate goals in a socially less painful way.

13.6 LOGISTICS CONSIDERATIONS

The technology of carbon sequestration and storage is more established than the technology of negative emissions (apart from afforestation). The theoretically very appealing feature of carbon sequestration and storage is that, if the fuel burnt is recently grown biomass, we can actually *remove* CO_2 from the atmosphere and produce energy.[23] This is very appealing, but the logistics of the storing part of the task should not be underestimated. The CO_2 concentration targets consistent with a 1.5–2 °C target imply that carbon sequestration and storage will have to offset 15–20 per cent of projected human emissions. This is a staggering amount, and the scale of the industrial enterprise to achieve this is little short of breathtaking. If CO_2 is stored in liquid form at a pressure of 100 bar, one cubic metre of compressed liquid CO_2 holds 0.6 tons of CO_2. This means that it would take 160 million cubic meters (that is a huge cube with a side of half a kilometre) *per day* to store away the world CO_2 emissions.[24] Even leaving cost considerations to one side, an obvious question is: 'Where are we going to put the stuff?' With a touch of tragic irony, the first port of call for storage are depleted oil and gas reservoirs. These reservoirs could in principle store 900 billion tonnes of compressed CO_2, the equivalent of twenty-five years of current emissions. To get some perspective, Mac Dowell et al. (2017) point out

> … in 2050 the [carbon sequestration and storage] industry will need to be larger by a factor of 2-4 in volume terms than the current global oil industry. In other words, we have 35 years to deploy an industry that is

---

[23] As I explained in Section 13.2, if we capture and store CO_2 produced by burning fossil fuels, we are at best carbon neutral (apart from 'frictions'). However, if we capture and store CO_2 produced by recently grown biomass, we are effectively putting underground CO_2 that was in the atmosphere 'a few years ago'. As usual, even producing energy while removing CO_2 is not a panacea: as the IPCC points out '[s]ome ambitious efforts to constrain atmospheric greenhouse gas concentrations may themselves impact ecosystems. In particular, changes in land use, potentially required for massively enhanced production of biofuels (either as simple replacement of fossil fuels, or as part of bioenergy with carbon capture and storage, BECCS) impact all other land ecosystems through competition for land.' IPCC Special Report, 2021, chapter 1, page 69.

[24] Hampshire-Waugh (2021).

substantially larger than one that has developed approximately over the last century …

In addition, there are limits to pumping speeds (how quickly the liquid CO_2 can be pushed underground) and to the availability of storage sites. Realistically optimistic estimates of how much of fossil fuel emissions can be captured and stored away per year therefore range between 10 and 15 per cent of total emissions. Lest you think this is too small to make a difference, remember that this would be a substantial fraction of the energy needed to produce our four material pillars (cement, plastic, steel and ammonia) – the four near-indispensable materials that are difficult to produce by non-fossil-fuel sources.

None of this implies that 'it cannot be done'. As I have explained in Chapter 3, this is just another example of the fact that we have to brace ourselves for major changes in our lives, in our economies and in our societies. These changes will be of different nature, and of different severity, depending on the scale of our abatement strategies, or lack thereof. But, given the sheer size of the task ahead, we must pay due care to ensuring that the transformation and adaption process is as smooth and painless as possible. *How* we approach net-zero is every bit as important as getting there – if for no other reason than unfair, inefficient or low-legitimacy policies can stop the decarbonization process dead on its tracks.

The attentive reader may have noted that I have made no mention so far of nuclear energy – a form of energy supply that produces no greenhouse emissions, and that could be applied for many of the energy-intensive uses for which renewables or forms of energy storage such as batteries are ill suited. We take a look at this option in the next chapter.

CHAPTER 14

The Role of Nuclear Energy

[Nuclear Energy] is the only known energy source that can supply the energy requirements for a technological civilization of several billion humans...
—Patrick Moore (Co-founder of Greenpeace)

Nuclear energy has no place in a safe, clean, sustainable future. Nuclear energy is both expensive and dangerous...
—Greenpeace USA

DESPITE THE FACT THAT MY FIRST AREA OF RESEARCH was in nuclear engineering, and I therefore have both a great interest in, and some knowledge of, the topic, the reader will have noticed that I have barely mentioned nuclear energy in my discussion so far. Much as I have dithered, I cannot defer mentioning the N word any longer, and I will offer my thoughts on the matter in this chapter. Before doing so, I must make two things clear. First, I do not intend to present a survey of all the possible sources of clean energy. I single out nuclear energy for attention because, apart from wind and solar, it is the main source of clean energy that can make a substantial global difference; because it is a 'firm' (as opposed to intermittent) energy provider; and because it does not compete for land. It is in this sense that nuclear energy is special – and this is probably why the co-founder of *Greenpeace*, Patrick Moore, says that it is the only known source of energy 'that can supply the energy requirements for a technological civilization of several billion humans'. Second, I do not intend to present in a short chapter a thorough treatment of the thorny problem of whether nuclear energy is *the* way to go to curb global warming – once again, a whole book could easily be devoted to the topic.[1] Rather, I want to look at the use of nuclear energy from the perspective that we have been building so far – namely starting from the conclusions that (i) we must reduce emissions rapidly and in large scale; (ii) that renewable sources of energy require some form of 'firm" energy supply alongside unless we are prepared to significantly over-scale their deployment; and (iii) that, even leaving cost considerations aside, there is a finite supply of land, and therefore wind farms, solar installations, forests and plantations of biomass compete with agriculture (and cities, and roads, and places of natural and historical beauty). Looking at the desirability or otherwise of nuclear energy in isolation makes little sense, unless these basic constraints are taken into account, and nuclear energy is compared to the feasible alternatives.

14.1 FISSION

There is another aspect of the problem that makes nuclear energy from fission absolutely key to an economics-based appraisal of what we should do about climate change. We have discussed at length that the timing of abatement depends strongly on how rich we are going to be in the future. As we have seen, our expectations of how rich we are going to be in the future and our aversion to uneven consumption together dictate who (us or our descendants) should bear the greater weight of the abatement burden. Since our central expectations see our descendants much richer than we are, a significant burden of the abatement effort is pushed to future generations – how significant, again, depending on our dislike for intergenerational unevenness in consumption. It is the 'tax-on-the-poor' argument again.

This way of looking at the optimal timing of the abatement problem should by now be familiar to the reader. However, these decisions are predicated on our grandchildren indeed ending up being (much) richer

---

[1] For what it's worth, my position is that a portfolio of solutions is the best way to tackle the problem of stabilizing and reducing CO_2 concentrations, and that nuclear energy should, with qualifications, be part of this portfolio. I am not able at the moment to elaborate on this position further (for instance, I cannot answer (yet) a question such as 'Should the "portfolio weight" of the nuclear contribution be 5 per cent or 40 per cent?'). Part of my current research is aimed at finding an answer to questions like this.

than we are now: and, as we have discussed in Chapter 10, if one had to pick something most economists do agree on, this assumption of positive, if not spectacular, output growth appears be a more solid expectation than most. So, barring big surprises, we expect our grandchildren to be richer, and hence better equipped to shoulder a substantial part of the abatement cost.

Let's remind ourselves, however, of the link between GDP growth and energy usage, that we have already discussed and that we will revisit in Chapter 15 – see, in particular, Fig 15.3. As it is clear from this graph, *continuous* extra growth (the 'magic sauce' that has allowed us to escape the Malthusian trap, and that is supposed to make us richer in the future) has historically been very closely associated with extra energy consumption. In simple terms: if we are going to be that much richer, we will have to consume a lot more energy. I am far more confident of this prediction than of virtually any other prediction one can make in economics. This, however, raises the obvious question: if we truly believe in our continued economic growth, where is this energy going to come from, once the fossil fuel resources are either depleted or, for very good reasons, left in the ground? Renewables are a big part of the answer, but, as we will discuss in Chapter 15, given the Earth's physical constraints, it is difficult to see how they could cater for the energy demands that we can project in, say, 2200 (or perhaps even in 2100). So far, in one form or another, virtually all the energy we have harnessed has come from the Sun. Yes, the energy from fossil fuels comes from breaking chemical bonds in exoenergetic reactions. But the energy to make the chemical bonds that we break when we burn the same fossil fuels still came, via photosynthesis, from the Sun. When we use hydroelectric energy, we exploit the fact that low-lying water evaporated thanks to the heat received from the Sun, and then came down as rain near the top of a mountain: the work to get the water 'up there' was ultimately done by the Sun.

What about wind power?' you may ask. Edmond Healey (1656–1742) understood as far back as the beginning of the eighteenth century that the heating effect of the Sun's rays is proportional to their angle of incidence on the Earth. He also understood that these differences in the heating of the Earth's surface at different latitudes were responsible for the trade winds – a far more convincing explanation than that of his contemporary Lister, who thought that the same winds were due to the daily respiration of the Sargasso seaweed.[2] So, also when it comes to wind energy, in the end it is still down to the Sun. In short, in the history of mankind almost all the energy we have used has come from the Sun.[3]

Now, our star does pour daily an enormous amount of energy on planet Earth – much more than we currently use, and, if we were able to capture it all, much more than we need now or in any foreseeable future.[4] However, there are thermodynamic limits to how efficiently we can extract this Sun energy, either in its direct form (via solar panels), or indirectly (via wind turbines). Even if pushed to their thermodynamic limits of efficiency, it is difficult to see how we will be able to convert enough of this theoretically bountiful energy supply to cater not just for our present, but also for our future energy demands. The key thing to keep in mind is that we must find energy not just for the 'easy' applications, such as electricity production, but also for Smil's recalcitrant four pillars of civilization – steel, cement, plastic and fertilizers – for aviation, for heavy-duty transportation (such as lorries and tractors) and for all those situations where the high-energy density of fossil fuels is difficult to replace. These near-future demands on renewables must also take into account that in a decarbonized world we will have to consume energy for tasks that have virtually no impact on our current energy budget: direct air capture, for instance, (of which we currently do essentially zero) requires a lot of energy; hydrogen could perhaps become a clean source of energy, but producing it requires a lot of input energy; extracting the *extra* critical minerals and rare earths to charge all the batteries that will power the clean electric cars and lots of other stuff will require energy for activities that do not currently enter our energy balance sheet.

---

[2] See in this respect Coopersmith's (2015) excellent book, page 57.

[3] One of the few sources of energy not related to the Sun is energy from tides, whose movements are due to the Moon's gravitational pull. In the abstract, tidal energy is huge. Putting it to useful application is very difficult. Another non-Sun-related energy source is geothermal energy, that comes from the radioactive decay of elements in the Earth's core. Because of this decay activity, the temperature of the Earth's inner core (more than 10,000 °F), is similar to the temperature at the surface of the Sun.

[4] The Sun pours on the Earth 173,000 watts (joules per second). This is 10,000 time the total human energy usage.

Admittedly, there are other, non-Sun-related sources of energy – such as tidal waves or the heat from volcanic activities. Large as they may be in theory, they are very difficult to convert into usable energy on a large scale and globally.[5] Nuclear energy offers the possibility of tapping onto energy of a completely different type, and (especially in the form of fusion) potentially in a close-to-unlimited scale.[6] So, if the expectations about output growth on which our economic analysis rests its conclusions are to be achieved, nuclear energy must implicitly be assumed to play a significant role – which is why we have to take a look at it.

This is clearly a contentious statement. As the quotes, both from sources close to Greenpeace, that open this section show, saying that opinions on the topic of nuclear energy are polarized is a quaint understatement, and, indeed, some of the objections to its use are both valid and obvious. However, when I ask my students to list in order of importance their reservations about nuclear fission, and I compare their list with mine, I find that the order of the items in our respective lists is almost reversed. Catastrophic accidents and the handling of nuclear waste are top of my students' worries. Geopolitical risk is at the top of mine (followed as a rather distant second by the handling of nuclear waste). Don't get me wrong: it is not that I believe that nuclear accidents will not happen any more. Unfortunately, if we use nuclear reactors, we *will* have new Chernobyls, no matter what regulations and passive safety systems we will put in place – it will happen simply because these beautiful systems and tough regulations will be operated and adhered to, respectively, by human-all-too-human actors.[7] I am aware of this – yet,

---

[5] Locally things can be very different: when, as a young man, I used to tour Iceland, I was surprised to find plentiful hot water in the humblest youth hostels. It was provided by geothermal energy, that today supplies 25 per cent of the total energy consumption of Iceland.

[6] If one takes a physicist's perspective, one could say that, since the Sun's energy comes from the fusion of hydrogen into helium, we have been using fusion energy all along.

[7] A good, non-technical, but serious and well-researched account written by a History Professor at Harvard University is given in Plokhy (2019). The book gives a clear account of how production targets that 'had to be met' induced the operators to engage in practices far removed from what the manual said. Then, more mistakes were made, and more accepted practices were overruled, when the situation in the reactor became patently critical.

I think that the geopolitical risks (read, military proliferation) outweigh the physical risks.

Let me be clear. I do not underestimate the risks of nuclear accidents, or the difficulty of storing nuclear waste safely for thousand of years. However, I think that we must put these risks in perspective – and that, when we do so, accident and storage risks are actually much smaller than risks we routinely accept in other aspects of our lives – and more to the point, than risks that we routinely accept for other energy sources. See, in this respect, the trade-off between deaths per year and greenhouse gas emissions shown in Fig 14.1 from the invariably good and reliable source 'Our World in Data' – and please note that the deaths per terawatt-hour reported for nuclear energy *include* both the Chernobyl and the Fukushima disasters.[8] What I find much more difficult to 'put in perspective' is the possible human cost of a nuclear war, the likelihood of which could be greatly enhanced by widespread diffusion of nuclear power plants.

To explain more precisely what I mean, let's start from the risk of nuclear accidents, and let's take the Chernobyl accident as a prototypical example of how badly a nuclear emergency situation can be handled (see the next paragraph in this respect). The human cost of the Chernobyl tragedy has clearly been huge, yet precise quantification is surprisingly difficult.[9] This is because most of the radiation-associated morbidity and

[8] The death rates from fossil fuels and biomass are based on state-of-the-art European pollution controls – so they are close to an 'as-good-as-it-gets' case, and are therefore extremely optimistic – in the sense that they flatter the dangers of these sources of energy. This over-optimism is not small change: the death rates from accidents related to carbon extraction in China are about fifty times as high as in Europe. For a discussion see OurWorldInData.org/safest-sources-of-energy.

[9] A word of caution: a lot of the assessment of the damage from Chernobyl has come from Ukrainian sources, and these sources have tended to paint a catastrophic picture of what happened. As an example, Viktor Sushko, deputy director general of the National Research Centre for Radiation Medicine (NRCRM) based in Kiev, Ukraine, has described the Chernobyl disaster as the 'largest anthropogenic disaster in the history of humankind…', a hyperbolic statement I find difficult to justify. Chernobyl was a Soviet-Union-run reactor in what is currently Ukraine. As the political climate between Ukraine and Russia is currently toxic, damage assessments from Ukraine must be taken with a large pinch of salt. In reality, according to the 2006 report of the UN Chernobyl Forums Health Expert Group: 'The actual number of deaths caused by this accident is unlikely ever to be precisely known.'

What are the safest and cleanest sources of energy?

Death rate from accidents and air pollution

Measured as deaths per terawatt-hour of electricity production.
1 terawatt-hour is the annual electricity consumption of 150,000 people in the EU.

Coal
36% of global electricity
24.6 deaths
↳ 1230-times higher than solar

Oil
3% of global electricity
18.4 deaths
↳ 613-times higher than nuclear energy

Natural Gas
22% of global electricity
2.8 deaths

Biomass
2% of global electricity
4.6 deaths

Hydropower
12% of global electricity
1.3 deaths
171,000 deaths from Banqiao Dam failure in 1975, China

Wind
7% of global electricity
0.04 deaths

Nuclear energy
10% of global electricity
0.03 deaths
Includes deaths from Chernobyl and Fukushima disasters

Solar
4% of global electricity
0.02 deaths

Greenhouse gas emissions

Measured in emissions of CO_2-equivalents per gigawatt-hour of electricity over the lifecycle of the power plant.
1 gigawatt-hour is the annual electricity consumption of 150 people in the EU.

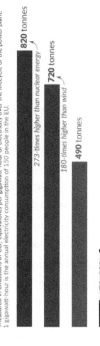

820 tonnes

720 tonnes
↳ 273-times higher than nuclear energy

490 tonnes
↳ 180-times higher than wind

78–230 tonnes

34 tonnes

4 tonnes

3 tonnes

5 tonnes

Death rates from fossil fuels and biomass are based on state-of-the art plants with pollution controls in Europe, and are based on older models of the impacts of air pollution on health.
This means these death rates are likely to be very conservative. For further discussion, see our article: OurWorldinData.org/safest-sources-of-energy. Electricity shares are given for 2021.
Data sources: Markandya & Wilkinson (2007); UNSCEAR (2008; 2018); Sovacool et al. (2016); IPCC AR5 (2014); Pehl et al. (2017); Ember Energy (2021).
OurWorldinData.org – Research and data to make progress against the world's largest problems.   Licensed under CC-BY by the authors Hannah Ritchie and Max Roser.

14.1 Death rates from accidents and pollution for different sources of energy (left graph), and greenhouse emissions in tons of CO_2 equivalent emissions to produce one gigawatt-hour of electricity over the lifetime of the plant. Source: Our World in Data.

mortality materializes over decades, and 'the current observation period is only slightly longer than the recognized minimum latency period of about 10 years for many of the cancers.'[10] A 2006 report by the UN and WHO estimated the number of the indirect deaths (on top of the approximately 50 deaths directly linked with the accident, and which are not disputed) to be around 4,000. After the publication of the UN-WHO report, the influential scientific journal *Nature* challenged its accuracy; in particular, it put in doubt its key estimate of the projected indirect death toll of 4,000. Several of the scientists and physicians cited in the UN-WHO report said that the document by the UN-WHO had either misrepresented their views or that their conclusions had been misinterpreted. For example, the full report had estimated another 5,000 deaths among people living farther from the accident, which was not mentioned in the press release. Since both sources are of high quality, and I cannot independently assess the relative merits of the two sides of the argument, let me take a conservative but realistic approach, and let me put the total number of indirect deaths at around 10,000.

Now, this huge number was in great part due to a near-criminal mismanagement of the crisis by the Soviet authorities, which, for several days after the accident, even denied that anything had happened at all. As one example among many of how the Soviet authorities managed the accident, the regulations released at the time about how to handle the contaminated meat read as follows. (Meat and milk were contaminated because radioactive material fell on the grass around Chernobyl, that was then eaten by cattle.) The Soviet bureaucrats came up with detailed manuals on how to deal with the contaminated meat, wool and milk. The respective industries were instructed to classify their produce as high, medium and low in terms of radiation. Meat with high levels of radiation was then to be shoved into a freezer, so that authorities could wait until the radiation level fell. What about medium and low-level-radiation meat? It was supposed to be mixed with non-contaminated meat and turned into sausages. This meat was labelled as fit for consumption and sent all over the country – and now comes the last touch – *but the instructions were that it should not to be sent to Moscow* (where the rule-making politicians and bureaucrats lived).

[10] The UN & WHO reports, 2006.

So, the mismanagement of the Chernobyl accident clearly played a big role in its (lack of) containment. However, I do not take much comfort from the fact that 'it was just due to human error'. The reason why I don't is simply because there is no guarantee that the next big accident may not occur in a country even less willing or able to manage the risks of an accident at a nuclear power plant. This is why it does not make sense to consider the safety of nuclear plants assuming a textbook compliance with safety standards. If we embrace nuclear energy worldwide, I think we will have to expect that somehow, somewhere more Chernobyls (more 10,000-death accidents) will happen again. This is clearly terrible. However, before saying that it is unacceptable, these large numbers should be compared with the number of deaths we routinely 'accept' in other parts of our lives. To put the numbers in perspective, 1.3 million people die every year on the world's roads. That is more than 100 Chernobyl accidents *every year*. More to the point, 4.2 million people die every year[11] due to outdoor pollutions – pollution that could be directly reduced by producing energy via nuclear fission power plants. As physicist David McKay used to say 'nuclear energy is dangerous, but not infinitely dangerous'. See again Fig 14.1. Yet, paradoxically, some of the countries (such as Denmark, Norway, Germany) that seem most reluctant today to 'go nuclear' are the ones with the highest safety standards and best-developed risk cultures. By contrasts, in China there are currently 49 nuclear reactors in operation, 17 are being built, and another 100 are planned to become operative by 2035. As for the country's safety standards and risk culture, the death rate from coal extraction in China is fifty times that of Europe per ton of carbon (please read again footnote 8 to put the fossil fuel mortality rate reported in Fig 14.1 in context).

One may object that there is no need for taking risks as great as those entailed by the nuclear energy industry because today we have viable sources of renewable energy that are probably cheaper,[12] and certainly safer. As I shall discuss in more detail in Chapter 15, however,

[11] WHO. This source is very conservative in its estimate. A recent study by Vohar et al. (2021) puts the global death toll from fossil fuel emissions at more than 8 million.

[12] Saying that they are cheaper is correct, but the costs in the production of nuclear energy have not fallen because the regulatory burden in the West has kept on increasing.

Energy consumption by source, France
Primary energy consumption is measured in terawatt-hours (TWh). Here an inefficiency factor (the 'substitution' method) has been applied for fossil fuels, meaning the shares by each energy source give a better approximation of final energy consumption.

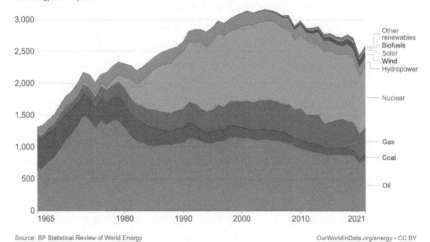

Source: BP Statistical Review of World Energy   OurWorldinData.org/energy • CC BY
Note: 'Other renewables' includes geothermal, biomass and waste energy.

14.2 Energy consumption by power source – France. Source: Our World in Data.

because of the intermittent nature of wind and solar power, relying *only* on renewable sources of energy requires a massive over-sizing of their capacity: if we have to do with zero sources of 'firm' energy (of which nuclear is by far the cleanest), we would require installations of renewables approximately six times as large than if both firm and intermittent energy were produced at the same time. (See Sepulveda et al., 2018, for a study focussed on the United States.)[13] Even leaving cost considerations to one side, this over-sizing creates strong competition (with agriculture and with reforestation) for physical space, especially if we want to future-proof our climate solutions, that is, if we take into account the projected growth in energy needs and population from today to the end of the century.

And let's be clear: if deployed in large scale, nuclear energy does make a huge difference in terms of emissions. Figs 14.2 and 14.3 show the

---

[13] For zero emissions without firm resources, 'the total required installed generation and storage power capacity with renewables alone would be five to eight times the peak system demand, compared with 1.3–2.6 times peak demand when firm resources are available'. Sepulveda et al. (2018).

Energy consumption by source, Germany

Primary energy consumption is measured in terawatt-hours (TWh). Here an inefficiency factor (the 'substitution' method) has been applied for fossil fuels, meaning the shares by each energy source give a better approximation of final energy consumption.

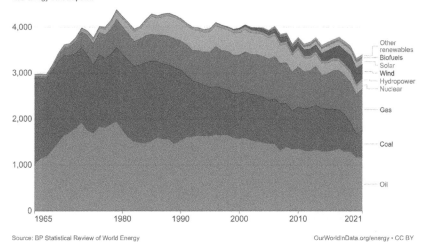

Source: BP Statistical Review of World Energy
Note: 'Other renewables' includes geothermal, biomass and waste energy.

OurWorldInData.org/energy • CC BY

14.3 Energy consumption by power source – Germany. Source: Our World in Data.

energy-source mix of energy consumption for two otherwise geographically and industrially very similar countries: Germany and France. After the Fukuyama accident, Germany has turned its back on nuclear energy, while France has stayed the nuclear course and, as of this writing, is still planning to expand its nuclear power capabilities.[14] As the figures show, despite the large effort to move into renewables, the lion's share of Germany's energy production still relies massively on fossil fuels. By contrast, oil- and coal-plant emissions to produce the electricity France consumes, which accounted up to the 1970s for almost 60 per cent of its electricity production, are now almost zero.

Another important observation: I have shown in Fig 12.4 how steep (and, at a global level, unprecedented) the decline in CO_2 emissions has to be in order to approximate the optimal policy recommended by the modern version of the DICE model – a policy, you will recall, that should just keep us below 2 °C by the end of the century. I have carried out an extensive (although non-systematic) search of the per capita emission

[14] In October 2021 President Macron announced a plan to add the new-generation micro-reactors to the energy-production mix.

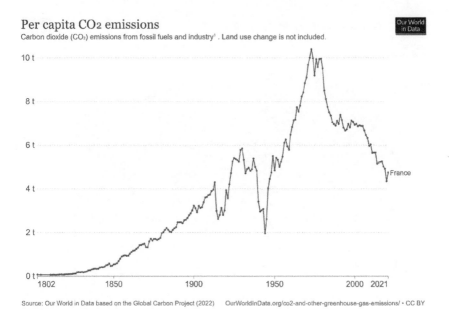

Per capita CO2 emissions
Carbon dioxide (CO₂) emissions from fossil fuels and industry¹ . Land use change is not included.

Source: Our World in Data based on the Global Carbon Project (2022)   OurWorldInData.org/co2-and-other-greenhouse-gas-emissions/ · CC BY

1. **Fossil emissions**: Fossil emissions measure the quantity of carbon dioxide (CO₂) emitted from the burning of fossil fuels, and directly from industrial processes such as cement and steel production. Fossil CO₂ includes emissions from coal, oil, gas, flaring, cement, steel, and other industrial processes. Fossil emissions do not include land use change, deforestation, soils, or vegetation.

14.4 Per capita CO_2 emissions – France. Source: Our World in Data on the Global Carbon Project (2022).

patterns for the countries covered by the excellent Our World in Data source. The only country for which I have been able to detect a pace of *voluntary* emission abatement anywhere close to what would be required to meet the 2 °C target has been France.[15] As Fig 14.4 shows, there has been a sudden, sustained and large drop in emissions starting with the 1980s. As Fig 14.5 then shows, this coincides with the sharp increase in energy provided by nuclear fission. (Fig 14.2 conveys a similar message using a different metric, energy consumption by power source.) Which brings me to the punchline: barring wars and disasters, strong reliance on nuclear energy has so far been perhaps the only way to reduce carbon emissions at a pace consistent with remaining within 2 °C warming by the end of the century. (Despite the massive investment in renewables,

[15] The other sharp drop in Fig 14.5 is associated with Second World War – not an emission-reduction option we want to consider.

Share of energy consumption by source, France

To convert from primary direct energy consumption, an inefficiency factor has been applied for fossil fuels (i.e. the 'substitution method').

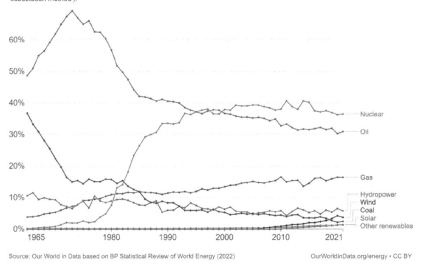

Source: Our World in Data based on BP Statistical Review of World Energy (2022)   OurWorldInData.org/energy • CC BY

14.5 Share of energy consumption by source – France. Source: Our World in Data.

the fall in per capita emissions from their peak for Germany has been of 40 per cent; for France it has been of 60 per cent.)

So, despite the unavoidable risks of nuclear energy, and given the gravity of the climate problem, a strong case can be made that the nuclear industry should have an important role in the portfolio of initiatives and partial solutions to tackle climate change.

Despite all of this, I do harbour very serious reservations about 'going nuclear' – and these, strangely enough, are hardly ever mentioned by my students.[16] What literally keeps me awake at night when I think of nuclear energy are the risks from using the by-products from nuclear energy production for military purposes. Once again, I do not lose much sleep about the risks of Switzerland or Sweden developing uranium enriching facilities. I am far more worried, however, when countries in unstable parts of the world, often rich in other energy sources, and often with few

[16] I often wonder whether this may have anything to do with my growing up in the darkest hours of the Cold War confrontation. At the time I was too young to remember it, but the Cuban missile crisis, which saw the Soviet Union and the United States a small step away from a nuclear confrontation, occurred four years after my birth.

apparent concerns for global warming, nonetheless find that they desperately need to add nuclear energy to their energy mix. Unfortunately, as Goldstone (2011) points out, 'to address climate change, nuclear energy will need to become much more widespread, so many new nations will need to join the nuclear "club", and indeed 61 nations without nuclear power, […] including developing nations around the globe such as Bolivia, Madagascar, and Yemen, have begun to explore the option of nuclear power through discussions with the International Atomic Energy Agency (IAEA). This presents the danger of greatly multiplying the number of nations with access to weapons materials.'[17]

Alarming as this might be, I do not see how this can be prevented: it is hardly realistic to envisage a supranational body authorizing countries to develop nuclear power plants based on their safety record and/or geopolitical risk. Even if such a supranational institution could be set up, it is difficult to imagine how it could enforce its deliberations. Therefore I fear that a world in which most countries had nuclear power plants, and the attending uranium enriching facilities, would be a vastly less stable one.[18] Admittedly, there have been proposals from the IAEA and Russia to establish international uranium enrichment facilities. The (very clever) idea behind these initiatives is to bring all enrichment capacity, *and ultimately all enrichment*, under international control. And, indeed, there is an International Uranium Enrichment Centre (IUEC) already in operation at Angarsk in Siberia, with Russia, Kazakhstan, Armenia and Ukraine as the participating states. The goal is to provide auditable supplies of low-grade uranium for power-generation

---

[17] Page 142.

[18] Natural uranium contains only about 0.7 per cent of the U-235 isotope, which is the main fissile isotope of uranium for the most common reactor designs. Light-water reactors require uranium enriched to 3–5 per cent. Research nuclear reactors usually require enrichment between 7 and 20 per cent, but there are exceptions (for instance, the ILL High-Neutron-Flux Research reactor in Grenoble where I used to conduct research in the 1980s, and which produces the world's highest continuous flux of neutrons for research use, requires enrichment up to 97 per cent). Weapon-grade uranium requires enrichment up to 90 per cent. Since the different isotopes of uranium only differ in the number of neutrons, they have the same chemical properties, and can therefore be separated only by physical processes, such as centrifugal selection. Fortunately, because of the small difference in mass between the isotopes, enriching uranium to military-grade levels is technologically not trivial.

use, but no enrichment facilities, to countries with little or no nuclear capabilities (and that should, hopefully, stay that way). Interestingly, the development of the Russia-led IUEC project at Angarsk (which occurred before the 2022 Russian invasion of Ukraine) had been seen positively by the United States. Unfortunately, I do not see how a determined country with powerful backers can be prevented from developing its own enrichment facilities. As the case of North Korea shows, the poverty of the country need not be an impediment. And, in all likelihood, this rogue, go-solo country would be in a geopolitically unstable part of the world. As for the wisdom in accepting dependence on a geopolitically aggressive country such as Russia for one's uranium enrichment (and hence energy supply), one has to look no further than the predicament Europe found itself in the winter of 2022.

Many (most?) economists come to the same conclusions I reach about the desirability of nuclear energy, but they often are less worried than I am about nuclear proliferation. In his recent book, for instance, MIT's Prof Pindyck[19] plays down the destabilization risks of too many states 'going nuclear' by claiming that sanctions against countries that want to acquire military nuclear capabilities are effective, and that the reprocessing or enrichment processes are complex enough to create a high barrier to entry. And, he claims, a country determined to gain access to nuclear weapons can directly build a reactor designed to produce plutonium, by-passing the nuclear-power-construction plant stage. So, in his view, nuclear *power* plants are very indirectly linked to nuclear military proliferation. Yet the strategy of building a power nuclear plant from which military-grade uranium can then be obtained seems to be already actively explored by the so-called hedger states. As Brewer, Miller and Volpe (2022) point out:

> [h]edgers develop the capacity to build the bomb for ostensibly peaceful purposes, such as fueling nuclear power plants [...]. Sometimes, they also develop nonnuclear missiles or space launch capabilities that can later be modified for nuclear delivery systems. Such investments underwrite an insurance policy against aggression by adversaries or abandonment by

---

[19] Pindyck 2022, page 154–255.

allies, *since much of the same technology can be used to build nuclear weapons later if the security environment deteriorates.*[20]

The same authors point to South Korea and Saudi Arabia as two countries that may be currently pursuing such a hedging strategy. Ultimately, the fact remains that countries in unstable regions of the world that feel threatened by hostile nuclear powers, without their own nuclear deterrent capabilities have to rely on the nuclear umbrella of their 'protectors' – on the 'kindness', that is, if not of strangers, at least of allies. In this situation, the temptation to build a nuclear insurance can be rational for each individual country, but highly destabilizing at the collective level.

In sum: *if* the production of enriched fissile material could be centralized and put under solid international control; and *if* the world found a way to prevent go-alone countries from developing their own enrichment capabilities,[21] I think that the nuclear option would have an important role to play in our attempts to control global warming. Currently, I do not see, however, how the conditions of both 'ifs' can be met, and I am therefore reluctant to look for the solution to a very serious problem (global warming) by sowing the seeds of an enormous one (a nuclear war). I have no objections to (many) more nuclear power plants being installed in stable countries, with low levels of corruption, high accountability and strong risk cultures. I just don't see how to limit the membership to the nuclear club only to the countries that satisfy these admission criteria.

[20] Brewer E, Miller N L and Volpe T, Ukraine Won't Ignite a Nuclear Scramble, *Foreign Affairs*, online edition, 17 November 2022, emphasis added.

[21] In the specific case of North Korea, its know-how for nuclear energy production was passed on to them by the then Soviet Union in the late 1960s. In the 1970s North Korea acquired a Soviet-era Scud missile from Egypt, and managed to reverse-engineer it to produce its two first missiles, the Hwasong-5 and the Hwasong-6. (Warrick J and Vitkovskaya J, North Korea's Nuclear Weapons, *Washington Post*, March 9, 2018.) A succession of US presidents and of diplomatic dispositions ranging from the conciliatory to the belligerent have then been unable to rein in the North Korean nuclear programme. And at the time of this writing we all know the difficulties of re-establishing negotiations with Iran after the previous nuclear accord was rescinded by President Trump.

What are the alternatives? If we accept that we must have 'firm' energy sources alongside renewable ones, and if we only consider well-proven and relatively established technologies, we are not exactly spoiled for choice: apart from nuclear fission, the process whereby CO_2 is captured at emissions and stored underground 'forever' is the most obvious candidate. But let's not forget that, after the various attending 'frictions' are taken into account, it is far less emission-friendly than nuclear energy, and presents significant logistical problems. If nuclear fission makes us uneasy because of proliferation risks, what about nuclear *fusion*, then?

14.2 FUSION

Fusion is the vaccine for climate change
—Chris Mowry (CEO of General Fusion)

There are many technologies that currently show promise in humanity's attempts to control global warming, but have not reached the stage of large-scale deployment. I have decided not to discuss in this book these nascent or unproven proposed solutions, because doing so involves building theories and projections on foundations that are speculative to begin with – usually, not a great strategy. My biggest omission, in this respect, is my failure to examine in some detail some forms of geoengineering – a big omission because these proposed solutions could be both cheap and quick to deploy, potentially making a difference in a year or two after deployment, rather than decades. Despite this, I have decided to make an exception for nuclear fusion, because, if the energy it produces could be economically harnessed, it would be totally transformative – hence the quote that opens this chapter.

Two lines of techy stuff: *fission* energy comes from splitting a suitable heavy nucleus into lighter nuclei and neutrons. As the lighter nuclei plus left-over neutrons have a lower total mass, and mass-energy must be conserved,[22] there is some 'left-over' energy, that we can use to boil

---

[22] The difference in mass is tiny. However, as the only Einstein equation everybody knows tells us, $E = mc^2$. In the formula c is the speed of light, which, as also everybody knows, is a huge number, and it is squared, which makes it even bigger. That is why even a small difference in mass is equivalent to a huge amount of energy.

some water in a turbine. The reaction is exoenergetic, in the sense that it produces more energy than what is needed to get it started.

Also with fusion we get energy from reaching a lower energy state, but in this case we combine superlight nuclei into slightly heavier elements. (The 'sweet spot' of minimum energy is attained for mid-size nuclei, around Fe.) The problem is that to break up a heavy nucleus (what you do with fission) you just have to bombard it with a neutron of just-right energy; however, convincing two isotopes of hydrogen (deuterium and tritium) to come close enough to fuse into a helium atom and a neutron is vastly more difficult, because the 'strong force' between nucleons is only felt at very short distances, and the weaker-but-longer-range electrostatic force between the positively charged protons creates a strong repulsive barrier.[23] The temperature to which these nuclei have to be brought for fusion to occur is *extremely* high (about 150 million degree Celsius, which means ten times hotter than the core of the Sun). Clearly, no structural material can withstand these temperatures. In stars, it is gravity that pulls the light nuclei together. (This may seem surprising, as the force of gravity is extremely weak. However, within stars the quantities of hydrogen are huge,[24] and gravity 'wins' by virtue of the sheer quantity of mass.) In fusion reactors the confinement of the plasma must be achieved by means other than gravity, such as super strong magnetic fields.[25] For someone with my background this is all really fascinating stuff, but for our purposes the only thing of relevance here is that, because of its very nature, fusion poses unparalleled technological challenges and it is not obvious that these difficulties will be overcome in the near future. Only expensive research will tell us how to crack this

---

[23] A nucleus is made up of neutrons (with no charge) and protons (positively charged). They are both referred to as nucleons, and all nucleons experience the very strong, but extremely short-range, strong force. Finally, isotopes are nuclei with the same number of protons – and hence the same *chemical* properties – but different number of neutrons – and therefore different *physical* properties, such as weight.

[24] This is not surprising, as 92 per cent of the atoms found in the universe are hydrogen; when one adds 7.1 per cent of helium atoms, everything else is almost a rounding error – a rounding error to which we owe our existence.

[25] Plasma is the fourth state of matter (neither solid, nor liquid, nor gas) and involves charged particles. It is the most abundant state in the universe, because it is the state of matter present in all stars, including the Sun.

nut – and whether the nut can be cracked at all in scale. And expensive research needs funding.

Now, there has been much talk in recent years of a 'surge' in funding for fusion projects. An October 2021 survey by the Fusion Industry Association reports that eighteen private firms have attracted $2.4 billion in funding for fusion projects – indeed, a record. Almost all the funding (and this is important) has come from private sources.[26] When people begin talking in billions, one immediately gets the impression that the figures in questions must be huge. They are anything but. A better way to characterize the sum of $2.4 billion is beer money – actually, not quite, since Americans alone spend $30 billion per year on beer. Other yardsticks to gauge the size of the investment in fusion research are the amount spent by Americans on Christmas trees ($6.1 billion in 2021);[27] on grooming American pets ($9.5 billion in 2021);[28] or the $1 billion spent on turkeys on Thanksgiving day alone. So, when put in perspective, this means that the invisible hand of the market is devoting a tiny amount to a project that could have a transformative impact on climate change.

This is not atypical. Many energy projects, much less financially risky than nuclear fusion, would have remained expensive niche curiosities had it not been for government intervention. Take solar panels. The first modern-era solar panels were installed in outer space in 1958 to power the Vanguard satellites. (This happened four short years after the first photovoltaic cells were invented.) The energy these panels could produce came with the exorbitant price tag of $300/watt. To put things in perspective, the company First Solar claimed in 2019 to be able to produce panels with a running cost of 40 cents/watt. How did this happen?

The free-market textbook tale is that, yes, the first solar panel may have been extremely expensive when first produced, and only justifiable because in outer space there are no alternatives. However, as the technology developed, the cost would go down a bit, extending the use of solar panels to another application with few alternatives (who knows, mountain refuges in the Alps). The industry would then expand a bit,

---

[26] See P. Ball, 2021, The Chase for Nuclear Energy, *Nature*, which provides an excellent survey.

[27] Finder.com using data from the National Christmas Tree Association.

[28] American Pet Products Association.

and, by doing so, would become a bit more efficient, thereby making the product economically viable for another sector (say, lighthouses). You get the drift: by small incremental steps the good in question would be transformed from a chunky, inefficient luxury item to a slick and infinitely superior mass commodity (as it has indeed happened to, say, personal computers, mobile phones or cars).

But this is not at all what happened with solar energy production. If mountain refuges and lighthouses had to wait for the magic of unaided 'learning by doing', they would still be, literally, in the dark. All over the world, government subsidies have played a key role in turning photovoltaic cells from the most expensive to one of the cheapest sources of energy. It all started in Germany, where historically both the Social Democrats and the Green Party have always pursued doggedly the solar route. As *The Economist* writes[29] '…[a]s of 2004, installations of any size could sell any amount of solar energy to the grid for EUR457 ($567) per megawatt-hour – about five times what it cost to generate electricity from coal at the time. The price was guaranteed for 20 years. The touchpaper was lit. And the rocket took off. By 2012 Germany had paid out more than â,¬200bn in subsidies. It had also changed the world. Between 2004 and 2010 the global market for solar panels grew 30-fold as investors in Germany and the other countries which followed its lead piled in.'[30]

What is the message here? That we tend to extrapolate the extraordinary allocation capabilities of the market from those goods and services where it *does* have an unparalleled success record, to, well, everything. To be sure, state-directed funding of economic initiatives has had, at best, a chequered record of success – pithily summarized in the slogan

[29] *The Economist*, How Governments Spurred the Rise of Solar Power, Technology Quarterly, July 2021.

[30] It is not just the case of energy production. UCL Economics Professor Mariana Mazzuccato has documented in her controversial but, in my view, excellent book *The Entrepreneurial State* (2013) the important role played by the government in facilitating economic growth. The book pulls no punches, as it argues that innovations in areas as varied as medicine or the Silicon Valley high tech products have benefitted in substantial ways from state help. Despite what some critics have said, the book should not be read, I believe, as making the case that the state can always channel resources better than the private sector (if it could, the Soviet Union of the 1980s would have been an economic powerhouse), but as a powerful corrective to the ideology that efficient allocation of resources is only achieved via private funding.

'governments are bad at picking winners'. But when it comes to financially high-risk, long-horizon, strategically important investments, there
are very few alternatives. The 'strategically important' part here is as
important as the 'high risk' and 'long-horizon' bits. Saying that something is strategically important (when it is not empty rhetoric, or a dis-
guise for protectionist measures), means that there are positive externalities associated with its production. And, as we have seen, markets do not
price externalities (positive or negative) properly. In these conditions,
government intervention of *some* sort[31] is not just desirable – it is simply
indispensable.[32]

Which brings us back to the pitifully small amounts invested in nuclear
fusion, especially in the United States. Solar panels and wind turbines
have been generously subsidized,[33] and to great effect, but only crumbs
have been left for fusion research. Yes, crumbs: when the US Department
of Energy trumpets *$50 Million for Fusion Research at Tokamak and Spherical
Tokamak Facilities*, we know that there is a problem: $50 Million is the
price-tag of a single top-end mansion in Bishops Avenue, Hampstead,
London.[34] In Europe the public funding is more generous, as EUR5.61
billion have been approved for the funding of ITER, the European fusion
research project for the period 2021–2027. But this still amounts to less
that EUR 1 billion per year for all of Europe. The amount per year spent
on European healthcare is 1,000 times larger. Or, if you prefer, EUR 1
billion per year is twice the amount spent on defence by that military
giant, Luxembourg. Why has this been the case? Why have taxpayers
been so much more generous with wind and solar subsidies than with
the funding of fusion research?

---

[31] The intervention doesn't have to be via subsidies; sometimes it can happen by creating
the 'missing markets', if one has a Coasian rather then Pigouvian view of externalities.

[32] I should add that some economists, such as UCL Professor Mariana Mazzuccato, whom
I mention in footnote 30, take a much more sanguine view, and argue that the role of
the state should be much wider than just fixing market failures.

[33] The subsidies for renewables worldwide exceeded $120 billion in 2017. IRENA
working paper, Energy Subsidies: Evolution in the Global Energy Transformation to
2050, January 2020 – an excellent reference on global subsidies, including to the fossil
fuel industry.

[34] In case you were wondering, the most expensive house in London – as of Autumn
2022 – was sold for £210m in January 2020.

As we are entering the murky waters of political policymaking I can only speculate here; but, if pressed, I would say that renewables can be 'sold' to voters much more easily than negative emission technologies (unless the negative emission technology in question is afforestation), and *infinitely* more easily than anything with the word 'nuclear' attached to it. If I am correct, this is a sad and dangerous state of affairs, because fusion energy, transformative as it would be, will *certainly* remain a constant thirty years in the future (as the joke goes), if private financing remains the only source of funding – and will be only marginally more likely ever to bring tangible fruits unless public funding increases dramatically.[35]

14.3 THE MILITARY THREAT FROM FUSION POWER REACTORS

Finally, what about the danger of military nuclear proliferation – the very danger that cools my enthusiasm for fission power reactors? Hydrogen bombs,[36] after all, are every bit as deadly as uranium or plutonium (fission-based) bombs; if anything, they are even more destructive. Would building a new generation of fusion power plant open the door to even more unchecked nuclear military proliferation? Does the winding road that leads to a nuclear fusion power plant eventually take us to the building of a hydrogen bomb?

Saying anything definite is almost impossible in this case, because no single fusion reactor has been built yet, and the potential for military repurposing of fusion power reactors are speculative at best. There are, however, some considerations that suggest that fusion power reactors are different and pose less of a proliferation danger. First of all, a nuclear

---

[35] The private firms who have obtained the $2.4 billion funding in 2021 are currently promising energy from fusion by the 2030s. I hope I am wrong, but I think that this is on the optimistic side – which, after all, is not surprising: if your (financial) existence depends on attracting private funding for a project such as nuclear fusion, an unlimited optimism must be one of your defining character traits. Or, to put it a bit more cynically, would you tell investors anything different?

[36] A short note about terminology. 'Atomic bomb' is a generic term often used to designate both fission and fusion devices, although more commonly used for fission bombs. I prefer not to use this term. The designations 'thermonuclear' and 'hydrogen' both refer to devices based on fission. I use them interchangeably.

hydrogen bomb requires the combination of a conventional fission device for the primary stage (fuelled by 235U or 239Pu), and a secondary stage thermonuclear part (containing deuterium and tritium, isotopes of hydrogen). Since the 235U isotope is rare (the natural abundance of 238U is 99.274 per cent, and of 235U is 0.72 per cent), the enrichment facilities needed for a conventional fission bomb are still required to build a hydrogen bomb. So, if a country's ultimate goal is to build a nuclear arsenal, there is no reason to go for a fusion reactor, as the much 'simpler' fission reactor will do the job.

Which brings me to the second point: we don't even know for sure whether fusion power reactors will ever see the light of day. If they do, formidable technological problems will have to be solved. These problems are vastly more difficult than those attending the construction of a fission bomb, which could be solved with the technology of the mid 1940s. So, the technological challenges of building fusion reactors naturally create an enormous barrier to entry. By near-starving its population, a 'rogue state' such as North Korea has managed to build fission bombs. But it is not easily conceivable that a future North Korea will be able to muster the technology of fusion power, and then use it for military purposes. And, in any case, if a country is hell-bent on producing a thermonuclear military device, a fusion power plant is not needed: the first hydrogen bomb, after all, was detonated in 1952, and, even if the claim is disputed, North Korea (that certainly does *not* have fusion power plants) maintains to have tested a thermonuclear device in 2016. In sum: I do not see fusion power reactors adding to the nuclear proliferation threat posed by fission reactors. We would not be opening another Pandora's box if we developed fusion power plants: we would simply be leaving the same box as gapingly open as, alas, it already is.

CHAPTER 15

Constraints

We have as little time as our great and finely articulated continent has space,
we must be as economical of the one as of the other, we must husband them …
[Settembrini to Hans Castorp]
> —Thomas Mann, *The Magic Mountain*, 1924, transl. H T Lowe-Porter

T HE APPROACH TAKEN BY ECONOMISTS when assessing the desirability of different abatement options implicitly assumes that we can deploy the optimal solution at any scale – if anything, as we 'do more and more of something' economies of scale and the process of 'learning by doing' might kick in and even facilitate the task. However, when the abatement effort is as big as what is required to tackle climate change, this should not be taken for granted. To clarify the point, let me make a contrived and extreme example: let's assume that wind turbines are determined by our economic analysis to be the most effective way to curb emissions. The next question is: in this wind-turbine-only world, is there enough physical space on which to erect the turbines? At first blush, the question may seem strange, but it is only after quantifying both the supply and the demand side of the equation (how much energy is required and how much can be provided if we fill all the available land with wind turbines) that we can give a meaningful answer.

An only slightly less contrived example is the following. It is widely recognized that, in order to limit global warming to 1.5–2 °C by the end of the century, negative-emission technologies – technologies, that is, which remove CO_2 from the atmosphere – are going to be needed. In this context the 'trillion tree project' is often mentioned, often as a get-out-of-jail card that will allow us to limit our emission-curbing efforts.[1] Planting trees sounds like one of the greenest and least painful decarbonization options on the table. However, a back-of-the-envelope calculation shows that planting one trillion trees requires as much land *as the whole of Brazil – the whole lot, not just the Amazon forest.*[2] Let's not get into the details of how desirable planting one-trillion trees may actually be (a serious analysis must take into account, for instance, the poor albedo of trees,[3] often lower than the surface on which the trees are planted; the competition for land with agriculture, and with solar and wind farms; the fact that only *growing* forests achieve a net subtraction of CO_2 from the atmosphere; and so on). The fact remains that devoting an area as large as the whole of Brazil to tree planting must have deep implications for land competition (with agriculture, and with large-scale installations of renewable energy plants, such as wind farms), and, therefore, on food prices.[4] Constraints of this type must be taken into account for a serious analysis of the climate-control problem.

---

[1] See, e.g., www.trilliontreecampaign.org/ for a very one-sided view of the benefits and feasibility of planting one trillion trees.

[2] Of course, once we have planted our trillion trees, it's not that we are done forever. Once the huge forest is fully grown and reaches 'steady state', a huge amount of carbon will have been *stored*, but no additional emissions will be captured. It would be time to find the space to plant another Brazil-worth of forests. In economics one says that you cannot fix a *flow* problem (the continuing emissions) with a *stock* solution (a one-off subtraction of CO_2, however large).

[3] 'Albedo' is a measure of how much of the incoming electromagnetic radiation from the Sun is directly reflected by the terrestrial surface. The albedo for the Earth as a whole is about 0.3 (meaning that on average 30 per cent of the incoming energy is reflected), but there are huge variations depending on the reflective surface. Trees, especially conifers, have poor albedo (about 0.1), lower than the albedo of grassland that they may replace, and *much* lower than snow-clad land, which can have an albedo as high as 80 per cent.

[4] How big are the effects of land competition on food prices? One can look at the effect of ethanol mandates in the USA, that require a growing fraction of the corn production to be diverted to the production of ethanol as a petrol substitute. (The US ethanol project in its entirety is tragically ill-conceived, and, if you really care about CO_2 emissions, you could just as well fill your tank with petrol, but this is another story.) Joint work by Profs Roberts and Schlenker (2010) suggests that the diversion of land in the USA to fulfil the corn production mandate of the ethanol programme could cause the price of staples (corn and its substitutes) to grow as much as 30 per cent. Obviously, it is the world's poorest populations that stand to suffer most from this increase in global food prices.

The examples I have just presented are stylized in the extreme, but they show clearly the nature of the problem: in the equations of the Integrated Assessment Models we have looked at there was no 'you-are-running-out-of-land' constraint, nor was there a 'you-are-running-out-of-resources' constraint. Discounted costs and benefits were the only considerations at play in deciding which abatement options were worth taking. However, the physical feasibility issue is by no means a trivial one.[5] In this chapter I will therefore try to answer the question: 'Even if we assume the best will to curb emissions, is our abatement effort going to encounter obstacles due to hard constraints, such as land or sea-bed availability? Are these constraints going to affect our ability to decarbonize as much as desired by 2040, or 2050 or 2100, or whenever?'

Taking these questions seriously is important. Concerned citizens all over the world, understandably, look with bated breath at the vagaries of political favour for or against the taking of serious climate action.[6] These fears are well founded. However, we are much less attuned to the worries coming from the practical difficulties we may encounter even if we are committed to carrying out an ambitious abatement programme – I call these the unexpected bumps on the decarbonization road. As usual when it comes to climate-related matters, the problem is complex and nuanced. I intend to present an aspect of it in its essential elements in the remainder of this chapter. The aspect I want to focus on is whether we will have enough physical space to put all the wind turbines and solar panels that we are going to need.

[5] There is a broader debate, which goes beyond the climate-change arena, about the sustainability of the path of economic growth the planet has experienced in the relatively recent past. Some of the literature is rather strident and economically ill-informed. Among the good-quality commentators one can certainly number Herman Daly, an ecological economist and Emeritus Professor at the University of Maryland, School of Public Policy who also served as Senior Economist in the Environment Department of the World Bank. His *Economics for a Full World*, 2015, is certainly worth reading for wider perspective about physical limits to growth.

[6] I harbour no doubts whatsoever that the 2020 US American presidential elections were won by President Biden. It is also true, however, that a few tens of thousand votes in some critical states (as few as 40,000 according to the count by Woodward and Costa, 2021) could have reversed the result. What would the future have been for climate action if President Trump, as the leader of the biggest economy in the world, had been put in charge of climate policy for another four years?

Before we get started we must get some common misunderstandings out of the way. Land availability constraints are seldom mentioned because, the received wisdom goes, they are non-binding (which means that we don't have to worry about where to put the solar panels and the wind turbines). This can be correct if we look at today's requirements, and at today's energy mix. But, surely, we want to future-proof our climate solutions at least over the lifespan of our children. So, what we really want are estimates of what fraction of a country's present and future energy budget could be catered for by renewables (not just today and not only if we use energy the way we do today) without running out of space. When we take these considerations into account, the question of land availability becomes more complex, and it is easy to see estimates that may be technically correct, but that should be strongly caveated. So, what are the things to keep in mind?

How much energy a solar panel or a wind turbine produces (give or take some variations) is pretty easy to estimate. Also how much land one solar panel or wind turbine requires is pretty straightforward to calculate. This gives us the energy per unit area. So, to see if 'there is enough land' we just have to divide the total energy required by the energy per unit of land. It is the numerator (the total energy required) that is tricky to estimate, and where it is easy to make mistakes. What can go wrong with this estimate? First of all, when we see figures about how much of a country's energy expenditure could be covered by renewables, often these figures refer to electric energy, which is only about 20 per cent of the total energy budget. To stop global warming we have to decarbonize the whole economy, not just the electric sector. This is just a school-boy error, and I won't spend any more time on it. I only mention it because it is more common than it should be.

Second, as I explain later in the chapter, if we want to use *only* intermittent renewable sources, without recourse to 'firm' sources of energy such as nuclear or gas, we have to scale up the size of their installations by a factor of five to ten.[7] This, of course, is because of the

---

[7] A source of energy supply is called 'firm' if it can provide energy at any time, on demand. No need to explain what 'intermittent' means. 'Dispatchable' is any form of energy supply that can be used as 'back-up' when there is a shortfall of intermittent energy. Batteries are an example of a dispatchable source of energy.

intermittent nature of the energy supply from renewables. This means two things: first, that any estimate of how much energy from renewables will be available requires a precise specification of how much energy will be needed from firm or dispatchable energy sources; second, that looking at average energy usage makes little sense: our renewable-based solution must be able to handle peak demand, not average demand. This is why, if we say that we don't want *any* fossil-fuel plants (even if fitted with carbon sequestration and storage devices), and that we don't like nuclear energy, the weight on the shoulders of renewables becomes *much* heavier. This key piece of information (the fraction of energy from firm or dispatchable sources) is rarely mentioned.

Third, as I said, it does not make sense to look only at the energy needs today: our energy solutions must be reasonably future-proofed. We don't know how much energy we will need in the future, but, if the economists' projections of economic growth are anything to go by, the future energy needs will be much greater than today. We shall discuss the link between economic growth and energy expenditure in Section 15.1 in some detail, but here I am just making the point that very often land-constraints assessments just look at how much energy we need today, and this is really not very meaningful (especially with large parts of the world that still have to escape poverty via economic growth).[8]

Fourth, a fully decarbonized world will have energy requirements that we do not have today. These have to be added to the tally, and they may not be small at all. For instance, I have already explained that negative emission technologies must play an important role in any scenario compatible with a 1.5–2 °C temperature increase by the end of the century. Direct Carbon Capture is one of the scalable technologies that could be called upon to deliver the required carbon removal in scale, and without competing for land. Unfortunately, one of the problems with Direct Carbon Capture is that it consumes *a lot* of energy (the other one is cost). Another call on renewables may come from the production of hydrogen – often touted as a possible 'green' energy source. It is still too early to say whether the enthusiasm (or the hype?) around hydrogen is justified. What we know for sure, however, is that its production is very

---

[8] Is this really the only way? See a discussion of 'degrowth' options in Section 11.3.

energy thirsty. So it is the charging of the batteries that we will need to provide a part of the dispatchable energy required to smooth the intermittent availability of energy from renewables. Now, if we don't want to make the carbon-emissions problem worse, all these new demands on our energy budget will have to come from renewables. We have to add these items to our list – something that land availability estimates seldom .

This is just a foretaste of things to discuss. I will come back to all of these points in what follows, but I wanted to warn the readers from the start against over-optimistic estimates.

15.1 HOW MUCH ENERGY?

As mentioned above, in climate change as everywhere else, we have to balance the two sides of the supply/demand equation. In economics, the assumption is always made that a sufficiently strong demand automatically creates its own supply: increasing demand for a good or service will not run into a permanent scarcity problem because the last item will have the price that just clears the market. So, if the demand for good X increases, the last item of X might become very expensive, (perhaps because we now have to source its raw input materials from deep down the Mariana Trench), but this same last item produced of the desired good or service will have the price that equilibrates supply and demand. In a well-functioning market economy there is no rationing, there are no queues for goods in limited supply, and no shelves full of products nobody wants to buy. Is this assumption going to work in the case of the global energy demand and supply?

To answer the question, we first have to ask ourselves how large the demand for energy is going to be. There are two ways to look at the question. The first (simple but unsatisfactory) approach is to look at the present energy consumption, and to ask ourselves whether we can physically provide this amount of energy with renewable (or net-zero emission) sources.[9] This approach, which has been taken by several researchers, is unsatisfactory because we want to provide energy to power not just today's world, but also the world of our (great-grand-) children.

---

[9] To be precise, one should speak of *power* (energy per unit time), rather than energy.

Estimating how much energy they will need is clearly not easy. Let's attack the problem using the by-now-familiar technique: 'When faced with a difficult problem that you can't solve, try an easier problem that you can't solve'. So, as a prelude, we are first going to answer the question: 'How much do we expect the economy to grow over the next decades (or centuries)?'

I have explained at length in Chapter 10 how difficult answering this question is. However, most economists seem to have a solid expectation that the world economy will continue to grow – most of the debate is about the exact pace of growth. Furthermore, if we believe that in the next decades the poorest areas of the world will significantly improve their economic conditions, the demographic dynamics discussed in Chapter 11 point to a (temporary but prolonged) increase in population.[10] So, the planet would be facing both an increase in population *and* an increase in energy consumption per person. I cannot see how the current extreme inequality in living standards between different parts of the world can be reduced without these demographic dynamics playing out. In any case, most Integrated Assessment Models produce their optimal recommendations *given a robust path of economic growth.* It only makes sense, then, to consider an energy demand consistent with the model-assumed growth in the economy.

So, let's take a state-of-the-art new-and-improved version of the DICE model, and let's see what it implies for global growth.[11] The results are shown in Fig 15.1. This figure shows the expected global output up to the year 2300, and the uncertainty around this growth, represented the upper and lower curves. If the distribution of output followed a normal distribution, a bit less than 70 per cent of the realizations of output would fall within the upper and the lower curve. Going back to our initial question, we therefore need to ensure that somehow we produce enough

[10] The current population of Africa is about 1.4 billion. If the current high rate of infant mortality decreases, as it always does as economic conditions consistently improve, but fertility remains high, as it tends to in the first phases of economic catch-up, it is not fanciful to see a population close to 3 billion by the end of the century.

[11] For the technically minded reader, the growth model grafted onto the original DICE model is described in Bansal and Yaron (2004), as adapted by Jensen and Traeger (2014).

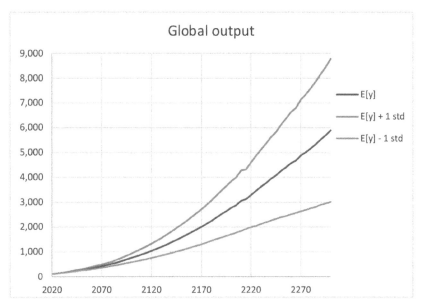

15.1 The expected global output up to year 2300, and its associated uncertainty, as obtained using a modern version of the DICE model.

'clean' energy to satisfy the vastly larger needs of the next centuries. You may object that projecting economic growth centuries ahead is probably foolhardy. Fig 15.2 shows that, even if we 'only' care about the next 100 years, we should still size our energy solutions to provide enough energy for a global output that may be ten times as large as today's.

So, let's assume that we have an order-of-magnitude handle on how much economic growth we can expect. This allows us to move to the next step. Throughout human history a growth in economic output has always been very solidly associated with a growth in energy expenditure. Economists get very excited about trying to establish whether there exists what they call 'Granger causality' between economic growth and energy expenditure: is economic growth causally responsible for greater usage of energy, or does the increase in energy usage propel the economic growth? The question is indeed interesting, but for our purposes we can content ourselves with the observation that there certainly exists a strong correlation (a much weaker concept than causation) between energy use and economic growth. The strength and clarity of the relationship is shown in Fig 15.3 (taken from the work of my colleague, Dherminder

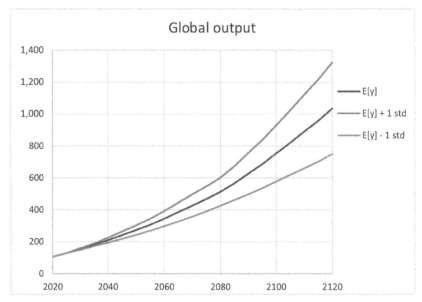

15.2 The expected global output up to one century from now, and its associated uncertainty, obtained using the same modern version of the DICE model.

Kainth (2021)), which shows the output growth (the logarithm of the ratio of the GDP for year i to the GDP in year 1965) against the growth in energy consumption (again, the logarithm of the ratio of the energy consumption for year i to the energy consumption in year 1965). In his work, which covers more than half a century of global data, Kainth (2021) tries to capture non-linearities in the relationship (this is the slightly curved red line in the figure), but for our purposes we can assume that we are just dealing with a straight line.

Keeping clear in the back of our mind the question we are trying to answer (are we going to find *physical* constraints to decarbonization), this relationship is extremely powerful. Given the output growth projected by the Integrated Assessment Model of our choice (shown in Figs 15.1 and 15.2 in the case of the modern DICE model), we can read off the straight line in Fig 15.3 (suitably extrapolated) what the energy requirements will be in a century's time (and if we are brave enough, even later).

Admittedly, this is a rough-and-ready estimate, which can be criticized on several accounts. For instance, there has been much talk about future economic growth being service-, not goods-led. Because of this, the

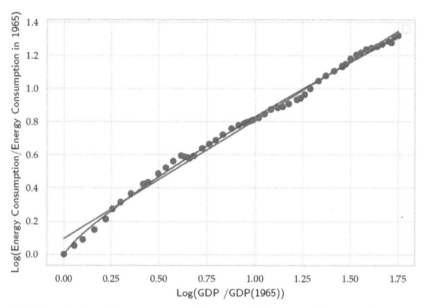

15.3 Normalized world energy consumption versus GDP expressed in terms of constant $2010 value from 1965 to 2020 (dots) along with power law fits (green and red continuous lines).

argument goes, we will require much less energy for this growth to happen: our 'carbon intensity' will decline. The argument, suggestive as it is, is far from convincing from a global perspective. First of all, many of the 'services' that the rich Western world seems to enjoy, such as exotic holidays, are far from being energy-light. Second, over the course of this century economic growth will hopefully spread to those parts of the world that have so far enjoyed so little of it. These regions will have to go through the goods-intensive phase of growth, exactly as China did and is still doing now. Third, the data in Fig 15.3 cover a period when a substantial part of the recorded growth is due to the developed world, where the transition from a goods to a service economy should already have taken place. Yet in the global data there is hardly any deviation from linearity (in logs). We can understand why this is the case by looking at Fig 15.4, which shows energy consumption per capita in different regions of the world. As the picture clearly shows, for some regions in the rich West energy consumption per person has stopped growing (and in the UK it even seems to be falling); however, in China and India it is still rising

273

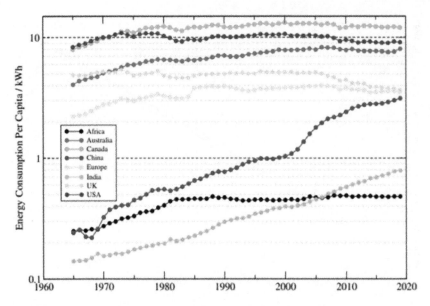

15.4 Energy consumption per capita in different regions of the world.

at a very fast pace. And, most important of all, in Africa there has been virtually no growth after the mid 1980s: when (I don't want to say 'if') sustained economic growth arrives in this part of the world, the quasi-linear upward trend (on a logarithmic scale) will continue for decades to come.[12] So, the relationship depicted in Fig 15.3, simple as it is, provides us with a very workable tool to explore future energy needs.

15.1.1 FROM ECONOMIC GROWTH TO ENERGY REQUIREMENTS.

Never try to walk across a river just because it has an average depth of four feet.

—Milton Friedman

How are we going to use this information? For a given projection of economic growth we can deduce how much energy this growth path will require. We can then make some assumptions about how much of this energy we want to be provided by renewable sources (wind and solar). (This is the bit about the role we want to allow firm energy supplies to

---

[12] A linear trend on a logarithmic scale obviously translates into an exponential growth in natural units.

play.) And, finally, we can explore whether land- and sea-bed availability poses binding constraints to these decarbonization plans.

Stated like this, it sounds easy, but let me state from the outset that carrying out this calculation properly is far more difficult than it may at first blush appear. As I said, we have to decide first whether we want to rely for electricity production *only* on renewables, or on renewables used alongside a background of always-available-on-demand ('firm') energy (such as nuclear, gas or coal, possibly with carbon sequestration and storage). The important point here is that electricity supply from renewables is highly intermittent, as so is demand. The energy produced by solar panels peaks around midday, which happens to be exactly when electricity demand is at its lowest. At this time of day, energy production is therefore higher than demand. As evening approaches, solar power generation then falls exactly when net demand increases. If we plot this mismatch as a function of time of day, it has a shape that, with Zodiac-sign-naming imagination, can be read as that of a duck (see Fig 15.5) – a duck whose neck has become more and more pronounced each year, as more solar capacity has been added over time.[13] And as for wind-turbine-generated energy, we cannot even base our planning on the broad time-of-day regularities available with solar power to schedule the back-up energy resources. So, if we want to gauge how many wind turbines or solar panels we have to install to meet this intermittent demand with the intermittent supply from renewables, knowing the *average* demand for electricity is no more useful than knowing that Milton Friedman's river is only four feet deep.[14]

This is why studies for the USA[15] (but broadly valid, *mutatis mutandis* to other parts of the globe) suggest that we would have to overscale the deployment of solar and wind installations by a factor of five to ten if

---

[13] This has a big impact on the cost-effectiveness of energy sources other than solar: utility companies are having to ramp up electricity production towards the evening, and this can cause stress on the grid. The non-renewable sources of energy (nuclear and coal) are only economic when they are running all the time, and the effective cost goes up a lot if they have to be used intermittently (and, sometimes, doing so is just plain impossible).

[14] The quote that opens this subsection is often attributed to Nassim Taleb, but Friedman came up with it a few decades earlier.

[15] See Sepulveda et al. (2018).

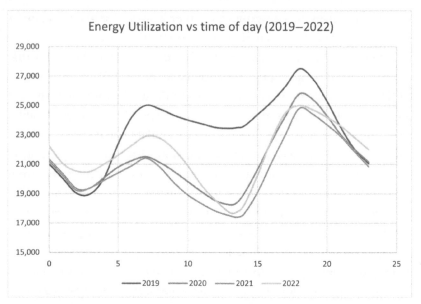

15.5 The 'duck curve': the daily pattern of electricity demand in California (megawatt) – first Saturday in February from 2019 to 2022. Data extracted from the California Independent System Operator (CAISO), reported in Elements.visualcapitalist.com.

we want to rely only on renewables. Given the intermittent and greatly variable nature of energy demand on the one hand, and of energy supply from renewables on the other, the less one can rely on 'firm' sources of energy, the more wind turbines and solar panels one is going to need – and, to achieve 'diversification', these must be located on wider and wider areas. (If, at a given point in time there is no wind at a given location, it hardly helps to have twice as many wind turbines in the *same* spot.) For the purpose of our analysis, the bottom line is that, if we wanted to rely only on renewables, just looking at the *average* energy requirement is not enough, and we have to scale up the electricity requirement by a substantial factor.

Then in our estimate we have to guess whether very-large-scale energy storage systems may come to commercial fruition in the medium-term future.[16] If they do, the reliance on firm sources of energy may be

---

[16] Large scale energy storage systems have to cater for vastly different timescales of energy supply, from minutes to weeks. They can be classified as mechanical (lifting a weight, typically water, so that its potential energy can be converted into kinetic energy – the

reduced, but the call on renewables to deal with the energy/supply mismatch by 'charging batteries' will be huge.

Next, we have to decide whether energy from renewables is going to be used not only for the applications we are today familiar with, but also for currently non-existing uses. We have seen, for instance, that virtually all the paths consistent with keeping the temperature increase within the Paris Accord 1.5–2 °C target require substantial removal of carbon from the atmosphere – something we are currently doing in absolutely negligible scale. To make a difference, carbon removal should take out of the atmosphere every year a significant fraction of today's emissions. One of the proposed technologies to remove carbon from the atmosphere is via Direct Carbon Removal, which, unfortunately, requires a lot of energy. Hydrogen could provide an important source of clean and 'fungible' (multi-use) energy, but it also requires a lot of energy to produce, as it is not found in its element form in the atmosphere.[17] If all these 'new' energy requirements are to be met by renewables, we have to add them to the total tally.

I could go on, but the point is that just counting how much energy is required from renewables (and therefore assessing whether there is 'enough land' for the attending installations) is not as simple as it may seem. Yet, the considerations I have touched upon are rarely mentioned in many optimistic accounts of how much energy the world may need by the end of the century. We are not talking about small change: if, by the end of the century, economic output is indeed going to be ten times as large as today, *and* we want to rely on renewables only, *and* we want to do a lot of Direct Carbon Removal, *and* we need to charge a lot of batteries to have dispatchable energy – then the energy requirement could easily be fifty times as large as today's. When these considerations and requirements are taken into account, loose constraints can quickly become binding.

Dinorwig pumped storage plant in Wales, for instance, can be ramped up in 16 seconds); electrochemical (batteries of various types); thermal (stored heat can be used to produce energy when needed, as with some new-design fission reactors); and chemical (whereby chemical bonds are created, as in the case of syngases – which are synthetic gas mixtures). For a good survey, see LDES and McKinsey & Company (2021).

[17] See Alverá (2021) for an interesting, if perhaps a bit uncritically positive, discussion of the potential uses of hydrogen as a source of energy.

15.2 SO, IS THERE ENOUGH LAND (AND SEA)?

All of this brings us back to the question we started from: is there going to be enough land (and suitable sea-beds) to host the solar panels and wind turbines needed to decarbonize the whole economy (not just the 'easy' electricity component)? And is a renewables-only solution going to be future proof – able, that is, to accommodate our presumably increasing energy needs?[18]

It is clear that any answer can at best be tentative: we have to make informed guesses about the dispersion of economic growth to the end of the century; on how much we decide to rely on fission nuclear energy; on whether significant technological breakthroughs will materialize; and so on. We also have to decide how much agricultural land we are willing to 'sacrifice' without unacceptable knock-on effects on food prices. Lancrenon et al. (2022) make a number of educated guesses, based on data available from the latest IPCC report and a number of reliable sources, and come up with a set of nuanced, but sobering, answers.

Their first conclusion is that the adequacy of renewables-only sources of energy to power the whole economy strongly depends on the population density of the region considered (they look at the USA, Europe, China, Japan and India). So, Japan, with relatively little 'suitable' land and a high population is in the worst predicament, with not enough available space to house, alongside its agricultural land, all the solar panels and wind turbines needed to cater even for today's energy requirements. At the opposite end of the spectrum there is the USA, that could cater for its whole energy needs with renewables all the way to the end of the century in the case of low growth (5th percentile), and for almost half a century in the 95th-percentile growth scenario. China, India and Europe are then in an intermediate situation, 'running out of space' in a few decades (Europe probably sooner than either India or China).

---

[18] A recent study by McKinsey (Land: A Crucial Resource for the Energy Transition, May 2023,) points out that, once regulatory, technical and environmental constraints are taken into account, of the German land potentially available for wind turbines, only 18 per cent remains usable. Similar reductions apply to other Western countries. Effective land availability can therefore be considerably smaller than what is assumed in most calculations, and in the estimates that follow.

Can energy from renewables be transported from renewable-energy-richer to energy-poorer regions? To some extent it can, but electrons cannot be sent down a pipeline as gas can, nor can they be put in tankers and shipped around the world. They can be transmitted down power lines, but not without significant losses. Currently, a few thousand kilometres is about as much as one can go without really big losses of power.[19] So, ideas such as covering millions of acres of the Sahara desert with solar panels would work if the energy were needed nearby. Sahara-generated electricity would be of little use, however, to power Japanese appliances.

As a sanity check, we can revisit the analysis of the availability of sea beds for wind turbines carried out by Cambridge physicist McKay (2009) for the United Kingdom that I presented in Section 15.2. First of all, let's remind ourselves that Britain is blessed with a total coastline few countries of the same size can boast, and is buffeted by winds described with British understatement as 'robust'.[20] As I mentioned, McKay makes an extremely aggressive assumption about the deployment of shallow and deep offshore wind turbines: in his scenario, one third of the British shallow waters (an area, as I pointed out, the size of a third of Wales) are going to be used to install shallow-water wind turbines. This means filling the equivalent of a strip 4 km deep *all around the coastline of the UK*. To this McKay adds deep-offshore turbine installations, exploiting sea beds with depths up to 50 meters (it is currently extremely difficult to locate wind turbines in deeper waters). Since the sea beds around the UK do not fall off very quickly (as far as wind energy goes, another lucky feature of the UK physical geography), the furthest turbines will be located only 50 km from the nearest shore. How much energy does this massive deployment of wind turbines produce? McKay calculates that doing all of this can realistically provide 50 kWh/d per person – that is to say, a little bit more than what the average UK citizen consumes (about 40 kWh/d) *just to drive her car*. Non-commercial transportation is

---

[19] Even with current transmission and distribution networks in the USA, the average amount of energy lost ranges from a minimum of 2.2 per cent (for Wyoming) to a maximum of 13.3 per cent (for Idaho). *Energy Information Administration.*

[20] The average UK wind speed is almost twice that of Italy, a country of similar size and length of coastline.

a sizeable fraction of the total energy expenditure, but the total energy expenditure for the average UK person is close to 200 kWh/d – and these are just *today's* energy requirements. And we have not factored in the overscaling of average energy supply from wind due to its intermittent nature, nor have we added the 'other' energy uses renewables may be called upon to fulfil in the future.

The important point from all of this is that there are many bumps along the decarbonization road, and some are more visible than others. We are all (rightly) attuned to the vagaries of the political process in the West and in the USA in particular, where a Trump-like president could easily derail the global abatement effort (given the free-riding nature of the global warming problem, one large defector is enough to sink the whole project). There are, however, some hazards that are less obvious. As we have discussed, the *global* reliance on rare earths to build solar panels, electric cars and wind turbines, but the *geographically localized* supply of the same elements together make up one such hidden bump on the road. In this chapter I have tried to shine some light on another possible bump on the road to net-zero that is hiding in plain sight: the availability of land, and the consequences that land competition can have. The point I have tried to make is not that the green transition is impossible. Simply, that it is more difficult to achieve than usually acknowledged.

CHAPTER 16

The Plumbing

E CONOMICS HAS A RATHER PATCHY RECORD of success when it comes to providing clear and effective guidance on big important topics of wide social import – and, admittedly, climate change is exactly one such problem. And the economics profession does itself a disservice when it cannot find a consistent voice even on topics that are infinitely simpler, narrower and more clear-cut than climate change, such as, say, the effect of minimal wage on unemployment, or whether the money-printing associated with the monetary experiment called Quantitative Easing will lead to inflation. Having said that, there *are* areas where the predictions of economics have been shown to work very well, and where economics has provided useful and effective policy guidance. One of the poster children of these success stories was the auctioning of the licences for the operation of the 3G mobile phone networks in the UK that occurred in 2000, when Gordon Brown was Chancellor of the Exchequer.[1] The advice that the government of the time obtained from professional economists from Oxford University and University College London was so good and useful that the government collected the equivalent of $36 billion, when the original expectations had been in the region of $4–5 billion. The US Acid Rain programme has by most accounts been another such success story, one at which we shall look in some detail for the insights it provides about what can work best in the case of climate-change control. One could present other instances

---

[1] For a very good, non-technical discussion of what can be an extremely technical topic, see Backhouse (2010), page 27 and *passim.*

of success, but the more relevant question is what all these 'success stories' have in common. Backhouse (2010) gives a nice characterization as follows:

> Spectrum auctions and market emissions are both, despite their size and importance, small in relation to the societies in which they have been created. In both cases, market participants were firms whose managers had learned the new rules about how to work within the new markets and whose activities could be closely monitored. In this context, economic expertise proved important in designing systems that could accommodate competing pressures and [...] could cause efficient responses to unexpected developments.[2]

In short, when the actors involved behave not too differently from how economics textbooks assume *all* people to behave, economics works pretty well. Things gets messy when Homer Simpson, not *Homo Economicus*, makes the choices. When it comes to the design of abatement policies, this suggests that economics may provide useful guidance about how to regulate firms, or how to create markets (say, in emissions) for professional agents; less so when it tries to predict how the *gilets jaunes* will react to a modest fuel tax. This is why one of the areas where economic analysis holds the greater promise is the regulation of large emitting corporations.

Doing this right is extremely important. The social cost of carbon does not tell us who should pay for the abatement cost, or where 'the money comes from'. And the term 'social cost of carbon' does not point automatically to a tax – the idea of social cost of carbon is silent in these important respects. In reality, there are many ways to 'collect the money', which differ in efficiency and social equity. For instance, suppose that we decide not to tax car fuel users, but to tax fuel-producing companies instead. If markets are perfectly competitive, then higher production costs will be reflected in higher prices for the goods produced. The consumers will still have to pay, but not exactly in the same proportions as if a tax on fuel had been imposed. If producers enjoy a significant profit margin, then the final outcome (who pays) will depend on whether

---

[2] Page 35.

they have 'pricing power' (in which case the price increases will again be passed on to consumers), or they don't (in which case the distribution to the shareholders will be hit). This, of course, has significant distributional effects, which are clearly important, but this is not what the social cost of carbon is about. The social-cost-of-carbon approach just assumes that whatever will have to be done to get the money, it will be done in an optimal way. Ultimately, we may decide to trade away some of this optimality in favour of distributional fairness: we may choose to pay a higher total price in order for its cost to be more equitably shared.[3] However, the more we stray from the optimal path, the higher the abatement mountain to climb becomes. And if we go about the abatement business in a ham-fisted manner, the final costs will end up being much higher for a given level of abatement, or the level of abatement for a given cost could be correspondingly lower. Given the scale of the task ahead of us, the difference in outcome between an efficient and an inefficient abatement strategy can make the difference between success and failure.

So, how can we go about implementing in an efficient way the strategies that we need to actually collect the amount of money for ton of CO_2 emitted suggested by the social cost of carbon? The first thing to understand is that often economists assume thorny problems away by requiring all their agents to be rational and well informed. However, in the case of climate change just invoking rationality on the part of all the actors helps, but does not solve the problem. Yes, the rational consumer of an economic textbook will make a clear-minded cost-benefit analysis between, say, the higher upfront cost and the lower running cost of a more efficient appliance, and will therefore respond appropriately to price incentives. However, because of the free-riding problem discussed in Section 1.1.3, a 'rational' emitting company will still calculate that,

---

[3] Economists get very excited about an arrangement being *Pareto optimal*: this means that no other arrangement can make any one happier without making someone worse off. When one first hears about it, it sounds great, but Pareto efficiency loses much of its bite (and appeal) when we discover that taking \$1 from Warren Buffet to lift 1,000,000 people out of starvation is *not* Pareto efficient. Also, Pareto efficiency is totally silent about what economists call the 'initial endowments', that is, how wealth happens to be initially distributed among the economic actors before the reallocations take place – not a reasonable starting point to analyze climate change. This is why I do not mention Pareto efficiency in what follows.

whatever other companies do, it is worth its while to produce cheap energy by emitting a lot of CO_2, even if the ultimate collective outcome will be disastrous: this is just the dismal logic of prisoner's-dilemma situations. This is why even a pure economics-inspired treatment of the climate-change problem cannot invoke a totally *laissez-faire* approach, and recognizes the government must step in with some clever institutional arrangements (subsidies, taxes, regulations, establishing emission markets, etc.). Faced with the problem of deciding how these interventions can be implemented, and which interventions are the most efficient ones, an economist is therefore faced with three questions: shall we regulate quantities? Shall we impose taxes or grant subsidies (price mechanisms)? Or shall we employ something cleverer, such as cap-and-trade? As we shall see, in the world of Microeconomics 101 – a world in which everybody is a rational utility maximizer and production costs and related quantities are perfectly known *by everybody* – the surprising result is that it doesn't really matter, as all these policies will bring about the same result, and, no matter which lever you choose to pull, this result is always the optimal one.

As we approach the real world (and we begin to look for answers in a book on Intermediate Microeconomics) we first realize that the costs of production and the demand functions are not perfectly known. In this sub-lunar world of imperfect information, important differences immediately arise among the three different ways of regulating emissions: why they do, and what we can do about them is the meat of this chapter. Even the book on Intermediate Microeconomics, however, doesn't hold all the answers we want, and we need to put in a bit more work. The main problem is that the more realistic descriptions *do* account for uncertainty (say, in the production costs), but still assume that everyone is perfectly rational. In reality, it is far from clear how rationally consumers and producers behave in the real world – where by 'behave' I mean, for instance, respond to (price) incentives. The purpose of the arrangements a social planner must come up with is therefore twofold. First, even if everybody is as rational and as well informed as the reader of this book, interventions are still needed because of the free-riding problem – which has its roots, not its solution, in perfect rationality. In addition, if some agents are not rational or correctly informed, then rules must be designed so as to overcome their cognitive biases. Not an easy task.

Before we get started, let me make clear why appeal to rationality will not necessarily get us very far if we want to find economic solutions to the problem of climate change. Compare and contrast the case for subsidies for renewables (say, solar panels) and for negative emissions. Subsidies have been extremely important in order to bring down the cost of solar panels, but, once the unit cost of electricity is competitive with fossil-fuel-based sources, they are in principle no longer needed. Things are a bit more complex than this, but you see my point: once solar panels have become competitive, a rational producer will decide that she can produce electricity more cheaply using solar panels, and will automatically do so without any further incentive. However, compare this with the case of a costly negative emissions technology or of a costly carbon sequestration and storage installation. Just subsidizing either of these initiatives will not increase their adoption. Without some form of mandate or incentive, an electricity producer will not rationally adopt a carbon sequestration and storage procedure *no matter how cheap*, because this will increase her production costs, and she will be at a commercial disadvantage with respect to the competitor who has not installed the same technology. It is true that, if everybody thinks this way, the collective result will be dismal, but the dire logic of the diners' dilemma (see again the discussion in Section 1.1.3) ensures that this is the dismal result that will be achieved.[4] So, yes, subsidies for carbon sequestration and storage or for a negative emission technology can work, but only after a stick or a carrot has been used to induce their adoption in the first place. To escape the bad outcome, the players engaged in a prisoner's or diner's dilemma require a 'coordinator' (someone to wield the stick or the carrot) to escape their predicament. Now, the stick could be a mandate for you to do something or a tax if you do something else; the carrot could be an incentive (say, a tax break) if you engage in some virtuous action. Which tool is more effective? Let's see.

---

[4] I have assumed that customers who purchase from electricity producers, and the producers themselves, are only motivated by money. This is not necessarily true.

16.1 REGULATIONS FOR IRRATIONAL CONSUMERS

Price mechanisms work very well with consumers when the only choice they have to face is how to respond here and now to a price change (say, an increase in the spot price of petrol). (This, after all, is the basis of the celebrated invisible-hand mechanism.) However, not all price mechanisms are that simple. Suppose that the government partially subsidizes the installation cost of a heat pump, which will give almost-zero future running costs to heat your house, but still requires, even after the subsidy, a hefty initial outlay. Then, for the scheme to work one must assume that consumers will trade off upfront costs and future benefits in a rational (or, at least, consistent) way. But this is exactly where cognitive bias (our 'mistakes in thinking') come to the fore with a vengeance. Here are some examples of 'consumer irrationality'.

In theory, a house builder who installs a more efficient (and more costly) heating system should be able to sell the more energy-efficient property at a higher price. In practice, buyers are observed not to give full credit in the purchase price for the money that they will save on lower heating bills. Therefore the efficient but costly energy systems are not installed in the first place. Those economists who like to cling on to the construct that consumers are rational can say that they are extremely impatient (so that tomorrow's benefit is so heavily discounted as to pale into insignificance compared with today's outlay). However, in a case such as this, the impatience invocation is a tiny fig leaf to cover the pudenda of a difficult-to-rationally-justify choice.

There is nothing special about house building. Studies have shown that drivers are reluctant to pay more upfront for cheaper-running cars unless the extra cost is recovered in as little as *one or two years* of savings on fuel. Similarly, homeowners tend not to invest in solar panels unless the installation cost is recouped in three or four years of lower energy bills.[5] Or, again, think of the rental market, where utility bills are paid by

---

[5] What could be at play here is not just what economists call inconsistent financial valuation, but plain and simple lack of capital – capital to invest in the more expensive but more efficient car or house or for the solar panels can also play an important role. This is why governments in countries such as the UK are starting subsidized programmes of house insulations. Where often decisional irrationalities melt away is when the setting moves from a laboratory experiment to the messy real-life

tenants, not by landlords. The latter have little incentive to put in place efficient heating systems because they are unlikely to obtain a higher rent from the tenant, who doesn't factor the lower gas bill in her evaluation of competing properties. More generally, a study by Golove and Eto (1996) has shown that consumers demand rates of return on the money they spend on energy efficiency ranging from 20 to 100 per cent. This means that the efficiency investment must often pay for itself in an unrealistically short time: sometime, as I said, in as little as one year. For the fun of it, one can work out the implied impatience discount rate, but more commonly, these behaviours go under the blanket rubric of cognitive biases.

From this it follows that, very broadly speaking, given the 'peculiar degree of impatience' displayed by consumers, abatement schemes whose success is predicated on individuals making a correct evaluation of present costs and future benefits, and responding rationally to price incentives, cannot be guaranteed, or even expected, to be very effective. If we insist on using the price mechanism in the case of the heat pump, the government may have to provide huge subsidies to induce consumers to make the switch. So, the reduction in carbon emissions would be obtained at too high a cost. 'Simple' price mechanisms, such as a straight tax on fuel, would work much better. However, we all know what fierce resistance these types of measures have encountered in the past – and we are all aware that they are often akin to a 'regressive tax', that hurts the poor more than the rich. And exhortations aimed at consumers to be more efficient (switch your lights off when you don't need them, turn the thermostat one degree lower) can help a bit, but come nowhere close to addressing the big problem.[6] As one example among many, think of the switch away from energy-expensive halogen bulbs to cheaper LED bulbs. To be effective, the switch had to be mandated at the production level, despite the fact that the electricity bill for consumers is lower with LED bulbs.

environment. This is at the root of the differences between the 'fast and frugal heuristics' of the bounded-rationality school, and the plain irrationalities of the behavioural economics school.

[6] As physicist MacKay used to say: 'If we all do a little, we achieve very little'. When it comes to climate change every little does *not* help.

Because of all these reasons, and because of the danger of irking voters with unpopular laws, the bulk of price-based climate regulations has been aimed at corporate entities. As corporations more closely approximate the textbook rational agents, economics is likely to have a lot more to say in this domain. And, as we shall show in Section 16.2, it certainly does.

16.2 REGULATION FOR RATIONAL EMITTING COMPANIES

How does one impose regulations on companies? Broadly speaking, either by directly regulating the amount of noxious activity they undertake (e.g., by imposing limits on CO_2 emissions); or by imposing taxes on the emission (or granting subsidies for the abatement) of noxious products, and relying on profit maximization to obtain the most efficient outcome. People who think that the state should have a big role to play in the arrangements of a society, tend to like a *dirigiste* approach, and to favour strong regulations; and people who tend to look at government actions as meddlesome interventions in its citizens' lives dislike regulations just as strongly – or perhaps a bit more. I do not have to spell out how these preferences map onto political affiliations, and we can therefore immediately understand why getting a dispassionate analysis of the effectiveness of regulations is far from easy.

The terms of the problem are very nicely illustrated by Weitzman (1974) when he writes

> I think it is a fair generalization to say that the average economist in the Western marginalist tradition has at least a vague preference toward indirect control by prices, just as the typical non-economist leans toward the direct regulation of quantities. That a person not versed in economics should think primarily in terms of direct controls is probably due to the fact that he does not comprehend the full subtlety and strength of the invisible hand argument. The economist's attitude is somewhat more puzzling. Understanding that prices can be used as a powerful and flexible instrument for rationally allocating resources and that in fact a market economy automatically regulates itself in this manner is very different from being under the impression that such indirect controls are generally preferable for the kind of problem considered in this paper. Certainly a

careful reading of economic theory yields little to support such a universal proposition.[7]

So, why is Weitzman surprised that economists should prefer a price mechanism to quantity mandates? Isn't that a bit like being surprised that the Pope is Catholic? What does economic theory have to say about this?

Let's get some basic facts straight first. To begin with, *if* the social planner knew perfectly how much it costs to produce a certain product, and what quantity of CO_2 emissions its production entails, then it would make absolutely no difference whether controls were put on quantities or on prices. To make the point clear, suppose that I knew without error that your car can run for exactly 20 kilometres with one litre of fuel. Let's also assume that the cost of petrol is $1 per litre. Then I could say that you can only travel 200 kilometres; or that you can use at most 10 litres of petrol; or that you can spend at most $10 on petrol – it would not make any difference at all: any of these regulations would obviously have *exactly* the same effect. Economists also often like to say that prices are superior planning instruments because they are supposed to economize on the cost of information (how does the government find out, for instance, about the intricacies of the industry it is trying to regulate?). However, if the relationship between prices and quantities were perfectly known, it would not be any easier to dictate prices rather than quantities, because *exactly the same information* is needed to choose either.

This is all true, but not very helpful. In the case at hand, our favourite strategy of trying to solve a difficult problem we don't know how to solve by looking at a simple problem that we don't know how to solve does not take us very far. For our toy model to have some bite we have to introduce from the start two complications: heterogeneity of abatement costs (for different firms abating the same amount of emissions entails different costs); and uncertainty on the part of the planner on cost of abatement faced by the different firms.[8] When these two features are added, it is no longer obvious whether price mechanisms or direct regulation is more

---

[7] Page 477.

[8] In reality, not even the firms themselves necessarily understand their own abatement costs well. This creates another layer of complexity.

efficient. As we shall see, the correct answer depends on both the cost curve (how much abating a bit more costs), and on the benefit curve (how much extra advantage we get from an extra bit of abatement). As a first approximation, whether direct rules or price mechanisms work better depend on the interplay between the shape of these two functions – and this is why Weitzman is surprised that economists should a priori prefer price mechanisms, while in reality, sometimes they work better, and sometimes worse.

Can we understand the nature of the problem a bit more clearly? In real life the entry-level model of perfect knowledge we started with does not help us very much, because in the messy world we live in we know for sure neither the cost of emission reductions nor the damage from a certain level of emissions, and this double uncertainty plays a key role in the optimal strategy. Note that it is not just that the planner doesn't know this: to a large extent even the emitter has a pretty hazy idea about her own abatement costs. Keeping this in mind, let's focus on the comparative advantage of price over quantity controls. We want to see under what conditions the difference in welfare from using prices rather than controls is positive. We also want to understand what has to happen for this difference to tilt the balance in the favour of regulations. In a few terse pages of clear thinking sprinkled with nothing more than first-year college maths, Weitzman (1974) obtained a simple but startling result, that could be expressed with a neat two-term formula. We don't even need the formula to understand the intuition behind it.

First of all, the formula says that, the more uncertain we are, the bigger the difference will be (of whatever sign) between the effectiveness of the two emission-reducing regimes. This makes sense, because we know that, if we were not uncertain at all, there would be no difference. Next, the formula shows that price mechanisms would work better if the curvature of the cost function is greater than the curvature of the benefit function. But in a situation when the curvatures are reversed, using price controls would be bad.

Let's try to understand what this really means. Fig 16.1 shows a schematic abatement-cost curve in the right panel, and a schematic abatement curve in the left panel. What do these curves represent? The units are arbitrary, but the respective qualitative shapes should make

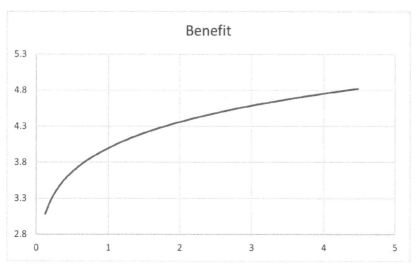

(a) The benefits of abatement – cost of abatement on the *x* axis.

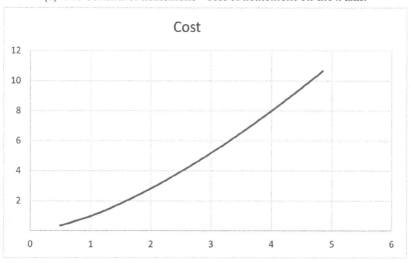

(b) The costs of abatement – 'amount' of abatement on the *x* axis.

16.1 The costs and benefits of abatement strategies.

sense: starting from the left-hand figure, which shows the benefits for increasing abatement efforts, we can see that the first bit of abatement is easy to achieve and brings about a lot of benefits (these are the 'low-hanging fruits' in the left part of the left panel). Note also that the slope of the benefit curve at the origin is greater (in absolute value) than the slope of the cost curve: as we begin our abatement efforts, the costs are low and the benefits high. However, after the easy benefits have been reaped, the benefits for a given effort become more and more difficult to achieve, and the benefit curve on the left levels off. Conversely, moving to the right-hand panel, the first abatement initiatives are relatively cheap, but as the abatement programme tries to reach further and further forms of energy production, the costs become greater and greater: the curvature has an upward concavity.

Now, the key insight from Weitzman was that it is the interplay between these two curvatures that matters. First of all, if the curvature of the benefit function were greater than the curvature of the cost function (as would be the case, for instance, if the cost function were almost linear), using prices as control could entail very big errors. When the benefit function is very curved 'the smallest miscalculation [in prices] results in either much more or much less than the desired quantity'.[9] Conversely, controlling prices makes more sense when the benefit function is almost linear. As Weitzman writes 'In such a situation it would be foolish to name quantities. Since the marginal social benefit is approximately constant in some range, a superior policy is to name it as a price and let the producers find the optimal output level themselves, after eliminating the uncertainty from costs.' Weitzman adds 'although there are plenty of instances where the price mode has a good solid comparative advantage [...], in some sense it looks as if prices can be a *disastrous* choice of instrument far more often than quantities can'.[10] So, preferring one mechanism to the other is by no means a foregone conclusion – hence, once again, Weitzman's surprise about the unquestioning propensity of economists to favour price mechanisms.

16.3 MOVING BEYOND PRICE OR QUANTITIES

It gets more interesting. Academic work that followed hot on the heels of Weitzman's original work showed that *combining* in a clever way price

---

[9] Page 485.
[10] Page 486, emphasis in the original.

mechanisms and regulation can be more efficient than either system in isolation.[11] To understand how this magic can come about, we have to think about how price or quantity controls can go wrong. The maths now get a bit messier, but the intuition remains simple: when abatement costs turn out to be higher than expected, price mechanisms bring about too little abatement; conversely, quantity mechanisms bring about too little abatement when abatement costs turn out to be lower than expected. A mixed system can get the best of both worlds by using licences (quantities) to guard against extremely high levels of emissions, while prices can provide an incentive to abate more than licences require, if the cost of abatement turns out to be low.

How can we turn this intuition into an efficient regulatory framework? This is where the idea of cap-and-trade comes to the fore. Licences to emit are first sold at an auction to emitting firms. Then a subsidy is established for those firms that emit less than is allowed by the licences; and a penalty is also levied from those firms that exceed their emission limits (what is allowed by the licences it bought). Finally – and this is often the contentious bit – firms can trade licences between each other.

Why is this part contentious? Because some people find distasteful that the right to emit can be bought. I understand the emotive response, but let's not forget the total emission cap still remains in place (because the total number of licences does not change, they only change hands), and the total level of emissions therefore does not increase. What happens is simply that the companies most efficient at reducing emissions can do so and have spare licences to sell in the market at a price higher than their costs of emission reduction. Similarly, the companies that find emission reduction very costly will buy licences from the efficient ones. The total expenditure suffered by the system as a whole for a given level of emissions can be greatly reduced *for the same level of total emissions*. Furthermore, there is now an incentive to invest in research

---

[11] The first paper in this soon-to-become-crowded field was by Roberts and Spence (1976), both Harvard economists. Michael Spence was later awarded a Nobel prize, in part for this work. In those happy days, one was able to publish in top journals by producing articles considerably shorter than *War and Peace*, and without having to quote hundreds of references – the 1976 paper by Roberts and Spence was a svelte fifteen-page article, with a grand total of *four* references.

and development to reduce emissions: any 'saved' licence, remember, can be sold and turned into cash.

It sounds terribly clever, and elegant. But can this work in practice in the case of global warming? There is a case study academics often point to in this context – a case study that has to do with the ups and downs of the famous acid-rain programme. Let's see what happened.

16.4 BUT DOES IT REALLY WORK? THE ACID-RAIN PROGRAMME

The idea that markets can play a positive and efficient role in bringing a problem such as global warming under control is neither obvious, nor popular among non-economists. Some critics feel that there is something perverse in using the market to fix a market failure – this is a logical *non sequitur*, but it has a superficial appeal. More generally, concern for the environment and global warming is often associated with a no-growth, anti-market agenda, which makes even considering market mechanisms suspect, when not heretic. Backhouse (2010) (quoting Oates (1992)) captures these attitudes well:

> In the early days of 'Environmental Regulation' [...] the role of economic analysis in the design and implementation of policies for the protection of the environment was viewed with suspicion, and in some instances with outright hostility, by many environmentalists. Economic forces were seen by many as the basic source of environmental degradation, and effective policy had to *combat these forces, not cooperate with them.* Much of the early legislation embodied this perspective. In the United States, for instance, the Clean Air Act of 1970 forbade the use of cost-benefit analysis in the determination of standards for environmental standards. Such standards were to be set [...] without regard to cost of attainment.[12]

As I think my reader has by now surely appreciated, I do not believe that markets are the solutions to all problems. I also think that they are the solution to fewer problems than many economists believe. However, it would be just as silly and ideologically driven to claim that, as we move away from the production of consumer goods, markets *never* work.

---

[12] Page xiii, emphasis added.

My position is that whether a market solution can work or not is an empirical, not an ideological, issue, and that every case should be considered on its merits, and in its specific institutional context. In this spirit, I believe that what we have observed in the case of the regulation to curb acid rain can give us useful guidance as to whether market solutions may work in the fight against climate change. In itself, looking at one case study does not prove anything. However, the significant similarities between the goals of reducing acid rain and the temperature of the planet gives us hope that what we can learn in one case can be transferred to the other. If this is indeed the case, the recommendations that economic analysis has given about how to reduce acid rain may be spot on also in the context of climate control.

So, what happened with acid rain?[13] When sulphur dioxide and various nitrogen oxides emitted in the production of electricity combine with rain water, the latter acidifies; this is harmful to humans, and has negative environmental effects.[14] When electricity is produced by burning coal, the amount of emitted oxides (we will mainly talk about sulphur oxides in what follows, but similar considerations apply to nitrogen oxides as well) depends on the quality of coal. Low-sulphur coal is more expensive, and in some areas of the USA more difficult and expensive to get hold of.

As early as the 1970s it became clear that sulphur oxide emissions had to be reduced, but, obviously, the baby-cum-bathwater solution of not producing electricity was not an option. So, different possibilities were explored to reduce the emissions of sulphur and nitrogen oxides. This reduction could be achieved in two ways: by applying scrubbers, that remove the oxides in the emission flue; and by substituting high-sulphur coal with low-sulphur coal. Both options were costly: the cost of scrubbers was significant, and scrubbers were effective mainly with high-sulphur coal; and low-sulphur coal, as mentioned, is more expensive than high-sulphur coal.

There are other important factors to take into account. Some electricity-generating firms were physically located close to low-sulphur coal mines, and for them the cost of using the low-sulphur variety was

---

[13] For a good discussion of the effectiveness of the US cap-and-trade programme and of its relevance to the climate-change problem, see also Stavins et al. (2021).

[14] The material in this section draws on Blakehouse (2010), page 22 and *passim*.

lower. Also, some plants were so designed that they could easily switch from high- to low-sulphur coal, but for others the switch was far more costly. So, there were different, imperfectly known costs to comply with whatever rules would be put in place – and while the producers may have had a better understanding of their cost structure than the regulators did, their knowledge was still far from perfect.

Given this background, in the 1970s the US Administration tried to bring the acid-rain problem under control by regulation (the 1970 Clean Air Act). The rules stipulated that *new* coal power plants could not emit more than 1.2 pounds of sulphur dioxide per million BTU (British thermal units) of energy generated. This is a clear case of a policy that has certainty of outcome (if it can be properly monitored), but uncertainty of cost. Despite its simplicity, as formulated the policy did not work. To begin with, since it only applied to new plants, power companies had strong incentives to prolong the life of old, dirtier and less efficient plants, which were not caught by the cap. In addition, they had no incentive to increase the efficiency of the existing (exempt) plants.

As emissions did not decline as hoped, in 1979 the rules were changed: first, those companies that were below their 1.2 pounds/ BTU million cap were no longer allowed to meet demand by burning high-sulphur coal, even if they stayed within the cap. Also, the new rules required new plants to be fitted with scrubbers. The intentions were commendable, but this delayed the installation of new, more efficient power plants, stretched out the lives of the dinosaur plants, and removed incentives to use low-sulphur coal (as we saw, scrubbers are only efficient with high-sulphur emissions). Again, the regulations were deeply unpopular, left huge scope for fierce political horse-trading, and, once again, turned out to be less effective than hoped for.

The regulatory regime changed with the 1990 Amendment to the Clean Air Act. The desired reduction in emissions was going to be achieved in two phases: in the first, the dirtiest power plants were required to reduce emissions by 3.5 million tons per year (again, a certain-outcome, uncertain-cost rule). However, in the second phase virtually all plants were going to be subject to a national (not plant) emission ceiling. This national ceiling was then translated into an allowance for each producer – so far, so unexciting. But the novel provision of the

Amendment was that permits would be issued to the operators, with each permit allowing them to emit one ton of sulphur dioxide – and the permits could be bought and sold freely in the market.

Electricity producers now faced a completely different set of choices. First of all, those energy firms that were able to produce energy more cheaply could sell permits to those who found the emission reduction more expensive (remember the geographical and technical differences faced by different producers). Second, it was now much easier to enforce compliance, as an electricity firm could no longer argue that it should be granted a special-status exemption: if for a given firm complying was really so difficult, after all, it could always buy permits in the market. Third, costly investment in innovations in scrubbing could now make economic sense: as a consequence, selfish, profit-maximizing producers would now seriously assess whether it was going to be worth their while to invest in the scrubbing technology – and many calculated that it would. The result was that scrubbers improved, their cost fell, and they became used more widely. In sum: not only were sulphur dioxide emissions finally brought under control,[15] but the target was achieved in a considerably more efficient way than via quantity regulation.[16] And, yes, abatement cost estimates produced before the introduction of the 1990 Amendment had to be substantially revised, but for once *downwards*: before the Amendment came into force the US Environmental Protection Agency had estimated the total cost of the acid rain programme at $6.1 billion. Eight years into the programme the total implementation bill ended up between $1.1 and $1.7 billion.[17]

---

[15] Emissions of SO2 have declined by 80 per cent since the early days of the Clean Air Act, despite the fact that electricity production increased greatly.

[16] As told, the account of the acid rain programme sounds a bit like a too-perfect just-so story. Matters, as usual, were more complex and, admittedly, emissions had begun to fall before the introduction of the licence scheme. For an informative, but very one-sided, account of the effectiveness of cap-and-trade schemes see, for instance, Kill et al. (2010). I warn the reader that their paper makes some valid points (especially when it discusses the chequered record of financial institutions in coming up with useful, as opposed to rent-extracting, products, or the conflicts of interest among different financial institutions that some of the climate derivatives entail), but it is far from balanced. The general consensus among economists is that traded-permits schemes, while not perfect, *can* be effective.

[17] Stavins et al. (2012).

What are the similarities between acid rain and climate change? One important feature both problems share is the very high uncertainty of costs and outcomes. This is very important. As we have seen, under certainty, there is a total equivalence between quantity-based or cost-based controls. This being the case, the more we depart from the certainty case, the more the differences between the two modes of achieving the same goal become important. But there are additional reasons why cap-and-trade can be very well suited to fighting climate change. The very 'democratic' nature of CO_2 emissions, which know no boundaries, make the problem essentially distributed (this, after all, was one of the causes of the free-riding temptation), and therefore difficult to tackle with a *dirigiste* approach. So, as Harvard economist Stavins and his colleagues point out:[18]

> "[...] the cap-and-trade model seems especially well suited to addressing the problem of climate change, in that emitted greenhouse gases are evenly distributed throughout the world's atmosphere. Emissions reductions anywhere make identical contributions to helping alleviate the problem, and there are no pollutant concentration hot-spots. The sheer number and variety of greenhouse gas-emissions sources heightens the practical difficulty of developing a comprehensive and effective command-and-control approach, and magnifies the cost savings that could be achieved by enlisting the market to find the least costly abatement options."

Unfortunately, today's political landscape is far more polarized and ideologically riven than in the 1990s, and, as a result, 'greenhouse-gas cap and trade appears to have been collateral damage in a wider set of policy and ideological battles'.[19] This is more than regrettable, because for a task as complex and as vast as climate control we really cannot afford to let the most efficient abatement policies become hostage to ideological prejudices. We have precious little room for manoeuvre to stay within the 1.5–2 °C warming target by the end of the century. If the lessons of the acid rain programmes are anything to go by, employing

---

[18] Ibid.
[19] Ibid.

an efficient or a ham-fisted regulatory emission policy can end up making the difference between success or failure. And, when it comes to global warming, we already have so many obstacles on the way to 1.5, that we should not engineer additional ones out of pseudo-economics prejudices or ideological preconceptions of what reality should look like. The case of the effect of minimum wage on unemployment mentioned in the opening paragraphs of this chapter is a clear example of how strong the temptation can often be to filter reality through ideological preconceptions. Cap-and-trade may not hold all the answers, but it is a valuable addition to our abatement toolkit and the emission-reduction task ahead would be far more daunting without it.

CHAPTER 17

Unfinished Business

There are more things in Heaven and Earth, Horatio,
Than are dreamt of in your philosophy.

—Willian Shakespeare, *Hamlet*, I.5 167–8

J UST AS HAMLET ADMONISHES Horatio that there are more things in Heaven and Earth than are dreamt of in his philosophy, so I should warn the reader that there is far more to climate change than can be captured in our economics models. The application of economics to real-world problems works best when 'objectives are precisely defined and, hardly surprisingly, when people behave in ways that correspond to the assumptions made in economic theory.'[1] In the case of global warming, the quantity that in economic analysis we try to maximize, the world's 'utility', patently fails to capture many important aspects of the phenomenon; and as for the economic actors, when it comes to climate choices their behaviour is a very far cry from how perfectly informed, fully-rational agents would approach the problem (with the voters' refusal the world over to countenance even modest carbon taxes the most obvious, but not the only, example).[2] Also, economic analysis is perfectly suited to identifying the root causes of global warming – as we have seen, the problems of the unpriced externalities and of free-riding.

---

[1] Backhouse (2010, page 17).

[2] In some countries, such as Italy, there is significant taxation of petrol at the pumps, but this has been in place for decades, and has nothing to do with the curbing of CO_2 emissions – it is just a form of unavoidable taxation (if one wants to drive) common to countries were levels of tax evasion are high.

This does not mean, however, that it will necessarily be as successful at identifying how these two problems can be solved. I am aware of all of this, but one of my points has been that modern economic analysis, *despite* its highly reductionist approach – despite all the stuff that it leaves out – still makes an important contribution to the global-warming debate by showing that prompt and large-scale abatement action is optimal. However, deciding how quickly and in what scale we should act is not the be-all and end-all of tackling global warming. In this chapter I touch on some of the important aspects that this type of one-dimensional analysis leaves out.

17.1 EQUITY

The economic approach to global warming prides itself for being non-moralistic, and instrumentally pragmatic: '*if these are your preferences and goals, and these are your constraints, this is what you should do*' is the approach it takes. So, for instance, when we discussed the social cost of carbon, I made clear that it should not be understood as a 'sin tax' to punish the bad emitters,[3] but as the most efficient way to 'spread the abatement pain' over generations (again, given our preferences). There is a lot to be said for the value-neutrality of the economics approach, if for no other reason than it clearly separates the ethical aspect (the choices we make, for instance, about how much we should care about future generations), from the instrumentally efficient consequences of these choices. Having said that, there are important aspects of the climate change problem that can awkwardly, if at all, be handled using the economics approach, even from a purely instrumental point of view. And, if we want to get the business of controlling climate change done, getting a handle on these aspects is at least as important as getting the social cost of carbon right. What am I referring to? Simplifying greatly, the economics analysis tells us whether it makes sense for us to invest heavily and promptly in climate-change abatement: the answer is 'yes, definitely'. Finance theory might suggest some helpful tools to achieve the required goals. But this still

---

[3] Don't get me wrong. Perhaps bad emitters *should* be punished, especially when they try to obfuscate the facts of global warming so as to be allowed to emit more. However, these are altogether different sets of considerations, outside the scope of economic analysis.

leaves the (politically and ethically, not technically) difficult questions of how the burden should be shared largely unanswered.

Now, when it comes to these ethical and political choices, I do not have the specialized knowledge or insights that would make my views more worthy of listening to than anyone else's. However, I want to share with my by-now-hopefully-less-perplexed, but still open-minded, reader some pieces of factual information on the basis of which our more difficult decisions can be made. We can start, for instance, with the observation that the populations that are likely to suffer most from climate change happen to be in some of the poorest areas of the world (as we have discussed, the Sahel, or the coastal area of the Indian sub-continent). At a stretch, we could try to model within an economics framework our dislike for inequality of consumption across different people. This could be achieved by making the utility function more complex, and introducing extra difficult-to-estimate parameters to reflect this additional dislike. I am doubtful that great insight could be achieved by adding this complication: we would be choosing the cross-sectional-inequality-aversion parameter to move the solution in a more reasonable direction (nothing wrong with this), but I do not immediately see what else we could obtain from the exercise. The answer (abate more) would be fully baked into the way we rephrase our question. Models, remember, are useful when they surprise us, not when they reassure us. And, in any case, even if the extra modelling complication did provide some unexpected insight, it would still model only a small fraction of what we would like to capture.[4] There are still important considerations that remain stubbornly outside an economics-based treatment. Consider the question, for instance, of *who* should bear the greatest burden of the abatement efforts. Currently the countries with the highest emissions per person are from the economically developed world, with several Arabic Gulf states, the United States, and Australia the top emitters per person. (China is responsible for a large fraction of the emissions, but its population is huge, and its emission intensity is only marginally higher than that of Europe. See Fig 17.1.) A complementary perspective is provided by Fig 17.2, that shows the annual

---

[4] This aspect is well discussed in Dasgupta (2008). Interestingly, it is dropped after the first few pages of the article.

emissions of CO_2 in 2017 (well before the distorting effects of the COVID pandemic.) The clear message from this figure is that the sub-Saharan countries currently make a negligible contribution to global emissions, yet are the countries that most desperately want to attain the level of economic well-being of the West. By a cruel twist of fate, they are also among the countries that stand to suffer most from global warming. But an arguably even more important piece of information is the *cumulative* emissions from different countries since the beginning of the Industrial Revolution shown in Fig 17.3 (the chosen date in the graph was 1751): again, it is clear that Africa and South America have contributed very little to the present CO_2 concentration problem.

Now, the West is beginning to accept that we should curb carbon emissions. But the developing world can point out that the economic development of the now-chastised West has been attained on the back of historically huge cumulative emissions. Taking away the punch bowl when the party gets rowdy is never popular: but it is positively infuriating when some of the guests have barely had their first sip. Not surprisingly, many developing countries see the request that 'now we should all stop CO_2 emissions' as a ploy by the rich West to remain richer and more powerful. I don't think that it is the case, but, leaving conspiracy theories to one side, the question of whether, and to what extent, past emission behaviours have a bearing on what we should do now is not a badly posed one. Economics cannot help here, yet there is little hope to getting poor countries on board with climate control (by telling them that they should stop deforestation, for instance), unless these questions are answered in a way that is perceived as equitable by all parties.

And, to remind ourselves that reality is always a bit more complex than how we would like it to be, Fig 17.4 shows the role of 'imported' emissions. To understand what this means, we must keep in mind that how much a given country emits only tells part of the story.[5] Suppose that a country imposes very tough emission limits, but does not curb the consumption of energy-intensive goods. Since these goods then have to be imported from somewhere, effectively the country with tough

---

[5] For a good discussion of imported emissions see Helm (2012).

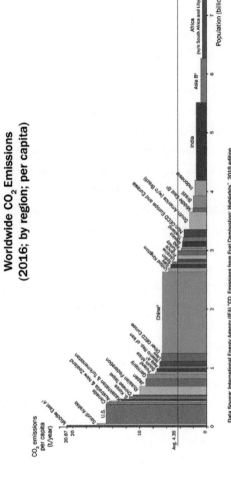

Worldwide CO₂ Emissions
(2016; by region; per capita)

CO₂ emissions per capita (t/year)

Data Source: International Energy Agency (IEA) "CO₂ Emissions from Fuel Combustion: Highlights". 2018 edition
Note: Emissions from energy-related CO₂ only; no other greenhouse gases
1) Middle East A: Bahrain, Oman, Kuwait, Qatar, United Arab Emirates
2) Middle East B: Israel, Jordan, Lebanon, Syrian Arab Republic, Yemen
3) Asia A: Brunei Darussalam, Malaysia, Mongolia, Singapore
4) Asia B: w/o Asia A, China, India, Thailand, Chinese Taipei, Indonesia, Korea, Japan
5) China: People's Rep. of China, Hong Kong

Version: 22-Feb-2019 by AQAL Group (https://aqalgroup.com) and Tom Schütz (http://tomschutz.eu)
This work is licensed under the Creative Commons Attribution-Share Alike 4.0 International License (CC BY-SA 4.0)

Population (billions)

17.1 CO₂ emissions per person by country. Population on the x axis, emission intensity (emissions per person) on the y axis. The size of each rectangle shows the total emissions from that country.

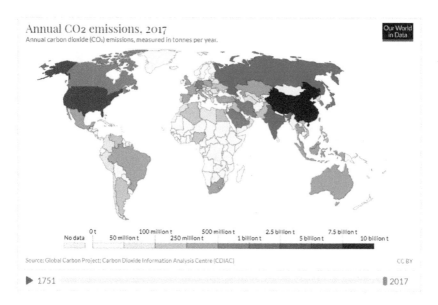

17.2 Annual emissions. Source: Our World in Data.

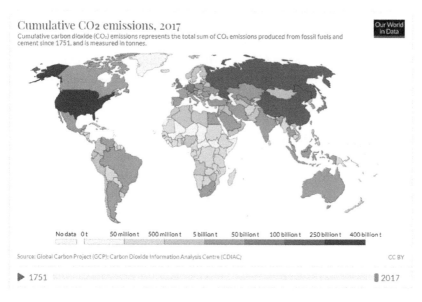

17.3 Cumulative emissions since 1751. Source: Our World in Data.

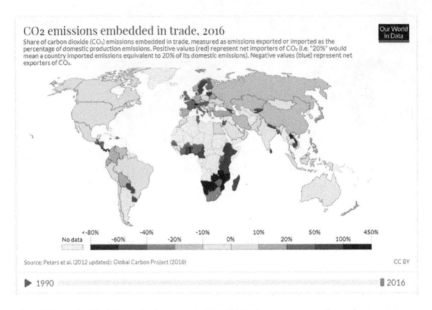

17.4 CO$_2$ embedded in trade. Source: Our World in Data.

emission regulations imports goods manufactured at high energy cost in other countries. And if the countries from which the goods are imported have lower emission standards than the importing country the net result for the planet is negative. To calculate consumption-based emissions we need to take into account where goods are produced and where they are consumed across the world. Whenever a good is imported we need to add all CO$_2$ emitted in its production to the emissions of the importing country, and subtract all CO$_2$ emitted from the tally of the exporting country. When we do so, we get a picture such as the one in Fig 17.4. Note that the some of the poster-children of emission control (such as Sweden and Switzerland) do not look quite as 'carbon-virtuous' any more once imported emissions are taken into account, and that both Russia and China are strong net exporters (so, they are, literally, doing some of the emission dirty work for someone else).

Where do all these graphs leave us? As always, one cannot derive an *ought* from an *is*. However, policies that do not take into account these basic facts are unlikely to garner any broad legitimacy. And this broad legitimacy can only come from solutions that are, and *are widely perceived to be*, fair by all parties.

17.2 CAN ONE DO GOOD WHILE DOING WELL?
THE ROLE OF FINANCE

As we saw in Section 3.2, any serious attempt to curb global warming will require very substantial investments – on the same scale of what we spend on defence, or education. Some of this funding will have to come from the private sector, some of it from the government, with plenty of room for creative partnerships. The role of a well-functioning financial sector is to channel investments to productive (or damage-reducing) activities. It is therefore a truism that the financial sector has an important role to play in the green transition. This does not necessarily mean, however, that, given the magnitude of the task ahead, financial engineering must deliver newfangled derivatives instruments or that path-breaking financial innovations are needed. Don't get me wrong: I have nothing against innovation *in general*. It is with the nature of innovation in the financial industry that I have a problem.

In the last decades the financial industry has been very good at coming up with ideas that have brought a lot of benefit – the problem has been that they have benefitted the financial industry itself, not their clients or society at large. 'I hear about these wonderful innovations in the financial markets and they sure as hell need a lot of innovation. I can tell you of two – Credit Default Swaps and CDOs – which took us right to the brink of disaster: were they wonderful innovations that we want to create more of?' These were the words with which the ex-Chairman of the Fed, Paul Volker, addressed in 2009 (right after the Big Crisis) representatives of the financial industry at the *Wall Street Journal Future of Finance Initiative* in the UK. 'The only thing useful banks have invented in 20 years is the ATM', was his final put-down. Indeed, it has been a sad reality of the last decades that the financial industry (especially in the so-called sell-side – roughly speaking, banks) has mainly come up with self-serving, rent-extracting devices to increase their profits. This is why I am not convinced that we need a new wave of complex financial products supposedly designed to facilitate the green transition. What we do need from the sell-side (again, banks) is an efficient distribution to the most suitable investors of the debt and equity instruments that will finance the transition. To some extent, the banking sector should also advise on how these instruments should be structured so as to enhance their appeal to ultimate investors. But the first and foremost task will be to place efficiently a lot of bonds and equity stock, and to make sure that there exists a liquid market for their trading – a 'job description' that a nineteenth-century banker (think of Mary Poppins' Mr Banks) would have been totally familiar with.

The buy-side (roughly speaking, the asset managers who invest the savings of their private and institutional clients) can also play an important, albeit different, role in facilitating the green transition. Things here are delicate. A large and growing fraction of investors actively demand that their funds should be invested 'ethically', or, at least with due regard to the reality of climate change. It is perfectly legitimate for the agents of these investors to channel their funds to firms with green credentials – it is actually more than legitimate: as fiduciary agents, it is their duty to do so. But what about those asset managers who are investing the money of investors who have not expressed a view about climate change? If the managers pursued a 'green agenda', would they be doing the best they could for those clients whose only stated concern is to make their money grow as quickly and safely as possible?

These questions are not theoretical. Laurence ('Larry') Fink, CEO of BlackRock (the largest asset managers in the world, with approximately 10 trillion USD under management), has been very vocal about his desire to steer companies (via voting right, but mainly simply by asset allocation) towards green practices.[6] This has not gone down well in conservative circles. In August 2022, the offices of the Attorney General of nineteen (Republican) states sent Mr Fink a letter[7] arguing that, by pursuing his green agenda in non-green-designated funds, he was neglecting the best interest of the people who had entrusted him with their money: 'Many of our laws state that a fiduciary must "discharge [their] duties solely in the interest of the participants and beneficiaries [...] for the exclusive purposes of [...] providing benefits to participants

---

[6] See, e.g., BLACKROCK, Corporate Sustainability, Committed to Sustainability, Our Partners on the Path to Net Zero, www.BlackRock.com/corporate/sustainability/committed-to-sustainability#.

[7] www.texasattorneygeneral.gov/sites/default/files/images/executive-management/BlackRock%20Letter.pdf.

and their beneficiaries [...]" The stated reasons for your actions around promoting net zero, the Paris Agreement, or taking action on climate change indicate rampant violations of this duty, otherwise known as acting with "mixed motives".'[8] And, in the view of the Attorney Generals, Mr Fink was clearly pursuing a *private* agenda: 'BlackRock appears to use the hard-earned money of our states' citizens to circumvent the best possible return on investment, as well as their vote. BlackRock's past public commitments indicate that it has used citizens' assets to pressure companies to comply with international agreements such as the Paris Agreement that force the phase-out of fossil fuels, increase energy prices, drive inflation, and weaken the national security of the United States. These agreements have never been ratified by the United States Senate. The Senators elected by the citizens of this country determine which international agreements have the force of law, not BlackRock.'[9]

BlackRock responded with a letter[10] signed by Delia Bass, Senior Managing Director, and Head of External Affairs. Leaving aside the arguments about voting rights (interesting but technical), and generic statements about how good BlackRock has historically been to its investors (true, but not very relevant), BlackRock's key response was: 'We believe investors and companies that take a forward-looking position with respect to climate risk and its implications for the energy transition *will generate better long-term financial outcomes.*'[11] So, BlackRock was saying, we are looking after your money in the best possible way because we believe that green assets, and companies that steer their policies in a green direction, will be financially successful. Or, in plain terms, their defense is that doing good is the best way to do (financially) well.

[8] Page 3 of the letter.
[9] Page 1 of the letter.
[10] I obtained an electronic copy of the BlackRock response letter from a colleague – thank you – but I have failed in my attempts to provide a URL for my readers. The only reference I could find on Google was: https://thetexan.news/wp-content/uploads/2022/09/BlackRock-Response-to-AGs-09062022_Final.pdf. When I tried to access the site of thetexan.news, I received the message 'Access denied - Error code 1020'. Considering that I have had no trouble in finding on the internet dozens of sources of the letter from the nineteen Attorney Generals, one may be led to conclude that BlackRock prefer to keep a low profile on this, and are not keen to have the issue discussed.
[11] Page 3 of the response, emphasis added.

Is this really the case? Superficially, it would seem very plausible: surely, firms, say, with 'stranded assets' (oil and gas in the ground that they may never be allowed to extract) surely bear (regulatory) climate-related risks that other firms do not experience. Isn't it a good (financial) idea to avoid them? Yes and no. It all depends on the discount at which these firms trade with respect to similar firms that are not exposed to the same risk. From a purely financial perspective – the perspective BlackRock says in its response that it embraces – the stock of stranded-asset firms may be so cheap, that it is worth investing in them despite the higher risk. It *may* – but is it? And, if it were, are BlackRock, and asset managers in general who avoid brown assets, leaving money on the table that their clients could collect?

The awkward truth is that we really don't know. Estimating the 'risk premium' – the compensation over the riskless return, that is, that investors demand for bearing risk – is the bread and butter of any asset manager. Academically, this is an area of vibrant research in asset pricing, to which I have made a small contribution (in the fixed-income area). So, why don't we deploy the best econometric tools of the trade to green and brown assets, and answer once and for all the question of whether investors also enjoy an extra return when they go green?[12] The problem is that estimating the risk premium is an extremely data-hungry exercise. When I explain to my students what measuring a risk premium is like, I say that it is like detecting a gentle breeze in the middle of a hurricane (the hurricane being the continuous buffetting of the price of an asset from unexpected news, while the risk premium imparts a gentle nudge in one direction or the other). It *can* be done, but fifty years' worth of data is skimpy – and ten years is ridiculously short. Alas, it has only been in the last decade and a half that climate concerns have become prominent in some investors' minds, and this is nowhere close to what is needed

---

[12] A priori it is far from obvious that this should be the case. If green assets do well in a state of high climate damage, then they act as hedges, and should command a *negative* risk premium – which makes sense: you pay for insurance above the actuarial value of the expected loss because it protects you in moments of need. As Amenc (2022) writes 'Low carbon investing products are typically built on the assumption that green stocks produce positive alpha. Economic theory contradicts this assumption: all else being equal, green firms should earn lower returns than brown firms because they provide non-pecuniary benefits and risk-hedging benefits to investors.'

to do a serious study. Which is why the results from many studies that have appeared so far are all over the map, with some suggesting that green investing is the road to riches, others that it is a money pit, and everything in between. My colleague, Prof Nöel Amenc, has carried out extensive research on this, and his conclusions are unambiguous: after 'adjust[ing] for the other factor exposures, we did not find much in the data in the way of a premium associated with a green or anti-green factor'.

Where does this leave us, as concerned citizens and investors? The fact that we cannot really tell whether investing in green or brown firms is financially advantageous or not suggests that the difference in (risk-adjusted) return is small. If that is the case, unless we actively oppose the efforts that are being made curbing climate change, what is wrong with giving our investments a green tilt (either by divesting from brown or investing in green firms)? Investing *only* in green firms would be difficult to justify on a purely financial basis (the lack of diversification would be too large: you would be putting too many of your eggs in the same green basket) – but any asset manager worth her salt knows that any theme investing simply means tilting the composition of the portfolio in a particular direction, not ditching everything else and going for broke. If anything, conscious that it is far safer to fail with the crowd than by oneself, active asset managers tend to be too cautious in departing from the 'market portfolio' – and they have often been accused of being closet index-huggers, while extracting fees for their supposedly superior stock-picking ability.

Does channelling one's money in a green direction really facilitate the decarbonization of the economy? Does it 'move the needle' in the fight against climate change? The obvious influence channel from buying (selling) green (brown) asset to fighting climate change is by making funding more expensive for brown firms (and therefore discouraging, say, the next oil exploration) and cheaper for green firms (thereby making investing in, say, the new wind turbine design cheaper). In a Western-style capitalist economy, where the allocation of funding to productive enterprises is mainly left to the market, this can in principle make a significant difference (the more so, the larger the number of green investors). Whether it does in practice is still open for debate, with academic work from top economists estimating the extra cost of capital anywhere from 0.004 to 1.5 per cent. Matters are different for an economy such as China, where the state has a much greater input in the allocation of resources, and in providing help and subsidies to 'strategically important' companies in times of trouble. This, therefore, opens the question of whether the unfettered mechanisms of the market as resource allocator are well suited for the task of bringing climate change under control. I look at this important question in the next section.

17.3 LIMITS OF THE MARKET

In western-style economies, we take for granted that there are no queues for the consumer products that we like, and no shelves full of goods nobody wants to buy. However, the more we think about it, the more we realize that there is something almost magical in how the uncoordinated and undirected actions of millions of agents should bring about such a felicitous allocative outcome.[13] Nobel-prize-winner Harvard Professor Schelling opens our eyes to the wonders of the market's ability to allocate efficiently in his *Micromotives and Macrobehavior*, a non-technical book that I warmly recommend to appreciate how amazing it really is that such an 'obvious' outcome should actually be obtained.[14]

The very success of the market in allocating resources effectively can, however, make us fall into the trap of complacency. Fist, we tend to forget that this outcome is not 'natural' and pre-ordained: for the allocative genius of the market to blossom suitable capitalist institutions and solid legal frameworks must develop alongside it. The fallacy that the allocative power of the market can arise 'spontaneously' once some impediments are removed has unfortunately been at the root of many grievous policy mistakes the developing world over.

The second market fallacy is as serious as the first. The ability of the unhindered (but regulated) market to provide us efficiently with the

---

[13] Sometimes, there *are* queues in western-style economies, such as the queues for returned Wimbledon tickets. These queues, however, are not unwanted, but engineered: they are a way of addressing problems of equity of accessibility for a coveted, but limited-supply, service – in this case, being able to admire Federer's grace on Central Court even if you are not oligarchly rich.

[14] See, in particular, chapter 1.

consumer products and services that we want has been taken to imply that it is always the most efficient way to direct our limited resources to obtain a socially desirable production outcome. In reality, the ability of the market to provide what we need has historically not been tested against intergenerational challenges – or for projects, such as nuclear fusion, that have return horizons much longer than the typical investor's. Markets are also not well suited to handle economic decisions that have geopolitical or strategic implications. To understand what I mean, we can look in some details at the case of the geopolitics of rare earths. I stress that, in doing so, I do not intend to give a satisfactory treatment of the supply-chain bottlenecks that influence the global availability of rare earths: full books have been written on the topic.[15] I only look in what follows at what the global (un)availability of rare earths can teach us about the limitations of free markets.

17.3.1 THE GEOPOLITICS OF RARE EARTHS. To start with, what are rare earths? They are a group of less-than-twenty elements: the fifteen lanthanide elements plus yttrium and a few 'invited guests', such as scandium, which are sometimes included and sometimes not. Their physics is very interesting, but we don't need to know anything else about their properties apart from the fact that they are essential for many industrial processes, notably in the production of rechargeable batteries for electric cars and in the functioning of wind turbines. In the prevalent direct-drive design, a single 3 MW turbine requires two tons of rare earths for its permanent magnets. Electric-car batteries 'only' require between one and two kilograms of rare earths to make the permanent magnets of the currently favourite design, but we expect that we will have to produce *lots* more electric cars than wind turbines in our brave new and green world. All of which is to say that the importance of these elements in the

---

[15] Similar considerations could be made about the incorrectly named critical minerals, such as copper, lithium, nickel or cobalt. Lithium, nickel and cobalt are crucial components of batteries. Rare earths are essential for the permanent magnets used in electric cars and wind turbines. 'Since 2010 the average amount of mineral resources needed for a new unit of power generation capacity has increased by 50% as the share of renewables in new investment has risen.' IEA (2021), *Critical Minerals: The Role of Critical Minerals in Clean Energy Transitions*, available at www.iea.org/topics/critical-minerals.

context of the tools we need to combat global warming (and much else) is well known and non-disputed.

Second, China has a very strong position in terms of proven reserves of rare earths,[16] but, as far as *reserves* go, no real monopoly. Rare earths are rare, but not *that* rare: Praseodymium, for instance, is four times more common than tin (9.5 parts per million in the Earth's crust), and Neodymium is almost as abundant as copper. (They are actually called 'rare' not because of their scarcity in the Earth's crust, but because they are difficult and costly to separate.) However, China has an *absolutely dominant* position in the world when it comes to the technology for their extraction, their highly specialized metallurgy and the whole supply chain. As Kalantzakos (2018) put it, when it comes to rare earths China is in effect 'an OPEC of one'.

Given this factual backdrop, we can fast forward to September 2010, when the simmering tensions between China and Japan about the disputed Senkaku Islands reached one of their periodic crisis points. On that occasion, for political leverage China 'unofficially' stopped its rare-earth exports to Japan. This was very serious, because, as the Japanese foreign minister admitted, Japan was at the time '[reliant] for 97 percent of these resources on China'.[17] This brought to the front pages of the international financial press the obvious fact that the West had become strongly dependent on the supply of the strategically important rare earths, and that China was in a position of total control over this supply. The spike in prices shown in Fig 17.5 gives an idea of how quickly global concerns about their continued supply grew. It was, in a way, a much needed wake-up call. However, if one looks at the part of the graph after the 2010–2011 spike one notices that prices went quickly back to normal. Just by looking at this graph, one may venture to guess that the West must have found alternative sources of rare earths, and therefore unshackled itself from its previous dangerous dependence. (You will note from the graph that by 2016 the prices of Europium

---

[16] There are 44m of metric tons of rare earths for China, against 22m for Vietnam, 21m for Brazil, 12m for Russia and 7m for India. The USA holds 1.5m. *Statista*, www.statista. com/statistics/277268/rare-earth-reserves-by-country/.

[17] Joint Press Availability with Japanese Foreign Minister Seiji Maehara, quoted in Kalantzakos (2018).

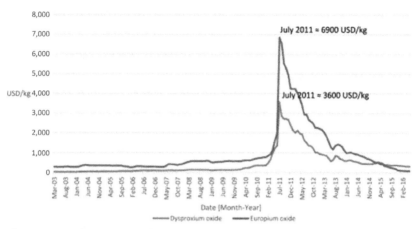

17.5 Prices of dysprosium oxide and europium oxide from 2003 to 2016. Source: ScienceDirect.com.

oxide, which had spiked to almost $7,000/kg, ended up *below* their pre-crisis levels.)

Nothing of the sort happened. After a lot of hand-wringing and solemn deliberations, as the situation normalized, prices went back to 'normal', and the market incentive to mine and process rare earths disappeared. The shares of companies such as Molycorp in the USA or Lynas in Australia, which had tried to exploit the higher prices to become active in the extraction and processing of rare-earths, fell from their highs of over $74 (Molycorp) and AUD 2.6 (Lynas) to cents in the dollar. Molycorp was finally forced to file for bankruptcy in 2015.

These have not been isolated cases: the mining of rare earths in the USA and in the West in general has been *abandoned*, not extended. What happened with the Californian Mountain Pass mine is an interesting example of the market logic behind this state of affairs. The mine was opened in 1952, and for decades provided the rare earths needed for the Cold War electronic and military industry. By 2002 the mine was closed, because the high costs of complying with California strict environmental regulations made it economically more attractive to import the same rare earths from a country such as China – a country with lower environmental standards but, arguably, a clearer strategic vision.[18] This is the same mine

---

[18] Green (2019), *The Collapse of American Rare Earth Mining: And Lessons Learned*, Defense News, www.defensenews.com/opinion/commentary/2019/11/12/the-collapse-of-american-rare-earth-mining-and-lessons-learned/.

that was reopened in 2008 by Molycorp. The company briefly benefitted from the 2011 spike in prices, but then was not able to be internationally competitive when prices reverted to pre-crisis level. We have already seen how the Molycorp story ended. As a result, the reserves are still there, but the logic of the market dictates that, despite their strategic importance, they still remain untapped.

The bottom line is that the West is still strongly dependent on China for its rare-earths supply, and the current low prices are predicated on the confidence that China will always be willing to 'play ball' as a member of international organizations such as the WTO, and continue in its role of supplier of rare earths to the world. I cannot tell how well-founded this confidence is: I can only wonder, for instance, what would happen if a military confrontation erupted between China and Taiwan, and the US defence commitments to Taipei were called into question. Let's not forget that the oil squeeze enforced by Arab countries in the 1970s had its origin in a geopolitical conflict, or that, in the space of a few short months in the second half of 2022, Europe suddenly found itself in an energy emergency after the sanctions imposed on Russia for the invasion of Ukraine prompted Russia to reduce drastically its gas supply.[19]

There is nothing unique about the dependence of the whole world on one supplier for its needs of rare earths. When it comes to the production of solar panels, China (again) provides 84 per cent of the world manufacturing capacity, and is dominant in every single aspect of their production: it produces 79.4 per cent of polysilicon (the raw material that has to be melted and cast into ingots); a staggering 96.8 per cent of the wafer sheets (the 200-micrometer layers of silicon required for the panels); 85.1 per cent of the cells that are obtained after doping;

---

[19] As Dr Samantha Gross, Director of the Energy and Security and Climate Initiative at the Brookings Institution, has pointed out to me in a private exchange, there *are* differences between dependence on oil or gas and dependence on rare earths: 'a crucial difference between critical minerals and fuels is how they are used and in what quantity. You need [some sort of] fuel *to run* the existing system, while you need critical minerals *to build* new. Thus disruptions in supply [of critical minerals] are less [severe for] the economy (although still not great, especially as we transition). You also use these materials in much smaller quantities, making stockpiling easier.' Emphasis added.

and 'only' 74.7 per cent of the final panels.[20] The conclusions of International Energy Agency in this respect are very clear: 'China has invested over USD 50 billion in new PV supply capacity – ten times more than Europe'; as a result of this, over the last decade the world solar panel manufacturing capacity has shifted from Europe, Japan and the USA to China. And what China produces is more than double than its internal demand for solar panels: so, China is effectively the single world supplier of one of the two most important renewable-energy tools in our fight against climate change. With what I consider a quaint understatement, the IEA concludes that 'the level of geographical concentration in global supply chains also creates potential challenges that governments need to address'.[21] In plain English, if, for whatever reason China decided to stop its exports of solar panels in the same way as Russia curtailed its supply of gas to Europe in 2022, the world would have nowhere to turn to.[22]

How did this happen? Because, by state-directed investment but without any intrinsic 'competitive advantage', China in the last decade has managed to bring down the production cost of solar panels (the 'learning-by-doing' process again) much more than its Western counterparts. As this happened, the price signal told Western consumers: 'Don't build your own solar panels, buy the Chinese ones'. The point here is that, just because the invisible hand of the market is extremely efficient at putting the latest mobile phone model – the one that we *really* want – in our pockets, it does not automatically follow that it is as good, or even *any* good, at tackling problems about which the price signal does not contain all the relevant information. The European dependence on imported Russian gas, and the associated tensions about the construction of the Nord Stream 2 pipeline, are another point in case: the price signal (yes,

---

[20] International Energy Agency, IEA (2022), Solar PV Global Supply Chains, IEA, Paris www.iea.org/reports/solar-pv-global-supply-chains, or, for fuller account its *Special Report on Solar PV Global Supply Chain*, August 2022.

[21] *Ibid.*

[22] As for wind turbines, China built more offshore wind turbines in 2021 than the rest of the world in five years. (Forbes, 26 Jan 2022, www.forbes.com/sites/davidrvetter/2022/01/26/china-built-more-offshore-wind-in-2021-than-every-other-country-built-in-5-years/?sh=244acf094634). As a result of this China now operates almost half of the world's offshore wind installations.

indeed, it *is* cheaper to buy gas from Russia than from elsewhere)[23] does not impound all the relevant considerations about the desirability of this dependence.

In a way, these considerations may seem too obvious to make. However, a common narrative presents the market as a universal supernaturally efficient allocator of resources, without distinguishing between those domains in which it is, indeed, extremely efficient from those where its effectiveness is much more open to doubt. Free-market zealots present a very selective interpretation of concepts such as Pareto efficiency and Walrasian equilibrium to argue that markets should *always* be left as unregulated as possible; that taxes and subsidies are *always* distortions; and that *all* government interventions are unnecessarily meddlesome at best, and noxious at worst. For these ideologues material improvement can only 'come not through St Paul's of Tarsus *sola fide*, but through Hayeck's *solo mercato*'.[24] But there is no evidence to support this. Yes, in some (many) cases government interventions in picking winners have been painfully bad (especially in countries with poorly accountable governments, and with high levels of clientelism and corruption). But a careful and open-minded analysis of how economic growth and innovation happens in Western-style economies shows that in many cases the role played by the government has been essential as an enabler and facilitator.[25]

If the reader needs further convincing, she can ponder on the following. Thanks to initially large government subsidies, electric energy from wind turbines and solar panels is now, not just competitive with, but cheaper than, electric energy from fossil fuels. I can confidently predict that in the next decades, as renewables technology develops more rapidly than in the super-mature fossil-fuel industry, the needle will

---

[23] Gas reserves have been identified in the Eastern Mediterranean (Egypt, Israel, Cyprus and Lebanon). At a pinch Liquefied Natural Gas imported from the USA could be used. But in the end, it all comes down to cost: the price signal unambiguously says: 'Buy Russian gas.'

[24] Bradford De Long (2022), page 5.

[25] See in this respect, Mazzuccato's well-argued *The Entrepreneurial State: Debunking Public vs Private Sector Myths* (2013). Prof Mazzuccato actually argues that the state should play a more interventionist role than just as an obliging fixer of market failure, ready to stand aside once the awkward fixing has been done – see the discussion below.

move even more decisively in favour of solar and wind. Now, let's leave all the environment and climate advantages of renewables to one side, and let's make a blinkered, one-dimensional, purely economic appraisal of the desirability of getting our energy from renewables. Since wind and solar energy is now cheaper than fossil-fuel energy, the sum of the (discounted) benefits over a long enough period of time of this cheaper energy will eventually outweigh the investment cost that we have paid in the past. Now, if the net-present-value analysis that is taught in business schools the world over (basically, 'add the discounted benefits, subtract the costs, and, if the result is positive, go for it') had been carried out some thirty years ago, it would have almost certainly pointed to wind and solar as very attractive business propositions.[26] But, if this is the case, why did the supposedly omniscient and efficient market have to be kick-started by subsidies? Why were the subsidies necessary in the first place? For the same reason why there is practically zero private-sector interest today in nuclear fusion:[27] because, much as the market may work well in providing goods and services when costs and benefits are immediately comparable and, preferably, not-too-separated in time, it is not as well suited to reaching an efficient allocation of resources when very-long-range, strategic, intergenerational, geopolitically important considerations come to the fore. Clearly China seems to have a clearer understanding of this than many Western countries. And, of course, no issue has ramifications that are more deeply intergenerational, strategic and geopolitically important than global warming. As Bordoff and O'Sullivan (2022b) write, three 'market failures' make unfettered markets poorly suited to dealing with the climate transition situation: 'First, the private

[26] One can quibble about the correct discount rate. However, given the huge economic advantage from cheaper energy *forever*, one would require a very high discount factor to make the costs larger than the benefits. One could also argue that we now know that renewables would become more than competitive, but we did not know this thirty years ago, and so the investors' hesitancy may have been well founded. To this, I would reply that everything we have learnt about technological innovation, from computers to cars to televisions, shows that prices go down, performance improves and the pace of improvement invariably defies expectations.

[27] As of this writing, there are a handful of private companies involved with nuclear fusion. To my knowledge the largest is Cambridge-Massachusetts-based Commonwealth Fusion Systems. From its internet site I understand that it employs 100 members of staff. The Shell group alone employs approximately 86,000 staff.

sector lacks sufficient incentives to build the infrastructure and other assets that most countries need to ensure their energy security. Second, market forces alone cannot encourage the building of the infrastructure required for a more orderly energy transition – infrastructure *that by definition may be obsolete before private companies have achieved a full return on investment.* And third, private firms and individuals lack strong enough incentives to curb emissions whose costs society bears.'[28]

In sum: the power of the market must certainly be harnessed to tackle the climate problem effectively, and I agree that private-sector incentives can play an important role in making the attending 'plumbing' as efficient as possible (recall the lessons from cap-and-trade). Exclusively market-based solutions, however, cannot be an answer to the climate problem by themselves. Much as free-market lobbyists and ideologues try to convince us of the opposite, *laissez faire* and self-regulation will not get us there. Government intervention and government money will have to play a key role – probably greater than some Western countries, such as the USA, are currently comfortable to accept.[29]

For anybody who is not blinded by ideological blinkers this should be uncontroversial – after all, as we saw in Chapter 1, a massive market *failure* is at the heart of the global-warming problem. I therefore debated at length whether this section of the book was worth writing at all. In the end, I concluded that stating what is obvious, while never thrilling, is, occasionally, necessary.

[28] Online edition, accessed 8th October, 2022. Emphasis added. This article also provides an interesting discussion of the 'government overreach' in the 1970s and 1980s (the Nixon and Carter years, respectively) in dealing with the energy crises ushered in by the oil embargo and the Iranian revolution. However, the authors' assessment of the effectiveness of the markets in the energy sector pays too little attention, in my opinion, to the global-warming dimension of the problem.

[29] Some economists, such as Prof Mazzuccato, advocate a much larger role for government than as the fixer of market failures, and envisage an activist entrepreneurial role for the state. See Mazuccato (2013), page 27 and *passim*. Her point is very well taken, but I may temper this enthusiasm for an expansive role for the state with the observation that, in states where corruption is high and accountability is low, government financing of large-sale projects can become the ideal distribution channel for bribes, for clientelism, and for state-protected criminal activities.

17.4 CODA: A POSTCARD FROM EASTER ISLAND

Much as I have tried to provide my readers with the tools to make up their own minds about what we should do about climate change, some of my preferences (and biases) must by now be evident. In particular, I believe that the increase in the total factor of production[30] at a rate greater than the growth in population that we have observed since the start of the Industrial Revolution has been little short of a miracle – particularly because, exactly as with miracles, we don't really understand how and why it happened. There are many aspects of present-day Western societies that can – and should – be criticized. However, as I already said, if I had to choose behind a Rawlsian veil of ignorance, I cannot think of another century when I would prefer to have been born. And if I were a woman, my preference would be ten times stronger. It is true that it is Western modes of production that are creating the global-warming problem – arguably one of the biggest problems humanity has faced in the last centuries. However, the same Western modes of production can also foster the innovations (more efficient solar panels and wind turbines, cheaper carbon sequestration or direct air capture, new forms of adaptation – and, one day, probably nuclear fusion) that we need to solve it. In the previous section I argued that the market alone will not get us there. But it is just as clear (to me, at least) that *without* the market and the institutions that come with it, we will not solve the climate-change problem without enormous pain.

As I have mentioned, some economists (decidedly a minority) believe my techno-optimism is misplaced. They believe that we are living on borrowed time, like someone who is enjoying a great standard of living by running a greater and greater debt on her credit card. We are depleting the resources of the planet more rapidly than they can be replenished, they maintain, and we are on a lemming-like march towards a not-so-distant cliff.

---

[30] We have encountered the total factor of production already: as you will recall, it is what is left unexplained in economic output, after the other factors of production (labour and capital) are accounted for. For a reminder, see the discussion in Section 10.3. Since both labour and capital have diminishing returns (the last labourer does not produce as much as the first), our only hope to grow output *per person* is through the increase in the total factor of production.

As the reader by now knows, I am not convinced by these arguments. First of all, I am not sure what we should count as 'resources': uranium, for instance, was a useless element less than a century ago; after we have found nuclear fission all of a sudden we have a new valuable resource. Deuterium and tritium do not count as resources today, but may become extremely valuable if we crack the fusion problem. Simply put: in a dynamic economy, we simply do not know what will be a valuable resource tomorrow. Even when it comes to land, the Malthusian view of declining marginal productivity doesn't really hold. In the United States fewer farmers cultivating less land have trebled food production between 1948 and 2017 – this corresponds to a rate of growth for the total factor of agricultural production of 1.47 per cent per annum, higher than for virtually any other sector of the US economy[31] (some other sectors have shown higher *growth*, but this has been because there has been an increase in either labour or capita). As the USDA explains, '[e]ven as land and labor used in farming declined, innovations in animal and crop genetics, chemicals, equipment and farm organization have enabled continuing growth in farm output'.

Am I completely certain that the rate of innovation discovery will keep us 'ahead of the game' in the decades and centuries to come? Of course I am not, and I think that it is a good mental exercise to keep the flame of doubt always flickering – this, at least, is what my background as a scientist has taught me. It is in this spirit that I would like to close this book by discussing what (probably) happened on Easter Island as a metaphor of what, despite my optimism, *may* be happening on our planet. My main source for the material I am going to discuss is the excellent work by Brander, Scott Taylor (1998), that I strongly recommend for the more technically inclined readers.

Easter Island (Rapa Nui) was discovered by Europeans in 1722. It is a tiny island, located some 3,200 km west of Chile, and with a present-day population of about 7,700 people. The reason why even schoolchildren know about such a small island is because of its enigmatic and enormous statues, that caused so much puzzlement for the first explorers – and

---

[31] US Department of Agriculture (2021), *A Look at Agricultural Productivity Growth in the United States, 1948–2017*. See the very comprehensive site www.usda.gov/media/blog/2020/03/05/look-agricultural-productivity-growth-united-states-1948-2017.

for generations of visitors and scholars after that. These statutes are enormous – the largest 'movable' one weighs more than 80 tons, and there exists an unfinished one of 270 tons in the quarry where it was being carved. The puzzlement is understandable: the population of 3,000 people the first Europeans found in 1722 seemed too small, and technologically too primitive, to have quarried, carved and transported over long distances the enormous statues. As for moving the statues, this would have required levers, rollers, wooden sleds and the like. All this stuff is made of wood. However, almost no trees were found on the island in 1722. And when the local residents were asked how the anthropomorphic statues had been built and transported, they answered that they had walked the distance thanks to supernatural powers.

The surprises were not over. It was later discovered (thanks to pollen records dated with carbon-decay methods) that in the distant past the now-almost-barren island had been covered by a large palm forest by the time the first Polynesian settlers arrived (around 400 AD). Archaeological reconstruction then indicated that the original small Polynesian population (perhaps as small as about fifty people) rapidly grew and flourished by using the plentiful trees for making canoes (to catch fish), dwellings, tools, etc. For the early settlers, these were the times when 'the living was easy', as it is estimated that subsistence activities did not take much of their time, leaving plenty of opportunity for activities such as carving huge statues and moving them over large distances around the island.

A few dates (established, again, thanks to pollen and carbon-dating records) then punctuate the following thousand years: most of the statues were carved between 1100 and 1500 AD – a period longer than the Industrial Revolution has so far lasted. As far as the fate of the forests goes, they were greatly reduced in size by 900 AD, and totally gone by 1400 AD. As forests thinned out, the diet of the islanders became poorer in proteins (less fish, for instance, was caught), and agricultural yield declined. The population, after attaining a peak of 10,000 around 1400 AD, began to decline in size.

In this reconstruction, the year 1500 is a watershed. As we have seen this is the time by when the carving of statues stops. But this is also the time when we find the first records of weapons, of fortified dwellings, and, probably, of cannibalism. When Capitan Cook visited Easter Island in 1774 (fifty years after the Dutch explorers had first documented its existence) the gigantic statues were no longer standing, but had been knocked over, and the population appeared smaller than half a century before. Apparently, the time of easy living was by then over, and life on Rapa Nui had likely become 'nasty, brutish and short'.

The accepted explanation for this reversal of fortune is simple. As Brander, Scott Taylor (1998) put it:

> ... Easter Island suffered a sharp decline after perhaps a thousand years of apparent peace and prosperity. *The population rose well above its long-run sustainable level and subsequently fell in tandem with disintegration of social order and a rise in violent conflict. [...]* 'Easter Island is a story of a society which – temporarily but brilliantly surpassing its limits – crashed devastatingly.' [32]

The paper by Brander and Taylor goes into a very nice analysis of what was so special about Easter Island (Polynesians colonized many islands, and none followed the same meteoric rise and fall), and point out that what was different about Easter Island was that the species of palm tree the colonizers discovered was particularly slow to grow (reaching maturity in about fifty years). With such a slow replenishment rate of resources, it is not difficult to harvest, cut, burn and consume more trees than can regrow. However – and this is a key point – when the initial stock of trees is high, this progressive depletion is far from obvious from one generation to the next. And when the cause of the decline in living standards is difficult to understand, finding a remedy is even harder: perhaps erecting more statues or organizing propitiatory festivals may seem an appropriate response, even if curbing 'overgrazing' would be the far more effective solution. As the study by Brander and Taylor shows, under the right (or, rather, wrong) conditions, a slow and protracted decline can quickly accelerate, unexpectedly leading to a 'devastating crash'.

Why should we be so interested in the fate of a tiny island with a population that, at its peak, barely reached the size of a very small town? Because there are indications that, *mutatis mutandis*, a similar pattern of overexploitation of resources, economic growth and sudden and 'unexplained' decay may satisfactorily account for much bigger instances

---

[32] Page 122, emphasis added.

of civilization 'rises and falls': perhaps the collapse of the Mayan Empire, the decline of the old Mesopotamian states, or the demise the Chaco Anasazi population[33] in the Southwestern United States can be explained as instances of a recurring pattern of overexploitation of finite or slowly regenerating resources.

This is interesting in itself. But the resonance of what may have happened to Easter Islanders, the Mayas, the Chaco Anasazis and perhaps many others clearly goes much deeper. May Easter Island be a metaphor for our own planet? Could we be depleting our resources more quickly than they can be regenerated? Are we missing the signs of a crisis that has been building up too slowly for us to notice, or to diagnose correctly?[34] Are we living it up, in short, on 'credit-card money'?

Drawing facile parallels is tempting and easy. However, as Brander and Taylor point out, for the 'catastrophic' solution to emerge from their model, several parameters (depletion rate, regeneration rate, population growth, etc.) must be in a precise range. For Easter Island, it is not fanciful to estimate that the parameters were indeed in the critical range. Carrying out a similar estimation for the planet as a whole, or for parts of it, is far more problematic – if at all possible. At a less mathematical and more institutional level, the ability of a society to adapt plays a key role in determining whether a crisis of the type that may have befallen the inhabitants of Rapa Nui can be averted. As far as we know, the people who lived on Easter Island when the times went from good to bad were not obvious examples of populations with the variety of resources and technological means to adapt effectively. Our modern world in its entirety is, at least in principle, much better placed to act, prevent and adapt. Once again, the 'miraculous' post–Industrial Revolution growth in the total factor of production is in this respect our best insurance policy. And, after all, the modern world does not rely on a one-trick-pony (the slowly growing palm tree) as the Easter Islanders did. This is why

---

[33] Today, the Chaco Anasazi civilization is hardly a household name among non-archaeologists, but, in its heydays, they built 'great houses' of more than 700 rooms and an impressive system of roads and trade.

[34] The reader may want at this point to go back to the quote by Machiavelli that opened Chapter 2, about the illness that eludes detection when it would be easy to cure, but, by the time it is apparent, becomes difficult or impossible to treat.

Brander and Taylor, after presenting a compelling explanation of what may have caused the demise of Easter Island, and after convincingly arguing that a similar pattern of growth and decline may have been followed by other civilizations the world over, in the end do *not* make the case that something similar could be occurring to our whole planet.[35]

Having said all of this, we cannot dismiss out of hand the possibility that, if not for the planet as a whole, at least for parts of it, the story of Easter Island may be part of a script that can be played out again with different actors – and this time on a far larger scale. And, as Brander and Taylor remind us in the closing words of their paper, the exceptional growth in the total factor of production upon which our hopes of continued prosperity rest has so far lasted for only 300 years: a far shorter duration than Easter Island's 'Golden Age'.

For the reasons I have explained, I don't believe that this is a central scenario. And I wouldn't even assign to it a keep-me-awake-at-night degree of likelihood. However, when we think about what to do about climate change, and use our terse and elegant models to give us guidance about the best course of climate action, keeping alive a remote-but-plausible flicker of doubt in the back of our minds is both helpful and – for lack of a better word – intellectually honest. I think that the way out of our climate predicament is to grow more, and better, not to embrace de-growth. But I may be wrong.

To conclude: the reader, who should know me by now, can perhaps guess what I am about to say. If we find that this nagging doubt does begin to make the quality of our sleep worse than it should be, my suggestion would be to invest the time and effort necessary to create a model to help us think straight. And (as a tongue-in-cheek closing remark), who knows: perhaps engaging in model building is just how the total factor of production has kept on growing in the short last few centuries.

[35] Brander and Taylor have not been the first to frame the history of Rapa Nui as a parable for the 'tragedy of the commons'. This interpretation probably goes back to the very first European visitors in the eighteenth century, and was then refined in the twentieth century using the language of game theory. It must be said that recent work – e.g., by di Napoli, Lipo and Hunt (2021), Callaway (2012) and Lipo, Hunt, Horneman and Bonhomme (2016) – has cast a revisionist doubt on the 'tragedy of the commons' story. Probably we will never know for sure. I have presented the account by Brander and Taylor not as the established truth, but as a reminder that we should always keep our minds open.

References

Aldy J E, Kotchen M J, Stavins R N and Stock J H, (2021), Keep Climate Policy Focused on the Social Cost of Carbon, *Science*, 373 (6557), 850–852

Alverá M, (2021), *The Hydrogen Revolution: A Blueprint for the Future of Clean Energy*, Hodder Studio, London, UK

Amenc N, (2021), *When Greenness Is Mistaken for Alpha: Pitfalls in Constructing Low Carbon Equity Portfolios*, working paper, Scientific Beta Publications

Axelrod R, (1984), *The Evolution of Cooperation*, Penguin Books, London

Ayres R, (2013), The Underestimated Contribution of Energy to Economic Growth, *Structural Change and Economic Dynamics*, 27, 79–88

Ayres R, (2016), *Energy, Complexity and Wealth Maximization*, Springer, Cham

Ayres R, (2017), Gaps in Mainstream Economics: Energy, Growth and Sustainability, in Shmelev S, (ed.), *Green Economy Reader: Lectures in Ecological Economics and Sustainability*, Springer, Berlin, 39–54

Backhouse R E, (2010), *The Puzzle of Modern Economics*, Cambridge University Press, Cambridge, UK

Bansal R, Kiku D and Ochoa M, (2019), *Climate Change Risk*, NBER Working Paper 23009, www.nber.org/papers/w23009, 1–75

Bansal R and Yaron A, (2004), Risks for the Long Run: A Potential Resolution of Asset Pricing Puzzles, *Journal of Finance*, 59 (4), 1481–1509

Barnett M, Brock W and Hansen L P, (2021), *Confronting Uncertainty in the Climate Change Dynamics*, working paper, University of Chicago, May 2021, available at https://larspeterhansen.org/lph_research/new-preliminary-paper-confronting-uncertainty-in-the-climate-change-dynamics/

Barr J M, (2018), *The Economics of Skyscraper Height*, Rutgers University working paper, available at https://buildingtheskyline.org/tag/urbanization/

Bonneuil C, Choquet P-L and Franta B, (2021), Early Warnings and Emerging Environmental Accountability: Total's Responses to Global Warming, 1968–2021, accepted for publication in *Global Environmental Change*, October 2021

Bordoff J and O'Sullivan M L, (2022a), Green Upheaval: The New Geopolitics of Energy, *Foreign Affairs*, January/February, 101 (1), 68–84

Bordoff J and O'Sullivan M L, (2022b), The New Energy Order: How Governments Will Transform Energy Markets, *Foreign Affairs*, Online edition, July/August

REFERENCES

Box G, (1979), Robustness in the Strategy of Scientific Model Building, in Lautner R L and Wilkinson G N (eds.), *Robustness in Statistics*, Academic Press, New York, 201–236

Bradford De Long J, (2022), *Slouching Towards Utopia: An Economic History of the Twentieth Century*, Basic Books, London

Bradley C, Canal M, Smit S and Woetzel J, (December 2022), *A Miracle of Widespread Progress: A 20-Year Journey of Health and Income*, McKinsey Global Institute

Brander J A, Scott Taylor M, (1998), The Simple Economics of Easter Island: A Ricardo-Malthus Model of Renewable Resources, *The American Economic Review*, 88 (1), 119–138

Callaway E, (2012), Easter Island Statues 'Walked' out of Quarry, *Nature*, https://doi.org/10.1038/nature.2012.11613

Carney M, (2021), The World of Finance Will Be Judged on the $100tn Climate Change, *Financial Times*, 30/31 October, 13

Caro R A, (1983), *The Years of Lyndon Johnson: The Path to Power*, Knopf, New York

Chandler D L, (2018), Explaining the Plummeting Cost of Solar Power, *MIT News*, available at https://news.mit.edu/2018/explaining-dropping-solar-cost-1120

Chang H-J, (2014), *Economics: The User's Guide*, Pelican Books, London

Cook E R, (2013), Megadroughts, ENSO, and the Invasion of Late-Roman Europe by the Huns and Avars in Harris W H (ed.), *The Ancient Mediterranean Environment between Science and History*, Columbia Studies in the Classical Tradition, Columbia University Press, New York

Coopersmith J, (2015), *Energy, the Subtle Concept: The Discovery of Feynman's Blocks from Leibniz to Einstein*, Revised Edition, Oxford University Press, Oxford

CoreEcon, (2017), *The Economy: Economics for a Changing World*, Oxford University Press, Oxford

Cornell B, (1999), *The Equity Risk Premium: The Long-Run Future of the Stock Market*, John Wiley, Chichester, UK

Corry O, (2017), The International Politics of Geoengineering: The Feasibility of Plan B for Tackling Climate Change, *Security Dialogue*, 48 (4), 297–315

Daniel K D, Litterman R B and Wagner G, (2018), *Applying Asset Pricing Theory to Calibrate the Price of Climate Risk*, NBER Working Paper 22795, www.nber.org/papers/w22795

Dasgupta P, (2008), Discounting Climate Change, *Journal of Risk and Uncertainty*, 37, 141–169

Dasgupta P, (2020), Ramsey and Intergenerational Welfare Economics, in Zalta Edward N (ed.), *The Stanford Encyclopedia of Philosophy* (Summer 2020 Edition), https://plato.stanford.edu/archives/sum2020/entries/ramsey-economics/

Dasgupta P, (2021), *The Economics of Biodiversity: The Dasgupta Review*, HM Treasury, London, available at www.gov.uk/official-documents

Deschenes O and Greenstone M, (2007), The Economic Impacts of Climate Change: Evidence from Agricultural Output and Random Fluctuations in Weather, *American Economic Review*, 97 (1), 354–385

Deschenes O and Greenstone M, (2011), Climate Change, Mortality, and Adaptation: Evidence from Annual Fluctuations in Weather in the US, *American Economic Review*, 103 (4), 152–185

Diamond J, (2005), *Guns, Germs and Steel: A Short History of Everybody for the Last 13,000 Years*, Vintage, London

Diamond J, (2019a), *Collapse: How Societies Choose to Fail or Succeed*, Allen Lane (Penguin Books), London

Diamond J, (2019b), *Upheaval: How Nations Cope with Crisis and Change*, Allen Lane (Penguin Books), London

Dietz S, Hope C, Stern N and Zenghelis D, (2007), Reflections on the Stern Review: A Robust Case for Strong Action to Reduce the Risks of Climate Change, *World Economics*, 8 (1), 121–168

DiNapoli R J, Lipo C P and Hunt T L, (2021), Triumph of the Commons: Sustainable Community Practices on Rapa Nui (Easter Island), *Sustainability*, 13 (21), https://doi.org/10.3390/su132112118

Eizenga D, (2019), Long Term Trends across Security and Development in the Sahel, *West African Papers*, no 25, OECD, September

Eliasch Review, (2008), *Climate Change: Financing Global Forests*, Earthscan, London and Sterling, VA

Folini D, Kubler K, Malova A and Scheidegger S, (2021), The Climate in Climate Change, *Environmental Economics eJournal* available at www.semanticscholar.org/paper/The-Climate-in-Climate-Economics-Folini-Kubler/9dd88113bcca0bb2c566463ec744065c6712a3eb

Forni L, (2021), *The Magic Money Tree and Other Economic Tales*, Agenda Publishing, Newcastle Upon Tyne, UK

Franceschini G, Englert M and Liebert W, (2013), Nuclear Fusion Power for Weapons Purposes, *The Nonproliferation Review*, 20 (3), 525–544

Freeman S, (2019), Original Position, in Zalta Edward N (ed.), *The Stanford Encyclopedia of Philosophy* (Summer 2019 Edition), https://plato.stanford.edu/archives/sum2019/entries/original-position/

Galagher K S, (2022), The Coming Carbon Tsunami, *Foreign Affairs*, January–February, 101 (1), 151–160

Gilboa I, (2010), *Rational Choice*, MIT Press, Cambridge, MA

Goldstone R J, (2011), Climate Change, Nuclear Power, and Nuclear Proliferation: Magnitude Matters, *Science & Global Security*, 19, 130–165

Gollier C G, (2013), *Pricing the Planet's Future: The Economics of Discounting in an Uncertain World*, Princeton University Press, Princeton, NJ and Oxford

Golove W H, Eto J H, (1996), *Market Barriers to Energy Efficiency: A Critical Reappraisal of the Rationale for Public Policies to Promote Energy Efficiency*, Lawrence Berkeley National Laboratories, US Department of Energy, Technical Report no LBL-38059

Gordon R J, (2016), *The Rise and Fall of American Growth*, Princeton University Press, Princeton, NJ and Oxford

Graeber D, Wengrow D, (2021), *The Dawn of Everything: A New History of Humanity*, Allen Lane, Penguin Book, London

Gruen L, (2021), *The Moral Status of Animals*, from *The Stanford Encyclopedia of Philosophy* (Summer 2021 Edition), Edward N. Zalta (ed.), URL https://plato.stanford.edu/archives/sum2021/entries/moral-animal/

Hampshire-Waugh M, (2021), *Climate Change and the Road to Net Zero*, Crowstone Publishing

Harrod R F, (1948), *Towards a Dynamic Economics*, London, Macmillan

Harvey H, (2018), *Designing Climate Solutions*, Island Press, Washington, Covelo, London

Helm D, (2012), *The Carbon Crunch*, Yale University Press, New Haven, CT

Hickel J, (2021), What Does Degrowth Mean? A Few Points of Clarification, *Globalizations*, 18 (7), 1105–1111

Howard H P and Sterner T, (2017), Few and Not So Far Between: A Meta-Analysis of Climate Damage Estimates, *Environment and Resource Economics*, 68 (1), 197–225

International Energy Agency (2021), Energy subsidies: Tracking the impact of fossil-fuel subsidies, available at www.iea.org/topics/energy-subsidies

Jaffe S, Minton R, Mulligan C B, Murphy K M, (2019), *Chicago Price Theory*, Princeton University Press, Princeton and London

Jensen S, Traeger C P, (2014), Optimal Climate Change Mitigation under Long-Term Growth Uncertainty: Stochastic Integrated Assessment and Analytic Findings, *European Economic Review*, 69, 109–125

Jollimore T, (2021), *Impartiality*, The Stanford Encyclopedia of Philosophy, Zalta E N editor, Fall 2021 edition, Metaphysics Research Lab, Stanford University

Kalantzakos S, (2018), *China and the Geopolitics of Rare Earths*, Oxford University Press, Oxford

Kemoe L, Okou C, Mitra P, Unsal F, (2022), *How Africa Can Escape Chronic Food Insecurity amid Climate Change*, IMF Insight and Analysis on Economic and Finance, https://blogs.imf.org/2022/09/15/how-africa-can-escape-chronic-food-insecurity-amid-climate-change/, 15 September

Kikstra J S, Waidelich P, Rising J, Yumashev D, Hope C, Brierly C M, (2021), *The Social Cost of Carbon Dioxide under Climate-Economy Feedbacks and Temperature Variability*, Environmental Research Letters, 16, JOP Publishing, 1–33

Kill J, Ozinga S, Pavett S, Wainwright R, (2010), *Trading Carbon: How It Works and Why It Is Controversial*, FERN working paper, available at www.fern.org/fileadmin/uploads/fern/Documents/tradingcarbon_internet_FINAL_0.pdf

Knutti R, Rogelj J, Sedlacek J and Fisher E M, (2016), A Scientific Critique of the Two-Degree Climate Change Target, *Nature Geoscience*, 9, 13–18

Koopmans T C, (1965), On the Concept of Optimal Economic Growth, *Academiae Scientarum Scripta Varia*, 28 (1), 1–75

Krugman, P R and Obstfeld, M, (2004), *International Economics – Theory and Policy*, Pearson, New York

Kuper S, (2021), The Next Big Political Battle? Real Carbon Taxes, *Financial Times Magazine*, 25 September, 6

Langmuir C H, Broeker W, (2012), *How To Build a Habitable Planet – The Story of Earth from the Big Bang to Humankind*, Second edition, Princeton University Press, Princeton, NJ, and Oxford

Laughner J, Neu J L, Schimel D, Wennberg P O, Brasanti K, et al. (2021), *Societal Shifts Due to COVID-19 Reveal Large-Scale Complexities and Feedbacks between Atmospheric Chemistry and Climate Change*, Proceedings of the National Academy of Sciences, PNAS November 16, 118, 46, available at www.pnas.org/content/118/46/e2109481118

Lawrence F, (2020), Truth Decay: When Uncertainty Is Weaponized, *Nature*, 578, Book review, 3 February, 28–29, available at www.nature.com/articles/d41586-020-00273-4

LDES and McKinsey & Company, (2021), *Net-Zero Power: Long-Duration Energy Storage for a Renewable Grid*, working paper, 1–76, November 22, available at www.mckinsey.com/business-functions/sustainability/our-insights/net-zero-power-long-duration-energy-storage-for-a-renewable-grid

Le Page M, (2020), Winter Ice in the Bering Sea Is Doomed to Disappear within Decades, *New Scientist*, accessed electronically at www.newscientist.com/article/2253501-winter-ice-in-the-bering-sea-is-doomed-to-disappear-within-decades/

Lipo C P, Hunt T L, Horneman R and Bonhomme V, (2016), *Weapons of War? Rapa Nui mata'a Morphometric Analyses*, Antiquity, 90 (349) 172–187

Mac Dowell N, Fennel P S, Shah N, Maitland G C, (2017), The Role of CO_2 Capture and Utilization in Mitigating Climate Change, *Nature: Climate Change*, published online, 5 April, 243–249

MacAskill W, (2022), *What We Owe the Future: A Million Year View*, OneWorld, London

Machiavelli N, (2006), *Il Principe*, Instituto della Enciclopedia Italiana, Bibioteca Treccani, Milan

Marshall T, (2015), *Prisoner of Geography: Ten Maps That Tell You Everything You Need to Know about Global Politics*, Elliot and Thompson, London

Mazzuccato M, (2013), *The Entrepreneurial State: Debunking Public vs Private Sector Myths*, Penguin Books, London

Mazzuccato M, (2018), *The Value of Everything: Making and Taking in the Global Economy*, Allen Lane, (Penguin Books), London

Meyer R, (2021), Carbon Tax, Beloved Policy to Fix Climate Change, Is Dead at 47, *The Atlantic*, July 20

Messner S, (1997), *Endogenized Technological Learning in an Energy Systems Model, Journal of Evolutionary Economics*, 7, 291–313

Michaels D, (2020), *The Triumph of Doubt*, Oxford University Press, Oxford

Morris I, (2015), *Foragers, Farmers and Fossil-Fuels: How Humans Evolve*, Princeton University Press, Princeton, NJ and Oxford

Nogrady B, (2021), Most Fossil-Fuel Reserves Must Remain Untapped to Hit 1.5 °C Warming Goal, *Nature*, News, 8 September

Nordhaus W, (1993), Rolling the 'DICE': An Optimal Transition Path for Controlling Greenhouse Gases, *Resource Energy Economics*, 15, 27–50

Nordhaus W, (2007), *The Challenge of Global Warming: Economic Models and Environmental Policy*, Yale University Press, New Haven, CT

Nordhaus W, (2009), *An Analysis of the Dismal Theorem*, Cowles Foundation discussion paper 1686, Yale University Press, New Haven, CT

Nordhaus W, (2021), Why Climate Policy Has Failed: And How Governments Can Do Better, *Foreign Affairs*, 100 (5), September–October, online edition

Notenstein E W, (1945), Population: The Long View, in: Schultz T W (editor), *Food for the World*, University of Chicago Press, Chicago, IL, 36–57

Oates W E, (1992), *The Economics of the Environment*, Edward Elgar, Aldershot, UK

Parry I (2021), *Five Things to Know about Carbon Pricing*, IMF Publications, Finance and Development, 1–5

Parson E A, Fisher-Vanden K, (1997), Integrated Assessment Models of Global Climate Change, *Annual Review of Energy and the Environment*, 22, 589–628

Patterson O, (1982), *Slavery and Social Death*, Harvard University Press, Cambridge, MA

Picketty T, (2014), *Capital in the Twenty-First Century*, The Belknap Press of Harvard University Press, Cambridge, MA and London

Picketty T, (2020), *Capital and Ideology*, The Belknap Press of Harvard University Press, Cambridge, MA and London

Pierrehumbert R T, (2010), *Principles of Planetary Climate*, Cambridge University Press, Cambridge, UK

Pindyck R S, (2013), Climate Change Policy: What Do the Models Tell Us? *Journal of Economic Literature*, 51 (3), 860–872

Pindyck R S, (2022), *Climate Future: Averting and Adapting to Climate Change*, Oxford University Press, Oxford

Pinker S, (2018), *Enlightenment Now: The Case for Reason, Science, Humanism and Progress*, Allen Lane, London

Plokhy S, (2019), *Chernobyl: History of a Tragedy*, Penguin Books, London

Ramsey F P, (1928), A Mathematical Theory of Saving, *Economic Journal*, December, 57–72

Rasmussen C, (2021), *Emission Reductions from Pandemic Had Unexpected Effects on Atmosphere*, NASA's Jet Propulsion Laboratory, November 9

Rawls J, (1971–1999), *A Theory of Justice*, Harvard University Press, Harvard, MA

Rebonato R, (2012), *Taking Liberties: A Critical Examination of Libertarian Paternalism*, Palgrave Macmillan, London

Rebonato R, (2014), A Critical Assessment of Libertarian Paternalism, *Journal of Consumer Policy*, 37 (3), 357–396

Rebonato R, Kainth D Melin L and O'Kane D, (2023), *Optimal Climate Policy with Negative Emissions*, EDHEC/ERCII working paper, available at https://papers.ssrn.com/sol3/papers.cfm?abstract_id=4316059

Rebonato R, Kainth D and Melin L, (2023), Climate Output at Risk, *The Journal of Portfolio Management* 49 (6) 32–59

Rebonato R Ronzani R and Melin L, (2023) Robust Management of Climate Risk Damages: Risk Management, *Springer Verlag Nature*, 25 (3), 1–43, September

Reuveny R, (2007), *Climate Change-Induced Migration and Violent Conflict*, Political Geography, 26, 656–673

Roberts M J, Schlenker W, (2010), *Identifying Supply and Demand Elasticities of Agricultural Commodities: Implications for the US Ethanol Mandate*, NBER working paper series, Working Paper 15921, available at www.nber.org/papers/w15921

Roberts M J, Spence M, (1976), *Effluent Charges and Licences under Uncertainty*, Journal of Public Economics, 5, 193–208

Robbins L C, (1932), *An Essay on the Nature and Significance of Economic Science*, Macmillan, London

Robinson J, (1982), Shedding Darkness, *Cambridge Journal of Economics*, 6(3), September 1982, 295–296

Royal Society, (2009), *Geoengineering the Climate: Science, Governance and Uncertainty*, RS Policy document 10/09, Issued: September RS1636, 1–98

Rudik I, (2020), Optimal Climate Policy When Damages Are Unknown, *American Economic Journal: Economic Policy*, 12 (2), 340–373

Schelling T C, (1978), *Micromotives and Macrobehavior*, Norton & Co, New York and London

Scheidel W, (2022), Does a Better Future Lie in the Prehistoric Past? book review of Graeber and Wengrow (2021), in *Foreign Affairs*, 101, (3), 187–193

Schubert K, (2019), *William D Nordhaus*: Intégrer le Changement Climatique dans l'Analyse Macroéconomique de Long Term, *Revue d'Economie Politique*, Vol 129, 887–908, available online at www.cairn.info/revue-d-economie-politique-2019-6-page-887.htm

Scott C J, (2017), *Against the Grain: A Deep History of the Earliest States*, Yale University Press, New Haven, CT and London

Sepuleveda N A, Jenkins J D, de Sisternes F J, Lester R K, (2018), The Role of Firm Low-Carbon Electricity Resources in Deep Decarbonization of Power Generation, *Joule*, 2 (11), 21 November, 2403–2420

Shapin S, (1998), *The Scientific Revolution*, University of Chicago Press, Chicago, IL and London

Shefrin H, (2023), *The Psychology, Science, and Economics of Global Warming: Fear, Bias, and Hope*, Cambridge Series in Quantitative Finance, R. Rebonato editor, Cambridge, UK

Sidgwick H, (1907), *The Methods of Ethics*, MacMillan, London

Singer P, (1979–1993), *Practical Ethics*, second edition, Cambridge University Press, Cambridge, UK

Smil V, (2008), *Energy in Nature and Society*, The MIT Press, Cambridge, MA and London

Smil V, (2018), *Energy and Civilization: A History*, The MIT Press, Cambridge, MA and London

Smil V, (2021), *Grand Transitions: How the Modern World Was Made*, Oxford University Press, Oxford

Smil V, (2022), *How the World Works: A Scientist's Guide to Our Past, Present and Future*, Viking Press, New York

Solow R M, (1974), The Economics of Resources or the Resources of Economics, *American Economic Review*, 64 (2), 1–14

Stavins R, Chan G, Stowe R, Sweeney R, (2012), *The US Sulphur Dioxide Cap and Trade Programme and Lessons for Climate Policy*, VOX EU, CEPR working paper, available at https://voxeu.org/article/lessons-climate-policy-us-sulphur-dioxide-cap-and-trade-programme

Stern Review, (2006), The Stern Review on the Economic Effects of Climate Change, *Population and Development Review*, 32 (4), 793–798

Stiglitz J E, Stern N, (2021), *The Social Cost of Carbon, Risk, Distribution, Market Failures: An Alternative Approach*, NBER working paper, Working Paper 28472, available at www.nber.org/papers/w28472

Taylor F W, (2005), *Elementary Climate Physics*, Oxford University Press, Oxford

Tegmark M, (2015), *Our Mathematical Universe*, Penguin Press, Allen Lane, London

Tirole J, (2016), *Economie du Bien Commun*, Presses Universitaire de France, Paris

Tol R, Frankhauser S, (1998), On the Representation of Impact in Integrated Assessment Models of Climate Change, *Environmental Modeling and Assessment*, 3, 63–74

Tomori V, (2021), Scientists: Don't Feed the Doubt Machine, *Nature*, 599, 9

van der Zwann B C C, Gerlag R, Klaassen G and Schrattenholzer L, (2002), Endogenous Technological Change in Climate Change Modelling, *Energy Economics*, 24, 1–19

von Neumann J and Morgenstern O, (1944), *Theory of Games and Economic Behaviour*, Princeton University Press, Princeton, NJ

Vohra K, Vodonos A, Schwatz J, Marais E A, Sulprizio M P, Mickley L J, Global Mortality from Outdoor Fine Particle Pollution Generated by Fossil Fuel Combustion: Results from GEOS-Chem *Environmental Research*, 195, 11075, available at https://doi.org/10.1016/j.envres.2021.110754

Wang X, Yang B, Ljungqvist F C, (2019), *The Vulnerability of Qilian Juniper to Extreme Drought Events*, *Frontiers in Plant Science*, 10, 45–62

Wasserman J, (2019), *The Marginalist Revolution*, Yale University Press, New Haven, CT and London

Watson J, (1980), editor, *African and Asian Systems of Slavery*, Blackwell, Oxford

Weart S R, (2008), *The Discovery of Global Warming*, revised and expanded edition, Harvard University Press, Cambridge, MA

Weil P, (1989), The Equity Premium Puzzle and the Risk-Free Rate Puzzle, *Journal of Monetary Economics*, 24, 401–421

Weitzman M, (1974), Prices vs. Quantities, *Review of Economics and Statistics*, 91, 1–19

Weitzman M, (2009), On Modeling and Interpreting the Economics of Catastrophic Climate Change, *Review of Economic Studies*, 41 (4), 477–491

Wilson E O, (1975), *Sociobiology: The New Synthesis*, Harvard University Press, Cambridge, MA

Wilson E O, (1975), *On Human Nature*, Harvard University Press, Cambridge, MA

Wilson E O, (2012), *The Social Conquest of the Earth*, W W Norton, New York

Wimsatt W C, (2007), *Re-Engineering Philosophy for Limited Beings: Piecewise Approximations to Reality*, Harvard University Press, Cambridge, MA

Woodward B, Costa R, (2021), *Peril*, Simon & Schuster, New York and London

Wootton D, (2018), *Power, Pleasure and Profit: Insatiable Appetites from Machiavelli to Madison*, Belknap Press, Harvard University Press, Cambridge, MA

Xu C, T A Kohler, T M Lenton, J-C Svenning and M Scheffer, 2021, Future of the Human Climate Niche, *Proceedings of the National Academy of Sciences*, 117 (21), 11350–11355.

Zhang Z, Moore J C, Huisingh D and Zhao Y, (2015), Review of Geoengineering Approaches to Mitigating Climate Change, *Journal of Cleaner Production*, 103, 898–907

Index

Volker, Paul, 307
Voltaire, 189
von Neumann, John, 114

Weitzman, Martin, 21, 23, 81, 288–292
wet-bulb temperature, 225

Williams, Bernard, 83, 157–158
Wilson, E. O., 158
wind power, 60–61, 242–244, 264–267, 275, 278–279, 313, 317–318
women, 72, 169, 171
World Meteorological Organization (WMO), 52